AF720463

Portuguese Emigration

Portuguese Emigration

Edited by
Leonidas Adair

STATES
ACADEMIC PRESS
www.statesacademicpress.com

Published by States Academic Press,
109 South 5th Street,
Brooklyn, NY 11249, USA

Copyright © 2022 States Academic Press

This book contains information obtained from authentic and highly regarded sources. Copyright for all individual chapters remain with the respective authors as indicated. All chapters are published with permission under the Creative Commons Attribution License or equivalent. A wide variety of references are listed. Permission and sources are indicated; for detailed attributions, please refer to the permissions page and list of contributors. Reasonable efforts have been made to publish reliable data and information, but the authors, editors and publisher cannot assume any responsibility for the validity of all materials or the consequences of their use.

Trademark Notice: Registered trademark of products or corporate names are used only for explanation and identification without intent to infringe.

ISBN: 978-1-63989-428-4

Cataloging-in-Publication Data

Portuguese emigration / edited by Leonidas Adair.
p. cm.
Includes bibliographical references and index.
ISBN 978-1-63989-428-4
1. Portugal--Emigration and immigration. 2. Portugal--Emigration and immigration--Political aspects. I. Adair, Leonidas.
JV8261 .P67 2022
325.469--dc23

For information on all States Academic Press publications visit our website at www.statesacademicpress.com

STATES
ACADEMIC PRESS

Contents

Preface

This book aims to highlight the current researches and provides a platform to further the scope of innovations in this area. This book is a product of the combined efforts of many researchers and scientists, after going through thorough studies and analysis from different parts of the world. The objective of this book is to provide the readers with the latest information of the field.

Portuguese emigration has increased ever since Portugal became a member of the European Economic Community. The main causes of increasing rate of emigration in Portugal have been global financial crisis, job insecurity, high unemployment and deteriorating working conditions. The economic crisis of 2008 and the budget cuts which followed were a major factor which has influenced migration. Since most of the emigrants are highly educated, their migration has caused a significant loss of human capital in Portugal. The main objective for migration has been to find employment and better opportunities abroad. This book includes some of the vital pieces of work being conducted across the world, on various topics related to Portuguese emigration. It aims to shed light on some of the unexplored aspects and the recent researches in this field. Scientists and students actively engaged in this field will find this book full of crucial and unexplored concepts.

I would like to express my sincere thanks to the authors for their dedicated efforts in the completion of this book. I acknowledge the efforts of the publisher for providing constant support. Lastly, I would like to thank my family for their support in all academic endeavors.

Editor

1

An Immigrant in America Yes, But Not an Emigrant in My Own Country! The Unbearable Weight of a Persistent Label

Graça Índias Cordeiro

Surprised by an Unexpected Category…

Boston, June 2014. I had just interviewed João Feitor, a retired, well-known Portuguese-American businessman, highly respected in the local community of Cambridge in the state of Massachusetts. With a remarkably successful career as vice-president of one of the largest American companies in its sector (UNICCO), and a life dedicated to the appreciation of Portuguese culture and to bringing together organizations of Portuguese origin, João Feitor represents the "self-made man" in the best American style, whose life has been reported in the local press as an example of the "personification of the American dream." (Mundo Português 2000).

He had made himself available to talk to me right from the beginning and picked me up early in the morning from Lechmere station, the end of the Green Line that connects one end of the small town of Cambridge to Boston. We headed toward his home, a beautiful villa in the suburbs, 5 minutes from the station. There we talked, with his wife, Fátima, until after lunchtime. It was raining heavily and I ended up accepting their return ride to Boston, carrying a box containing a selection of documents from his personal archives that he kindly lent me so I could make copies. On the return trip, and without my having asked anything about that subject, he said abruptly:

> But there is one thing I won't stand for: I don't mind being an immigrant here. In fact, I'm proud of it. That's what I am. But ... calling me an emigrant? In my own country? I don't accept that. I'm no emigrant. I'm as Portuguese as those who live there, no more or less. (Interview JF 2014-Jun-05)

G. Í. Cordeiro (✉)
Centro de Investigação e Estudos de Sociologia (CIES-IUL), ISCTE Instituto Universitário de Lisboa (ISCTE-IUL), Lisbon, Portugal
e-mail: graca.cordeiro@iscte-iul.pt

And he told me how in his hometown, Vila Franca do Campo, in São Miguel Island, Azores, the mayor, his long-time friend, had invited him one summer to the opening of a welcome party for emigrant communities with those words written on a banner, and how he had refused to attend, despite his friendship with the mayor. "I don't wear the emigrant's hat. I don't feel less Portuguese than others and don't want to be treated like that". This was what he told his friend, explaining that it was nothing personal. The following year, a similar party was organised, with a banner bearing the phrase "welcome to the non-resident Portuguese community"...

The topic of this short conversation was unexpected for me. I was in the middle of an ethnographic study on the movement to establish the label "Portuguese Speaker" as a category of the US Census in the state of Massachusetts[1]. My approach began in the place where this movement had emerged, and aimed to understand views of Portuguese-speaking immigrants and their descendants about this appeal, which was led by the Massachusetts Alliance of Portuguese Speakers (MAPS), a social-service non-profit organization (NPO) based in Cambridge. I would uncover the point of view of these "new Americans" through analysis of historical and ethnographic sources. The aim was to understand a complex process of identity construction – as well as the transformation of the category Portuguese on American soil over the past decades – in one of the states where "800,000 Massachusetts residents speak Portuguese (...) the second-most commonly spoken foreign language in this state after Spanish" (Margolis 2013, 84, 235).

Despite having gone through some excellent bibliographical references on Portuguese emigration to the United States (Monteiro 1987; Baganha 1988) as part of this study, my point of view was that of the immigrant, which made all the difference. A substantial part of my fieldwork was dedicated to understanding what it meant for my interlocutors to be American, to become a US citizen, and how "being Portuguese" or "of Portuguese origin" was part of "successful integration" into American society. Despite my fieldwork leading me to interact with different speakers of Portuguese as variously an official, native or heritage language, a closer relationship with the Portuguese-American community was inevitable. This led me to discover dimensions I had not even thought of addressing, such as the question raised by João Feitor. The sudden reference to this category of emigrant, invoked and refused outright, gained even more relevance because it coincided with Cláudia Pereira and Joana Azevedo's invitation to participate in a colloquium on Portuguese emigration, which they organised at the ISCTE-IUL [University Institute of Lisbon], in Lisbon. I felt I was far from questions about emigration, as I was focused on the experience and local projects of immigrants and their descendants on American soil. I was suddenly faced with the obvious fact that "every immigrant is an emigrant, every alien is a citizen, every foreigner is a national", to quote Roger Waldinger

[1] "From ethnic minority to linguistic majority: Portuguese speaking identities and urban change in Massachusetts (20–21th century)" January–July 2014, supported by University of Massachusetts, Boston and Luso-American Developement Foundation through a Grant for lecturing and research in US.

(2015, 37), and that the ambivalent relationship between these two categories is the source of the tension revealed clearly in the way John Feitor disclosed his feelings.

Inspired by this short conversation, I have accepted the challenge of thinking about this ambivalent and tense relationship between being simultaneously immigrant and emigrant, being Portuguese in the host society and American in one's homeland. Hence, my purpose is to help to clarify the paradoxical fact with which I was faced: why is "being Portuguese" in the US seen as an inclusion factor in the host society, according to many reports, while being an "American emigrant" in Portugal appears to be an exclusion factor among domestic residents who are considered "more" Portuguese? More specifically, the reflection that follows explores the relationship between these two statuses – which, while equally ambivalent, have moved in opposite directions: that of the emigrant, with prevailing negative connotations constructed over many years, perhaps even centuries, in a country characterised by a long history and experience of emigration; and that of the immigrant, which has much more positive connotations and is particularly prominent in certain regions and cities of a "nation of immigrants" (Kennedy 1963). Because they are relational concepts that can only be properly grasped from a certain point of view, this reflection takes the standpoint of the city of Cambridge, MA, where the most important Portuguese community in Greater Boston has been building its life and its history for more than a century.

Ambivalences and Stigmatizations

In the USA, Portuguese-Americans are proud of being immigrants or descendants of immigrants, seeing themselves as a small part of the endless process of building this huge nation of immigrants. In the city of Cambridge, MA, whose city mission is "value and support racial, socio-economic, cultural and religious diversity", and which has been led since 2008 by the "nation's first black, openly lesbian mayor (and the first Black female mayor in Massachusetts)"[2], this sentiment is even stronger. In the early 1970s, Gilberto Velho, a reputed Brazilian anthropologist who did fieldwork among the immigrant Portuguese community in this city, noted that even then Cambridge stood out for its "dominant ethos characterised by an appreciation of "individualism of difference" (...) with a deliberate effort to build a unique style" (1994, 42). The positive meaning of the immigrant status in a city like Cambridge, which is intensely cosmopolitan, is something explicitly assumed by those who live in or frequently visit this city.

On the contrary, emigrant status does not seem to fit well with the self-identity of Portuguese immigrants. The word emigrant seems to be an imposed hetero-classification, which is often contested, and even refused, by Portuguese immigrants – especially when they visit their mother country. The contrast between the uses of immigrant status – which is chosen and thought to connote integration – and

[2] https://www.cambridgema.gov/CityCouncil/citycouncilmembers/denisesimmons

emigrant status – which is imposed and thought to connote exclusion from other Portuguese people – deserves our attention. The short exchange with John Feitor made me aware of other stories I have heard about social interactions between Portuguese residents and non-residents that show how uncomfortable Portuguese non-residents are with this stigmatised label.

Just as in the US (the nation of immigrants), in Portugal (a nation of emigrants[3]), there is also a deep ambivalence about everything related to the theme of immigration (Martin 2011, I). This theme triggers ambivalent feelings and judgments. In both countries, immigration concerns the incorporation of some "others" regarded as foreign – either because they are of foreign origin, or because they choose to live/reside in a foreign country. This type of mobility – which is not only residential but also, and above all, social – raises attitudes and discourses that can be positive and even myth-making, and which extol the migrant's success and capabilities. But these attitudes and discourses can also be negative and even stigmatizing, loading onto the migrant the weight of being an "outsider" with fewer rights than those "established" in the land they arrived in or the land they abandoned (Elias and Scotson 2008). This apparently simple ambivalence shows the complexity of socio-spatial mobility phenomena that must be defined and analysed from a relational perspective (Stock 2006) and not from an essentialist and dichotomous one (Leeds 1975). Choosing to examine the point of view of those who are moving, their self-perceptions, their experiences, their self-identification – rather than the field of imposed ascriptions –is the way to get closer to this relational perspective. This is a valuable strategy for understanding the construction of complex and multiple identities (Noivo 2002, 258).

I cannot help but think of Paulo Filipe Monteiro's words which, in 1980, took their perspective as a source of reflection on emigration studies in Portugal, emphasizing the ambivalence of the emigrant's situation: "The phenomenon of emigration, even more than most social phenomena, seems to present great ambiguity and variability as its principal features" (Monteiro 1994, 55).

In his small and lucid book *Emigration: The eternal myth of return* (1994), Monteiro questions the idea that an immigrant is also an emigrant. The transitory nature of the "emigrant" status for those who leave, and its permanence for those who stay, clearly shows the dissociation between the two statutes: the emigrant's point of view is, after all, the immigrant's point of view:

> The view that the emigrant is marked above all by a connection to the country of origin is the point of view of the host countries, which see them mostly for their ethnic difference; this is the Portuguese elite's point of view, they are the ones interested in this link, and it has been the ethnographer's, by profession: e.g., it is almost everyone's [point of view] except the emigrants'. Studies on emigration, often ethnographic, ethnic or political, have maintained this view. (Monteiro 1994, 19)

[3]After a brief period from 1980 onwards – when Portugal attracted significant flows of immigrants – emigration once again became seen as a 'structural constant' of Portuguese society in scientific and political discussion. This trend has been particularly pronounced since 2008, with the worsening of the Portuguese economic crisis.

In another essay on the Portuguese-American community in the state of Connecticut (a neighbouring state of Massachusetts) – which unfortunately has never been published in a book – Paulo Monteiro (1987) tries to trace the route of emigrantsto the USA back to the village in the Lousã mountains where they supposedly came from originally, and finds it impossible.

This led him to declare, in a later interview, "I found neither the famous Portuguese communities nor even Portuguese people; I found Luso-Americans" (Pereira 2016); or, to use a more native category, Portuguese-Americans, as Monteiro fully embraces the term these people use to identify themselves, rather than the national Portuguese categorization.

A more micro-level approach to each person's individual experience carries the risk of observing something that only exists in the mind of the observer, and which does not correspond to the actual experience of the observed. Those thought of as emigrants in the sending society are absent, and their daily lives go on mostly in another country – that of the receiving society. Thus, the emigrant emerges as a figure imagined by those who stay, and this representation has a real impact on interaction with those who are classified as such. Those represented as emigrants not only feel they do not fit the representations made of them, but also react against such representations, discourses and related attitudes, which turn out to be discriminatory.

From a brief glance at the meagre existing literature on this topic, it is possible to see how the term emigrant carries with it a whole history of stigmatization in Portugal. This remains true despite a change in the government's official discourse since the 1980s which was intended to alter a designation that "contained in itself a pejorative meaning, denoting an image of a second-class, poor and often illiterate citizen" (Santos 2004, 67).[4] But while the emigrant has been accorded greater dignity in the Portuguese State's official speeches – and while a policy of rapprochement with Portuguese emigrants, now referred to as "communities around the world", has been implemented through the creation of services and bodies to support these communities – the pejorative use of this term is still widespread in Portuguese society. The quote below, taken from a speech by Correia de Jesus (1988), Secretary of State of the Portuguese communities at the time, clearly shows this negative meaning:

> That the term has a negative meaning is recognised by us, residents, and by the majority of the emigrants themselves. If you ask us: 'Are you an emigrant?' – we will promptly respond that we're not, as if refuting a slur. And I can tell you that at the end of a youth summer school for Portuguese descendants held last summer, when asked about what they liked the most in the course, one of the participants replied without hesitation: 'they never called me the son of an emigrant.'" And when I was in Brazil, already as Secretary of State for the Portuguese Communities, the most applauded statement, in all circumstances, was that "for this government there are no emigrants, there are only Portuguese people. (Correia de Jesus 1988, 15)

[4] Exemplified by Prime Minister Cavaco Silva at the presentation of the XI Constitutional Government Program, on August 26, 1987: "Our companions who live and work abroad are respected communities that contribute to the wealth and development of the countries where they are and to magnify the name of Portugal. They are the modern expression of our universalist and humanist vocation". See Vanda Santos 2004, 66–7.

Edite Noivo's reflections (2002) on first-person accounts of Portuguese immigrants in Australia and Canada (p. 268–9) – and even on her own experience of an interaction with a bus driver in Portugal, which ended with the shouted insult "Damned emigrant!" (Maldita emigrante)' (266) – also carry significant weight. Which leads to the conclusion that "Most narratives about return visits to Portugal are replete with such tales of social and cultural marginalization. In the end, visits to the homeland seem to both appease and reactivate the pains of uprooting" (Noivo 2002, 268).

Although the official politically correct designation might have been transformed by replacing emigrant with "non-resident Portuguese", the prejudice and stigmatizing image associated with the word emigrant remain. Although Portugal's accession to the European Community has transformed emigrants to European countries into European citizens, and despite all the national political discourse of whitewashing and rehabilitating the term, the negative stereotype remains: one does not grant dignity to a population group by decree or by official decision.

In fact, these two terms – immigrant and emigrant – are by no means equivalent. For ordinary individuals, these two categories seem to be two sides of the same coin, even they have completely different meanings. Their complementarity is only apparent: it is a contradictory complementarity, both in terms of their usage, the meanings they carry, the emotional support they mobilise, and even in the forms of power they reveal. Emigrant is clearly a hetero-classifying, decontextualised category imposed by others, while immigrant comes across as a self-classification normally used with a positive sense. This is one of the reasons why the category of immigrant is more inclusive than that of emigrant, even though it is used in the host country. In this sense, as Paulo Monteiro said so well, the emigrant's point of view is, after all, the immigrant's point of view. Immigrant appears as a category of self-identification used by the person him/herself, while the emigrant category is used by those external to the individuals who are thus classified.

Hence emigrant is an imposed category used to mark exclusion from the group of non-migrant Portuguese: "I might be an immigrant but I'm not an emigrant. What is this? This mania for excluding us…?, João Feitor says impatiently in our conversation, maintaining that dual citizenship (dupla nacionalidade) should reflect an equivalence that in reality it does not.

My Whole Life Is Here: Belonging to a Portuguese-American Home

The purpose of this text is just to open up a few reflections that I had during my fieldwork in the Boston area. I could not resist drawing inspiration from Maria Ioannis Baganha's critical view of Portuguese emigration statistics (1991), which stressed the higher quality and reliability of the American equivalents. In a similar sense – as an urban anthropologist more sensitive to individual experience in particular living places and to the "articulation between the place whence a migrant originates and the place or places to which he or she goes" than to migrant flows (Brettell 2000, 98) – I would consider the perceptions of Portuguese Americans from Cambridge, MA of the emigrant category as a reliable source enabling deeper reflection on the theme of emigration.

Once again, I recall Paulo Monteiro's statement that a Luso-American, or a Portuguese-American, is not a Portuguese person, but an American with Portuguese ethnicity (1987). Ethnic origin is one of the dimensions fundamental to the construction of American identity. Being Portuguese-American – or Azorean-American, as many from the Azores prefer – is therefore a way of being American. In a reflection on his previous study of the Portuguese-American in Connecticut, Monteiro clearly explains how this ethnic differentiation has nothing to do with the idea of "Portugality" or the myth of a "Portuguese community" or even of a diaspora. Rather, these ideas are part of the rhetoric fuelled by the Portuguese Government, "who have always been interested in the emigrants' remittances and, therefore, very interested in feeding this idea that they were linked to us", always implying that "they" would or "should return" (Pereira 2016). Indeed, it is clear that the notion of the emigrant is irrevocably associated with this nationalist rhetoric about "Portuguese communities spread across the world" and, in that sense, it is completely foreign to the local realities of integrating Portuguese immigrants.

We have to look at this particular place – the East side of Cambridge Street and its surroundings – so we can see the "attachments and connections between people and place" and the "worlds of meaning and experience" (Cresswell 2004, 11) of Portuguese-Americans and/or Azorean-Americans. These experiences reflect the real-life migrant's links to particular places "such as their villages of origin and the urban neighbourhoods in which they settle in the host society (....) not the entire national territories of the countries they move from and to" (Brickell and Datta (2011) cit. in King (2012, 31). Even though being Portuguese is a multiscale form of belonging, it is not so much connected with the Portuguese nation in the abstract, as with the current life and memories of the village and/or region of origin, a place mostly visited in certain seasons, at certain moments in the migrant's life. Migration types change a lot: permanent migration turns into seasonal migration; a return turns into a re-emigration, etc. Like the many retired immigrants who, during their working life, stayed for decades without visiting their homeland and are counted as permanent immigrants, João Feitor – who lives during the summer in Vila Franca do Campo – can now be considered a seasonal emigrant. Life-cycle dynamics challenge efforts to draw up migration typologies, requiring us to be flexible in our categorizations.

Although João Feitor has lived in a comfortable villa in Medford, a suburb of Cambridge, for some years, he explains that it is almost as if his house were a hotel "because my whole life happens in [central] Cambridge". It is there that he continues to be the director of the Filarmónica de Santo António Inc. Cultural Centre and of Cambridge Portuguese Credit Union (CPCU). He is the person who says the first words before the Saint Anthony procession and is the one who makes the solemn speech accompanying the raising of the flag on June 10, the Day of Portugal and the Communities. Boston's flag-raising event used to be held at the Cambridge City

Hall in the Mayor's presence – in recognition of the fact that Boston's Portuguese community live mostly in this nearby town and not in Boston itself – but today it takes place at the City Hall in Boston[5] proper. João Feitor is a reference point, not only because he is a true ethnic entrepreneur with a remarkable capacity for achievement, but also because he has helped numerous Portuguese and Cape Verdean immigrants obtain work, a home and even US citizenship. Moreover, he was at the heart of the resumption of Portuguese traditions in Cambridge in the 1970s and 80s – part of the process of creating a Portuguese ethnicity, which today is part of the multiculturalism so particular to this small town. Renowned for his leadership skills, JF is part of a small, particularly active group, which in recent decades has set up clubs and associations, and resurrected dormant festivities such as the Impérios das Crianças (Empires of the Children), the Festa de Santo Cristo (Festival of Holy Christ), and the Saint Anthony's Day festivities. They have invented celebrations like the Portugal Day Parade, and supported the creation of the Portuguese school and folkloric dance group Corações Lusíadas[6] (The Lusiad Hearts), not to mention coordinating the collective effort to build the modern church of Santo António in several stages, which an entire community came together to pay for in full. These activities took place in the context of the renovation of dilapidated houses in an old working-class neighbourhood in the far east of Cambridge, which was densely occupied by one of the most intense waves of Portuguese immigrants to the US nearly 40 years ago.

This neighbourhood remains the most important cluster of Boston's ethnic Portuguese community – containing all the Portuguese restaurants, travel agencies, funeral directors, bakeries, the Saint Anthony church, the Valente's library branch, shops – and is referred to in a Boston local gastronomic guide as the "Portuguese boulevard" (Morgenroth 2001). All these activities continue to be supported by many former residents of these few blocks, which neighbour MIT and are now undergoing an accelerated process of gentrification.

Pride in being an immigrant and the valorization of Portuguese descent are clear signs of full integration into American society. The American citizenship which João Feitor is so proud of makes him an American in body and soul. It allows him to leave behind the transition period during which he had a green card, which granted him various rights as a US resident but not the desired US citizenship with all rights, whose acquisition entailed (until 1981) relinquishing Portuguese citizenship. Feitor's pride in being an immigrant is, in this case, not only the pride in having built a successful career from scratch – as a newcomer from his native island in the Azores – but also in having contributed to the construction of a Portuguese-American community that values both citizenships in this town.

[5] The Boston Portuguese Festival – held since 2004 under the auspices of the Boston Consulate General – resumed some of these activities initiated by the Cambridge Portuguese community, with some minor changes. One of them was the transfer of the Portugal Day Ceremony, along with the hoisting of the flag, to the City Hall in Boston instead of Cambridge.

[6] Directed by Sérgio and Fátima Soares.

Along with Villar, I agree that "the Portuguese-American community is a strategic and positive space that belongs to both societies at once" – a kind of "public home which provides a synthesis for this either/or" (Villar 2012, 242). As this author pointed out based on the analysis of three Portuguese-American autobiographies, this sense of community "emerges as the site where a performance of self-representation takes place" (ob. cit., 234) – a performance connected with local cultural memories and not with political discourses of national identity in either country. Moreover, local cultural memories operate on both sides of the ocean – in receiving and host societies alike – in many different ways. Beyond the image of two sides of the same coin connecting two countries, two cultures, two different languages, we come across a place/community collectively created through a historical process of creative synthesis between two or more experienced and practiced places (Stock, op. cit.). These places are locally rooted in concrete spaces, and are considered by all concerned as the Portuguese-American or American-Azorean home, where the immigrant category is welcome, but where the emigrant does not fit.

Final Remarks

There is no doubt that the Portuguese migrant experience in Massachusetts is a transnational process. Migrants are living in "trans local spaces" within their own personal and institutional networks that span the Atlantic Ocean, connecting places in the Azores or the mainland with neighborhoods in New England cities in several ways. This so-called transnationalism involves migrant activities which, as Portes says, "are not limited to economic enterprises [such as sending and receiving remittances or setting up a business back home], but include political, cultural and religious activities as well" (Portes 1999: quoted by King 2012, 25).

In fact, those in the Portuguese-American community "transgress geographic, political and cultural borders", in the words of Caroline Brettell (2000, 104), combining in a single social field "home and host society as a single arena of social action" (Margolis 1995, 29, cit. in Brettell 2007, 104). The many forms of mobility and communication between Cambridge – the focus of the sense of Portuguese-American belonging in Greater Boston – and the island, city, village or parish that he/she belongs to, nurture this sense of dual membership, which is framed by the welcomed status of dual citizenship.

Portuguese-Americans like to be Portuguese in Portugal as well as American in the US – or Portuguese-Americans. They have positive feelings of attachment simultaneously to their homeland and to the host society. But they agree that they don't like to be emigrants in their own country and we can anticipate, along with Edite Noivo, that there is a "risk of a sense of cultural homelessness" because the "migrant sense of belonging is dissociated from the perceptions prevailing in the homeland" (Noivo ob. cit., 259). As she pointed out:

> …residence abroad is being reconstructed by residents in Portugal as a boundary between the 'fully Portuguese' and 'contaminated Portuguese' as if the 'territorial boundaries of Portuguese nation are superimposed on to social boundaries in ways that fragment the community by projecting a form of otherness onto the non-resident population. (Noivo 2002, 265)

Accordingly, "foreignization" of the emigrants is part of a process of "othering" which creates a powerful label used in every dimension of social life, including careless uses of them in social media, political discourses and, even, scientific texts. This process deserves a wiser reflection about the meanings of being an emigrant as well as its impacts in everyday life.

"Migration is too diverse and multifaceted to be explained in a single theory" (King 2012, 11). It is thus necessary to overcome categories used in the study of complex forms of socio-spatial mobility (Stock ob. cit.) – categories that are inextricably linked to strictly national perspectives (Glick-Schiller 2005). We must also diversify the scales at which we view "kaleidoscopic phenomena" – to use the term Ulf Hannerz employs to characterise the cultural diversity and heterogeneity of the city, where "the multitude of parts again and again take on new configurations" (1980, 15). For this reason, looking "closely and within" (Magnani 2002) the meanings of being an immigrant from an individual perspective no doubt help us think about the various effects of population classifications and their real impact on social and labour integration in specific towns. As Brettell said, "managing migration is as much a local issue as it is a national and global issue" (2007, 54) and should be more about managing integration than managing flows (ob. Cit., 53).

In the Portuguese case, the blurred image of emigration (Baganha 1991), the myth of return and its financial function (Pereira 1971, 56 cit. in Monteiro 1994, 8), as well as the naturalization of a phenomenon looked as if it were obvious by common sense, have all contributed to conflating the "rhetoric of the State" and "the rhetoric of the emigrants". This has left in the shadows "the shockingly understudied other side, which refers to what [emigrants] actually do, the many paths they have followed, where and how they have organised and organise their work, investments, family, housing and social lives, what they have lost and what they have won" (Monteiro ob. Cit., 59). With this brief reflection on the immigrant category – a reflection that arose from a concrete case – I hope to have contributed to the study of the social construction of the "emigrant" category in what has been called the "Portuguese diaspora". I also hope to have enriched a Portuguese-American history whose undiscovered and unworked sources harbour a wealth of diverse experiences that remain under-explored.

Acknowledgments and Funding I thank the Department of Anthropology, UMass Boston for their hospitality to this research project, which is the basis of the following text: "From ethnic minority to linguistic majority: Portuguese-speaking identities and urban change in Massachusetts (20th–21st century)" and especially Tim Sieber, as well as Isabel Fêo Rodrigues, from Umass Dartmouth, for their help with the field work between January and July 2014; my thanks also go to the Luso-American Development Foundation for a Grant for lecturing and research in the US, without which it would not have been possible to proceed with this research. Thank you to Cláudia Pereira and Joana Azevedo for the invitation to be part of this publication as well as the useful comments that helped improve the text, which remains my full responsibility. Finally, all my gratitude to my interlocutors in the Boston area and in particular to Fátima and João Feitor for the immense patience they showed in the long conversations we held in their home.

The research for this chapter was funded by the Luso-American Development Foundation, FLAD, with a grant for lecturing and research in the US in the 2014 Spring Semester at the Department of Anthropology, Umass Boston. Translated from Portuguese by Raquel Mendes and Dave Tucker. The chapter's translation was funded by the Fundação para a Ciência e a Tecnologia, through Strategic Funding: UID/SOC/03126/2013. The proofreading of this chapter was funded by the Portuguese Emigration Observatory (Observatório da Emigração).

References

Baganha, M. I. (1988). *International labor movements: Portuguese emigration to the United States 1820–1930*. PhD History, University of Pennsylvania.

Baganha, M. I. (1991). Uma imagem desfocada – a emigração portuguesa e as fontes sobre a emigração. *Análise Social, 26*(112–113), 723–739.

Brettell, C. B. (2000). Theorizing migration in anthropology. The social construction of networks, identities, communities, and globalscapes. In C. Brettell & J. F. Hollifield (Eds.), *Migration theory. Talking across disciplines* (pp. 97–135). London: Routledge.

Brettell, C. (2007). Adjustment of status, remittances, and return: Some observations on 21st century migration processes. *City & Society, 19*(1), 47–59.

Correia de Jesus, M. F. (1988). *Conferência proferida aos cursos de defesa nacional de Lisboa e Porto* em 17 e 19 de Março de 1988. https://comum.rcaap.pt/bitstream/10400.26/2735/1/NeD46_ManuelFilipeCorreiaJesus.pdf. Accessed 4 Sept 2016.

Cresswell, T. (2004). *Place, a short introduction*. Malden: Blackwell Publishing.

Elias, N., & Scotson, J. L. (2008). *The Established and the outsiders* (Volume 4 of the collected works of Norbert Elias). Dublin: University College Dublin Press.

Glick-Schiller, N. (2005). Transnational urbanism as a way of life: A research topic not a metaphor. *City & Society, 17*(1), 49–64.

Hannerz, U. (1980). *Exploring the city. Inquiries toward an urban anthropology*. New York: Columbia University Press.

Kennedy, J. F. (1963, August 4). A Nation of immigrants. *New York Times*.

King, R. (2012). *Theories and typologies of migration: An overview and a primer* (Willy Brandt Series of Working Papers in International Migration and Ethnic Relations. 3/12).

Leeds, A. (1975). La sociedad urbana engloba a la rural: especializaciones, nucleamientos, campo y redes; metateoria, teoria y métodos. In J. E. Hardoy & R.P. Schaedel (Comp.) Las ciudades de America Latina y sus areas de influencia a través de la historia (pp. 317–336). Lima: S.I.A.P.

Magnani, J. G. (2002). De perto e de dentro: notas para uma etnografia urbana. *Revista Brasileira de Ciências Sociais, 17*(49), 11–29.

Margolis, M. L. (2013). *Goodbye, Brazil. Émigrés from the land of soccer and samba*. Madison: The University of Wisconsin Press.

Martin, S. F. (2011). *A nation of immigrants*. Cambridge: Cambridge University Press.

Monteiro, P. F. (1987). Luso-Americanos no Connecticut: questões de etnicidade e comunidade. *Povos e Culturas, 2*, 765–913.

Monteiro, P. F. (1994). *Emigração. O eterno mito do retorno*. Oeiras: Celta Editora.

Morgenroth, L. (2001). *Boston neighborhoods. A food lovers' walking, eating and shopping guide to ethnic enclaves in and around Boston*. Guilford: The Globe Pequot Press.

Mundo Português. (2000). Vol. 6, nr. 82.

Noivo, E. (2002). Towards a cartography of Portugueseness: Challenging the hegemonic center. *Diaspora, 11*(2), 255–275.
Pereira, M. H. (1971). *Livre cambio e desenvolvimento económico*. Lisboa: Cosmos.
Pereira, C. (2016). O mito das comunidades portuguesas: entrevista com Paulo Filipe Monteiro, *OEm Conversations With*, 5. Lisboa, Observatório da Emigração, CIES-IUL, ISCTE-IUL. http://observatorioemigracao.pt/np4/5612.html. Accessed 5 Sept 2016.
Santos, V. (2004). *O discurso oficial do Estado sobre a emigração dos anos 60 a 80 e imigração dos anos 90 à actualidade*. Lisboa: ACIME (Observatório da Imigração 8).
Stock, M. (2006). L'hypothèse de l'habiter poly-topique: pratiquer les lieux géographiques dans les sociétés à individus mobiles. *Espaces Temps.net*, Textuel. https://www.espacestemps.net/articles/hypothese-habiter-polytopique/. Accessed 5 Sept 2016.
Velho, G. (1994). Trajetória individual e campo de possibilidades. In G. Velho (Ed.), *Projeto e metamorfose. Antropologia das sociedades complexas* (pp. 31–48). Rio de Janeiro: Jorge Zahar.
Villar, C. R. (2012). Janus and the Portuguese Emigrant. The Autobiographies of Portuguese Immigrants in the United States. *Luso-Brazilian Review, 49*(2), 232–250.
Waldinger, R. (2015). *The cross-border connection. Immigrants, emigrants, and their homelands*. Cambridge, MA: Harvard University Press.

2

New Migration Dynamics on the South-Western Periphery of Europe: Theoretical Reflections on the Portuguese Case

Russell King

Introduction

Grateful to the editors for the invitation to write this concluding chapter, I first want to make it clear that my perspective in doing so is that of a partial outsider to the rich and vibrant field of Portuguese migration studies. Whether this yields any advantage in my reading of the dynamics of Portuguese migration, it is for the reader to decide. Optimistically, my semi-outsider status, bringing in a range of comparative and theoretical perspectives, offers a useful counterpoint in a book pretty much entirely produced by Portuguese authors working within Portuguese universities and research institutes. I also position myself as a partial outsider to the majority authorship of this book, most of whom are sociologists or have received a predominantly sociological training. As a geographer, I bring to the table a broader comparative view of the migratory phenomenon: comparison not just regionally and between countries but also in terms of diverse methodologies and scales of analysis.[1] This is not to denigrate the importance of sociology or any other discipline, absolutely not, and in fact sociology has been at the forefront of the development of the interdisciplinary field of migration studies; but I do believe that the perspective of the geographer has been under-valued within the social sciences generally, even if there are signs that this is now changing (see, for instance, Favell 2008, 262).

Having set out my stall, the chapter continues as follows. The next section delves into the core-periphery model, a concept which is at once beguilingly simple and also complex when interrogated in diverse and changing historical and geographical contexts. Core-periphery structures are used to elaborate Portugal's somewhat

[1] These arguments are more fully developed in King (2012, 2019).

R. King (✉)
School of Global Studies, University of Sussex, Sussex, UK
e-mail: R.King@sussex.ac.uk

ambiguous position in what I have previously and perhaps contentiously labelled as the 'Southern European migration model' (King 2000). My conclusion, briefly, is that Portugal's position within this model is sustained, albeit with more exceptions than the other Southern EU countries. The key difference is that Portugal is also the hub of its own 'Lusophone' migration system, which gives it a 'semi-peripheral' position within global migration patterns. The subsequent section shadows the structure of the book. Here I attempt to draw out key theoretical insights and findings from the chapters in the various sections of the book – on 'old' and 'new' Portuguese emigrants, high-skilled and labour migrants, and questions of migratory identity. The final part of the chapter nominates four areas which, in an ideal world (and a much longer book!) could have been accorded more emphasis – the spatial patterning of Portuguese migration origins, the issue of return migration, the gender perspective and the relationship between migration and development.

On Cores and (Semi-)Peripheries: A Portuguese Perspective on the Southern European Migration Model

Like the rest of Southern Europe (King 1982), Portugal illustrates the tension between dependency on the one hand and development on the other, such that its style of economic and social progress has been labelled 'dependent development' (Holland 1979). Dependency theory has its roots in the Latin American *dependencia* school of, amongst others, André Gunder Frank (1967) and its re-application via the core-periphery model to the global scale by Wallerstein (1974) in his historical world-systems model of capitalist (under)development, in turn re-applied to the European scenario by Seers et al. (1979). Seers et al. introduced an explicit geographic analysis, mapping the core-periphery system in a series of maps and diagrams (see, especially, Seers 1979, 4–5, 17, 21) which distinguished flows of migrants, trade and tourists between European countries classified as 'core' (France, West Germany, Belgium, the Netherlands, Luxembourg, Switzerland, Austria, Sweden, Norway, Denmark), 'periphery' (Ireland, Portugal, Spain, Greece, Yugoslavia, Turkey) and 'semi-periphery' (Finland, Italy and – controversially – the UK). This classification is far from water-tight, and the danger of 'fixing' it in cartographic form is that the static map obscures its dynamic nature. Particularly fluid and ambiguous is the category of semi-periphery – a point I shall return to presently with reference to Portugal and this country's complex migration dynamics.

At the root of the core-periphery model is the process of uneven spatial development which, many Marxist-inspired scholars argue, is intrinsic to the capitalist system. Spatial polarisation in and around the core is driven by economies of scale and agglomeration; this process of cumulative causation generally outweighs overspill effects to the periphery. Selwyn (1979, 37) stresses that 'core-periphery systems, whilst not unchanging, are very persistent', due to the fact that the resultant spatial inequalities are underpinned by 'very deep rooted economic, social and political structures'.

As Seers (1979) and others have more recently emphasised (eg. King 2015 and, in this volume, Pereira and Azevedo, Chap.), migration is perhaps the most important of the flows linking peripheral to core countries in an asymmetric relation of power which ranges across political economy, economic geography and social inequality. Moreover, migrant labour has a cyclical function, flowing into the core countries at a time of economic expansion, and blocked and 'returned' during a recession. Thereby, economic fluctuations in the core are transmitted to the periph-ery, which acts as a disadvantaged shock absorber protecting the core (Selwyn 1979, 38). However, this is only one of a range of migration mechanisms which can be interpreted through the core-periphery lens, as can be seen by the case of Portugal.

In its simplest form, and generalisable (with partial exceptions) across all four main Southern European EU countries (Spain, Portugal, Italy and Greece), this migration-centred model has moved through several distinct phases over the past century and more.[2]

Stage 1 is the transatlantic cycle of emigration from Southern Europe which started in the mid-to-late nineteenth century, in the footsteps of, and overlapping with, major emigration flows from Northern European countries. Whereas the Northern Europeans settled mainly in North America, Southern Europeans' destinations were in both North and South America (except for Greeks who mainly went to the United States). For the Portuguese, the key transatlantic destinations were Brazil, the US and Canada. Across the four Southern European countries, the transatlantic cycle reached its apogée in the decades spanning the turn of the century. It then faded into pulses interrupted, in chronological order, by World War I, the Great Recession and World War II, with a final phase during the 1950s and 1960s. Its partial reappearance in very recent years, as part of the so-called 'fourth wave' of emigration, will be commented on below.

Although these nineteenth- and early-twentieth-century migrations were largely born out of poverty and unemployment – so a typically global-scale periphery-to-core migration – for the Portuguese there was also colonial settlement migration, especially in Brazil, with professional involvement in farming, business development and administration. Sapelli (1995, 31–32) wrote that these early Southern European migrations were historically significant in that they created a 'culture of emigration' which endures to the present day.

Stage 2 is the postwar phase of European labour migration, concentrated in a much shorter time-frame of circa 1950–1973. As portrayed by Seers (1979, 4, 6, 23–24), this was the classic periphery-core spatial model functioning across a South–North divide within Europe. These were 'Fordist' migrations of an era of marked industrial expansion in the core economies of Europe, whose factories and construction sites became reliant on labour sourced not only from the 'near periphery' of Southern Europe but also, in the cases of the UK, France and the

[2] The analysis that follows draws partly on King (2015), with additional insights from Pereira and Azevedo, this volume, Chap.

Netherlands, from an 'outer periphery' of colonial and former colonial territories. France and West Germany were the main magnets drawing in supplies of South European migrant labour: in the case of France mainly from Portugal, Spain and Italy (as well as Algeria, Morocco and Tunisia); in the case of West Germany from Italy, Greece, Yugoslavia and Turkey. From a sending-country perspective, Portugal had a highly diversified set of destinations, especially at the start of this period (USA, Canada, Brazil, Venezuela, Angola, Mozambique) whilst, within Europe, France was the main receiver of Portuguese emigrants, followed by West Germany and Luxembourg.

According to figures for this period culled from the OECD's migration observatory, which I have analysed in detail elsewhere (King 1984, 1993), Portugal's peak emigration phase was 1969–1971, when over 150,000 migrated per year to other European countries. In 1973, when these labour migrations were brought to a close by the oil crisis, the 'stock' of Portuguese workers living abroad in Europe was 469,000 (compared to 858,000 Italians, 582,000 Turks, 535,000 Yugoslavs, 527,000 Spaniards and 332,000 Greeks). However, unlike emigration from most of these other countries, which was shaped by bilateral recruitment agreements, most Portuguese emigration to Europe, especially to France, was clandestine, due to the restrictions on 'free' emigration imposed by the fascist regime then in power. The demise of that regime in 1974 coincided with the end of the Fordist era of intra-European mass labour migration.

For the remainder of the 1970s, throughout the 1980s and into the 1990s, we see a much more diversified set of migration processes in stage 3 of the 'Southern European migration model'. Return migration was initially the dominant flow, driven by a variety of factors: recession and unemployment in the North European host countries, the prospect of a better future in the now-developing economies of Southern Europe, and the more cultural, emotional and life-stage factors which are also an intrinsic part of return decision-making. In the case of Portugal, returns from recession-bound Europe were massively outnumbered by the estimated half-million *retornados* who repatriated from the newly independent colonies in the mid-1970s. The Portuguese migration profile also differed from that of the other three Southern European countries at this time in one other important respect – emigration continued at quite a high level. This fact reflected, on the one hand, the ongoing strength of the Portuguese culture of emigration and its diversified array of destination countries and, on the other, the country's status as a weak member of the European economic periphery, lagging behind the progress achieved by Spain, Italy and even Greece at this juncture. Switzerland became an important destination for Portuguese emigration, in addition to the former key European targets of France, Germany and Luxembourg.

Finally, in this complex interplay of return-emigration-immigration which characterises the Portuguese 'third wave', we see the relatively new phenomenon of immigrants arriving in Portugal – from Brazil, the former African colonies and, after 1990, some East European countries where new emigration possibilities suddenly opened up after the collapse of the communist regimes. The scale of this immigration, however, has been lower than in Spain, Italy and Greece. Apart from the economic factor mentioned above, geography also plays an explanatory role in this differentiation. Located at the south-western periphery of Europe, bordering only one other country and distant from the 'new' migration access routes across the Mediterranean (to southern Spain and Sicily) and from neighbouring Eastern European countries (to Italy and Greece), Portugal was geographically 'out on a limb' in this new era of immigration to Southern Europe.

The suddenness, scale and epoch-making nature of the Southern European 'migration turnaround' to net immigration in the 1980s and 1990s (see King et al. 1997) gives support to reclassifying the Southern European countries as 'semi-periphery' since they are no longer confined purely to the status of suppliers of migrant labour to the 'core' countries of Europe. This is not the only rationale for viewing Southern Europe, including Portugal, as semi-periphery, as we shall see shortly. Before that, let us record the occurrence of stage 4 of the Southern European migration model, which refers essentially to the last decade or so.

Although the Eurozone financial crisis of the late 2000s was the defining moment of the 'fourth wave', Pereira and Azevedo argue in Chap. that the fourth cycle of Portuguese emigration started around 2001, with the stagnation of the economy and rising unemployment, as well as the currency switch from the escudo to the euro in Portugal. I would concur with this, also on the basis of evidence from the other Southern EU countries where, well before the financial crisis, one could observe a more deep-seated structural crisis of youth unemployment and lack of hope for the future, especially amongst unemployed graduates (see, for example, Conti and King 2015). Meanwhile, in Portugal, according to figures presented by Pereira and Azevedo, annual emigration rose from around 50,000–60,000 in the early 2000s to reach 110,000–120,000 in the mid-2010s – rates comparable to those of the 'emigration boom' in the late 1960s.

Portugal as a Migration Semi-periphery

Although the basis of my argument in the foregoing section has been that Portuguese migration dynamics can be best understood within the combined framework of the core-periphery model and the four-stage Southern European migration regime, there are certain unique features which characterise the Portuguese case. These specifically Portuguese features lead to the classification of Portugal as semi-periphery on the following grounds.

First and foremost, Portugal has historically had a Janus-faced position in the global hierarchy of metropolitan cores and dependent peripheries. Less than half a century ago, so within the living memory of many older Portuguese, the country was the metropolitan core with its own colonial periphery. First Brazil and then Goa and the African colonies were lost and, with the revolution of April 1974, the axis of Portuguese international relations was inverted. In Stuart Holland's words, 'from being the nominal centre to a major African periphery, Portugal became a minor nation state on the periphery of Europe to which, by geography and culture it had always belonged' (1979, 139). Holland's somewhat glib dismissal of the Portuguese colonial era as an aberration from the country's 'true place' on the periphery of Europe plays down the impact of Portugal's long period of colonialism on the country's kaleidoscope of migration flows, both 'out' and 'in', over the four waves portrayed above and highlighted in several chapters in this book.

Still today, Portugal looks both to Europe, especially since its membership of the EU from 1986, and outwards to Latin America and Africa; it is not only European but also Atlantic and, arguably, Mediterranean in its vision and identity. This reinforces its multi-faceted and intermediate positionality within the core-periphery system, and is reflected in the way it continues to send various types of migrant to places as differentiated as the UK, Switzerland, Brazil and Angola, and receives migrants from the Portuguese-speaking world as students, professionals and labourers.

In their landmark paper arguing for Portugal to be classified as a semi-peripheral country in the global migration system, Góis and Marques (2009) draw attention to the country's integration, as both a sender and receiver of migrants, in several subsystems of regional and global significance.[3] However, key to their argument is the identification of a 'Lusophone migration system'. Especially over the past two to three decades, new flows, moving along pathways of an older colonial system based on a common language, have bonded the Portuguese-speaking countries together, with Portugal at the core of this system.

Following Arrighi (1985), Góis and Marques (2009, 27) maintain – and I agree – that the semi-periphery is neither a new nor a transitional or residual category within the core-periphery model but, rather, a distinct and permanent feature of the world system. Portugal, with its unique location on the south-western periphery of Europe, its history as a colonial metropole and its heterogenous, shifting and mixed migration flows, rather well exemplifies this theoretical point about the validity of the notion of semi-periphery.

Four other migratory features confirm Portugal's status as a semi-peripheral country. The first is its experience of immigration flows from other (semi-) peripheral countries. The largest of these inflows are from the Eastern European periphery – that which lies within the EU (Poland, Romania etc.) – and from a non-EU 'outer' periphery (Ukraine, Moldova, Georgia etc.). Additionally, in Chap. by Queirós, we learn of the migration of Portuguese construction workers to neighbouring

[3]This includes, according to their schematic map (Góis and Marques 2009, 31), the following systems: (i) the Western European one of Portuguese emigration to France, Germany, Luxembourg, the Netherlands, Switzerland, the UK and Spain; (ii) the North American one, also of Portuguese emigration (USA and Canada, the latter country inexplicably omitted by the authors); (iii) the Latin American realm of both emigration and immigration (Brazil both directions, emigration to Venezuela); (iv) the African colonial system of origin countries for migration to Portugal (Cape Verde, Guinea Bissau, São Tomé, Mozambique and Angola, the last of these now a receiver of Portuguese emigrants); (v) an Eastern European source area for recent immigration to Portugal (Ukraine, Moldova, Romania); and (vi) an Asian source area (China, India, Pakistan and Bangladesh).

north-west Spain, which can be seen as an interesting case of migration to a bigger, contiguous neighbour within the semi-periphery.

The second 'semi-peripheral' feature is the phenomenon of replacement migration. Góis and Marques (2009, 41, 43) document the close link between Portuguese migration to Switzerland and Cape Verdean migration to Portugal, often involving workers engaged in the same economic sector. The interdependence or 'structural coupling' of these two migrations occurs because of the membership of Portugal and Switzerland in a common labour circulation area, whilst Cape Verdean migration to Portugal continues the colonial relationship.

A third type of migration, which Portugal has pioneered in Europe, is that of 'posted workers'. Quite different from the well-researched history of Portuguese labour migration to France or North America, this arises due to the way that Portuguese companies act as labour subcontractors for big European construction companies, using the advantages of lower Portuguese wages and willingly mobile workers to 'post' contingents of labourers to construction sites within the European free movement area (Marques and Góis 2017, 74–75). Over the years 2007–2011 Portuguese posted workers were the largest nationality within the EU, averaging over 60,000 per year, mainly to France, Germany, the Netherlands and Spain.

Finally, we can observe how Portugal, like a number of other Southern European countries, increasingly functions as a transit country for migrants who move there from countries of the less-developed world, and use it as a short- or long-term stop-over before moving northwards to more prosperous Northern European countries. In the Portuguese case, migrants of this kind typically originate from Brazil, China, South Asia and the Portuguese African ex-colonies. Whilst Góis and Marques (2009) describe this 'redistributive' function of Portugal in general terms, a recent paper by McGarrigle and Ascensão (2018) documents the specific case of Punjabi Sikhs who use Lisbon as a 'translocality' to stay for a while during their long-term migratory journeys to other European countries such as Germany and the UK.

Highlights of the Book

In this section of the chapter I review the contents of the book and pick out some of the stand-out features of the chapters, especially from the point of view of their theoretical insight and empirical originality. This is an inherently subjective exercise and no doubt my biases will be evident.

At a general level, the book functions as an excellent state-of-the-art on Portuguese emigration. It brings together for an English-language readership much of the best recent Portuguese scholarship on migration, packaged neatly within five themes: new patterns, skilled migration, labour migration, postcolonial continuities, and identities. The various chapters exemplify a range of methodologies, appropriate for a topic – migration – that has many facets and is therefore best studied via 'mixed methods' (Vargas-Silva 2012; Zapata Barrero and Yalaz 2018). Some chapters are desk studies, others present their own quantitative survey data, some rely on in-depth qualitative interviews and yet others personify a more ethnographic, humanistic or even autobiographical approach.

The part of the book – New Patterns of Portuguese Emigration – sets out the broad theoretical, historical and statistical context. In their opening chapter, Pereira and Azevedo help us to understand the key features of recent Portuguese emigration, its structural factors, the characteristics of its diverse flows and bipolar destinations – 'North' to 'old' (France) and 'new' (UK) Europe, and 'South' along routes first mapped out by the history of Portuguese colonialism (Brazil, Angola). This historically multi-layered diaspora results in the Portuguese being the most numerous immigrant (foreign-born) group in Brazil and Luxembourg, the second largest in Switzerland and the third largest in France. In terms of structural factors, the authors unpick the ultimately devastating impact of the 2008 financial crisis when, in the following years, Portugal and other peripheral European countries (Spain, Greece, Ireland, Latvia and Lithuania) entered a period of austerity and economic entrenchment which resulted in very high rates of youth unemployment and hence enhanced emigration potential. But behind this severe conjunctural crisis lay another one, more deep-seated – the blocked career, and life, aspirations of a whole generation of young people, especially those with higher education whose investment in long years of study had not led to employment opportunities in their own countries consonant with their aspirations.

Pereira and Azevedo broadly accept the notion of Portugal's location within the 'Southern European migration model' (King 2000, 2015) but, along with the succeeding chapter by Pires, they also challenge it by pointing out some 'deviant' features of the Portuguese case. Three points seem key here. First, the immigration phase of this historical model (1980s–2000s) was less marked in Portugal. Second, emigration from Portugal continued at a high rate, even during the immigration phase. And third, whilst most Portuguese emigration has continued to be directed northwards to Europe, an important channel opened up towards the global South, especially the Portuguese-speaking countries therein. On the basis of migration flow data on immigration, emigration and returns for the years 2013–2015, Pires contends in Chap. that Portugal is more akin to Eastern EU countries such as Lithuania, Bulgaria and Romania. This is an intriguing indication of the 'uniqueness' of Portugal as a 'Western' and/or 'Southern' European country, but this comparison is based on recent and short-term data and may have only temporary validity.[4]

Pires' contribution is otherwise notable for its forensic statistical detail on Portuguese emigration and an ability to place these trends in a European and global comparative perspective, something that few authors have done. What is most portentious in his chapter, however, is contained in the final few paragraphs. The combination of continued high emigration (in the absence of significant

[4] Kurth (1993) makes a more historically grounded comparison between the Southern and Eastern peripheries of Europe, in which for example, there is a (far-from-exact) historical analogy between the Southern European countries' transition from Fascism to democracy and an open economy (including mass migration flows) in the earlier postwar decades and the Eastern periphery's transition – more a revolution in fact – from communism to democracy after 1989.

counterbalancing of immigration and return migration) with a fast-declining birth rate (which has halved since 1980) have pitched the overall Portuguese population into decline – a loss of 215,000 people over the period 2010–2015. With such a constellation of negative economic and demographic variables – high (youth) unemployment, a shrinking working-age and employed population, a stagnant GDP, a total fertility rate at 1.3 (cf. the replacement level of 2.1 children per woman), a rapidly ageing population and the migration trends already mentioned, the overall future for Portugal suddenly appears extremely uncertain.

In other Chap by Peixoto and 11 others, attention shifts to the transnational perspective, including return migration. Deriving from the project intriguingly titled 'Back to the Future', the authors' analysis focuses on the extent and characteristics of recent Portuguese migration. Through the now-popular transnational lens, the chapter seeks to understand the relationships that emigrants retain and develop with their home country. In the latter part of the chapter, the authors' particular emphasis on return migration is a much-needed contribution given that, as is pointed out, only 8% of the Portuguese migration literature concerns return migration. The coverage here is based on analysis of two questions administered in the 2011 Portuguese Census about prior residence. Some useful new insights are revealed – to cite just one example, recent returnees are younger than in the past – but, as a desk study, this obviously misses the depth of primary qualitative research.

Part of the book contains a clutch of chapters which are at the heart of the volume's main message – the recent switch to a more highly skilled emigrant profile. Setting aside for the moment the inherently problematic task of defining 'skill' in a migratory (or any other) context, and acknowledging once again the subjectivity of my own perspective, two chapters stood out for me by virtue of their originality. Pereira (Chap.) presents much-needed primary research on the emigration of Portuguese nurses, mainly to the UK. This is a gender-specific skilled-migration niche which has its own particular structuring factors, namely the high quality of Portuguese nursing training, and the switch in the UK's nurse recruitment from traditional overseas sources such as India and the Philippines to 'free-movement' EU countries. But, as the author convincingly shows, this specific type of skilled migration is simultaneously reproducing existing socio-economic inequalities and developing new professional and geographical disparities. As with the global migration of care and health workers, this is a periphery to core movement in which, to put it in the simplest of terms, 'Portugal trains nurses, and Britain takes advantage'.

Delicado, in Chap., uses the theoretical standpoint of 'Portugal as semi-periphery' to frame her analysis of the emigration of Portuguese scientists. National policies to encourage the training of scientists abroad, combined with intra-EU scientific mobility schemes, led to a high rate of outward movement. But, at the same time, as Delicado stresses, the Portuguese scientific system, perhaps more so than its Southern European neighbours, worked hard to attract foreign scientists to Portugal. In more recent years, the economic crisis and resulting austerity measures led to cuts in funding for higher education and research, so that a net brain drain has re-emerged as the dominant trend. An interesting question concerns the origin of scientists who are migrating to Portugal. The answer is, mainly from other (semi-)peripheries: Brazil in Latin America; Spain and Italy within Southern Europe; several Eastern European countries (eg. Romania, Bulgaria, Russia, Ukraine); and Asia, mainly India and China. Despite certain attraction factors (climate, culture, low cost of living by European standards), few researchers move to Portugal from the Northern 'core' countries. One can surmise that low stipends are the main reason, since this is a highly cited reason for the non-return of Portuguese scientists working/studying abroad (Gomes 2015).

An other part is on lower-skilled labour migration: two interesting chapters, both of which problematise, in different ways, conventional categorisations of forms of migration and their longer-term outcomes. Chapter, by Queirós, was mentioned briefly above. Here I want to spell out more clearly what I found fascinating about this multi-sited ethnography of Portuguese construction workers who have moved sequentially across borders (Portuguese-Spanish, then Spanish-French) as they navigated the years of the Portuguese and Spanish economic crises.

Queirós follows the inspiring statements of Marcus (1995) on multi-sited research and Fitzgerald (2006) about ethnography with migrants. Based on the 'transregional' cross-border space of north-west Portugal and the adjacent region of Galicia in Spain, he traces the evolution of an occupationally driven migration system of Portuguese builders and construction workers up to and through the crisis years of 2008–2010. A diversity of cross-border mobilities – weekly, fortnightly, longer-term – is observed but, as the economic crisis (which impacted the building industry more seriously than any other sector) developed, many of the migrants moved on to France, where Queirós set up another site of ethnographic research. In this way he exemplifies Marcus' entreaty to 'follow the people' – in this case migrants – but also following the 'connections, associations and relationships' of the research participants across space and boundaries. I was particularly taken by Queirós' notion of his participants' 'bulimic' pattern of experiencing time and space through circular migration: on the one hand working hard and accumulating money on construction sites abroad, denying themselves pleasure or non-essential spending; on the other hand, on weekends or holidays back in Portugal, restoring self-esteem by relaxing, sleeping, drinking, socialising and spending money ostentatiously. At the same time, the volatile nature of construction work, with its unpredictability, authoritarian work culture and lack of human dignity, results in a kind of 'identity de-structuring' and, when the building boom collapses, forces the workers to 'move on', rendering them, in Queirós' words, 'true contemporary nomads'.

In Chap., Marques further problematises the notion of skill through a study of Portuguese entrepreneurial activities in Luxembourg. The story of the Portuguese migration to Luxembourg is a rather hidden element in the overall history of labour migration in Europe. Recruited from the 1960s on, mainly to work in the steel and construction industries, by 2013 Portuguese were the largest immigrant group in the country, accounting for 37 per cent of all foreigners and 16 per cent of the Luxembourg population. Characterised by a generally low level of formal education, the Portuguese have, nevertheless, embedded themselves fairly successfully in the economic and social fabric of the country, including a growing trend to entrepreneurship, mainly in hotels and restaurants. This is exactly where the question of skill arises. If 'higher-skilled occupation' is proxied by education, as it often is (third-level education being the defining criterion), then this excludes an alternative conceptualisation of skill which refers to the 'actual' skills – management, responsibility, scale of financial turnover etc. – involved in running an enterprise. Hence the entrepreneurial route is a way for erstwhile labour migrants to achieve socio-occupational mobility through this 'intermediate' status somewhere between 'high' and 'low' skilled. This is the main theoretical point I wish to draw out from this chapter.

The next two chapters of the book – are on 'postcolonial continuities' in migration and focus on the two main 'Lusophone system' channels of post-crisis migration, to Brazil (Chap. by Rosales and Machado) and Angola (Chap. , by Candeias et al.). Both illustrate the interconnections between timing and economic trends in shaping new migration flows. In the case of Brazil, it was the coincidence of the ongoing crisis in Portugal with a boom in Brazil, partly due to the Soccer World Cup (2014) and the Olympics (2016). In the case of Angola, it was due to the oil boom, which drew in Portuguese migrants especially across the years 2005–2013. Recent Portuguese migrations to Angola and Brazil also illustrate a point I made earlier about the complex articulation of migratory forms that characterise the semi-periphery, and the way these North-to-South migrations challenge the normative premises of both economic migration theory and postcolonial studies. Hence, Portugal functions as both an old and a new periphery for South–North intra-European migration, it acts as a metropolitan core for immigration flows from ex-colonial and East European peripheries yet it also exhibits enduring colonial-era power relationships in sending its own migrants to those parts of the fast-developing global South where its cultural-linguistic influence is strong, and where there are also jobs and business opportunities.

For Brazil, the migrants, based on Rosales and Machado's survey data, are a predominantly higher-educated group and are differentiated by the two main destinations selected for the survey – Rio de Janeiro and São Paulo. In the former city the migrants tend to be in the academic, educational and scientific sectors, whereas in the latter there is a bigger involvement in the business sector. Alongside the economic motives, Portuguese also move to Brazil to experience a somewhat different lifestyle in an environment which is nevertheless reasonably familiar linguistically and culturally, yet tinged with new images of beautiful landscapes and happy-go-lucky people.

Although the 'old colonial' link is shared by both Brazil and Angola, in the latter the pull factors for this North–South migration are less to do with culture or colonial nostalgia, and more related to new opportunities opened up for Portuguese skilled workers in the oil industry, as Angola is the fifth largest oil producer in the world and the second in Africa after Nigeria. In actual fact, as Candeias et al. relate, the recent Portuguese emigration to Angola operates at two class/skill levels: on the one hand middle-class expats with high levels of technical and professional expertise who live in luxury housing; on the other, working-class labour migrants who can capitalise on their 'Portuguese' origins and credentials to get quite well-paid jobs. These characteristics make the 'new' Portuguese emigrants in Angola older than those in Brazil, and two-thirds are men. And unlike the Portuguese in Brazil, who are on the whole well-integrated, in Angola there is weak integration and the maintenance of strong ties with Portugal.

Finally, in Part V of the book, the focus is on 'Identities' – a complex topic indeed. In other Chap. Sardinha, following in the footsteps of pioneering research of Christou (2006) on Greek-American 'returnees' to Greece, looks at the broadly parallel case of second-generation Portuguese-Canadians who relocate to Portugal in a quest for self-discovery. Once again, the Portuguese economic crisis intervened, turning these optimistic 'homecoming' trips into nightmares of disillusionment, resulting in yet another migratory round, either of 're-return' back to Canada, or 'twice-migration' to another (European) destination. Through longitudinal interviews and ongoing contact with his research participants, Sardinha charts the complex reality of their migratory trajectories, revealing how standard models of migration origin and destination are repeatedly 'reversed' and recycled by these sequences of moves. Sardinha closes his contribution by speculating what future cycles of migration may continue his subjects' migratory peregrinations.

Sardinha is not coy about acknowledging his own positionality – as a second-generation Portuguese-Canadian who has 'returned' to Portugal – as part of his research study. This auto-ethnographic stance is taken further by Cordeiro in her chapter, in which she considers the 'unbearable weight' of being classified as an 'emigrant', and by implication 'less Portuguese' than non-emigrants, in Portugal. This is a subtle exploration of the cognitive dissonance between being seen as an 'immigrant' in the United States, and as an 'emigrant' by the Portuguese in Portugal. Perhaps surprisingly, Cordeiro and her key informants identified much more positively with being an 'immigrant' in the USA – a country founded on immigration, which therefore becomes an inclusive concept – than being labelled an 'emigrant' in Portugal, which is seen as a term of exclusion, of 'othering', of being 'outside' the 'true national family'. This 'imposed hetero-classification', which is often contested or rejected by those Portuguese who live outside of Portugal, is especially painfully felt when visiting their hometowns. In contrast to many 'migrant-identity' studies which tend to make assertions about migrants' feelings of belonging along the lines of (taking the Greek-American case, Christou and King 2014, 210) 'when I'm in America I feel Greek, but when I'm in Greece I feel American', Cordeiro opts for the inverse identificatory construction as somehow 'ideal' and more reflective of a positive dual identification: 'Portuguese-Americans like to be Portuguese in Portugal as well as American in the US'.

Four Topics on Which More Could Have Been Said

Although the book presents a remarkably thorough and well-structured account of Portuguese migration routes, old and especially new, there are certain themes that are under-represented. I nominate four such themes, acknowledging yet again the subjectivity of my perspective, since these topics correspond to some of my main research interests in migration studies.

The first of these is the patchy coverage of return migration. There is a compre-hensive treatment of the statistics on returns by Peixoto et al. in Chap. , and then Sardinha in Chap. deals in depth with a very specific type of return – of the sec-ond generation born in Canada. But we learn little – perhaps because it is still too early to tell – of the return propensities of the recent emigrants who are mainly younger and highly educated fleeing the Portuguese economic crisis. This is also important in the light of a key point made at the end of Pires' Chap., regarding the uncertainty of the country's economic and demographic future.

Second, a more geographical point: I was surprised by the lack of attention given to the spatial origins of the various recent outflows. We know from the extensive Portuguese migration literature that the prewar and postwar emigrations to North America were heavily concentrated from the Azores, whilst the mass migrations of the 1950s, 1960s and 1970s to France and other West European countries were sourced mainly from rural areas of mainland Portugal. But where in Portugal do the more recent outflows come from? Probably much more than in the past from urban areas, given the more educated character of the emigrants, but the evidence is missing.

Gender is my third axe to grind. Like all social processes, migration is fundamentally and unavoidably gendered. Men and women migrate for different – as well as sometimes the same – reasons, and migration is an act that is also – often unappreciatedly so – relational as regards gendered family and other personal relations. One issue with incorporating a gendered analysis into the study of migration is whether to have a separate chapter on 'gender' (or on 'migrating women' or for that matter on 'migrating men') or to ensure that gender is mainstreamed throughout the chapters. I think it fair to say that, with the exception of Chap. on the emigration of Portuguese nurses, gender remains in the background throughout most of the book and perhaps could have been given more attention.

Finally, there is scope for more to have been said about the relationship between migration and Portuguese economic and social development. Once again, there are fleeting references (when discussing 'brain drain', remittances and return migration) but no thorough-going dedicated analysis. What does the latest round of Portuguese emigration – the fourth wave – mean for the long-term evolution of Portugal as a (semi-)peripheral country at the south-western margins of Europe?

Acknowledgments This chapter is based both on a keynote lecture entitled 'New Migration Dynamics on the Southern Periphery of Europe', delivered to the Conference on Contemporary Portuguese Migration, held at the Instituto Universitário de Lisboa (ISCTE-IUL) on 12–13 March 2014 and partly on several of the chapters of this book, most of which originated as papers to the conference.

References

Arrighi, G. (1985). *Semiperipheral development: The politics of Southern Europe in the twentieth century*. London: Sage.

Christou, A. (2006). *Narrratives of place, culture and identity: Second-generation Greek-Americans return 'home'*. Amsterdam: Amsterdam University Press.

Christou, A., & King, R. (2014). *Counter-diaspora: The Greek second generation returns 'home'*. Cambridge, MA: Harvard University Press.

Conti, F., & King, R. (2015). Of mentalità and raccomandazione: Comparing the emigration and internal migration of Italian graduates. *Studi Emigrazione, 52*(197), 121–140.

Favell, A. (2008). Rebooting migration theory: Interdisciplinarity, globality, and postdisciplinarity in migration studies. In C. B. Brettell & J. F. Hollifield (Eds.), *Migration theory: Talking across disciplines* (pp. 259–278). New York: Routledge.

Fitzgerald, D. (2006). Towards a theoretical ethnography of migration. *Qualitative Sociology, 29*(1), 1–24.

Frank, A. G. (1967). *Capitalism and underdevelopment in Latin America*. New York: Monthly Review Press.

Góis, P., & Marques, J. C. (2009). Portugal as a semi-peripheral country in the global migration system. *International Migration, 47*(3), 21–50.

Gomes, R. M. (Ed.). (2015). *Entre a periferia e o centro: percursos de emigrantes portugueses qualificados*. Coimbra: Imprensa da Universidade de Coimbra.

Holland, S. (1979). Dependent development: Portugal as periphery. In D. Seers, B. Schaffer, & M.-L. Kiljunen (Eds.), *Underdeveloped Europe: Studies in core-periphery relations* (pp. 139–160). Hassocks: The Harvester Press.

King, R. (1982). Southern Europe: Dependency or development? *Geography, 67*(3), 221–234.

King, R. (1984). Population mobility: Emigration, return migration and internal migration. In A. M. Williams (Ed.), *Southern Europe transformed: Political and economic change in Greece, Italy, Portugal and Spain* (pp. 145–178). London: Harper and Row.

King, R. (1993). European international migration 1945–90: A statistical and geographical overview. In R. King (Ed.), *Mass migration in Europe: The legacy and the future* (pp. 19–39). London: Belhaven Press.

King, R. (2000). Southern Europe in the changing global map of migration. In R. King, G. Lazaridis, & C. Tsardanidis (Eds.), *Eldorado or fortress? Migration in Southern Europe* (pp. 1–26). London: Macmillan.

King, R. (2012). Geography and migration studies: Retrospect and prospect. *Population, Space and Place, 18*(2), 134–153.

King, R. (2015). Migration and Southern Europe – A center-periphery dynamic? In M. Baumeister & R. Sala (Eds.), *Southern Europe? Italy, Spain, Portugal and Greece from the 1950s to the present day* (pp. 139–169). Frankfurt/New York: Campus.

King, R. (2019). A geographer's perspective on migration, identity and space. In T. Linhard & T. Parsons (Eds.), *Mapping migration, identity and space* (pp. 329–354). New York: Palgrave Macmillan.

King, R., Fielding, A., & Black, R. (1997). The international migration turnaround in Southern Europe. In R. King & R. Black (Eds.), *Southern Europe and the new immigrations* (pp. 1–25). Brighton: Sussex Academic Press.

Kurth, J. (1993). A tale of two peripheries: Southern Europe and Eastern Europe. In J. Kurth & J. Petras (Eds.), *Mediterranean paradoxes: The politics and social structure of Southern Europe* (pp. 225–242). Providence: Berg.

Marcus, G. (1995). Ethnography in/of the world system: The emergence of multi-sited ethnography. *Annual Review of Anthropology, 24*, 95–117.

Marques, J. C., & Góis, P. (2017). Structural emigration: The revivial of Portuguese outflows. In J.-M. Lafleur & M. Stanek (Eds.), *South-North migration of EU Citizens in times of crisis* (pp. 65–82). London: SpringerOpen.

McGarrigle, J., & Ascensão, E. (2018). Emplaced mobilities: Lisbon as a translocality in the migration journeys of Punjabi Sikhs to Europe. *Journal of Ethnic and Migration Studies, 44*(5), 809–828.

Sapelli, G. (1995). *Southern Europe since 1945: Tradition and modernity in Portugal, Spain, Italy, Greece and Turkey*. London: Longman.

Seers, D. (1979). The periphery of Europe. In D. Seers, B. Shaffer, & M.-L. Kiljunen (Eds.), *Underdeveloped Europe: Studies in core-periphery relations* (pp. 3–34). Hassocks: The Harvester Press.

Seers, D., Schaffer, B., & Kiljunen, M.-L. (Eds.). (1979). *Underdeveloped Europe: Studies in core-periphery relations*. Hassocks: The Harvester Press.

Selwyn, P. (1979). Some thoughts on cores and peripheries. In D. Seers, B. Shaffer, & M.-L. Kiljumen (Eds.), *Underdeveloped Europe: Studies in core-periphery relations* (pp. 35–43). Hassocks: The Harvester Press.

Vargas-Silva, C. (Ed.) (2012). *Handbook of research methods in migration*. Cheltenham: Edward Elgar.

Wallerstein, I. (1974). *The modern world system*. New York: Academic.

Zapata Barrero, R., & Yalaz, E. (Eds.) (2018). *Handbook of qualitative research in European migration studies*. Amsterdam: Springer.

3

"I Was Enthused When I 'Returned' to Portugal, But I'm Leaving Disillusioned": Portuguese Migrant Descendant Returnees from Canada and Narratives of Return, Re-return and Twice Migration

João Sardinha

Introduction

Throughout the 1980s, 1990s and first half of the 00s, Portugal became a country affected by growing globalisation, development and modernisation. Its inclusion in the European Union brought about benefits to the country that included the modernisation of both the public and private sectors as well as that of the country's infrastructure, all aided by EU financial transfers. In conjunction with this financial influx, major international events also gave the country unprecedented visibility. Such was the case with the World Exposition of 1998 (EXPO 98) and the EURO 2004 football tournament, both of which contributed towards the development of various parts of the country, as well as drawing the world's attention not only to the events themselves but also to the host country.

Drawn by the newly-generated prosperity of this period, Portugal witnessed the return of a significant number of its emigrants – not only of first-generation migrants, but also of their offspring, some of whom had left Portugal as young children, while others had been born in the country of immigration. It is this latter group of migrants I focus on in this article. "Returning"[1] to Portugal at a time of economic growth, many migrated with full awareness of the opportunities that could be found, many often possessing plans of how they could contribute to the country's growth and vice versa – about how Portugal could contribute to their own personal growth. For

[1] I am fully aware that one cannot return to a place one never departed from. Thus the term "return", when referring to the sons and daughters of migrants, will be used to imply ancestral homeland return or return to one's ancestral roots.

J. Sardinha (✉)
Instituto de Ciências Sociais (ICS), Universidade de Lisboa (UL), Lisbon, Portugal
e-mail: jmsardinha@ics.ul.pt

some, however, such ambitions and beliefs were discarded in the wake of the economic crisis that loomed over Portugal from the mid-2000s until very recently. As a consequence, new mobility trajectories, consisting of re-return and twice migration,[2] became common in the lives of some returnees.

At the height of the period of economic crisis, high unemployment and increased emigration resulted from the economic downturn. Estimates show that in 2013, for example, around 110,000 Portuguese nationals departed for other shores (Pires et al. 2014), a figure that surpasses annual emigration statistics from Portugal's emigration heyday of the 1960s and early 1970s. Among Portuguese emigrant descendant returnees, the economic crisis led to job losses, to the closing down of businesses, as well as to individuals not being able to find work. The consequences of the crisis upon this group were thus no different from those experienced by society at large.

Taking the above points into consideration, in this article I aim to analyse narratives of return, re-return and twice migration. I set out to do this via the examination of stories and opinions collected through in-depth interviews and casual conversations held from 2008 to 2015 as part of two related projects. To support my arguments, I will rely on the narrative accounts of six Portuguese migrant descendants from Canada who have re-returned or twice migrated after having resided in Portugal for an extended period of time.[3] I have named these participants António, Carla, Marco, Natália, Nelson and Teresa.[4] Through this examination, I set out three primary goals of analysis: (1) to reflect on issues of attraction to and settlement in Portugal at a time when growth and prosperity were defining factors of return. The discussion will centre here on processes of integration and perceptions of Portugal and Portuguese society, past and present; (2) to examine the reasons behind acts of re-return/twice migration as provided by the interviewees, taking into account the impacts of the economic crisis; (3) to analyse the resources available to these individuals when it comes to making the decision to either return to Canada or move to another country. To achieve this third analytic goal, interactions between transnational network constructions and negotiations – factors that may facilitate mobility – are taken into consideration. The aim will thus be to understand how interactions, constructions and negotiations influence the mobility choices of these individuals at a time when social capital is particularly needed – at a time of economic downturn.

---

[2] Building on the concept developed by Bhachu (1985), I use the term "twice migration" to refer to migrants who migrated first to one country before migrating again to another to seek further life opportunities.

[3] The reduced number of research participants for this analysis is due to the fact that, out of the 22 Portuguese-Canadian returnees interviewed between 2008 and 2015, only these six participants had already moved out of Portugal by the time my fieldwork came to an end in 2014. I additionally point out that among these 22 participants, others also expressed a desire to leave Portugal due to the economic situation, while others were taking steps towards doing so. These individuals, however, remained in the minority, as most participants had no desires or plans to leave Portugal.

[4] In order to maintain anonymity, the participants of this study have been given pseudonyms.

Methodological Considerations

Ethnographic research is at the heart of this investigation. Relying on the qualitative method of in-depth interviewing as the primary source of data, complemented by information gathered through casual conversations with participants, this research has as its central aim the unveiling of meanings encoded in the act of return and re-return/twice migration and the construction and maintenance of personal networks (Christou 2004). This research thus relies on storytelling and the gathering of opinions, with discussion focusing on the conceptualisation of nation, place and culture, as well as dynamics of belonging and identity constructs in the migrants' network (re)building, both when moving to and out of Portugal.

Given that the author and researcher is also a Portuguese emigrant descendant who returned to Portugal from Canada, an additional methodological issue should be considered: the researcher/author's position as an "insider-outsider-within", a position that was particularly important in the recruitment of participants since members of my own personal networks of descendant-returnee migrants both participated in the study and provided links to other interviewees. My "insider-outsider-within" position further implies that I have personal experiences and "rootedness" within the same social context (of return) as the subjects that make this work auto-ethnographic. Auto-ethnography enhances participant research this owed to the fact that the researcher is seen as one of the researched – a boundary crosser (Reed-Danahay 1997).[5]

The participants this article focuses on were all interviewed twice. The first round of interviews, carried out between 2008 and 2012, took place when all interviewees were still residing in Portugal. Thus, all interviews were carried out face-to-face. Follow-up interviews that took place after 2013 were either carried out via Skype or Facebook, or face-to-face whenever participants were in Portugal on holiday.

Semi-structured interview guides were used to steer the interviews. The first round of interviews was guided by questions focusing on (1) integration issues, (2) negotiations of identity and belonging, and (3) local and transnational network construction and maintenance. The second round of interviews focused on the impact of the economic crisis in Portugal and its influence on mobility, and specifically its role in encouraging re-return/twice migration.

In providing a brief characterisation of the participants and their mobility paths, first, all six were born between the years 1973 and 1983 and all returned to Portugal between the years 1995 and 2003 unaccompanied. In 2013–2014, four of the

---

[5]Although this ethnographic research technique may bring with it limitations due to the lack of neutrality of the "insider looking in" (Dyson 2004), these limitations are outweighed by what I consider to be the technique's methodological appropriateness for the research, given that it can provide an additional layer of authenticity, reinforced by self-reflexivity and research awareness from an "insider" perspective (Denzin 1997; Ellis and Bochner 2000). As Hammersley and Atkinson (1983) point out, the social world cannot be researched without the researcher being a part of it.

participants re-returned back to Canada, the other two having twice migrated (one to the United Kingdom and the other to France). Of the four who re-returned to Canada, three returned to the same location they originally departed from, the other to another part of Canada. Lastly, while the participants returned to Portugal single, five out of the six have re-returned or twice migrated with their spouse or common-law partner, two with children as well.

The Lead-Up to the Crisis

For the offspring of Portuguese emigrants, "homecoming" is often seen as a superlative act; the realisation of ethnic completeness (Christou 2006a; Sardinha 2011a, b). This is particularly the case for those who dream of returning to an often idealised version of Portugal first imagined in the emigration country. Once the return is accomplished, however, pre-return idealisations may be contested by the realities of everyday life which may be very different from what was preconceived. As Christou (2004, 54) points out, "exilic" spaces can extend to the "idyllic" space of the ancestral homeland, which is the source of ethnic belongingness; but once the "real" return takes place, disillusionment and disappointment may become the dominant reactions: indeed, the "dream" may even become a "nightmare" (Christou 2006b) when the expected does not come to fruition.

Asked to discuss the reasons why they had "returned" to Portugal and what they were expecting upon settling in the ancestral homeland, participants most commonly described the lure of prosperity, of being able to succeed, and the belief that the Portuguese labour market held more professional opportunities for them. Also talked about was the desire to participate in the development and growth of the country, especially at the local level – in the communities their parents had departed from – where it was felt their involvement could make more of a difference. Moreover, interviewees also described wanting to "return to roots" (Wessendorf 2007) and to live out "being Portuguese in Portugal" (Sardinha 2011a, b). It is common for second-generation migrant descendants to relate nostalgically to the parents' place of origin, especially when their upbringing has been strongly transnational in nature. Such strong connections to roots might even be the motor that drives their desire to live in the country of their ancestry; to be ensconced in roots, where one expects to find the ideal homeland and the socio-cultural elements one thinks defines it – the same elements that served as the backbone of their sense of belonging during their transnational childhoods and adolescences. Building up to becoming "roots-migrants", such individuals tend to draw from everyday translocal experiences while growing up, be they those experiences fostered at home, in the company of fellow emigrants and/or during short holidays in the ancestral homeland (Wessendorf 2007).

Returning to their roots in the hopes of grounding themselves socially and culturally, however, is seldom a clear-cut accomplishment. As Wessendorf (2007) points out, the adaptation of migrant descendant returnees' highly translocal everyday lives to their parents' country of origin cannot be neglected. It is especially important to consider how these individuals deal with the discrepancies between their images of the homeland prior to migration and the actual realities they encounter once they settle there.

Although growing up surrounded by "Portugueseness" in Canada, both in the household and in the community, participants in this study commonly talked about being drawn to the ancestral homeland by what they saw in Portugal during holidays – times when experiences often serve to reinforce romanticised images of the country previously created at a distance, through familial and community transmissions in the diaspora (Afonso 1997, 2005; Santos 2005; King and Christou 2008; Sardinha 2011a). During these short stays, activities are more often than not "carnivalised" occurrences, as seldom are holidays "lived experiences" that permit "normalness" (Sardinha 2011a, b, 2014a). A commonly held perception, therefore, was that of people in Portugal living better, more enjoyable lives in comparison to the lives they themselves had in Canada. Carla (born 1973) expresses this very sentiment:

> To me, there were no wrongs in Portugal. Everybody seemed to have a pretty good life. You wanted a bank loan to buy a house, they'd throw in some extra money for the furniture. Everybody was 'living high off the hog', as the old saying goes. The country received international attention because of things like EXPO 98, EURO 2004, we would come here in the summer and everybody had money to rent a house in the Algarve during the month of August, going out every night and stuff. It was a better life than in Canada … at least I was led to believe that … but it was all smoke and mirrors.

What Carla perceived to be a "relaxing, laidback Portugal" when in the position of a holidaying returnee was quickly revealed to be otherwise upon moving to Portugal and being confronted with everyday life. As King and Christou (2008, 18–19) emphasise, second-generation homecomings needs to go beyond the notion of "an emotionally compelling existential project" and the myth-laden mission of return. This is due to the fact that upon facing the realities of everyday life in the ancestral homeland, many returnees will witness preconceived notions of the mythical/historic homeland – which often only mirror the subjectivities of migrant belongings – clashing with their new surroundings (Markowitz and Stefansson 2004).

In describing the origins of such clashes, the respondents particularly referred to conflicts encountered at an institutional level. For example, societal and organisational "let-downs" deriving from encounters with the "inner workings" of Portuguese society and the state – ranging from bureaucracy, to lack of honesty, to corruption – were described as having brought about disillusionment and rupture. In the words of António (born 1979):

> I moved (to Portugal) because I loved the place, and I still do. But the more time I spent here, the more I realised I didn't really know the place. You look at the Vasco da Gama Bridge and you think wow! Right? But then you realise that bridge is still not paid for and over the years, certain people made a lot of money off of it. It's no secret to anyone. I never thought about the justice system when I came here, but when you get here, you quickly find out it doesn't work, there's corruption at all levels, people give jobs to their friends who don't know a thing about what they're doing. It happens inside the government. We're supposed to believe things are going to be rosy forever in a country like that?

What Markowitz and Stefansson (2004) refer to as "the unsettled paths of return" – a phrase used to describe returnees' experience when confronted with the unexpected – are very much evident in António's narrative. António's words go beyond describing disillusionment with the unexpected, however, as they cast doubt on the country's present and future fortunes due to what is perceived as its negative functioning.

Misguided perceptions of the Portuguese job market were also highlighted. Some of the returnees said they had moved to Portugal thinking that their know-how and educational capital would permit them to enter the high end of the labour market, only to be confronted with the fact that things are not so straightforward once in Portugal. Natália (born 1980) recounted her experience:

> When you move to Portugal, you start at ground zero. Everyone else here is already set up in one way or another. They have their "connections", their "cunhas", as they say here, and we all know how valuable that is in Portugal. So you try to work your way up in an honest manner and you quickly find out that that's not how it works. I worked as a journalist in Portugal for a couple of years and it's a world of fierce competition that promotes exploitation. So as things got worse and people started losing their jobs … I mean, I knew of people who were making pretty good money, were let go and then couldn't land a job paying minimum wage. People with a lot of experience in the business. How was I supposed to compete with that? The only way would have been to subject myself to making even less.

Natalia's quote reflects a common sentiment – that migrant descendants are at a disadvantage upon returning to Portugal due to not having the right social capital or "cunhas" (individuals who assist in furthering one's professional advancement), as well as due to difficulties in penetrating already established social networks.[6] Thus, Natalia's experience mirrors the experiences recounted by some of the other participants, of having put in a lot of work to get to where they are professionally in Portugal, and to now see it all hit a "stumbling block" or "dead end". Among our participants, some lost their jobs, others closed down businesses, others couldn't find work, while others simply got tired of jumping around from job to job with no security and labour rights, all owing to the economic crisis overshadowing Portugal. Employment is the main concern for these individuals. It was described by them as the primary factor that had led them to pursue further mobility. The next section will examine this issue.

Re-returning/Twice Migrating: Transnational Networks and Reasons for Mobility

> I had a language school. That's how I made a living. When people and families start losing their jobs and getting taxed to the bone, they're going to look at where they can cut spending. Right there, the English classes for the kids is one of the first things to go. This town, a

[6] Research carried out by Tsuda (2004) on the return of Japanese-Brazilians (Nikkeijin) back to Japan as well as Christou's (2006a) work on Greek-Americans' return to Greece have noted similar tendencies.

> medium sized town, has been hit particularly hard by the economic crisis. Without students, I couldn't pay the bills, so I closed the doors. Contributed to the city with yet another empty building, packed up my things and returned to Canada.

Marco (born 1979) saw an opportunity when he left Canada in 2001 to live and set up a business in his parents' hometown. Portugal provided him with an opportunity, but one that did not last as long as he would have liked. Marco's situation was one not uncommon to crisis-hit Portugal. The difference between Marco and others in Portugal with similar stories is that Marco had an alternative country he could turn to – a "safety net country"; a form of "life insurance" possessed through dual citizenship, ready to be activated when needed.

Elsewhere I have argued that return migration often serves to fortify the transnational self, but in reverse. Where once the returnee invested in making contacts with Portugal and keeping Portuguese culture alive while in the diaspora, in the post-return period efforts are often made to keep the familial country of immigration present via contacts, dealings and lifestyle choices (Sardinha 2011b, 2014a). This is to say that returnees' migration experiences seldom end with return, for there is always another country to which one is tied. The past one often took for granted in the familial country of immigration may become fortified through maintained ties with individuals who are left behind, through maintained interest in events and occurrences back where one came from, as well as through confrontations with socio-cultural differences in the ancestral homeland.[7] As Cassarino (2004) points out, return migrations are more often than not part of a system of ties and exchanges distinguished by ongoing circuits of mobility (not always of a physical nature), as opposed to being definitive acts of resettlement.

In the narratives collected, it was often implied that mobility is an integral part of migrants' life strategies – even if not urgent in nature, it is a strategy they "hold in their back pockets". As Levitt and Glick Schiller (2003) point out, the degree to which an individual wishes to be transnational depends on the extent to which he/she wishes to be attached to the transnational social space and one's level of involvement in it. Defined as spaces in which there is ongoing dissemination of transnational meanings and symbols through social and symbolic ties, transnational social spaces are key to helping maintain multi-fold transactions that traverse borders (Pries 1999, 2001; Faist 2000). Investment in such a space is often a key tactic for gaining or maintaining "mobility capital". These individuals' transnational spaces are preserved through relations maintained in Canada and elsewhere that have facilitated a re-return/twice migration. The following three narrations – first from Marco, second from Natália, and third from Teresa (born 1983) – demonstrate how this works in the case of re-return:

---

[7] As a number of authors (Potter 2005; Conway and Potter 2007) have come to argue, the differentiation and non-acceptance of return migrants leads to a process of "othering"; that is the marked marginalisation of the returnees as outsiders who are perceived as being different to the indigenous population. This may lead to the returnee turning inward, leading to the realisation of difference between the individual and the society returned to, which in turn leads the individual to become closer to the country returned from (Sardinha 2011a, b, 2014b).

> Before I moved to Portugal, I lived in Edmonton where I went to college and I worked in restaurants as well. I have some friends there that I've always kept in contact with, who helped me out when I got back there. You don't have to look very hard to realise that Edmonton and (the province of) Alberta is filthy rich because of the Tar Sands (petroleum). Everybody's looking for workers so it's easy to find work. It's the complete opposite of Portugal. Having friends there who basically guided me and told me to go talk to this guy and that guy was very important. We're lucky to have another country to go to such as Canada, where we know people that can lend a hand if need be.
>
> In Toronto, with the Portuguese community being so big, there's all kinds of ethnic media. I know a lot of those people. I was sometimes even asked by the Portuguese media in Toronto to look into things for them in Portugal since I worked in the business. This is always a good thing, for if you're helping someone now, the day might come when they'll help you out. I mean it's no coincidence that I ended up finding work with an organisation that works for the Portuguese community (upon going back to Canada). That's the thing, you return to Portugal but you don't disconnect from where you came from, the place and the people ... Even when you are away, you still maintain contact with everyone through the internet, Facebook, that sort of thing.
>
> Up until he had to close down his butcher shop, my husband used to say: 'I will never leave Portugal'. But things started going downhill pretty fast. My parents have this back and forth lifestyle with a house here and a house back in Canada. If they had decided to sell everything and move (to Portugal) permanently, I don't know if we would have gone back. We have a big family there, one of the biggest Portuguese families in that part of Canada, and there's a lot of solidarity. My husband is not even a butcher there anymore. He works with my uncle in his cement business and makes more money than if he were a butcher. For the time being, we're also still living in my parent's house.

The three citations above have one commonality: they all express the importance of social networks and the role they played when making the re-return. Marco highlighted the importance of his friend, Natália the Portuguese community and Teresa her family. These quotes also emphasise the importance of networks in acquiring work in particular, but not exclusively. Teresa, who re-returned with a family, also drew attention to having a place to live upon arrival. Writing on ancestral homeland return, King and Christou (2008) outline three key challenges to be overcome if the "return of social realism" is to be successful: finding a place to live (a real sense of home in the homeland); economic security (a job); and a circle of friends. In making the re-return, we again witness the importance of the exact same variable.

Another point worth drawing attention to is the fact that these individuals nurtured their transnational networks at a distance, something that today is facilitated by modern technologies – namely the internet and telecommunication technologies. Using technological means of communication results in mobility that is spatially, temporally, and infrastructurally anchored, but globally distributed. Being able to see and talk to someone thousands of kilometres away at the click of a button, and being able to know what is happening as it happens in real time, helps link individuals together, facilitating exchange and reinforcing transnational ties (Somerville 2008). Access to news and information via technology provides proximity to occurrences of a social and cultural nature. As pointed out by Williams et al. (2008), people are often pragmatic about how technology fits into their current practices and it can help them accomplish what they want to accomplish in life. The authors further suggest that the degree of technological use is often influenced by family, friends, and individual interests. Being close to family and friends and/or being up-to-date on issues that affect the individual, or are of interest to the people back in the country of departure, may therefore become a priority for these descendants for strategic reasons, namely to facilitate a possible re-return if need be.

Beyond re-return, migrants may want access to multiple mobility strategies – the luxury of being able to pick between two or more options, with the ultimate aim being to find the best place to live at any given time. To exemplify this, I turn to António, who explained the following:

> Well I kind of knew things weren't going to work out for me (in Portugal) when I finished my PhD (in Political Science), but I wasn't limiting myself to Portugal nor to Political Science. I could've tried applying for a post-doc, but together with my partner, who is French, we decided to go back to Montreal, thinking it would be the best option for us. Portugal was on a downward spiral (economically) and it was a good idea to get out while we were ahead. On a more personal level as well, I had started to mistrust a lot of things about the country, from government to academia … it just wasn't healthy for me. In the end, leaving ended up being a wise decision. (…) The future of academia is in ruin in Portugal. But anyway, I got out of academics altogether. Portugal paid for my PhD. and it will never see that return. In Montreal I started working for an insurance company but my partner wasn't all that happy there – she couldn't find the right job, that sort of thing – so we packed up again and moved to France where I'm doing the same thing I was doing in Montreal and everyone's happy.

António identified Portugal's economic downturn – which had produced an environment he felt he could not strive in – and personal factors brought about by the country's "bad governance" that were affecting his well-being as the key reasons behind his decision to leave Portugal and go back to Montreal. Montreal, however, was not his "final" destination. Having a partner who is a French national also facilitated migration to France. His mobility flexibility was equally influenced by a second person who became another key player in the mobility negotiations. Thus, from António's mobility options and patterns, it can be argued that terms like "return", "re-return" and "forever" are incompatible. This is due to the multiplicity of lived-in and travelled-through personal maps, and to the negotiations and transactions carried out in transnational social spaces. The sense may be one of always being in transit, lured by the ephemeral state of "quest" that is often driven by global contemporary societies and, in some situations, the combined condition of youth, trying to find oneself, and the search for place – one that will permit prosperity, tranquillity and personal and collective growth (Pessoa 2004). Having anchored places or residency as back-ups at any given time in their lives gives António and his partner the security that enables them to have a flexible approach to career changes and options. As Hannerz (1990, 239) points out, such mobile participants will more often than not maintain a position of openness towards divergent cultural experiences, searching out contrasts rather than uniformity. Such transnational meanderings often imply that such individuals will gain the propensity to feel at home in a variety of contexts (Giddens 1991) as long as where they are provides the conditions they desire, something António felt Portugal, in the current time, could not fulfil.

Like António, Nelson (born 1979) opted to twice migrate, explaining in the following narrative why he and his wife chose to do this:

> After I decided to stop playing (professional football), we decided that it would be best to go somewhere that would give me an opportunity in life. We could have gone back to (the province of) British Columbia – all my family is there – but it was too far away from Portugal. My wife had spent a couple of years studying in Wales, so it was an easy decision. They facilitate everything there, not like here (in Portugal) where everything's a nightmare. I finished high school there and then got into university to study Sports Science and, through that programme, I landed a job with a top-flight football club. All this within three years, basically. Can you imagine this happening here in Portugal? I can't. (…) Still, if you ask me if I want to go back to Portugal, the answer is yes. I'm a sucker for the punishment. Portugal is like that bad boy that all the girls want, you know? … Or like that (popular) saying in Portuguese: 'The more you hit me, the more I like you'? That's Portugal (laughs).

What we take from Nelson's statement is his feeling of needing to leave Portugal because Portugal could not provide what he needed to succeed. He points out the efficiency and organised way of life in Wales that has permitted him to grow professionally in a short period of time, contrasting that with the lack of efficiency and disorganisation he found in Portugal.

Another point worth highlighting is Nelson and his wife's decision to move to Wales instead of Canada, primarily owing to the proximity of the United Kingdom to Portugal, a proximity that allows them to visit Portugal with more regularity and at lower travel costs in comparison to the west coast of Canada. As various authors (Baldassar 2001; Christou 2006a, b; Condon and Ogden 1996; Duval 2004) have pointed out, return visits can be perceived as transnational exercises through which social spaces are constructed, linked, and maintained. When these spaces become anchored in the ancestral homeland, they end up playing key roles in constructing return desires. Nelson and his wife's choice of moving to Wales over Canada is part of that strategy; of being close to Portugal in order to facilitate more regular contact, with the objective of someday returning to Portugal again. What we witness, therefore, is the desire to return to the ancestral homeland, no different from the desire Nelson had possessed before making his initial move to Portugal from Canada. The difference this time around is the fact that he now has a different vision and outlook towards the country he again yearns to live in. Asked why he would rather be living in Portugal than Wales or Canada, he replied:

> Because it's where I feel most at home; it's the country and the culture I was raised on and raised in as well. It's basically where I feel I belong, you know … even if things are a mess. Plus there's all that good stuff I'm sure you get from everyone you talk to: the sea, the sun, the food, the lifestyle, Benfica – who doesn't love that? Someday we'll go back … we'll see.

The aspiration to someday returning to Portugal is thus defined by feelings of being at home in the ancestral homeland – where the clarification of the "self" is consummated through being surrounded by familiarity, through comfort and through being a part of a greater whole, factors that seem to outweigh the negatives associated with Portugal. Such grounded attachment leads to questions about patterns of second returns to ancestral homelands, and about the extent to which positives associated with Portugal outnumber the negatives to the point where someday these individuals return, once again, to Portugal.

Conclusion

The objectives of this article have been threefold: to observe the return to Portugal of six descendants of Portuguese migrants from Canada at a time of economic prosperity in the ancestral homeland; to analyse the causes and patterns of re-return / twice migration during the recent period of economic downturn that overshadowed Portugal; and to draw attention to the transnational networks and ties available to these individuals that have facilitated their re-return/twice migration.

Upon returning to Portugal, the returnees described being confronted with the "real lived-in version of Portugal", which was dissimilar to what they had learned to appreciate about their ancestral homeland at a distance or during holiday visits: that it was relaxed and laidback. Upon settling, positive preconceptions often got deflated and replaced by adjectives such as "bureaucratic", "dishonest" and "corrupt", reflecting perceptions that brought about disillusionment and rupture with the society returned to. Such disillusionment was particularly highlighted in relation to the job market, where it was felt they were at a disadvantage due to not having the right connections or social capital.

Beyond the integration struggles described, recent disillusionment was also thought to have been brought about by the economic crisis – often thought to have been caused by the often unprincipled inner workings of Portuguese society and the country's poor governance – which, in turn, led to individuals losing their jobs, closing businesses and not finding work in Portugal. To leave Portugal, and search out opportunities elsewhere, became the natural alternative.

As this article has highlighted, mobility is often dependent on the strength of social networks and the social capital an individual can accumulate (Cassarino 2004; Morosanu 2010). If networks across borders are nourished, transnational links will persist (King and Christou 2008). Investing in and maintaining transnational spaces is thus a key tactic for gaining "mobility capital". This is where returnees are at an advantage, for they have come from a country (in this case, Canada) where they have maintained networks that have assisted in constructing the transnational self. Judging by their circulation patterns and networks, these migrants have thus become what Klimt (2000) terms "transmigrants", maintaining relations of a familial, social and organisational nature that traverse borders.

Mobility strategies may consequently have become unpredictable, determined not only by a logic of comfort in which economic survival – rather than living out one's roots in the country of ancestry, which was once given greater importance – becomes an overarching factor, but also by one's ties. This is the case for the two participants who ended up migrating to a third country. The decision to do so was not made blindly. Added to the equation, in both situations, was the fact that the wife of one participant, and the legal partner of the other, had ties to the two respective countries. The primary reason for twice migrating is no different from the main reason for re-returning – to improve one's life, above all economically; but one reason that did differ was articulated in Nelson's explanation that he opted for Wales in order to be physically closer to Portugal.

The initial act of returning to Portugal may therefore be nothing more than an act of self-discovery (Sardinha 2011b) happening in the "here and now", but one where the near future is kept in mind – and where transnational links are always maintained so they are ready to be activated if necessary. If the "here and now" is defined by economic hardship, then re-activating one's transnational status, mobilising any transnational social capital one possesses to one's benefit, and thus prompting further mobility – a re-return/twice migration – becomes a natural process.

One question now remains to be answered: will these individuals and their families give Portugal another chance? Or perhaps equally important to ask is: given their experiences and expectations, will they ever see Portugal as capable of providing them with the life they most desire in the land of ancestry?

Acknowledgments and Funding The results analysed in this article derive from two separate phases of fieldwork: a first phase carried out from 2008 to 2012 as part of the author's post-doctoral research project entitled "The Return of the Portuguese Second-Generation to Portugal: Identity, Belonging and Transnational Lives", and a second phase, as part of the Fundação para a Ciência e a Tecnologia (FCT) funded project "REPOR – Luso-descendant 'Returnees' in Portugal: Identity, Belonging and Transnationalism" (PTDC/ATP-GEO/4567/2012), carried out from 2013 to 2015. The proofreading of this chapter was funded by the Portuguese Emigration Observatory (Observatório da Emigração).

Bibliography

Afonso, S. (1997). *A Segunda geração e o regresso. A geografia do actor de fronteira*. Coimbra: Master's dissertation in Sociology, Faculty of Economics, University of Coimbra.

Afonso, S. (2005). A segunda geração e o regresso: motivação e vivências. In M. Marujo, A. Batista, & R. Barbosa (Eds.), *Proceedings of 1st international conference. The voice and choice of Portuguese immigrant women* (pp. 117–127). Toronto: University of Toronto.

Baldassar, L. (2001). *Visits home: Migration experiences between Italy and Australia*. Melbourne: Melbourne University Press.

Bhachu, P. (1985). *Twice migrants: East African Sikh settlers in Britain*. London: Tavistock Publications.

Cassarino, J.-P. (2004). Theorising return migration: The conceptual approach to return migrants revisited. *International Journal on Multicultural Societies, 6*(2):253–279.

Christou, A. (2004). Reconceptualizing networks through Greek-American return migration: Constructing identities, negotiating the ethnos and mapping diaspora—Theoretical challenges regarding empirical contributions. *Spaces of Identity, 4*, 53–70.

Christou, A. (2006a). *Narratives of place, culture and identity: Second-generation Greek-Americans return 'home'*. Amsterdam: Amsterdam University Press.

Christou, A. (2006b). American dreams and European nightmares: Experiences and polemics of second-generation Greek-American returning migrants. *Journal of Ethnic and Migration Studies, 32*, 831–845.

Condon, S. A., & Ogden, P. E. (1996). Questions of emigration, circulation and return: Mobility between the French Caribbean and France. *International Journal of Population Geography, 2*(1), 35–50.

Conway, D., & Potter, R. (2007). Caribbean transnational return migrants as agents of change. *Geography Compass, 1*(1), 25–45.

Denzin, N. K. (1997). *Interpretive ethnography: Ethnographic practices for the 21st century*. Thousand Oaks: Sage.

dos Santos, I. (2005). Being a part of several 'worlds': Sense of belonging and wedding rites among Franco-Portuguese youth. *Narodna umjetnost. Croation Journal of Ethnology and Folklore Research, 42*(1), 25–45.

Duval, D. (2004). Linking return visits and return migration among Commonwealth Eastern Caribbean migrants in Toronto. *Global Networks, 4*(1), 51–67.

Dyson, M. (2004). Dare to be different: Write an auto ethnography. In S. McLeod (Ed.), *Making spaces: Regenerating the profession. Proceedings of the 2004 Australian teacher education association conference* (pp. 187–194). Bathurst: School of Teacher Education/Charles Sturt University.

Ellis, C., & Bochner, A. (2000). Autoethnography, personal narrative, reflexivity: Researcher as subject. In N. K. Denzin & Y. S. Lincoln (Eds.), *Handbook of qualitative research* (pp. 733–768). Thousand Oaks: Sage.

Faist, T. (2000). *The volume and dynamics of international migration and transnational social spaces*. Oxford: Oxford University Press.

Giddens, A. (1991). *Modernity and self-identity. Self and society in the late modern age*. Cambridge: Polity.

Hammersley, M., & Atkinson, P. (1983). *Ethnography: Principles in practice*. London: Tavistock.

Hannerz, U. (1990). Cosmopolitans and locals in world culture. In M. Featherstone (Ed.), *Global culture: Nationalism, globalization and modernity* (pp. 237–251). London: Sage.

King, R., & Christou, A. (2008). *Cultural geographies of counter-diasporic migration: The second generation returns 'home'* (Sussex migration working paper) (Vol. 45). Brighton: University of Sussex, Sussex Centre on Migration Research.

Klimt, A. (2000). European spaces: Portuguese migrants' notions of home and belonging. *Diaspora: A Journal of Transnational Studies, 9*(2), 259–285.

Levitt, P., & Glick Schiller, N. (2003). *Transnational perspectives on migration: Conceptualizing simultaneity* (Working paper 3-09J). Princeton: Princeton University/Center for Migration and Development.

Markowitz, F., & Stefansson, A. D. (Eds.). (2004). *Homecomings: Unsettling paths of return*. Lanham: Lexington Books.

Morosanu, L. (2010). Mixed migrant ties: Social networks and social capital in migration research. *CARIM IV Summer School on Euro-Mediterranean Migration and Development (2009)*, Best Participant Essays Series AS 2010/43, Robert Schuman Centre for Advanced Studies, European University Institute. http://cadmus.eui.eu/bitstream/handle/1814/14048/CARIM_ASN_2010_43.pdf?sequence=1 Accessed 2 Feb 2015.

Pessoa, I. (2004). Adeus Macau! Repercussões de um percurso migratório nas trajectórias sociais de jovens portugueses. In *Actas dos ateliers do V Congresso Português de Sociologia* (pp. 39–47). Lisboa: Associação Portuguesa de Sociologia.

Pires, R. P., Pereira, C., Azevedo, J., & Ribeiro, A. C. (2014). *Emigração Portuguesa. Relatório Estatístico 2014*. Lisboa: Observatório da Emigração e Rede Migra/Instituto Universitário de Lisboa (ISCTE-IUL)/CIES-IUL and DGACCP.

Potter, R. (2005). Tale of two societies': Narratives of adjustment among second generation return migrants to St. Lucia and Barbados. In R. Potter, D. Conway, & J. Phillips (Eds.), *The experience of return migration: Caribbean perspective* (pp. 89–108). Aldershot: Ashgate.

Pries, L. (1999). New migration in transnational spaces. In L. Pries (Ed.), *Migration and transnational social spaces* (pp. 1–35). Aldershot: Ashgate.

Pries, L. (2001). The approach of transnational social spaces: Responding to new configurations of the social and the spatial. In L. Pries (Ed.), *New transnational social spaces: International migration and transnational companies* (pp. 3–33). London: Routledge.

Reed-Danahay, D. E. (1997). Introduction. In D. E. Reed-Danahay (Ed.), *Auto/ethnography: Rewriting the self and the social* (pp. 1–20). Oxford: Berg.

Sardinha, J. (2011a). Neither here nor there: Identity constructions, conceptions of 'home' and the transnational lives of second-generation Luso-Canadians and Luso-French in Portugal. In

I. M. Blayer, F. C. Fagundes, T. Alves, & T. Cid (Eds.), *Storytelling the Portuguese diaspora: Piecing things together* (pp. 153–174). New York: Peter Lang.

Sardinha, J. (2011b). 'Returning' second-generation Portuguese-Canadians and Portuguese-French: Motivations and senses of belonging. *Journal of Mediterranean Studies, 20*(2), 231–254.

Sardinha, J. (2014a). "Even if the only thing for me to do here was to milk cows": Portuguese emigrant descendant returnees from Canada narrate pre-return desires and motivations. *Diaspora, 17*(3), 316–339.

Sardinha, J. (2014b). Securing networks or networks of security? Portuguese emigrant descendant returnees negotiate transnational positioning. *InterDISCIPLINARY Journal of Portuguese Diaspora Studies, 3*(2), 413–432.

Somerville, K. (2008). Transnational belonging among second generation youth: Identity in a globalized world. *Journal of Social Sciences, 10*, 23–33.

Tsuda, T. (2004). When home is not the homeland: The case of Japanese Brazilian ethnic return migration. In F. Markowitz & A. Stefansson (Eds.), *Homecomings: Unsettling paths of return* (pp. 125–145). Lanham: Lexington Books.

Wessendorf, S. (2007). 'Roots-migrants': Transnationalism and 'return' among second-generation Italians in Switzerland. *Journal of Ethnic and Migration Studies, 33*, 1083–1102.

Williams, A., Anderson, K., & Dourish, P. (2008). Anchored mobilities: Mobile technology and transnational migration. In J. van der Schijff & G. Marsden (Eds.), *DIS '08 proceedings of the 7th ACM conference on designing interactive systems* (pp. 323–332). New York: Association for Computing Machinery.

4

Portuguese Emigrants' Political Representation: The Challenges of the External Vote

Marco Lisi, Ana Maria Belchior, Manuel Abrantes, and Joana Azevedo

Introduction

The participation of emigrants in national political systems has become an increasingly important topic (Bauböck 2005; International IDEA 2007; Lafleur 2013) Indeed, most consolidated democracies recognise the right of emigrants to vote in national elections (Blais et al. 2001; International IDEA 2007), and there has been a growing tendency to broaden the political rights of emigrants over the last few decades, particularly in the electoral arena (Spiro 2006; Bauböck 2007; Lafleur 2013).[1]

[1] This chapter is based on data provided by Portuguese government institutions, the Directorate General of Internal Administration (*Direcção Geral da Administração Interna*, DGAI), the National Electoral Commission (*Comissão Nacional de Eleições*, CNE), and the Directorate-General of Consular Affairs and Portuguese Communities (DGACCP).

M. Lisi (✉)
Faculdade de Ciências Sociais e Humanas (FCSH), da Universidade NOVA de Lisboa and Instituto Português de Relações Internacionais (IPRI), Lisbon, Portugal
e-mail: marcolisi@fcsh.unl.pt

A. M. Belchior
Instituto Universitário de Lisboa (ISCTE-IUL), Centro de Investigação e Estudos de Sociologia (CIES-IUL), Lisbon, Portugal
e-mail: ana.belchior@iscte-iul.pt

M. Abrantes
Universidade de Lisboa, Instituto Superior de Economia e Gestão (ISEG), Investigação em Ciências Sociais e Gestão (SOCIUS/CSG), Lisbon, Portugal
e-mail: mabrantes@socius.iseg.utl.pt

J. Azevedo
Instituto Universitário de Lisboa (ISCTE-IUL), Centro de Investigação e Estudos de Sociologia (CIES-IUL), Observatório da Emigração, Lisbon, Portugal
e-mail: joana.azevedo@iscte-iul.pt

We refer to external voting rights as 'the active and passive voting rights of qualified individuals, independently of their professional status, to take part from outside the national territory in referenda or in supranational, national, subnational, or primary elections held in a country of which they hold citizenship but where they permanently or temporarily do not reside' (Lafleur 2013: 31).[2] Although there are various theoretical and normative studies on external voting (Barry 2006; Bauböck 2005; Lafleur and Martiniello 2009; López-Guerra 2005; Rúbio-Marin 2006; Spiro 2006; Lafleur 2013), empirical work suggests that the development of external voting depends more on contextual factors rather than on normative arguments (Tager 2006; Rhodes and Harutyunyan 2010; Lafleur 2011). In other words, while existing theoretical and normative studies are concerned particularly with the legitimacy of the external vote, they fail to consider why and how it is implemented. Moreover, there is a scarcity of work on actual voting practices and on the (positive and negative) impacts of electoral system designs on emigrant voting.

Where studies of the external vote exist, they focus mostly on countries that are undergoing processes of consolidation or where external voting is a very recent phenomenon (International IDEA 2007; Collyer and Vathi 2007; Smith 2008). Finally, most of the studies concern with the effects of external voting focus on the inclusion of emigrants in one specific country (Escobar 2007; Itzigsohn and Villacrés 2008). Overall, then, existing work tends to neglect the question of the broader 'success' of voting abroad, in particular as a means of improving political representation and participation.

In this chapter, we will examine the adoption and evolution of external voting in Portugal. We will also evaluate its success and identify the reasons behind the lack of reforms to improve the practice of out-of-country voting. We believe that this case study is worthy of examination for several reasons. First, Portugal was one of the first countries to extend voting rights to emigrants. The external vote was recognised in Portugal following the establishment of democracy in 1974, with the election of representatives of the emigrant community in the legislative elections of 1976. Second, Portugal has been characterised by significant emigration flows. According to the most recent data collected by the the Portuguese Emigration Observatory (Observatório da Emigração) based on the latest estimates by the United Nations, in 2015 the number of emigrants born in Portugal surpassed 2.3 million. About 22% of Portuguese nationals live outside the country (Observatório da Emigração 2017). However, if emigrants' descendants are factored in, the Portuguese communities abroad consist of about five million people. According to an estimate based on data from 2017, there are 1.375 million Portuguese nationals residing abroad with a potential right to vote.[3]

---

[2] One essential characteristic of external voting is the opportunity to exercise a right without having to be physically present in the nation's territory. Therefore, external voting does not cover cases where emigrants have the right to participate in home country elections on condition that they return to the nation's territory to cast their votes (as in Italy before 2006).

[3] The estimate is based on data provided by Portuguese government institutions, the Secretary of State for Portuguese Communities, the Directorate-General of Consular Affairs and Portuguese

There is also another peculiarity that makes the Portuguese case particularly interesting. This is related to the fact that Portugal, in contrast to other European countries, did not make the transition from an emigration to an immigration country. As several studies have noted (Peixoto 2007; Pires et al. 2010), although emigration flows have experienced different cycles and some discontinuities, the number of Portuguese citizens that moved abroad has remained relatively high – even during the decades with highest immigrant inflows. The financial and economic crisis and the austerity policies that hit the country in 2011 led to a huge increase in emigrant outflows: a peak of around 120 thousand departures in 2013, followed by a progressive descent, to around 100 thousand in 2016 (estimates by Pires et al. 2017). Moreover, the fact that the main political parties have remained the same over the democratic period allows us to concentrate on the specificities of electoral rules and actors' interests. Finally, it is worth noting that there are few systematic studies about the Portuguese external vote and how electoral reform may improve the quality of emigrant representation. This is generally an understudied phenomenon and the Portuguese case is not an exception. There are few studies about Portuguese emigrants and their relationship with home-country politics – especially about their electoral participation – and those that exist tend to be essentially descriptive (Malheiros and Boavida 2003; Lobo 2007). Our study intends to fill this gap through research that explores the adoption and implementation of emigrants' political rights, as well as examining how electoral reform may improve the quality of emigrant participation and representation (Lisi et al. 2015; Belchior et al. 2017).

Why did Portugal enfranchise its citizens abroad? What are the characteristics of external voting in Portugal? How have these voting rights evolved? What are the main shortcomings of external voting and the problems/controversies associated with the practice of out-of-country suffrage? An analysis of the Portuguese experience provides an opportunity to answer these questions and to contribute to the debate about the emigrant vote. Moreover, an in-depth case study may shed more light on how the external vote can promote higher levels of inclusion and participation among emigrants, greater respect for the rule of law, and fairer political representation. Last but not least, a qualitative analysis is also well-suited to examining the factors that inhibit the improvement of emigrant representation and potential reforms of the electoral system design.

This study offers a detailed analysis of the development of external voting and the influence of the electoral system on the relationship between the emigrant community and elected representatives. The main argument is that external voting has displayed significant shortcomings that have prevented the fair political representation of Portuguese emigrants. Moreover, it will be argued that, although the debate on external voting reforms has been a constant feature of the political agenda, the

Communities (DGACCP), embassies, consular services and the Directorate General of Internal Administration (latest data available in November 2017). Citizenship is a prerequisite for participating in elections from abroad. As in Italy, the Portuguese nationality law stipulates that a child born to a Portuguese parent is automatically a Portuguese citizen. Since 2017, grandchildren of Portuguese nationals abroad can also request Portuguese citizenship.

conflicts between different political parties' interests have made it difficult to find a solution to improve voting methods for out-of-country electoral districts.

This study relies on extensive empirical material based on different types of sources on external voting. In particular, we draw on academic literature, the press, political parties' records, parliamentary and emigrant associations' documents, official statistics on electoral participation, as well as semi-structured interviews with members of parliament (MPs) and consultation with public officials.[4]

The following section examines the full range of external voting procedures, highlighting the advantages and disadvantages of each method, and the scope for reforming electoral laws. The third section describes the origin and development of emigrant voting rights in Portugal, while the fourth evaluates the success of external voting. The fifth focuses on recent debates about electoral reform. The conclusions summarise the main findings and suggest lines of research that are worth exploring in the future.

The External Vote in Theory: Electoral Laws and Procedures

With the expansion of external voting policies, the scholarly literature has paid growing attention to the factors that led to this worldwide development and to the implications of external voting for the functioning of contemporary democracies. Within this research we can identify three main explanations that may help us understand the reasons behind the external vote's implementation. The first is based on procedural and institutional arguments and it emphases the importance of international and domestic norms that have promoted emigrants' rights to participate in home country elections. As Lafleur has noted (2013: 33–36), most of these international instruments – such as treaties and conventions – do not require states to adopt external voting policies. However, two factors have been particularly important for the implementation of expatriate voting. The first is the influence that European institutions have had in recent decades, namely through the documents drawn up by the Council of Europe and the European Union. The second is related to the constraints imposed by constitutional norms. As in the case of the electoral system at the domestic level, the constitution may include principles or norms – such as the need for approval through a referendum or the requirement of an absolute or qualified majority – that make it difficult to implement the external vote.

[4] The interviews were carried out between January and April of 2010. We interviewed one representative from each Portuguese party with parliamentary representation, with the exception of the CDS-PP (who did not respond to the request): José Cesário (PSD), Paulo Pisco (PS), Helena Pinto (BE) and António Filipe (PCP). We obtained relevant details and clarifications from officials of the following public institutions: the Electoral Administration of the Directorate-General of Internal Administration (AE-DGAI), the National Commission for Elections (CNE), the Commission for the Registration of Portuguese Voters Abroad (COREPE) and the Council of Portuguese Communities (CCP).

The second explanation is based on an economic perspective. This suggests that the implementation of external voting has been motivated by dependence on emigrants' remittances. Yet comparative studies have found that states with a low level of remittances have also implemented the external vote (Collyer and Vathi 2007). Finally, several authors have pointed out the importance of political factors (Tager 2006; Rhodes and Harutyunyan 2010; Lafleur 2011; 2013). According to this third explanation, political parties' interests and the dynamics of competition may help us understand the development and content of external voting legislation. Moreover, emigrant associations and lobbies can also play an important role in the debate on emigrants' enfranchisement. As several studies have shown (Rhodes and Harutyunyan 2010; Lafleur 2011), we need to consider which combination of variables can better explain the adoption of external voting in a particular country and its development over time.

The implementation of external voting is linked to several methods and operational procedures. The electoral norms that regulate voting mechanisms for citizens residing abroad can be included in national constitutions, but they are more often part of non-constitutional or administrative legislation (Nohlen and Grotz 2007: 67–68). One of the most important issues in an electoral law is how it converts votes into mandates. As regards the emigrant vote, there are usually two possibilities: one is to establish a number of districts abroad, which serve to convert votes into mandates; another is to distribute emigrant votes among existing national districts and then to convert them according to the electoral rules used in the national territory. As Nohlen and Grotz (2007) underline, each method has a distinct logic: while the first emphasises the extra-territorial nature of the emigrant vote, the second places greater emphasis on being situated within the national territory as a requisite for suffrage. The first method also allows the political actors to control the impact of emigrants' votes on the final results, while the second is more uncertain in terms of parties' electoral performance.

More often than not, emigrant votes are counted within national districts (Nohlen and Grotz 2007: 70; Collyer and Vathi 2007). In such cases, external votes are apportioned to national electoral districts and included in the vote count of the district that was the emigrant's last place of residence before leaving the country. There are exceptions to the last place of residence rule, however: external votes may be counted for the electoral district corresponding to the capital city, for instance, or for those districts with a total number of voters below the national average. When these other counting methods are used, it is harder to assess the nature of the relationship between emigrant voters and MPs, and the impact of the external vote on final election results.

The choice of administrative procedure is also crucial for the implementation of the external vote (Thompson 2007). There are generally four alternative voting methods for citizens residing abroad: (1) the personal vote; (2) the proxy vote; (3) the postal vote, and (4) the electronic vote. All these different methods present both advantages and disadvantages. In the personal vote an elector must attend at a polling station in person – normally in a diplomatic or consular building – in order to cast his/her vote. This mechanism usually ensures the highest level of transparency but it requires emigrants to travel to vote, which may be particularly difficult in very large countries (such as the US, Brazil or China) or where the network of diplomatic or consular representation is less dense.

The postal vote has logistical advantages and its costs are usually relatively low, but it does not offer the same level of security and confidentiality as the personal vote. In Italy, where this method has been adopted, the widespread use of a 'preferential voting' system in the 2006 elections has been cited as an example of how this system cannot guarantee voting freedom and secrecy (Tarli Barbieri 2007: 139). Another disadvantage of this procedure is that it can be overly lengthy, and may not work well in countries where the postal services are unreliable or inefficient. This has been observed in the Portuguese case.

By contrast, the proxy vote is easy to organise and implement and relatively inexpensive. Voting by proxy means that an elector can appoint someone to vote for him/her at his/her polling station. Each elector needs to tell his/her proxy which candidate(s) to vote for. The biggest problem with proxy voting is that it cannot ensure transparency and secrecy, and thus calls into question the principles of fairness and equality (Lafleur 2013: 22). Finally, the electronic vote also minimises costs and it can ensure rapid results and greater mobility. However, it has logistical and security-related disadvantages and it can raise issues of voter equality (Braun 2007). Spain is one of the few European countries (along with Austria, France, the Netherlands and Switzerland) to have implemented pilot projects to allow emigrants to cast ballots through the Internet. According to the 'Voting From Abroad Database' collected by IDEA (International Institute for Democracy and Electoral Assistance), only 8 countries out of 216 currently use this method, and in Europe only Switzerland has adopted it.[5]

Overall, the choice of method depends not only on the electoral formula and system of voter registration, but also on the geographical distribution of emigrants, as well as the cultural and political traditions of the national community. It should be noted that some countries allow a variety of voting methods to take account of host country peculiarities and to ensure that emigrants are as well represented as possible.

According to the IDEA database, as of 2017 there are circa 155 countries that grant their citizens residing abroad the right to vote. Among these, 75 provide for the conventional personal vote only, which is cast at polling stations set up especially for elections. There are 22 countries that provide only for the postal vote, one with only the electronic vote and another five allow only proxy voting. Finally, 39 countries – 18 of them European states – provide for two or more voting methods.

This brief outline of external voting systems shows the main characteristics of external voting policies. However, as Nohlen and Grotz (2007) suggest, it is necessary to consider not just legal factors, but also political factors related both to the logistics and organisation of elections (political-procedural factors), as well as to party strategies and the dynamics of the party system (political-institutional fac-

[5]A complete database of voting methods around the world can be found at https://www.idea.int/data-tools/data/voting-abroad

tors). It is also important to take into account how successfully electoral laws enable the political representation of emigrants. Only with an understanding of the limits and constraints on emigrants' representation can reform proposals be improved.

How can we assess the success of the external vote? In order to evaluate how well electoral mechanisms represent citizens living abroad, it is important to consider three main dimensions. The first is related to the fairness and freedom of elections. Since Dahl's seminal contribution (Dahl 1971), there is a consensus that democratic elections imply the lack of significant fraud and coercion and that competition between diverse social and political groups must occur transparently and must be unbiased. The second important dimension is the equality of representation. The focus here is on whether emigrants have adequate representation compared with citizens living in the home country. Therefore, this dimension can easily be evaluated by considering the degree of proportionality of the external vote. The third element used in our study is based on the level of participation. Several scholars have argued that the impact of electoral systems on citizens' mobilisation is a fundamental aspect of the quality of contemporary democracies, not only because it fosters civic engagement and guarantees the transmission of people's interests, but also because it boosts government responsiveness (Powell 2000; Norris 2003; Beetham and Landman 2008). In the following, we will examine the implementation and development of external voting policies in Portugal and we will use these three criteria to evaluate the shortcomings of emigrants' representation and the prospects for reforming expatriate voting.

The Adoption of the External Vote in Portugal

Before examining the experience of external voting in Portugal, it is crucial to have some idea of the importance and characteristics of Portuguese emigration. Portugal has been a country of emigration since the second half of the nineteenth century. Between 1850 and 1975 two main cycles characterise the move abroad of Portuguese emigrants. The first occurred between 1850 and 1930 and was dominated by a transatlantic flow, mainly towards Brazil. The second cycle started after World War II, lasted until the end of the authoritarian regime in 1974, and concerned mostly European countries (France, Germany and Switzerland). In this period, and in particular from the mid 1960s until 1973, a massive flow of Portuguese nationals left the country. The third cycle began at the start of the democratic period and lasted until 2000. As noted earlier, Portuguese emigration has remained relatively high even during the period of economic growth experienced after access to the European Community. A fourth cycle of Portuguese emigration began in the 2000s, increasing in 2011 with the 'Great recession' and reaching its peak in 2013. Today Portuguese emigrants are distributed across more than 140 different countries worldwide.

During the authoritarian regime (1926–1974) there was little interest in the enfranchisement of Portuguese nationals living abroad. Salazar's New State (*Estado Novo*) did not explicitly recognise citizens' rights to emigrate and always attempted to control emigration flows for both political and economic reasons (Santos 2004; Pereira 2009, 2014). The dictatorship adopted an ambivalent emigration policy based on the discretionary powers assigned to the Emigration Board (*Junta de Emigração*) and on ill-defined regulations. On the one hand, the authoritarian regime officially restricted emigration in order to strengthen the colonial empire (in particular after the beginning of the colonial wars) and to retain control over the labour force with the aim of attaining the economic objectives of the state, particularly in agriculture and industry. On the other hand, emigration was encouraged not only because it served the nationalist component of the rhetoric elaborated under Salazar's dictatorship, but also because it limited the impact of the economic crises, especially after the regime's failed attempts to modernise the Portuguese economy (Malheiros and Boavida 2003).

Examining this emigration policy adopted by the New State helps us to understand the strong association between Portuguese nationals living abroad and right-wing political forces. As Table shows, the Social Democratic Party (Partido Social Democrata, PSD) has always gained the most votes in out-of-country districts with an average share of 44%.[6] Its strongholds are countries outside Europe,

Table: Electoral results in extraterritorial districts (percentages), Legislative Elections (1976–2015)

	Political party					
Year	BE	PCP	PS	PSD	CDS	Turnout
1976	–	6.3	28.7 (1)	41.4 (3)	18.6	86.8
1979	–	8.0	18.8 (1)	58.7 (3)	–	66.8
1980	–	7.8	12.7 (1)	70.6 (3)	–	61.8
1983	–	8.9	18.3 (1)	41.1 (3)	24.4	45.4
1985	–	9.1	14.5 (1)	33.8 (2)	29.4 (1)	30.0
1987	–	7.0	15.4 (1)	53.0 (3)	14.8	26.5
1991	–	4.3	17.8 (1)	65.7 (3)	9.0	32.6
1995	–	4.1	25.4 (1)	49.8 (3)	4.2	23.8
1999	0.5	3.8	48.2 (3)	33.9 (1)	3.2	23.5
2002	0.8	3.3	33.7 (1)	48.2 (3)	4.3	24.4
2005	1.7	3.0	43.7 (1)	38.2 (3)	3.4	24.7
2009	3.8	3.2	35.9 (1)	34.2 (3)	4.2	15.2
2011	2.3	2.8	30.0 (1)	41.2 (3)	4.9	16.9
2015	3.6	3.6	20.0 (1)	44.0 (3)	–	11.7
Average	2.1	5.4	25.9	43.7	10.9	35.0

Source: Ministry of the Interior (DGAI/MAI). Percentages include blank and invalid votes. Notes: (1) In parentheses the number of seats obtained by each party. (2) The two right-wing parties (PSD and CDS) formed a pre-electoral alliance in 1979 and 1980 under the label of Democratic Alliance (Aliança Democrática), and in 2015 under the label of Portugal à Frente. Also the PCP has usually formed electoral coalitions with left-wing parties or with the greens (since 1983). (3) The average is calculated only for the years in which the parties competed alone

[6] Despite its name, the PSD is a centre-right party. The PSD and the PS are the two largest parties in Portugal.

especially the United States, Latin America and Africa. By contrast, the Socialist Party (Partido Socialista, PS) has never been able to obtain the same level of support in extraterritorial districts as it achieved within the national territory. However, since the 1990s the two parties have competed more equally in European countries, where Portuguese emigrants display more leftist orientations. Overall, in out-of-country districts the two main parties have achieved a higher share of the vote than at the national level. In other words, small parties have always experienced huge difficulties in gaining support and communicating their message to the emigrant community, with the partial exception of the small right-wing Democratic and Social Centre (Centro Democrático-Social, CDS) during the first decade of the democratic regime. The Portuguese Communist Party (Partido Comunista Português, PCP) and the Left Bloc (Bloco de Esquerda, BE, a new left-libertarian party born in 1999) have never obtained seats in out-of-country districts.

Beyond the legacy of the authoritarian regime, it is worth emphasising that after the 'Carnation Revolution' of 25 April 1974, the move abroad of important personalities and political groups linked to the authoritarian regime enhanced the traditional dominance of conservative parties among Portuguese emigrants. In addition, the low levels of education and the low economic and professional background of those living and voting abroad have also benefited right-wing parties.[7] Consequently, the right has traditionally displayed a higher level of support for the introduction of external voting, whereas left-wing forces have been more skeptical.

Overall, Portugal's experience of the legalisation of the vote for emigrants was marked by two key moments (Malheiros and Boavida 2003: 467). The first was the passage of the first electoral law in 1976 during the transition to democracy, while the second crucial moment came in the 1990s, when emigrants' electoral rights were expanded to include participation in European and then presidential elections.

External voting rights for Portuguese emigrants were established with the first electoral law adopted after the fall of the authoritarian regime. This was a consensual issue among political parties and experts involved in the development of the first electoral law, which was used to elect the Constituent Assembly on 25 April 1975. The reasons for allowing Portuguese emigrants to exercise their voting rights were twofold. The first was related to the evolution of domestic politics following the regime change and consisted in a willingness to establish equal political rights, as well as opportunities for the effective participation and inclusion of all citizens. As the experience of other recent democracies shows, democratic transitions are often associated with the establishment and implementation of emigrants' political

[7] It is worth noting that the second generation of Portuguese emigrants displays some important differences compared to the first generation: while the first emigration cycle was based on male rural workers who left their country permanently, the second wave was more balanced in terms of gender and included a higher proportion of emigrants engaged in the industrial sectors (Baganha 2003: 148–150). In addition, the move abroad was more temporary and the exchanges with the home country more dense. This partially explains why the PS has improved its vote share in European countries in recent decades.

rights.[8] The second argument was based on the importance of emigrants for the Portuguese economy. Remittances represented a good share of the country's GDP between 1950 and 1970 and has subsequently been a crucial source of revenues for many families, especially in the uncertain period following the fall of the dictatorship. As other studies have emphasised (Calderón Chelius 2003), this argument has often been used to strengthen loyalty towards the home state and to stimulate ties between emigrants and their home country, especially in poor states (such as Mexico or Cape Verde).

Yet the electoral rights of Portuguese citizens living abroad initially only concerned legislative elections, as the military retained control over the (s)election of presidential candidates during the first decade of democracy. Apart from that, two main factors limited the use of external voting elections beyond legislative contests, namely for the direct election of the President and for national referenda. The first was the threshold of a two-thirds majority imposed by the Constitution in order to implement the electoral law reform. The second was related to the different interests of the main political parties. Under the Portuguese constitution, a consensus between the two main parties was needed in order to allow emigrants to vote in presidential elections and referenda. As a consequence, the expansion of voting rights was significantly influenced by the strategic calculations of the different political actors involved.

The first important change of the external vote that expanded emigrants' political rights occurred with the approval of Law 14/87, which allowed emigrants living abroad who do not opt to vote in another European member state to vote in European elections (see Table).[9] Moreover, the Council Directive 93/109/EC (6 December 1993) permitted European citizens to choose whether to vote for European elections in their state of residence or in their home country. The first time that Portuguese emigrants elected MPs to the European Parliament was in 1987.[10] In general, the PS has performed better in these elections than in legislatives ones, mainly because Portuguese citizens living outside Europe were not allowed to vote until the 2009 European elections. However, as in legislative elections, small parties have obtained a decreasing proportion of votes and turnout has also declined, with a strikingly low emigrant participation rate of 2.9% registered in the 2009 European elections, followed by a 2.1% registered in the 2014 elections.

The second major expansion of external voting concerned the election of the President of the Republic. Traditionally, the position of the right has been to defend the participation of emigrants in presidential contests, while the left has opposed it.

[8] See, for example, several Eastern European and Latin American countries that introduced external voting in the 1990s (International IDEA 2007). The case of Portuguese ex-colonies such as Cape Verde, Mozambique and São Tomé and Principe are also of relevance here, as all adopted external voting after the establishment of the democratic regime.

[9] The Maastricht Treaty approved in 1991 also established the right of emigrants to vote and run as candidates in European and local elections in their country of residence.

[10] These elections took place in Portugal and Spain only because of their entry into the European Community in 1986.

Table: Main laws regulating the external vote in Portugal

Laws	Year	Type of election	Main changes
Decree-law 95c/76 (30 January)	1976 (1976)	Legislative	Establish emigrants' right to vote in legislative elections
Decree-law 319-A/76 (3 May)			
Law 14/87 (29 April)	1987 (1987)	European	Establish emigrants' right to vote in European elections
Directive 93/109/CE			
IVth constitutional revision and Organic law 3/2000	1997 (2001)	Presidential Referendum	Establish emigrants' right to vote in presidential elections and referenda
Organic law 5/2005	2005 (2009)	European	Eligibility criteria: voting rights expanded to citizens living outside Europe
			Voting methods: in person
	2005 (2006)	Presidential	Clarification of eligibility requirements
Organic law 3/2010	2010 (2011)	Presidential	Reduce voting period (2 days)
			Changes in eligibility criteria
			Changes in the rules for establishing polling stations

Note: in parentheses the year of the first election that applied the new regulation

As a rule, the PSD has consistently supported broadening the emigrant vote since the 1980s as well as the adoption of the postal vote (Cruz 1998: 204). As mentioned above, this is because of the broad support that it has traditionally received from extraterritorial districts (Lobo 2007). Those who have opposed broader voting rights have argued that reform will unfairly increase the impact of the emigrant vote on election results. Emigrants could be decisive in a presidential election if that election is based on a majoritarian system, particularly in highly competitive contests. To this was added the argument that there were technical problems with the implementation of the external vote based on the personal vote, therefore calling into question the legitimacy of the final result (Malheiros and Boavida 2003: 476). In addition, the fact that Portugal's nationality law is based on *jus sanguinis* criteria was an argument used to imply that even people with very weak ties to Portugal can obtain citizenship. Finally, another argument deployed by those opposing reform was emigrants' lack of knowledge about national political life and the distance that separated them from the political parties, a problem that would be aggravated in 'second order' elections, in which levels of participation by the national electorate have been traditionally very low.

Despite the initial criticism of the socialists, the implementation of external voting for presidential elections became possible through an agreement between the PS and PSD on electoral system reform. In particular, the 1997 constitutional reform (fourth revision) made it possible to introduce single-member districts, corresponding to the (unfulfilled) expectation of the adoption of a mixed electoral system (Cruz 1998; Martins 2004; Sampaio 2009). With regard to external voting, this constitutional change made it possible for emigrants to vote in presidential elections and national referenda. In fact, the drafting of the electoral law of 2000 (Organic Law 3/2000), which originated with the fourth constitutional revision, was a key turning point in terms of broadening the right to vote of Portuguese citizens living abroad. The first time that this law was applied was in the 2001 presidential elections.

How can we explain the strategic convergence between parties with regard to the expansion of emigrants' voting rights? Some important developments related to the domestic political scene have to be emphasised. First, the consolidation of democracy seems to have had a significant impact on the scope for electoral reform (Malheiros and Boavida 2003: 477). Institutional and governmental stability allowed the parties to adopt a more open position and to favour the expansion of emigrants' voting rights. Second, the party system has evolved and become more bipartisan, with the two main parties winning the bulk of total votes (Jalali 2007). Finally, from the 1990s onwards, there was growing recognition of the emigrant community's socioeconomic importance to Portugal. This led to growing support among the political parties for emigrants' right to political equality (interviews with PSD and PS MPs), and the government reinforced its commitment to the communities abroad with the creation in 1996 of a consultative and representative body, the Council for Portuguese Communities (Conselho das Comunidades Portuguesas). Emigrant associations have also been able to increase their political visibility, especially in longstanding destination countries where various Portuguese generations coexist such as France and the USA.

Evaluating the External Vote in Portugal

After considering the adoption of external voting and the expansion of emigrants' political rights, this section assesses the technical characteristics of voting procedures and evaluates their performance over the democratic period. Due to the lack of comprehensive reforms (Freire et al. 2008), voting abroad and its successive reforms have been characterised by several problematic features, especially in terms of voting procedures. As this section demonstrates, these shortcomings have significant implications for making emigrants' voting rights effective.

The Constitution approved in 1976 established the principle of proportionality so as to better reflect social pluralism and more effectively represent the different political forces (Cruz 1998). This law has a general character and applies equally to citizens living both inside and outside the national territory. In order to achieve this objective, the electoral formula was also 'constitutionalised' through the adoption of the d'Hondt method. The constitutionalisation stipulates that electoral reforms require two-thirds approval by the legislature, making it harder to alter the formula used to convert votes into mandates.

How proportional is the external vote in Portugal compared to the national territory? Generally speaking, the Portuguese electoral system has been considered relatively proportional (according to the Gallagher index, the average disproportionality between 1976 and 2015 was 4.8). The average district magnitude is 10.5 (for the 2015 elections) but there are variations among the districts.[11] Apart from a small number of large districts (in Lisbon and Oporto), which have a higher level of proportionality, Portugal is otherwise split up into either average-sized or small constituencies (Martins 2004; Jalali 2007; Freire et al. 2008).

As regards the delimitation of districts, the commission charged with drafting the electoral law established two extraterritorial districts for citizens living abroad. Since 1976, these districts have elected four MPs: two for the European and two for the non-European host countries.[12] The European and extra-European districts are the smallest compared with the national ones (with two MPs each), and very disproportional (Martins 2004; Martins and Mendes 2005). In practice, the high disproportionality of the extraterritorial districts means it is impossible to elect representatives from the smaller political parties; only the two largest parties are able to do so.[13]

Given the number of Portuguese emigrants living in the two extraterritorial districts and the low number of MPs elected in these districts, the principle of proportionality was not strictly respected. This decision may be explained by the fear that Portugal's large emigrant community would be in a position to elect a large proportion of MPs, and this would be unfair since emigrant voters do not live in their home country (Lobo 2007: 83–84).

As regards voting procedures, the laws that regulate the external vote establish different voting methods: while in legislative elections emigrants vote by post (and have done so since 1976), in presidential elections they can only vote in person. In this case voters have to attend the polling station nearest to their place of residence in order to cast their vote. The Organic law 3/2000 also establishes a three-day voting process. As for the postal vote, voters have to fill in their ballot, which they receive 2 or 3 weeks before the election, and must then post it to the embassy or consulates in the host country, from where it is delivered to the Ministry of Interior where the votes are counted (Decree Law 95 C/76, article 8). The implementation of this voting procedure has been problematic, with several cases of illegal practices, especially where local notables or party structures were able to organise the vote collectively (in a 'syndicate vote')[14]. Moreover, the fact that the procedure

---

[11] In comparative terms, the Portuguese system is slightly more disproportional than other European countries with similar setups (4.58 disproportionality and an average district magnitude of 27.8). See Freire et al. (2008). The values of disproportionality and district magnitude are based on the 'least squares index (LSq)', a tool developed to measure the amount of disproportionality generated by an election outcome, by which is meant the disparity, if any, between the distribution of votes at the election and the allocation of seats. Source: https://www.tcd.ie/Political_Science/people/michael_gallagher/ElSystems/Docts/lsq.php

[12] This option was also adopted in other Portuguese speaking countries (Angola, Cape Verde and Guinea Bissau). Institutional isomorphism for laws governing citizens residing abroad is quite common, particularly when there are strong cultural and linguistic ties (see also Tintori 2011).

[13] This is also shown by Lijphart's effective threshold (1994). In Portugal, the value is 9.8 (the average between 1976 and 1999), while for the two external districts it is 25.

[14] 'Syndicate vote' is the practice of politicians registering a group of people (who are not necessarily eligible to vote) and then voting for them collectively.

adopted for legislative elections is different from presidential contests makes the practice of the external vote incongruent.

Besides the inequality between citizens in the home country and external electors and the lack of transparency, one of the main problems of voting abroad is related to emigrants' steady electoral demobilisation from the 1980s onwards. Indeed, turnout levels in legislative elections outside the national territory have declined significantly: while the rate of emigrant participation in the first post-transitional legislative elections in 1976 was around 82%, for the 1987 elections it declined to 26.5%, and in 2009 to 15.2%, while in 2011 the level of participation was 16.4%, and in 2015 the figures reached a historical low at 11.7%.[15] Although the trend towards increasing rates of abstention also characterises participation patterns within the national territory, it is worth noting that the intensity of this phenomenon in extraterritorial districts was significantly stronger than in domestic electoral districts and it also began considerably earlier. As a consequence, from the end of the 1980s national political forces and emigrant representatives began to discuss the need to reform the existing law to stimulate greater levels of participation and equality. Despite the lack of empirical studies, the causes of the decline in electoral participation in extraterritorial districts are to be found not only in voting procedures, but also in registration mechanisms (see below) and in the role played by political and civil society actors in mobilising voters.

Another problem associated with the low levels of participation concerns eligibility criteria. Overall, all citizens above the age of 18 can vote, a policy that is internationally widespread (Blais et al. 2001). It is important to note that unlike citizens residing in the home country, emigrants are not obliged to register, mainly because it is hard to monitor electoral registration abroad (Malheiros and Boavida 2003: 471). For external voting, registration occurs mainly at consulates, embassies or other designated centres, and it can be done any time up to 60 days before an election. Given the dispersion of Portuguese emigration and the weaknesses of the consular network, a substantial proportion of citizens living abroad does not register. For example, around 242,852 Portuguese citizens resident abroad registered for and were entitled to participate in the 2015 legislative elections, while a 2017 esti-mate put the total number of Portuguese nationals living abroad at 1.375 million[16]. This means that in practice, the eligibility criteria established for Portuguese nation-als living abroad did not favour the mobilisation and integration of the Portuguese emigrant community.

Contrary to the electoral law for legislative elections, voting abroad for the presidential election presents more exclusive rules in terms of eligibility. According to

[15] Figures of emigrants' turnout are based on the proportion of citizens living abroad who are enfranchised and who cast a ballot in home country elections (Bauböck 2007: 2398–2399).

[16] No such estimate was available for 2015. The estimate is based on data provided by Portuguese government institutions, the Secretary of State for Portuguese Communities, the Directorate-General of Consular Affairs and Portuguese Communities (DGACCP), embassies, consular services and the Directorate General of Internal Administration (latest data available in November 2017).

the fourth constitutional reform, voters must prove the existence of 'effective ties to the national community' (art. 121). The law approved in 2005 clarified this requirement by establishing that citizens can be held to have effective ties with the national community when: (a) they live in a country of the European Union or in an officially Portuguese-speaking country but ceased living in Portugal less than 15 years ago; (b) they live in any other country but ceased living in Portugal less than 5 years ago; or (c) they have gone to Portugal and stayed there for at least 30 days over the last 5 years, and can prove they can speak Portuguese (Law 5/2005 of 8 September 2005). Overall, the regulations regarding proof of effective ties to the community are not very clear and the criteria have been interpreted rather broadly (Mendes and Miguéis 2005: 11–12).

As for the relationship between MPs and emigrants, representatives of external districts have emphasised that it is impossible to represent the interests of citizens living in four different continents. Electoral campaigns have been concentrated in a small number of locations with a higher number of Portuguese residents (Paris, Brussels, São Paulo, Newark and New Bedford). The costs associated with organising abroad, the shortage of activists and human resources, and the low potential benefit in terms of votes amplify dramatically the isolation of regions where party penetration is less robust or nonexistent, and emigrant voters tend to remain less informed. A question mark hangs over the role of organisations representing Portuguese emigrants. On the one hand, they are expected to build community and encourage participation in home country politics among the local emigrants. On the other, their own existence as representatives may render voting in home country elections less necessary. By stimulating political engagement and awareness, these associations may activate the political rights of emigrants in their host country.

Our interviews with PSD and PS MPs indicate that electoral districts for the external vote need to be reformed in order to improve emigrants' representation. However, there is no consensus on the best way of strengthening MP-emigrant links. The disagreements are related not only to the number of districts (one or more), but also to the number of MPs that emigrants should elect. This debate, however, has been linked to the change of the electoral law that has long dominated the agenda on the reform of the political system (Cruz 1998; Freire et al. 2008; Freire 2019). Although electoral reform has been a recurring theme in debates about how to improve the political system, the external vote has not been a centrepiece of electoral reform proposals put forward to date. While there is convergence between parties about the need to maintain the degree of proportionality, issues related to the proximity between voters and elected representatives – specifically the type of electoral district (single-member vs multi-member) and preferential voting – have been highly contested (Martins 2004; Sampaio 2009).

It should be noted that both issues have been addressed from an exclusively national point of view, even though they are more problematic for the extraterritorial districts, especially due to the impact of the (weak) ties between emigrants and their representatives on turnout. The main reason for this is probably that external electoral districts have had a historically negligible impact on election results. Political parties and specialists alike have tended to neglect this dimension, not only because competition within these districts is limited but also because electoral outcomes are highly predictable. The fact that all MPs elected in extraterritorial districts between 1975 and 2015 belonged to the PSD or PS, with only one MP from the CDS elected in 1985 (see Table), has had a negative impact on the level of competition, as well as on parties' efforts to mobilise and inform Portuguese emigrants.

Two main conclusions emerge from this evaluation of external voting. First, there have been several problems in the implementation of emigrants' voting rights, especially with regard to fairness, political equality and turnout. The design of the electoral system for the external vote has limited the effective representation of emigrant communities, mainly due to the inconsistencies of (and controversies about) voting methods and the relationship between MPs and citizens. Second, political factors have played a crucial role in the debate about how best to represent this community, as well as in blocking electoral reform. This can be seen not only in the 'politicisation' of external voting, but also in the confrontation between the parties of the left and right, and the strategic calculations underlying the stances adopted by the political parties. It is noteworthy, for example, that the PS supported extra-European emigrant voting in presidential elections only when its demand for the personal vote was acceded to, while the PSD criticised this procedure when the PS proposed the same voting procedure for the parliamentary elections. Overall, the implementation of the external vote has displayed significant shortcomings, which have been brought to light by the incongruent reforms implemented during the democratic period.

Improving External Voting: The Recent Debate

The debate on the electoral law for external voting emerged again when the PS put forward a proposal in 2007 to adopt the personal vote not just for presidential but also for legislative elections (Draft Law 562/X). As mentioned earlier, there had already been a debate about voting procedures for citizens residing abroad when the legislation on presidential elections had been approved. On that occasion, left-wing parties supported the personal vote, while the PSD and the CDS-PP defended more permissive procedures, considering other voting methods such as postal voting.

The main argument in favour of the change proposed by the PS was that the personal vote would guarantee greater rigour and transparency. José Lello, the Socialist MP who authored the draft law, referred explicitly to vote fraud in Brazil during the 2005 legislative elections as an example of the problems with the existing electoral law. The underlying argument was that the existing law made it easier for parties to organise 'vote syndicates' and thereby distort the free choice of emigrant voters (*Público*, 23 September 2008). But there was another argument based on uniformity of methods, as it was deemed unacceptable that there should be two different procedures governing the external vote. Finally, José Lello highlighted that one of the problems with the postal vote was that it forced voters to choose a candidate long before the elections took place, when the electoral campaign was only just taking off. This meant it was harder for Portuguese citizens living abroad to be informed about and gain a clear picture of party stances and candidates' programmes. The socialists underlined that the high number of null votes was evidence of this problem: null votes accounted for around 8% of votes cast in the 2005 elections, compared with less than 1% for the previous presidential election. In 2015 elections, null votes accounted for circa 11% of votes.

Several parties and emigrant associations highlighted the logistical and organisational challenges presented by the new voting method, which reduced the electoral participation of Portuguese citizens living abroad. Indeed, the reform of the electoral law had been preceded by a decision, approved on 15 March 2007, to restructure the consular network, which led to the closure, merging and downgrading of various consular representations. Moreover, the Socialist government also decided to reduce the cost of dispatching electoral campaign material to emigrant communities. These measures produced public contestation among emigrant associations and lobbies, particularly in France and the US.

Despite the opposition of the main parties of the right and of the emigrant associations, the Socialist majority succeeded in getting the proposal approved in December 2008 with the support of all left-wing parties, while the PSD and CDS-PP voted against. However, President Cavaco Silva (of the right) vetoed the new law, on the grounds that not only was this reform not politically timely (it was an election year), but it also encouraged the electoral demobilisation of emigrants since the consular network would be unable to meet the logistical demands. The main criticisms expressed by the president echoed those of the parties of the right, namely that it would become harder for Portuguese emigrants to find polling stations. In his message to the parliament justifying his veto, Cavaco Silva highlighted the fact that the personal vote was associated with lower levels of participation as compared to the postal vote. A final issue he raised in his statement was the difficulty of finding alternative places to cast votes that would guarantee transparency and the inviolability of votes.

Whether or not to adopt the electronic vote was a key issue in the electoral reform debate. Indeed, José Lello criticised this method when presenting the Socialist draft law for two reasons: first, because there was evidence that the electronic voting system was not secure or transparent, as some European countries have shown;[17] and second, because inequality among citizens would increase, since the Internet was not widespread among the Portuguese emigrant communities.

The presidential veto made it harder to approve the law since a two-thirds parliamentary majority is required to pass organic laws. This impasse led the PS to give up on the reform, particularly in view of the upcoming electoral cycle in 2009. The reform of external voting was again at the centre of the political agenda in the period preceding the 2011 presidential elections. Given their disagreements on voting methods, the main parties adopted a 'minimalist' approach with the aim of implementing only minor and marginal changes. The new law (3/2010, 15 December)

[17] The UK, France and Ireland encountered problems with this new method and therefore decided to abandon the experiment.

reduced the voting period from 3 to 2 days for presidential elections, and increased the number of voters required to establish a polling station (from 1000 to 5000). This law also abolished the requirement to have an effective linkage to the national community for those who have been living in Europe for more than 10 years or outside Europe for more than 15 years, thus increasing the inclusiveness of voting for citizens residing abroad. This reform was approved by the main governing parties (PS, PSD and CDS-PP), while both radical left parties either abstained (in the case of the Left Bloc, BE) or rejected (Portuguese Communist Party, PCP) the proposal, stating that it was too close to the election day.

During the XIII Legislature (inaugurated after the 2015 elections), another important change occurred with indirect consequences for the expansion of eligibility for the external vote. Decree Law n.° 71/2017, which revised the Nationality Law, was passed, allowing grandchildren of Portuguese emigrants to acquire Portuguese citizenship.[18]

Finally, regarding eligibility criteria, in 2018 the government presented a proposal to implement the automatic registration of national citizens residing abroad. If it is adopted, this change will increase the number of registered voters abroad from circa 318,000 to 1.375 million voters (68% of new registered voters are resident in Europe, and 32% outside Europe)[19]. In addition, the debate on voting methods – in particular the adoption of electronic voting – is still ongoing. After the petition discussed by Parliament on this topic in 2016, the PSD proposed to give emigrants this possibility and the Socialist government agreed to implement a pilot to test this procedure[20].

Conclusions

Emigrant voting rights throughout the world have increased over time. This has also happened in Portugal, which recognised this right during the transition to democracy, in time for the first democratic legislative elections. As in the Spanish case, the fall of the authoritarian regime gave the biggest impulse to the enfranchisement of

[18] Criteria for granting nationality by effect of will to grandchildren of a Portuguese national: Individuals born abroad with at least one second-degree ancestor of the Portuguese nationality who has not lost this nationality, and who wish to be granted Portuguese nationality, shall meet the following requirements cumulatively: a) To declare that they want to be Portuguese; b) To have an effective connection with the national community; c) To register his/her birth in the Portuguese civil registry, after recognition of the connection to the national community (Decree Law n°71/2017).

[19] The estimate is based on data provided by Portuguese government institutions, the Secretary of State for Portuguese Communities, the Directorate-General of Consular Affairs and Portuguese Communities (DGACCP), embassies, consular services and the Directorate General of Internal Administration (latest data available in November 2017).

[20] See https://www.publico.pt/2017/06/04/politica/noticia/governo-pondera-modelopiloto-para-testar-voto-electronico-dos-emigrantes-1774550

Portuguese emigrants. In addition, the economic importance of remittances led political actors to implement emigration policies in order to sustain the allegiance of citizens living abroad towards their home country.

Two main problems affected the full inclusion and equality of emigrants' political representation: the lack of representativeness of the electoral system, on the one hand, and the limitations of and incongruencies posed by voting methods, on the other. These shortcomings also have important implications for the level of participation of Portuguese citizens living abroad, which has displayed a significant decrease over the last decades. These conclusions confirms previous findings (Smith 2008; Bolzman 2011; Tintori 2011) which indicate that the procedural and organisational aspects of electoral laws are a key to determining the success of the external vote.

It should be noted that political parties were crucial actors for determining the content of the external voting legislature and its (possible) reform. This work has shown that the main reasons underlying the difficulty of reforming have been not just the 'constitutionalisation' of electoral rules, but also the conflict between the main political parties over emigrant suffrage rights. Indeed, there has been a strong divergence among political actors along partisan lines, particularly as regards voting methods. Traditionally, while the PS and radical left parties (PCP and BE) have favoured the personal vote, the PSD and CDS-PP have been more open, backing the postal vote and, more recently, the adoption of electronic voting. Therefore, strategic considerations represent an important barrier against the improvement of external voting – a conclusion that confirms the findings from other empirical studies (Tager 2006; Rhodes and Harutyunyan 2010; Lafleur 2013). The limited impact of emigrants' vote on final electoral results, the low levels of civil society mobilisation and the characteristics of Portuguese emigration – in terms of both socio-economic background and geographical distribution – help explain why the reform of external voting has been blocked by political parties' interests. Finally, the main political actors did not recognise the autonomy of the external vote with respect to the domestic electoral system, relegating this problem to the general debate about the need to improve political representation at the national level.

This study has served to illustrate that there are limits on the representation of emigrants, namely in terms of participation, proportionality and the efficacy of voting methods. Therefore, the reform of external voting is an important step towards the improvement of the quality of contemporary democracies through a greater inclusiveness and equality among citizens. Moreover, the analysis of the activities of parties, MPs and other institutional actors with regard to emigrant communities provides further elements for understanding the relationship between emigrants and their representatives and patterns of mobilisation.

Acknowledgments and Funding A version of this chapter was originally published in *South European Society and Politics* (Lisi et al. 2015). This chapter includes further analysis over a longer period.

This chapter is part of the study "Portuguese Emigrants' Political Participation and Citizenship" (2009–2011), undertaken at the Centro de Investigação e Estudos de Sociologia (CIES-IUL),

ISCTE – Instituto Universitário de Lisboa (ISCTE-IUL), and financed by the Portuguese Emigration Observatory (Observatório da Emigração). The proofreading of this chapter was funded by the Portuguese Emigration Observatory (Observatório da Emigração). The authors would like to thank the DGAI, the CNE, the DGACCP, the CCP and the OEm for their support and cooperation. The authors would also like to thank also the anonymous reviewers and Imiscoe Series editors for their useful comments on a previous version.

References

Baganha, M. I. (2003). Portuguese emigration after World War II. In A. C. Pinto (Ed.), *Contemporary Portugal. Politics, society and culture* (pp. 139–157). Boulder: Social Sciences Monographs.

Barry, K. (2006). Home and away: The construction of citizenship in an emigration context. *New York University Law Review, 81*(11), 11–59.

Bauböck, R. (2005). Expansive citizenship: Voting beyond territory and membership. *Political Science and Politics, 38*(4), 683–687.

Bauböck, R. (2007). Stakeholder citizenship and transnational political participation: A normative evaluation of external voting. *Fordham Law Review, 75*(5), 2393–2447.

Beetham, D., & Landman, T. (Eds.). (2008). *Assessing the quality of democracy*. Stockholm: IDEA.

Belchior, A. M., Azevedo, J., Lisi, M., & Abrantes, M. (2017). Contextual reasons for emigrants' electoral participation in home country elections: the Portuguese case. *Journal of Contemporary European Studies, 26*(2), 197–214. https://doi.org/10.1080/14782804.2017.1413641.

Blais, A., Massicotte, L., & Yoshinaka, A. (2001). Deciding who has the right to vote: A comparative analysis of electoral laws. *Electoral Studies, 20*, 41–62.

Bolzman, C. (2011). The transnational political practices of Chilean migrants in Switzerland. *International Migration, 49*(3), 144–167.

Braun, N. (2007). E-voting and external voting. In International IDEA (Ed.), *Voting from abroad: The international IDEA handbook* (pp. 217–233). Stockholm: International Idea.

Calderón Chelius, L. (Ed.). (2003). *Votar en la distancia: la extensión de los derechos políticos a migrantes, experiencias comparadas*. Mexico City: Instituto Mora.

Collyer, M., & Vathi, Z. (2007). Patterns of extra-territorial voting. *Working Paper* T22, Sussex Centre for Migration Research.

Cruz, M. B. (Ed.). (1998). *Sistema eleitoral português: debate político e parlamentar*. Lisbon: Imprensa Nacional.

Dahl, R. A. (1971). *Polyarchy, participation and opposition*. New Haven: Yale University Press.

Escobar, C. (2007). Extraterritorial political rights and dual citizenship in Latin America. *Latin American Research Review, 42*(3), 43–75.

Fierro, C. N., Morales, I., & Gratschew, M. (2007). External voting: a comparative overview. In International IDEA (Ed.), *Voting from abroad: The international IDEA handbook* (pp. 11–35). Stockholm: International Idea.

Freire, A. (2019). Electoral systems and political reforms: Portugal in comparative perspective. In A. C. Pinto, & C. P. Teixeira (Eds.), *Political institutions and democracy in Portugal* (pp. 55–76). Palgrave Macmillan.

Freire, A., Moreira, D., & Meirinho, M. (2008). *Para uma melhoria da representação política. A reforma do sistema eleitoral*. Lisbon: Sextante.

International IDEA (Ed.). (2007). *Voting from abroad: The international IDEA handbook*. Stockholm: International Idea.

Itzigsohn, J., & Villacrés, D. (2008). Migrant political transnationalism and the practice of democracy: Dominican external voting rights and Salvadoran hometown associations. *Ethnic and Racial Studies, 31*(4), 664–686.

Jalali, C. (2007). *Partidos e democracia em Portugal 1974–2005*. Lisbon: Imprensa de Ciências Sociais.

Lafleur, J.-M. (2011). Why do states enfranchise citizens abroad? Comparative insights from Mexico, Italy and Belgium. *Global Networks, 11*(4), 1–21.

Lafleur, J.-M. (2013). *Transnational politics and the state. The external voting rights of diasporas*. London: Routledge.

Lafleur, J.-M., & Martiniello, M. (Eds.). (2009). *Transnational political participation of immigrants*. New York: Routledge.

Lijphart, A. (1994). *Electoral systems and party systems: A study of twenty-seven democracies, 1945–1990*. Oxford: Oxford University Press.

Lisi, M., Belchior, A. M., Abrantes, M., & Azevedo, J. (2015). Out of sight, out of mind? External voting and the political representation of Portuguese emigrants. *South European Society and Politics, 20*(2), 265–285.

Lobo, M. C. (2007). Portugal: extended voting rights and decreasing participation. In International IDEA (Ed.), *Voting from abroad: The international IDEA handbook* (pp. 83–87). Stockholm: International Idea.

López-Guerra, C. (2005). Should expatriates vote? *The Journal of Political Philosophy, 13*(2), 216–234.

Malheiros, J. M., & Boavida, M. J. C. (2003). El voto, arma del pueblo: La participación política de los emigrantes portugueses. In L. Calderón Chelius (Ed.), *Votar en la distancia: La extensión de los derechos políticos a migrantes, experiencias comparadas* (pp. 457–487). Mexico City: Instituto Mora.

Martins, M. M. (2004). *Participação política e democracia. O caso português (1975–2000)*. Lisbon: Instituto Superior de Ciências Sociais e Políticas.

Martins, M. M., & Mendes, M. F. (2005). *30 Anos de democracia. Retrospectiva das eleições para a Assembleia da República (1975–2005)*. Lisbon: Comissão Nacional de Eleições.

Mendes, M. F., & Miguéis, J. (2005). *Lei eleitoral do Presidente da República: actualizada, anotada e comentada* (3rd ed.). Lisbon: Comissão Nacional de Eleições.

Nohlen, D., & Grotz, F. (2007). The legal framework and an overview of electoral legislation. In International IDEA (Ed.), *Voting from abroad: The international IDEA handbook* (pp. 65–76). Stockholm: International Idea.

Norris, P. (2003). *Electoral engineering. Voting rules and political behavior*. Cambridge: Cambridge University Press.

Observatório da Emigração. (2017). *Portuguese Emigration Factbook 2016*. Lisbon: Observatório da Emigração, CIES-IUL, ISCTE-IUL. https://doi.org/10.15847/CIESOEMFB2016.

Peixoto, J. (2007). Dinâmicas e regimes migratórios: o caso das migrações internacionais em Portugal. *Análise Social, XLII, 183*, 445–369.

Pereira, V. (2014). *A ditadura de Salazar e a emigração. O Estado português e os seus emigrantes em França (1957–1974)*. Lisbon: Círculo dos Leitores.

Pereira, V. (2009). Ineficiência, fragilização e duplicidade. O velho Estado Novo perante a nova imigração para a França (1960–1968). *Ler História, 56*, 43–68.

Pires, R. P., Machado, F. L., Peixoto, J., & Vaz, M. J. (Eds.). (2010). *Portugal: atlas das migrações internacionais*. Lisbon: Tinta-da-China.

Pires, R. P., Pereira, C., Azevedo, J., Vidigal, I., & Veiga, C. M. (2017). *Emigração Portuguesa. Relatório Estatístico 2017*. Lisbon: Observatório da Emigração e Rede Migra, CIES-IUL, ISCTE-IUL. https://doi.org/10.15847/CIESOEMRE042017.

Powell, G. B. (2000). *Elections as instruments of democracy*. Yale: Yale University Press.

Rhodes, S., & Harutyunyan, A. (2010). Extending citizenship to emigrants: Democratic contestation and a new global norm. *International Political Science Review, 31*(4), 470–493.

Rubio-Marín, R. (2006). Transnational politics and the democratic nation-state: Normative challenges of expatriate voting and nationality retention of emigrants. *New York University Law Review, 81*(1), 117–147.

Sampaio, N. (2009). *O sistema eleitoral português. Crónica de uma reforma adiada*. Lisbon: Alêtheia.

Santos, V. (2004). *O discurso oficial do estado sobre a emigração dos anos 60 a 80 e emigração dos anos 90 à actualidade*. Lisbon: Alto-Comissariado para a Imigração e Minorias Étnicas.
Smith, R. C. (2008). Contradictions of diasporic institutionalization in Mexican politics: The 2006 migrant vote and other forms of inclusion and control. *Ethnic and Racial Studies, 31*(4), 708–741.
Spiro, P. J. (2006). Perfecting political diaspora. *New York University Law Review, 81*(1), 207–233.
Tager, M. (2006). Expatriates and elections. *Diaspora: A Journal of Transnational Studies, 15*(1), 35–60.
Tarli Barbieri, G. (2007). Il voto degli italiani all'estero: Una riforma sbagliata. In R. D'Alimonte & A. Chiaramonte (Eds.), *Proporzionale ma non solo: Le elezioni politiche del 2006* (pp. 121–159). Bologna: Il Mulino.
Tintori, G. (2011). The transnational political practices of "Latin American Italians". *International Migration, 49*(3), 168–188.
Thompson, J. (2007). The implementation of external voting. In International IDEA (Ed.), *Voting from abroad: The international IDEA handbook* (pp. 113–126). Stockholm: International Idea.

5

The Fourth Wave of Portuguese Emigration: Austerity Policies, European Peripheries and Postcolonial Continuities

Cláudia Pereira and Joana Azevedo

Introduction

Few studies have addressed recent emigration from European countries. The refugee crisis and migratory pressure have helped keep academic attention over the last few decades focused on immigration, asylum, reception and integration in Europe. However, these dynamics promoting entries into European countries coexist with other fairly significant dynamics promoting departures from these countries. The sovereign debt crisis coupled with austerity policies that asymmetrically affected Europe's peripheral countries have exacerbated the phenomenon of emigration in various European countries.

These migrant outflows can be observed in the peripheries of Europe – in Ireland (western periphery), Spain, Italy, Greece and Portugal (southern periphery), Poland, Bulgaria, Romania and Latvia (eastern periphery). The migrants that make up these flows have primarily emigrated to Western and Northern European countries, such as Germany and the United Kingdom. More specifically, their migrations have for the most part shifted towards major cities – to London, a "eurocity", in the United Kingdom's case (King et al. 2016). It is important to analyse the impact of inequalities on these outflows, reconciling the perspective of the destination countries with that of the countries of origin and relating this to more widespread processes of socioeconomic globalization.

Our book aims to counter the invisibility of emigration from European countries in the literature by examining the particularities of the Portuguese case. We seek to understand the structural and conjunctural factors that characterise the fourth wave of Portuguese emigration, comparing Portugal's experience of emigration with that of other Southern and Eastern European peripheral countries. We highlight the

C. Pereira (✉) · J. Azevedo
Instituto Universitário de Lisboa (ISCTE-IUL), Centro de Investigação e Estudos de Sociologia (CIES-IUL), Observatório da Emigração, Lisbon, Portugal
e-mail: claudia.pereira@iscte-iul.pt; joana.azevedo@iscte-iul.pt

significant volume of outflows in the fourth wave of Portuguese emigration, the direction of these flows, and the profiles of current emigrants. These flows are concentrated within Europe – in both old (France) and new emigration destinations (United Kingdom),[1] but are also significant outside Europe in historical destinations with post-colonial continuities (Angola and Brazil). Therefore, the fourth wave of Portuguese emigration moves predominantly from southern to northern Europe, but also from the Global North to the Global South. It is argued that the economic recession that followed the 2008 financial crisis played a decisive role in these recent emigration dynamics, together with other factors that are discussed extensively by the authors in this book.

The book compiles the work of authors from different academic backgrounds who have conducted empirical research on Portuguese emigration using a wide variety of extensive and intensive methods. Namely, national and international statistics, large-scale questionnaires, in-depth interviews and ethnography – thus seeking to diversify the range of methodological perspectives and strategies used to understand emigration today. The research presented in this book includes a greater diversity of methodological strategies than did studies of the old waves of emigration. For example, the use of large-scale surveys involving more than 6000 respondents, which enables us to compare Portuguese emigrants living in different countries, as Peixoto et al. do in Chap. 3 (REMIGR 2017). Also, the use of national and international statistics that allow us to compare the Portuguese with other immigrants living in the same country, as Pires and Pereira do in Chaps. 2 and 5, respectively.

Emigration to countries in the three continents of America, Africa and Europe has been a structural feature of Portuguese society since around the nineteenth century – and it has been a large-scale phenomenon both geographically and demographically. In this volume we analyse the similarities and differences between different migratory cycles. For instance, Sardinha and Cordeiro, in Chapters 12 and 13 respectively, discuss the identities of both the old emigrants and their descendants in North America. We also look to the old routes of Portuguese emigration to South America, Africa and Europe that have become attractive again to recent migrants (see Lopes, Queirós, Rosales et al. and Candeias et al. in Chaps. 6, 8, 10 and 11, respectively).

It is important to provide the key statistical data on Portuguese emigration today in order to better contextualise it within the topics discussed in the book. There are a total of 2.3 million Portuguese emigrants (stock) according to the United Nations (Observatório da Emigração 2018, 31). The calculation of this figure employs the statistical concept of an emigrant, i.e. an individual born in Portugal residing in

[1] The United Kingdom has been a destination of Portuguese emigrants since the 1960s, although at that time it received much lower numbers than France or Germany. It was only after 2011 that the UK's population of Portuguese emigrants grew dramatically to levels that exceeded those seen in other countries. The majority of Portuguese emigrants living in the UK before 2011 were in the Northeast and Southeast of England, as well as in the southern islands of Jersey and Guernsey, and were primarily concentrated in London (Almeida 2007; Beswick and Pozo-Gutiérrez 2010).

another country (cf. United Nations 1998). If we add the descendants of emigrants to the total number of emigrants the resultant figure is between five million and 5.5 million (Pires et al. 2014, 79).[2] The number of Portuguese nationals who moved out to other countries in 2016 was 100,000, as Pires shows in other Chap. Between 2008 and 2016 an average of 97,000 Portuguese migrants left the country per year. It is also important to note the number of Portuguese people who have moved back to the country: between 2001 and 2011 more than 233,000 returned to Portugal, according to Peixoto et al. in their chapter on transnationalism and returns. As Lisi et al. point out in other Chap., there are 1.375 million Portuguese nationals residing abroad with a potential right to vote in home elections.

Compared to other European countries, Portugal has a small population (roughly ten million), but it is the country in Europe (after Malta) with the second highest emigration rate, and the 12th highest in the world (Observatório da Emigração 2015). About 22% of Portuguese nationals live outside the country (Observatório da Emigração 2018, 31). The Portuguese are indeed one of the most numerous groups of immigrants resident (stock) in historical countries of Portuguese emigration, such as Brazil and Luxembourg, where they constitute the largest foreign-born population in the country (Observatório da Emigração 2017b, 42–44). They are also one of the largest immigrant groups resident in Switzerland, where they are the third most numerous population, and France, where they are the third largest.

For the first time, this volume brings together authors who have studied previous cycles of Portuguese emigration and now examine today's emigration (such as Rui Pena Pires, João Peixoto and José Carlos Marques) with scholars who started their research during the current cycle. The book thus adopts a comparative perspective on the new wave of Portuguese emigration, examining it from the point of view of those who also studied previous waves, and thus benefiting from longitudinal knowledge of this phenomenon.

Recent research shows us that we are currently seeing the fourth wave of Portuguese emigration. The challenge we set out to meet in this book was to characterise this new cycle, helping to explain its emergence and future prospects. In this chapter we begin, in the first section, by traversing through both past and pres-ent cycles of Portuguese emigration, and highlight key issues relating to the ongoing fourth wave. Namely, (i) the economic-financial crisis of 2008 and the resultant austerity policies; (ii) South-North emigration in Europe and Portuguese emigration compared with that from other southern and eastern peripheral European countries; (iii) the reassessment of the "South European model" of migration for the Portuguese case, together with the insights of the model's author, Russell King, in other Chap.; and (iv) Global North-South emigration. In the second section, we analyse highly

[2] Few countries provide data on the descendants of immigrants born in – and with the nationality of – the destination country. Australia, Canada, Denmark, the USA and New Zealand provide some information about the origin of immigrants, although sometimes using very broad categories that refer more to a linguistic-cultural universe (in the case of Portugal the set of Portuguese-speaking countries) than a particular country. Other relevant data for this purpose are consular registers, which include, in addition to Portuguese emigrants, their spouses and descendants (Pires et al. 2017, 79).

skilled and less skilled emigration along the old and new routes of Portuguese emigration by presenting (a) the statistical data on the school education and occupations of emigrants by country, (b) the conclusions on the topic by the book's authors. In the final section we introduce the contents of the book's chapters.

The Historical Waves of Portuguese Emigration

Portugal became a country of emigration in the second half of the nineteenth century. Between its beginning in 1850 and 2000, the history of Portuguese emigration has been characterised by three major waves or cycles (Pires et al. 2011).

The first cycle took place between 1850 and 1930 and followed a postcolonial trend, in which most Portuguese emigrants went to Brazil. This so-called transatlantic cycle, saw a significant volume of Portuguese nationals leaving the country as part of the Great European labour movement to the American continent. As emigrants from Northern Europe left for the Unites States (USA) or Canada, Southern European emigrants followed suit, but an even larger number went to the former South American colonies, which for the Portuguese meant Brazil (cf. Baganha and Marques 2001). The highly unequal distribution of resources motivated the Portuguese to migrate, enticed by the success narratives circulated by previous emigrants, job opportunities and existing migration networks (Peixoto 2000). They were mainly male rural labourers who emigrated permanently due to the difficulty of crossing the Atlantic Ocean to Brazil in this period, among other constraints (Baganha 2003). About two million Portuguese nationals then emigrated to these countries – a very high proportion of the Portuguese population of the time.

The second cycle took place after the end of World War II, between around 1950 and the fall of Portugal's dictatorship in 1974. During this cycle Portugal became one of the main suppliers of migrant labourers in Western Europe (to France and Germany). It was in this cycle that emigration reached its peak between the end of the 1960s and the beginning of 1970s – these record numbers were only reached again in 2011, during the current fourth wave. This second cycle was characterised by the emergence of barriers and restrictive emigration policies enforced by the authoritarian Portuguese regime at the time. These conditions forced the Portuguese to emigrate clandestinely, mostly to neighbouring European countries.

The beginning of this cycle, in the 1950s and 1960s, was probably the period when Portuguese emigration was most global in nature because there was a diversification of destination countries across America, Africa and Europe. There were outflows to Venezuela, Canada, South Africa, Angola, Mozambique and the rest of Europe while emigrants continued to travel to the US and Brazil. At the end of this cycle, flows were concentrated in Europe, and principally in France (Baganha and Marques 2001; Rocha-Trindade 1976). The volume of legal emigration had tripled by the end of this second cycle: from 1956 to 1964, an annual average of 42,000 Portuguese departed and between 1965 and 1973 this average tripled to 126,000 per year (Observatório da Emigração 2018, 17–18).

During this second wave of Portuguese emigration and the latter part of the first wave, Portugal was under a dictatorial regime. In this second cycle, in a context of economic stagnation and weak modernization, the only way to find better working conditions was to emigrate to nearby Northern European countries like France and Germany. This tendency was part of a broader displacement of the labour force from semi-peripheral Southern Europe to more industrialised Northern Europe, as is taking place in the current fourth cycle. By the end of this cycle, Portuguese emigration had begun to decline following the country's transition to democracy, which created expectations of better living conditions. In addition, the world oil crisis that began in 1973 provoked the closure of borders in many Northern European countries, limiting options for Portuguese emigrants (Peixoto 2000; Pires et al. 2011). This second cycle included more emigrant women than the previous one as well as a higher proportion of Portuguese emigrants in industrial sectors (Baganha 2003). Due to the proximity of other European countries to Portugal, the movements were more temporary. In the absence of reliable statistics, it is estimated that between 1950 and 1974 more than 1.8 million Portuguese nationals emigrated to traditional destinations, principally France and Germany, but also Brazil, the United States, Canada, Angola and Mozambique (Baganha 1994).

The third cycle of Portuguese emigration started after the beginning of democ¯ racy in 1974, with the end of political obstacles to emigration, and lasted until around 2000. The start of the free movement of people within the European Union took place during this cycle. Portuguese integration into the EU in 1986 led to an increase in emigration and a surge in the entry of immigrants into Portugal. At that time, researchers' attention was focused on this new movement of immigrants arriving in Portugal; this is why this is the least studied period of Portuguese emigration. Still, emigration continued to be a consistent feature of Portuguese society: between the 1980s and the end of the century, about 20,000 Portuguese migrants left the country per year. In the beginning of the 1990s the outflow reached 45,000 departures per year but dropped again from the mid-1990s, settling to around 20,000 by the end of the decade (Baganha and Marques 2001, 90; Observatório da Emigração 2018, 17–18). Flows were directed primarily to Switzerland and then spread to other European countries, including France and Germany, where networks of emigrants from previous cycles were already consolidated.

The second and third cycles of emigration were not restricted to the Portuguese but common to emigrants from other countries, particularly from the Southern European periphery. The post-war migration of workers from non-industrialised countries included Portuguese but also Spanish, Italian and Greek nationals emigrating to the industrialised countries – such as Germany and France – in search of manual labour. This is theorised in the "Southern European model of migration" by King and analysed by him in greater detail in ohter Chap.

Research on the three initial phases of Portuguese emigration is dominated by historical studies that seek to reconstitute the past and monographic studies that analyse past migrants' identities. References to research conducted on Portuguese emigrants living in about 140 countries may be found in publications that review the field (Rocha Trindade 1984; Baganha and Góis 1999; Peixoto 2012; Candeias, Ferreira and Peixoto 2014; Candeias et al. 2014).

In the wave of studies on Portuguese emigration that has emerged over the past few years, some authors have attended to the issue of identity among Portuguese emigrants and their descendants. They have studied the religious festivities celebrated by Portuguese emigrants from the Azores living in North America, and the newspapers, TV and radio produced by Portuguese emigrants and their descendants, among other examples (Leal 2017 ; Ferreira 2016). In other Chaps. of this book, Queirós and Rosales et al. draw attention to the identities of – and the meanings of social and professional (de)mobility among – the Portuguese in Spain, France and Brazil. In Chap., Sardinha looks at the descendants of emigrants who tried to live permanently in the idealised homeland of the parents, Portugal, and left disillusioned, continuing to experience transformations in their identities. Cordeiro deepens our understanding of the (dis)identification of emigrants with the category of "emigrant" and the social meaning attached to it by citizens in Portugal.

The Fourth Wave of Portuguese Emigration

Portuguese emigration is now in its fourth cycle. We argue that the fourth cycle of Portuguese emigration started around 2001 with the stagnation of the European economy and consequent increased unemployment – a period that coincides with the end of the circulation of the national currency, the escudo, and the beginning of the Eurozone's common currency, the euro. The number of Portuguese nationals leaving the country increased exponentially in 2011, the second phase of this cycle, at the time of the country's sovereign debt crisis and ensuing economic containment policies, which accelerated the growth of the unemployment rate. For the first time, the number of Portuguese nationals leaving the country reached the same level as during the previous peak of Portuguese emigration in the 1960s: an average of 115,000 Portuguese nationals emigrated per year between 2013 and 2015.

During the first phase of this wave, the number of Portuguese nationals moving to other countries began to increase progressively, rising from 45,000 in 2001 up to 90,000 in 2007 – double the number emigrating at the start of the decade.[3] During

[3]The data collected by the Portuguese Emigration Observatory (Observatório da Emigração) is obtained from the institutions responsible for immigration statistics in destination countries. More precisely, it is based on the information about Portuguese entries that the annual estimates of total Portuguese emigration are drawn up by Emigration Observatory, which are generally higher than the estimates produced by the Instituto Nacional de Estatística (Portuguese National Statistics Institute) (INE). Figures on permanent Portuguese emigration published by the INE and Eurostat – whose numbers are based on those of the INE – are underestimates. This becomes clear when they are compared to those calculated by the Emigration Observatory based on records of Portuguese arrivals in destination countries. The main source of information used by the INE to estimate international migrations to and from Portugal is the "Inquérito ao Trabalho" (Labour Force Survey), conducted by sampling. In the case of immigration, the results thus obtained are subsequently

this period, emigration continued to be predominantly European, flowing to the traditional destinations of Germany, France and Switzerland and one new country, Spain. In fact, Spain also became the destination to which the Portuguese emigrated most often in the first decade of the twenty-first century. Three thousand Portuguese nationals moved to Spain in 2001, and by 2007 that number had risen to 27,000, revealing enormous growth in 6 years.

Portuguese nationals who emigrated worked in civil construction and services (Pinho and Pires 2013). With the financial crisis of 2008, which greatly affected the construction sector, many Portuguese emigrants lost their jobs and either returned to Portugal or re-emigrated to England or France (see Queirós' chapter). Emigration to Spain fell over the following years, although it continued to be one of the five main destination countries for Portuguese emigrants.

Emigration decreased from 2008 to 2010 – as it did globally among OECD countries affected by the financial crisis – although the figure remained at a high plateau of over 70,000 Portuguese emigrants per year. The second phase of this cycle began in 2011, when a large increase in Portuguese emigration combined with low levels of immigrant inflows to produce negative net migration. The dynamics of Portuguese emigration from 2011 onwards are analysed in more detail in the following sub-section.

In this book we have challenged various authors from different disciplinary areas – all of whom are conducting research in this field – to reflect on Portuguese emigration today. The book's fourteen chapters reveal analytical themes that we feel must be highlighted in order to understand recent Portuguese emigration:

(i) the impact of the 2008 economic-financial crisis and austerity policies;
(ii) south-north emigration in Europe;
(iii) north-south emigration outside Europe and post-colonial continuities;
(iv) the importance of reassessing the existing Southern European migration model;
(v) highly skilled and less skilled migration along the new and old routes of Portuguese emigration;
(vi) emigrants' and their descendants' identities.

The fourth and current wave of Portuguese emigration will be characterised below by its distinguishing features.

---

corrected after comparison with the administrative records of entries held by the Serviço de Estrangeiros e Fronteiras (Immigration and Borders Service). For emigration, not only is there no national administrative register that allows a similar adjustment, as mentioned earlier, but – as the inquiry procedure is indirect – since those who have left cannot, by definition, be questioned. The result of this asymmetry in statistics on exits and entries has resulted in an underestimation published by Eurostat that is then used to calculate net migration. Hence it is probable that net migration is lower than recorded in both national and European statistics (Observatório da Emigração 2017a).

The numbers of Portuguese nationals emigration per year, as calculated by the INE and Emigration Observatory, are presented in table E.2, here: http://observatorioemigracao.pt/np4EN/1315/

During the 10 years between 2004 and 2013 Portugal became one of the EU and EFTA countries with the highest negative net migration. In absolute terms, only Poland, Greece and Spain had higher negative values for net migration, and if we discount returnee flows of emigrants, Poland and Romania are the only countries to lag behind Portugal (Observatório da Emigração 2015, 12–13).

Based on destination countries' permanent inflow data, between 2008 and 2012 an annual average of 80,000 Portuguese nationals emigrated, and in 2013 this number reached a peak of approximately 120,000 (both estimates).

Two facts distinguish the demographic impact of recent Portuguese emigration in both the country of origin and the destination country. First, as already mentioned, compared to other European countries, Portugal has a small population (roughly ten million), but it is the country in Europe with the second highest emigration rate (after Malta), and the 12th highest in the world (Observatório da Emigração 2015). Second, following the financial crisis of 2008 the Portuguese have become one of the most numerous nationalities entering European countries.

According to the most recent data available, in 2014 Portuguese nationals constituted the majority of new immigrants in France. In 2016, the Portuguese made up the second largest national group entering Luxembourg, the fourth-largest in Switzerland and the seventh-largest in the United Kingdom. Outside Europe, they were also the tenth-largest national group in Brazil (Observatório da Emigração 2015, 38).

Among the main factors that help explain this high number of Portuguese nationals leaving since 2011 we should highlight three factors. First, Portuguese emigration has not ceased since the 1960s, even when counterbalanced by immigration in the 1980s and 1990s. Second, the sovereign debt crisis and austerity measures implemented after 2011 – which followed the financial crisis and affected the countries of the peripheral south of Europe, including Portugal – swept heightened unemployment and consequent drastic reductions in job offers into the country. Third, there was a second, more structural and permanent, crisis – that of unemployment among young qualified Portuguese people, which led many to seek employment outside the country (King 2015).

The Economic-Financial Crisis of 2008 and Austerity Policies

The concentration of Portuguese emigration in Europe increased following Portugal's integration into the European Union in 1986, and its citizens' subsequent entitlement to free movement within EU countries. The research conducted by the book's authors shows that two changes later occurred in Portugal – as they did in all the peripheral countries of Europe – that played a decisive role in increasing the outflows: the entry into the Eurozone (2000); and the recession caused by the sovereign debt crisis and austerity policies implemented in the country, which had the greatest impact from 2011 onwards.

When the majority of European countries adopted the common currency, the Euro, in 2000, the competitiveness of Southern European countries declined and their employment rates fell (cf. Teixeira et al. 2014; Mamede 2016; Gibson et al. 2014; Reichlin 2014). The availability of Community funds – created to mitigate this problem – also fell, because the European Union now had more or less the same budget divided by more countries. Portuguese exports became more expensive due to the high value of the euro (Mamede 2016) and the European Union ceased to be a space of economic convergence. Industry became less competitive, further exacerbating unemployment (Teixeira et al. 2014). With a rise in the unemployment rate and constraints on the labour market, a significant part of the population of the Southern European countries sought employment in the countries of Western and Northern Europe. However, the outflows of emigrants declined with the financial crisis of 2008, whose global impact led to a reduction of employment across European countries (Herm and Poulain 2012; OECD 2011, 30).

Nevertheless when economic recovery was underway in Western and Northern European countries such as Germany and the United Kingdom, some 3 years later the countries of the South started to experience a sovereign debt crisis due to the use of external loans. This led to austerity policies that resulted in turn in the curtailment of growth[4] – in other words, in decreased employment and consequently increased emigration to countries with employment offers. The recession and austerity measures that affected Portugal further entrenched uncertainty about the future, prompting many to seek to leave the country. At an international level, the link between emigration and recession concerned various authors (Bygnes 2015; Bartolini et al. 2016; Triandafyllidou and Gropas 2014; Lafleur and Stanek 2016; King et al. 2016; Parutis 2014; Triandafyllidou and Isaakyan 2016). The first findings about the relationship between the financial crisis and the increase in Portuguese emigration began to emerge in 2014 and research has continued ever since (Gomes et al. 2015; Peixoto et al. 2016; Oliveira et al. 2016; Canavarro et al. 2014; Pereira 2015; Pires et al. 2015; Ganga et al. 2016; Justino 2016; Santana-Pereira and Horta 2017; Marques and Góis 2013; Leite et al. 2017; Farcas and Gonçalves 2017).

There was one push factor that was particularly significant in prompting such a high number of people to leave the country during the period of economic austerity: the accentuated growth of the unemployment rate among young people. The unemployment rate among this group rose by 21 percentage points between 2008 (16.7%)

---

[4] More precisely, due to the economic and financial crisis in international markets since 2008 and the inability of the Portuguese government to incur debt at reduced rates, the Portuguese authorities requested financial assistance from the EU in 2011. An Economic Adjustment Programme was negotiated with a team of officials from the European Commission, the European Central Bank and the International Monetary Fund, together known as the Troika. Financial rescue plans were negotiated for seven countries besides Portugal, namely Greece, Cyprus, Ireland, Hungary, Latvia, Romania and Spain (cf. https://ec.europa.eu/info/business-economy-euro/economic-and-fiscal-policy-coordination/eu-financial-assistance/which-eu-countries-have-received-assistance_en). This financial assistance to aid economic growth and restore investor confidence was provided between 2011 and mid-2014.

and 2013 (38.1%) (PORDATA-INE 2017). By comparison, unemployment among adults aged 25–64 was lower in 2008 (6.9%) and by 2013 had increased by only 8 percentage points. At the same time, the total unemployment rate grew by 9 percentage points between 2008 and 2013, from 7.6% to 16.2% (PORDATA-INE 2017). This resulted in a shrinking labour market with far fewer job offers, pushing many working-age Portuguese nationals to emigrate in search of employment opportunities.

In qualitative terms, working conditions have become more precarious due to the austerity imposed by EU policies to combat the economic recession. More specifically, greater flexibility has been granted for indemnity where jobs have been eliminated; salaries have been cut and working hours increased; vacation and 13th-month subsidies have been reduced; and career progression has frozen (cf. Pedroso 2014). These measures were implemented to combat the deficit and reduce external dependence. Yet according to a study on the impact of austerity on the economy, the welfare state and the performance of the Portuguese state in general, these measures also instigated "more poverty, more unemployed with less benefits, [and] substantial cuts in old age pensions and the national health service: austerity and recession bring growing social problems while reducing public responses to these problems" (cf. Pedroso 2014, 1).

One of the consequences of these poorer working conditions is visible in the construction sector, which has suffered a huge decline. Because government-supported projects and housing construction practically came to a halt, a large number of workers were forced into unemployment and left the country. Indeed, among Portuguese people with the lowest school qualifications, those working in the civil construction sector were among those most affected by austerity, which led many of them to emigrate from 2011 onwards to Angola, Spain, the UK and France.

Additionally, Portuguese society is one of the most unequal in the EU in terms of wealth distribution. The deceleration of GDP growth and increasing precariousness of working conditions have further exacerbated this situation (Carmo et al. 2018). The severity of unemployment in Portugal is "transforming into a structural variable that affects other economic and social dimensions, such as income inequality" (Carmo and Cantante 2015, 49).

Increased inequality in Portugal has contributed to processes of deprivation, which have not only led to the emigration of the less skilled, but also to the outflow of highly skilled, middle-class Portuguese nationals. In Portugal, as in other peripheral European countries, the middle-class is at permanent risk of sudden impoverishment (Estanque 2016). This macro-dimension factor lay behind the decision of many highly skilled Portuguese professionals in different sectors to seek employment in other countries.

In Portugal, austerity policies were accompanied by political rhetoric encouraging emigration on the part of the governments that implemented them. Thus, in 2011, politicians from the conservative coalition (*Portugal à Frente*)[5] within the

[5] Portugal à Frente was a right-wing electoral alliance formed by the Social Democratic Party (PPD/PSD) and CDS-PP.

Portuguese government encouraged young people to "leave their comfort zone" and go abroad in search of new opportunities: first, by the Secretary of State for Sports and Youth, Alexandre Mestre, who declared that "if we are unemployed, we have to leave the comfort zone, and go beyond our frontiers", and then by Miguel Relvas, Deputy Minister and Minister for Parliamentary Affairs, who affirmed that "[for] those who believe that they can find [opportunities] outside their country, in a relatively short timeframe, with the prospect of return if necessary, but who can strengthen their education, can confront other cultural realities, [this] is extraordinarily positive" (*Jornal de Negócios* 2013). These discourses encouraging departure were reinforced by the Prime Minister at the time, Pedro Passos Coelho. In the face of growing unemployment that hit young people extremely hard, particularly in the education sector, Passos Coelho suggested that unemployed high school teachers move to Portuguese-speaking countries such as Brazil or Angola, grasping the opportunities of "the Portuguese language market". Opposition political parties strongly condemned these declarations and mobilised around the topic of emigration in both their discourses and political action.

In this context of uncertainty – which comprised limited opportunities for social mobility, unstable labour market integration, a strong contraction of the welfare state, and the absence of professional opportunities – emigration emerged as a strategy adopted to overcome this socioeconomically restrictive scenario.

South-North Emigration in Europe

The majority of recent empirical research has focused on Portuguese nationals who have emigrated within Europe. The statistics suggest that in 2010 – and up until 2016 – more than two thirds of Portuguese emigrants resided within European countries. In terms of flows, more than 85% of Portuguese nationals who left the country during these years were migrating within Europe.

The data reveals a movement of Portuguese emigrants from Southern Europe to the North of the continent. According to King, there is a historical sequence of migration common to Spain, Greece, Italy and Portugal, which the author theorised as the "Southern European model of migration". This sequence started in the aftermath of the Second World War (King 2000), and is currently in its fourth stage, the "'New emigration' of young, well-educated people seeking employment and new lifestyle experiences in North Europe, since the nineties, accelerating after 2008 (King 2015, 139)". In King's words, the three previous stages of Southern European migration can be summarised as movements of emigration (1st phase), return (2nd phase) and immigration (3rd phase). In further detail,

> Emigration, mainly low-skilled labour migration, to North-West Europe and other parts of the world (…), 1945 to the early-mid seventies. Return migration, seventies and eighties: but some forms of return are still ongoing such as 'retirement return' and the 'pseudo-return' of the second generation, born abroad of migrant parentage. Immigration from a

> wide variety of countries worldwide, (…), eighties to today, but slackening off since 2008. (King 2015, 139)

In the current phase of "new emigration", King suggests that two crises have coincided, one conjunctural and another structural, both economic. The emigration of skilled young people from Southern Europe was the result of the 2008 financial crisis, but it also reflected a deeper structural crisis present for around two decades – that of graduate unemployment (King 2015, 158).

This model fits within a "centre-periphery framework", according to King in Chap. The geographic peripherality of these Southern European countries combines with their economic "peripherality" to produce fragile economies, as revealed in the aftermath of the 2008 financial crisis, when their structural dependency on the economies of the "centre" – i.e. Northern and Western European countries (King 2015) – became clear. In fact, during this period the UK, Germany, France and Switzerland were the countries that most attracted the emigrants of Southern European countries (Domínguez-Mujica and Gracía 2017, 42). The dependency of these countries is also explained by the push factor mentioned earlier: the four Southern European countries have the highest youth unemployment rates in the European Union (EU) (ranging from 31% to 48% in 2015) (Bartolini et al. 2016, 3).

Some authors have already drawn attention to parallel emigration from other peripheral European countries in the same period. Starting with the southern periphery, the recent emigration of Italians has been researched from the perspective of their insertion in the labour market of their destination country, such as Germany (Castellani 2018). The recent emigration of Spanish nationals to the UK, Germany, Norway and other core countries has been studied with a focus on the highly skilled, among other themes (Christiane and Oliver 2017; Cortes et al. 2015; Bygnes 2015; Faraco Blanco 2014; González-Ferrer 2013; Herrera 2014; Ros 2013). From the Western periphery, the recent emigration of Irish nationals – mainly to the UK – has been profiled and related to previous cycles of Irish emigration (Glynn et al. 2013). Other researchers have developed comparative analyses of emigrants from Southern and Eastern European peripheral countries to Western and Northern European countries following the crisis of 2008, which has opened up broader perspectives on migratory dynamics within the European continent (Bygnes and Erdal 2017; Bartolini et al. 2016; Lafleur and Stanek 2016; King et al. 2016; Parutis 2014; Raffini 2014; Triandafyllidou and Gropas 2014; Triandafyllidou and Isaakyan 2016).

Although there are similarities, there are also significant differences between the Southern European countries with respect to migration which will be further analysed in the following sub-section. As Jean-Michel Lafleur and Mikolaj Stanek observe in their book, *South-North Migration of EU Citizens in Times of Crisis:*

> transformations between pre and post crisis in migration patterns are not uniformly visible in the case of Southern European countries. The case of Portugal differs significantly from others due to the larger volume of migration flow compared to its overall population. [...] Unlike other Southern EU Member States, migration from Portugal has never ceased. (Lafleur and Stanek 2016, 217)

In Chap., Pereira compares the emigration of Portuguese nurses with that of Spanish, Italian and Romanian nurses occurring at the same time and heading to the same core countries in Europe. By combining data on both emigration and immigration, Pires compares the overall migration profile of Portugal with that of other European countries in Chap. He concludes that Portugal is placed not in a similar position to that of Southern European countries but rather to that of Eastern European countries, whose populations mainly move out and into which few immigrants move in. This contrasts with the other Southern European countries, where people leave to other countries but a considerable number of immigrants also enter.

Reassessment of the "South European Model" of Migration for the Portuguese Case

The South European model of migration was developed at a time, around 1990, when these countries were all predominantly sending countries – countries of emigration – but were also starting to become receiving countries – countries of immigration (King 2000). The model enabled researchers to identify that all of these countries had experienced similar migration processes since the aftermath of the Second World War, as described above.

With the financial crisis of 2008 and the ensuing austerity policies, there was a visible increase in the number of those leaving Southern European countries while at the same time immigrants and refugees continued to arrive, although these latter flows were not observed in the Portuguese case. In Portugal there was an exponential increase in Portuguese nationals as well as immigrants leaving the country, but the number of entries of migrants into the country fell (cf. Pires and Espírito-Santo 2016). The post- financial crisis immigration movements of 2008 differentiated Portugal – which had a low volume and flow of immigration – from the trend observed in Spain, Italy and Greece, where migrants continued to arrive in larger numbers.

For this reason, in the comparison of the gross emigration rate with that of the immigration rate in each country, Spain, Italy and Greece fall under the migratory profile of countries with more immigration than emigration, while Portugal is among the countries with more people leaving than entering. In terms of the balance between emigration and immigration, Spain, Italy and Greece have profiles similar to those of Belgium, France, Holland and Slovenia, where immigration surpasses emigration. By contrast Portugal, with a high gross emigration rate (23%) and low gross immigration rate (8%),[6] has a migratory profile more similar to that of Lithuania, Romania, Bulgaria and Poland.

[6] Gross emigration rate: stock of permanent emigrants in any given year as a percentage or a ratio of the resident population of the country of origin in this same year. Gross immigration rate: stock of permanent immigrants in any given year as a percentage or as a ratio of the resident population of the destination country in this same year.

The particularity of Portugal's position within global migration patterns has also been studied in the context of the Lusophone migration system, in which Portugal has migration networks with countries in the Global South where the Portuguese language is spoken, such as Brazil and Angola (Góis and Marques 2009). Recent re-emigration from these two countries is analysed in other Chapters. This data and the results of research presented in this book suggest that it is important to reassess the application of the South European model of migration to Portugal.

North-Global South Emigration

North-South emigration is another of the features that distinguishes Portugal from other Southern European countries. Today's emigration to Angola, Mozambique and Brazil continues to receive little attention from researchers (Åkesson 2016; Santos 2013; Peixoto et al. 2016). In Chap., Candeias et al. show that within the growth process of Portuguese emigration that led the country back to negative net migration in 2010, outflows to the Global South, although not dominant, played a relevant role. These flows – clearly stimulated by the 2005–2015 economic recession as well as by the severe austerity measures applied between 2011 and 2014 – were mainly to Portuguese-speaking countries, especially Angola, which was the main destination (despite the fall in migration flows observed after 2013–2014).

The authors demonstrate that, from a broader theoretical perspective, recent migration from Portugal (a former metropolis) to Angola (a former colony) is a strong example of North-South migration that challenges some classical premises espoused by both migration theories and post-colonial studies. The profile of emigration that emerges seems to support the theory that the emergence and development of North-South migratory movements relate to the economic expansion and increasing integration of parts of the Global South into global economic, political and even technological networks. At the same time, the authors find little evidence to back up the theory, suggesting that recent Portuguese emigration to Angola is largely a form of ancestral return, that is, a form of migration that mostly involves people who have some kind of specific ex-ante knowledge of and/or affective bond with Africa connected to previous migratory processes involving family or friends who settled there during the colonial period.

Rosales and Machado (other Chap.) look into the transatlantic movements between Portugal and Brazil, arguing that despite the differences between new and former contingents, history, the existence of colonial and post-colonial ties, and the shared language seem to play an important role for emigrants. The postcolonial representations of the "new" emigrants reproduce "old" colonial reifications of a stratified relationship, expressed nowadays in the derogation of some Brazilian institutions and the simultaneous exoticization of the "Brazilian easy way of life".

Highly-Skilled and Less Skilled Migration Along New and Old Routes of Portuguese Emigration

In both academic research on recent Portuguese emigration and in the media, increasing attention has been given to highly-skilled people leaving the country even though many Portuguese people with only elementary or secondary education continue to emigrate. In this section we summarise the available statistics, we compare the level of education of Portuguese nationals with that of other immigrants within the same country and also with Portuguese nationals in other countries.

Skilled Portuguese workers' main reasons for emigration are varied and are principally (i) to get a job, (ii) to work in their area of education, (iii) to study, or (iv) to progress in their professional career. These drivers of migration have been revealed by recent research projects on Portuguese emigration in times of crisis (Ganga et al. 2016; Oliveira et al. 2016; Peixoto et al. 2016; Pereira et al. 2015; Lopes 2014; Pereira 2015).

Between 2001 and 2011 there was considerable growth (70%) in the proportion of Portuguese-born migrants with high educational attainment, i.e. a shift from 7% to 11%. Still, Portuguese migrants with a basic level of education make up the largest group (62%). More than a quarter (27%) had a medium level of education (Observatório da Emigração 2015, 96–97). The most recent statistics about qualifications among Portuguese emigrants are those from the 2011 census, which were harmonised for analysis by the OECD through the DIOC database. However, the latest censuses refer to Portuguese emigrants who are already residents in their destination countries and do not include those who have recently arrived there.

The pattern of Portuguese skilled migrants is very heterogeneous and varies according to their destination country, as Pires shows in Chap. In 2010/2011 the proportion of Portuguese-born migrants with high educational attainment was 7% in France, 6% in Switzerland and 4% in Luxembourg, compared to 38% of those living in the United Kingdom. The two main current destination countries, the UK and France (in terms of permanent inflows, 2016), thus have very different profiles when it comes to the qualifications of Portuguese nationals residing there: 38% and 7% respectively have higher education qualifications. In France the proportion of Portuguese immigrants with only basic education (70%) is much higher than the proportion of those with higher education, while in the UK the proportions are similar, with 35% having only basic education (Cândido 2018, 11).

We may compare Portuguese emigrants with the other immigrants living in the same destination country in order to achieve a broader, more comparative, analysis. In a study about the USA, Espírito-Santo and Pires show that, like immigrants from Latin American countries, Portuguese emigrants tend to have low levels of formal education – in contrast to the generally high qualifications of European and Asiatic immigrants (Espírito-Santo and Pires 2014, 49, 61). This is understandable when we take into consideration the low formal education levels of the Portuguese in the 1970s, the time of the largest outflow to the USA (idem, 49). But so far studies of

Portuguese emigration have lacked comparisons with other immigrants within the same country, and for that reason few illustrative cases are presented in this book.

On another scale of comparison, of all destination countries for Portuguese emigrants, in 2001 the UK had the largest proportion of qualified Portuguese nationals (19%) followed by the USA (11%) (Espírito-Santo and Pires 2014, 69). In her chapter in this book, Delicado shows that the USA and UK have been the top destinations for Portuguese scientists. In 2011 the countries with the largest proportion of highly qualified Portuguese immigrants were the ones in which the Portuguese arrived recently, i.e. 1 year ago or less, such as UK and Norway (Observatório da Emigração 2015).

Moreover, the largest increase in Portuguese emigration happened from 2010 onwards and thus, unfortunately, there is still no census data that reflects this movement. The only data available on Portuguese emigrants who have recently entered into European countries that record their school qualifications are those from France, relating to 2012. The Portuguese were the lowest qualified among all recently-arrived immigrants, together with the Turkish: in both cases only 14% had higher education (Brutel 2014).

Only in the next censuses will we be able to access more accurate information about the qualifications of Portuguese emigrants who left the country from 2011 onwards. As the UK is the main destination and at the same time the country with the highest number of qualified Portuguese emigrants, we estimate that the number of Portuguese emigrants with higher education will have increased in this country. Once new census data is released we will also be able to assess the effects of Brexit, and in particular the impact of restrictive UK immigration policies on the entry of Portuguese emigrants into the country.

When it comes to the relation between qualifications and occupations, most Portuguese emigrants have predominantly less skilled jobs. This is related to the fact, mentioned earlier, that the majority have either only basic or medium levels of education. In 2010/2011, only about a fifth (19%) of employed Portuguese-born migrants had highly- or very highly-skilled occupations (managers, professionals and technicians). Still, as happens with the variable of qualifications, this highly-skilled occupational structure[7] is very different across destination countries, ranging from 10% in Luxembourg and 27% in United Kingdom to more than 40% in Denmark, Sweden and Ireland (Observatório da Emigração 2015, 94–96).

Two of the three chapters on skilled emigration in this book reveal that the United Kingdom is the top destination for a particular professional group of Portuguese emigrants: for Portuguese nurses, according to official statistics – Chap. by Pereira – and, together with the United States, for Portuguese scientists, according to a survey – Chapter, by Delicado. The "new" emigration of highly skilled Portuguese emigrants along an "old" route – to France – is analysed in Chapter by Lopes.

[7] ISCO 1/2/3 (OECD levels of classification).

What This Book Is about

The book is divided into five parts, with chapters organised by themes related to recent Portuguese emigration:

(a) New patterns of Portuguese emigration: A broad perspective;
(b) The labour market and Portuguese emigration: Highly skilled and less skilled migrants;
(c) Portuguese emigrants: Postcolonial continuities;
(d) Portuguese emigrants: Identities;
(e) Final reflections.

The first section presents a broad perspective on the new profiles of Portuguese emigration. These chapters relate the austerity measures taken following the financial crisis to increased levels of Portuguese emigration, and offer insights on the position of Portugal as a sending country in one of Europe's peripheries. They also address issues related to the country of origin, such as return migration and emigrants' rights to political representation in Portugal.

In Chapter, "Portuguese Emigration Today", Pires theorises about recent Portuguese emigration and immigration. He also discusses its evolution since 1974, the year that the Portuguese government stopped being a dictatorship and became a democracy, paving the way for new migratory dynamics. He bases his analysis on a statistical data set drawn both from origin and destination countries as well as international organisations. His first main finding is that Portuguese emigration became mainly European. Portugal's entry into the Eurozone and the financial recession towards the end of the last decade led to a reduction in job creation, and emigration consequently accelerated as way of filling this gap. Pires concludes that Portugal's position is similar to that of East European countries, where the population mainly leaves and few foreigners enter, resulting in a strong negative net migration rate – the inverse of what happens in most West and North European countries. He finishes by discussing migration and demography, and by proposing public policies concerning emigration and immigration.

In Chap., "New emigration and Portuguese society: transnationalism and return", by Peixoto et al., presents findings of a research project on Portuguese emigration carried out from 2013–2015 called "Back to the future: new emigration and its relationship with Portuguese society". It analyses Portuguese emigrants who moved to countries in Europe (UK, France and Luxembourg), South America (Brazil), and Africa (Angola and Mozambique). Based on a large-scale questionnaire survey with more than 6000 respondents the authors characterise recent Portuguese emigrations. Moreover, they analyse the official statistics from the Portuguese Census in 2001 and 2011 on returning emigrants. These extensive methods were complemented by 45 semi-structured interviews.

This broad sample taken from six countries provided a comparative perspective on the "new" routes of Portuguese emigration. More precisely, on the kind of transnational relationship the new emigrants have with Portugal based on the links they maintain with their home country and new patterns of return.

The first main conclusion is that the new emigrants engage in two main transnational practices: visits to the country of origin and remittances. While it is possible to identify changes in the mobility patterns of some emigrants and an eventual decrease in their transnational financial practices with Portugal, other emigrants keep the home country as a reference point of their social lives and hold on to returning as a goal.

The second main conclusion concerns the number and diversity of returns. Between 2001 and 2011 more than 233,000 Portuguese emigrants returned to Portugal. One key profile is embodied by the Portuguese emigrants who returned from traditional destinations in the 1960s and 1970s, such as France, who are mostly from older age groups, have low levels of formal education, and are retired. These characteristics constitute the most representative returnee profile, accounting for 48% of the total over the decade. The second main profile is embodied by the Portuguese emigrants coming from new emigration destinations (39%), such as the UK and Spain, who are mainly young adults with heterogeneous skills. Compared to emigrants matching the previous profile they have more formal education, are younger, are more often men and more often unemployed. The third key profile is of returnees (13%) from countries both within Europe (e.g. Italy) and outside Europe, the so-called "Lusophone" countries (e.g. Angola and Mozambique). They are mostly male, with an average age between that of the previous two profiles, and have the highest level of education.

In Chapter, "Portuguese Emigrants' Political Representation: The Challenges of the External Vote", Lisi et al. analyse the e representation of Portuguese emigrants in home-country elections during the democratic period (1976–2017). Over the last few decades, emigrants across the globe have gained expanded voting rights in home-country elections. The authors analyse the evolution of external voting both during the "old" waves of emigration (external voting was implemented in 1976, at the beginning of the third wave of Portuguese migrating abroad) and during the "new", recent wave of emigration. Furthermore, they evaluate the performance of the electoral system and the current limitations of Portuguese emigrants' political representation.

Lisi et al. suggest that a combination of political and socio-economic factors explains the implementation of external voting in the Portuguese case. The interests of political parties and the low level of civil society engagement lie behind the failure of electoral reforms and of attempts to overcome the shortcomings of external voting. The new wave of Portuguese emigration has reopened the debate about emigrants' political representation, leading recently to the expansion of eligibility and reassessment of voting methods.

The second section of the book takes a deeper look at the labour market insertion of highly skilled and less skilled Portuguese emigrants.

In Chapter, "A New Skilled Emigration Dynamic. Portuguese Nurses and Recruitment in the Southern European Periphery", Pereira presents the role of recruitment agencies in the profession apparently most affected by recent skilled emigration: nursing. The author combines intensive and extensive methodologies. She collected official statistics from the six main destination countries and analysed the evolution of outflows of Portuguese nurses – most of whom were women. In addition, she conducted ethnography in London, interviewing and doing participant observation among qualified Portuguese emigrants in 2013, and later interviewing 20 Portuguese nurses in 12 countries by Skype. Pereira proposes that the recent mass emigration of nurses is a trend common to other peripheral countries in Europe, namely Spain, Italy and Romania. The majority of nurses from all these countries, and likewise the Portuguese, have moved to the UK. Secondly, Pereira argues that this happened mainly due to a macro "pull factor", when the UK put up obstacles to employing nurses from outside European countries – historically the Philippines and India – and recruiters had to search inside the European continent.

In Chapter, "Migrating to Complete Transitions. A Study of High-Skilled Youth Migration to France", Lopes argues that Portuguese youth emigrate as a way to complete the transition to adulthood. He focuses on skilled Portuguese emigrants who have moved to France, using extensive and intensive methodologies – namely a questionnaire survey and biographical interviews. Teixeira Lopes' main finding is that a strong push factor prompting young people to leave the country is the "blocked transition to adulthood". This means encountering impediments to finding a stable job in the country and the consequent difficulty of becoming economically independent, marrying and parenting. Emigrating to France allows these young people to fully become "adults".

In Chapter, "'Pulled' or 'Pushed'? The Emigration of Portuguese Scientists", Delicado's main finding from the analysis of outflows of Portuguese scientists is that Portugal is a semi-peripheral country according to the definitions of migration-systems theory. The country both receives and sends scientists abroad, but many more researchers have left the country than have moved to Portugal. Delicado collected national statistics and has combined these with data from a questionnaire survey and in-depth interviews. Setting these migrations in the context of scientists' international mobility, she compares the role of pull and push factors in their decision to move, mainly to the USA and UK. Delicado ends by deepening the articulation between the macro perspective of national and international policies and the micro perspective of the scientists interviewed, critically analysing the advantages and disadvantages of the brain drain from peripheries to centres.

In Chapter, "Working Class Condition and Migrant Experience: The Case of Portuguese Construction Workers", Queirós lends visibility to a very significant social reality, but one that has remained practically invisible: the contemporary experience of Portuguese male construction workers abroad. The outputs are based on a multi-sited ethnography that took place during two different periods: the first between 2007 and 2008, when these workers moved from Portugal to Spain; and the second in 2014, when they re-emigrated to France after the financial crisis. These outflows to Spain and France reflect the global trend of Portuguese emigration in general, for which Spain became the top destination in the early 2000's and France one of the main five countries the Portuguese moved to after austerity policies were implemented in Portugal in 2011, as Pires shows in his chapter. Queirós' first conclusion is that the emigration of construction workers in both countries is temporary and circular; the author calls them the true "nomads" of today. Queirós' second conclusion is that the new work patterns and work-related mobilities ushered in by recent transformations in the civil construction sector – both at national and European level – apparently reinforce the subordinate integration of southern countries' economies and their workers in the larger European economy. This is due to existing social and economic inequalities between the sending and receiving countries inside the EU. He relates how the collective feeling of inferiority and the interiorization of social inequalities makes the moral and physical violence of everyday life in the workplace "normal", so it becomes naturalised. His final conclusion is that these work-related transformations – which lead to job instability and constant socio-geographic displacement – have a negative impact on workers' production rhythms as well as on their self-esteem.

In Chapter, Marques analyses the "Entrepreneurship among Portuguese nationals in Luxembourg". The majority of the small businesses owned by Portuguese emigrants are hotels and restaurants, followed by trade and construction companies. Entrepreneurship is particularly visible and important for labour integration in a country where the Portuguese are the largest immigrant population. The data is based on a survey carried out in 2012. Marques presents two main conclusions. First, transnational relations are weak because of the divergence between the time of demand and the time of supply of goods and services – and this is due to the type of business activity that predominates among these emigrants, i.e. mainly activity in the retail and hotel sectors. Secondly, these migrants' entrepreneurial activities have arisen from the identification of specific opportunities in the labour market, where they worked previously as employees, and the low level of bureaucratic difficulties they face.

The third section explores a distinguishing feature of Portuguese emigration: the "new" movements to "old" (former) colonies, namely Brazil and Angola.

In Chapter, "Contemporary Portuguese Migration Experiences in Brazil: Old Routes, New Trends", Rosales and Machado deepen our understanding of postcolonial settings through the perspective of Portuguese emigrants who have recently moved to São Paulo and Rio de Janeiro in Brazil. The data are drawn from a multi-sited ethnography of Portuguese emigrants from Lisbon and Porto living in these two cities, combined with questionnaires and statistical analysis. This old route, to Brazil, was the main path followed by the Portuguese for more than a century, from about 1850 until 1960. After 2011 the Portuguese once again started to emigrate to Brazil. While an old destination, there are now new trends in the social stratification of Portuguese emigrants who have moved to Brazil, as well as in their identities and strategies. Furthermore, their cultural practices are heterogeneous and differ between the two Brazilian cities. The authors conclude that in spite of new Portuguese emigrants having different tendencies to the "old" ones, colonial representations also structure their postcolonial perceptions of Brazil.

In Chapter, "Portuguese emigration to Angola (2000–2015): Strengthening a specific postcolonial relationship in a new global framework?", Candeias et al. present and discuss the contours and characteristics of recent Portuguese emigration to this African country (2000–2015). The chapter begins with a brief historical, demographic, social and political survey of Angola that also clarifies the migration nexus between Portugal and its former colony. The chapter's second part contextualises Portuguese emigration to Angola based on available statistics and on reviews of existing academic literature. The third section analyses the migration process and emigrant profiles. The study relies primarily on data gathered in a questionnaire survey involving a sample of 579 Portuguese citizens who migrated to Angola between 2000 and 2015. Particular attention is given to indicators concerning the dynamics of integration, the relations that the emigrants continue to uphold with Portugal and also the complex post-colonial nature of the process, which involves explicit and implicit links with the pre-independence period. Some of the chapter's main conclusions enable us to draw up a profile of Portuguese migrants in Angola: they are mostly male, over 35 years of age, and have a considerable level of academic and professional qualifications; also, most of them moved to Angola for professional reasons.

The fourth section of the book addresses the identities both of Portuguese emigrants in North America and of emigrants' descendants, the called "second generation".

In Chapter, "“I Was Enthused When I 'Returned' to Portugal, but I'm Leaving Disillusioned": Portuguese Migrant Descendant Returnees from Canada and Narratives of Return, Re-return and Twice Migration", Sardinha analyses the young Canadian descendants of Portuguese emigrants who decided to move to Portugal at the beginning of the twenty-first century. They are descendants of Portuguese migrants who went to Canada during the second wave of emigration. This was the period during which the highest number of Portuguese nationals moved to Canada: the early 1970's (cf. Vidigal 2018, 5). Afterwards, many emigrants decided to return to the country in the 1980s, 1990s and 2000s, as did their sons and daughters – the focus of this chapter. Sardinha's research draws on in-depth interviews carried out longitudinally from 2008 to 2015. He explores their processes of integration and perceptions of Portuguese society. He finds that with the economic crisis the migrant descendants questioned their settlement, with some going back to Canada and others migrating to other countries. The descendants idealised a mythical notion of their parents' homeland nurtured by transnational activities related to Portugal in Canada, by holiday visits, and by the narrative of prosperity and modernity about the country that spread between the international events of Expo 1998 and the Euro 2004 football tournament, which made Portugal attractive to immigrants. On emigrating to Portugal they were confronted with everyday life in the country and further disillusionment with the bureaucracy and limitations in the job market. Sardinha concludes that these descendants decided to leave Portugal by making use of their transnational social capital and reactivating transnational networks.

In Chapter, "*An Immigrant in America Yes, But Not an Emigrant in My Own Country!* The Unbearable Weight of a Persistent Label", Cordeiro examines the interplay of simultaneously being a Portuguese "immigrant" in the USA and an "emigrant" from the USA in Portugal. As "two faces of the same coin", these two categories reveal symbolic relations of power. The author describes ongoing ethnographic fieldwork in Greater Boston, where she has researched the relations between identity, ethnicity and migration. In the case of the Portuguese-American in the USA, their status as "immigrants" in this huge "nation of immigrants" is perceived positively and used proudly; while in the homeland, Portugal, being an "emigrant" carries with it an historical (mis)representation of having left the country due to economic difficulties and low levels of formal education, and is thus generally a stigmatised category. The author concludes that perceptions of these two concepts, immigrant and emigrant, go beyond the dictionary definition used in migration statistics. The content of these categories differs according to migrants' nationalities and according to social and historical contexts.

The final reflections by King in Chapter, "New Migration Dynamics on the South-Western Periphery of Europe: Theoretical Reflections on the Portuguese Case", set "new" and "old" Portuguese emigration within a broader comparative framework. First, King contextualises the historical evolution and geographical destinations of Portuguese emigration within the comparative perspective of the "Southern European migration model". He details the model's four stages, showing how the countries from the southern periphery of Europe (Spain, Italy, Greece and Portugal) have structural aspects and processes in common. Secondly, King theorises Portuguese emigration, demonstrating how it fits into the core and (semi-) periphery systems. His main finding is that what distinguishes Portugal from the other Southern European peripheral countries is the "coexistence of Portugal's status as the metropolitan core of a (post)colonial periphery and its (semi)peripheral situation within Europe". King goes through the book's chapters, drawing links with existing studies of migration. He concludes by identifying what is missing from ongoing studies of Portuguese emigration, laying out a research agenda for future studies to address: the spatial origins of the emigrants in the country, return migration, the question of gender, and the relationship between emigration and economic and social development.

This edited volume draws attention to this new historical period of Portuguese emigration. Each of its chapter helps us reflect on the complex features of Portuguese emigration today, raising new questions that we hope may inform future debates.

Funding The proofreading of this chapter was funded by the Portuguese Emigration Observatory (Observatório da Emigração).

References

Åkesson, L. (2016). Moving beyond the colonial? New Portuguese migrants in Angola. *Cahiers d'études Africaines, 1*(221), 267–286.

Almeida, J. C. P. (2007). Citizens of the world: Migration and citizenship of the Portuguese in the UK. *Portuguese Studies, 23*(2), 208–299.

Baganha, M. I. (1994). As correntes emigratórias portuguesas no século XX e o seu impacto na economia nacional. *Análise Social, XXIX*(128), 959–980.

Baganha, M. I. (2003). Portuguese emigration after World War II. In A. C. Pinto (Ed.), *Contemporary Portugal. Politics, society and culture* (pp. 139–157). Boulder: Social Sciences Monographs.

Baganha, M. I., & Carlos Marques, J. (2001). População. In N. Valério (Ed.), *Estatísticas históricas portuguesas* (pp. 33–126). Lisbon: Instituto Nacional de Estatística.

Baganha, M. I., & Góis, P. (1999). *Migrações internacionais de e para Portugal: o que sabemos e para onde vamos*. Revista Crítica de Ciências Sociais, 52/53. http://www.ces.uc.pt/myces/UserFiles/livros/243_Baganha_G%F3is 98%3A99.pdf. Accessed 15 Sept 2017.

Bartolini, L., Gropas, R., & Triandafyllidou, A. (2016). Drivers of highly skilled mobility from Southern Europe: Escaping the crisis and emancipating oneself. *Journal of Ethnic and Migration Studies, 43*(October), 1–22. https://doi.org/10.1080/1369183X.2016.1249048.

Beswick, J., & Pozo-Gutiérrez, A. (2010). Migrant identities, sociolinguistic and socio-cultural practices: Spanish and Portuguese Migrations to the South Coast of England. *Portuguese Studies, 26*(1), 41–59. (J. Beswick & M. Dinneen [Eds.], Portuguese-speaking Diaspora in Great Britain and Ireland: Special Issue).

Brutel, C. (2014). Les immigrés récemment arrivés en France. *INSEE Première,* 1524. http://www.insee.fr/fr/ffc/ipweb/ip1524/ip1524.pdf. Accessed 14 Sept 2014.

Bygnes, S. (2015). Are they leaving because of the crisis? The sociological significance of anomie as a motivation for migration. *Sociology, 51*(2), 258–273. https://doi.org/10.1177/0038038515589300.

Bygnes, S., & Erdal, M. B. (2017). Liquid migration, grounded lives: Considerations about future mobility and settlement among Polish and Spanish Migrants in Norway. *Journal of Ethnic and Migration Studies, 43*(1), 102–118. https://doi.org/10.1080/1369183X.2016.1211004.

Canavarro, A., Areia, M., & Pereira, M. (2014). Dossier temático: A nova vaga da emigração portuguesa. *População e Sociedade, 22*, 1–237.

Candeias, P., Góis, P., Marques, J. C., & Peixoto, J. (2014). Emigração portuguesa: bibliografia comentada (1980–2013). 01/2014. *SOCIUS Working Papers*. Lisbon.

Candeias, P., Ferreira, B., & Peixoto, J. (2014). Emigração portuguesa: o que temos vindo a estudar e o que nos falta saber – uma análise bibliométrica entre 1980 e 2013. *População e Sociedade, 22,* 11–34. http://www.cepesepublicacoes.pt/portal/pt/obras/populacao-e-sociedade-n-o-22. Acessed 15 Sept 2017.

Cândido, A. F. (2018). Portuguese skilled migration in DIOC 2010/11, *OEm Fact Sheets*, 8, Observatório da Emigração, CIES-IUL, ISCTE-IUL. https://doi.org/10.15847/CIESOEMFS082018. http://observatorioemigracao.pt/np4/6119.html. Accessed 13 July 2018.

Carmo, R. M. d., & Cantante, F. (2015). Desigualdades, redistribuição e o impacto do desemprego: tendências recentes e efeitos da crise económico-financeira. *Sociologia, Problema e Práticas, 77*, 33–51. https://doi.org/10.7458/SPP2015773311.

Carmo, R. M. d., Sebastião, J., Azevedo, J., Martins, S. d. C., & Costa, A. F. d. (2018). *Desigualdades Sociais: Portugal e a Europa*. Mundos Sociais: Lisboa.

Castellani, S. (2018). Scivolando verso il basso. l'inserimento lavorativo dei nuovi migranti italiani e spagnoli in Germania durante la crisi economica. *Sociologia Del Lavoro, 149*(February), 77–93. https://doi.org/10.3280/SL2018-149006.

Christiane, H., & Oliver, W. (2017). The role of argumentation and institutions for labour migration in the European Union – Exemplified by Spanish labour migration to Germany. *International Migration, 55*(S1), 69–85. https://doi.org/10.1111/imig.12338.

Cortés, A., Moncó, B., & Betrisey, D. (2015). *Movilidad Transnacional de Jóvenes Españoles y Latinoamericanos: una Comparación en Contextos de Crisis*. Madrid: Centro Reina Sofía Sobre Adolescencia Y Juventud.

Domínguez-Mujica, J., & Gracía, T. P. (2017). The economic crisis and the Southern European migration model. In B. Glorius & J. Domínguez-Mujica (Eds.), *European mobility in times of crisis: The new context of European South-North Migration* (pp. 17–48). Bielefeld: Transcript.

Espírito-Santo, I., & Pires, R. P. (2014). Estados Unidos da América, *OEm Country Reports*, 2, Lisboa, Observatório da Emigração, CIES-IUL, ISCTE-IUL. https://doi.org/10.15847/CIESOEMCR022014.

Estanque, E. (2016). Onde pára a classe média? Breves notas sobre o conceito e a realidade portuguesa. *Sociologia, Problemas e Práticas, 2017*(83), 37–54. https://doi.org/10.7458/SPP2017839971.

Faraco, B. C. (2014). Neue migration. Junge Spanier/Innen in Berlin. In C. Pfeffer-Hoffmann (Ed.), *Arbeitsmigration aus Spanien vor dem Hintergrund der Migrationsprozesse seit 1960* (pp. 214–234). Berlin: Mensch & Buch.

Farcas, D., & Gonçalves, M. (2017). Motivations and cross-cultural adaptation of self-initiated expatriates, assigned expatriates, and immigrant workers: The case of Portuguese migrant workers in the United Kingdom. *Journal of Cross-Cultural Psychology, 48*(7), 1028–1051. https://doi.org/10.1177/0022022117717031.

Ferreira, S. (2016). *A emigração portuguesa e os seus meios de comunicação social: breve caracterização* (OEm Working-Paper, 2). Lisboa: Observatório da Emigração, CIES-IUL, ISCTE-IUL. https://doi.org/10.15847/CIESOEMWP022016. http://observatorioemigracao.pt/np4/5097.html. Accessed 19 Sept 2017.

Ganga, R., Silva, J. P., Gomes, R., Vaz, H., Lopes, J. T., Silva, S., Cerdeira, L., et al. (2016). Portuguese scientists' migration: A study on the 2008 crisis aftermath. *International Migration, 54*(6), 43–55. https://doi.org/10.1111/imig.12271.

Gibson, H. D., Palivos, T., & Tavlas, G. S. (2014). The crisis in the euro area: An analytic overview. *Journal of Macroeconomics, 39*, 233–239. https://doi.org/10.1016/j.jmacro.2013.09.014.

Glynn, I., Kelly, T., & MacÉinrí, P. (2013). *Irish emigration in an age of austerity*. Cork: University College Cork.

Góis, P., & Marques, J. C. (2009). Portugal as a semi-peripheral country in the global migration system. *International Migration, 47*(3), 21–50. https://doi.org/10.1111/j.1468-2435.2009.00523.x.

Gomes, R. M., Lopes, J. T., Vaz, H., Cerdeira, L., Ganga, R., de Lourdes, M. M., Magalhães, D., et al. (2015). *Fuga de cérebros: retratos da emigração portuguesa qualificada*. Lisboa: Bertrand.

González-Ferrer, A. (2013). *La nueva emigración española. Lo que sabemos y lo que no*. Fundación Alternativas. http://digital.csic.es/handle/10261/93167. Accessed 8 Mar 2018.

Herm, A., & Poulain, M. (2012). Economic crisis and international migration. What the EU data reveal? *Revue Européenne des Migrations Internationales, 28*(4), 145–169. https://doi.org/10.4000/remi.6171.

Herrera, M. J. (2014). Migración cualificada de trabajadores de España al extranjero. In J. Arango, D. M. Malapeira, & J. O. Alonso (Eds.), *Inmigración y emigración: mitos y realidades. Anuario de la Inmigración en España* (Vol. 2013, pp. 99–109). Barcelona: CIDOB (Barcelona Centre For International Affaris).

Jornal de Negócios. (2013, January 17). As várias declarações de apelo à emigração. *Jornal de Negócios*. http://www.jornaldenegocios.pt/economia/detalhe/as_varias_declaracoes_de_apelo_a_emigracao.html. Accessed 7 Apr 2014.

Justino, D. (2016). *Emigration from Portugal: Old wine in new bottles?* Washington, DC: Migration Policy Institute.

King, R. (2000). Southern Europe in the changing global map of migration. In R. King, G. Lazaridis, & C. Tsardanidis (Eds.), *Eldorado or fortress? Migration in Southern Europe* (pp. 1–26). London: Macmillan.

King, R. (2015). Migration and Southern Europe – A center–periphery dynamic? In M. Baumeister & R. Sala (Eds.), *Southern Europe? Italy, Spain, Portugal and Greece from the 1950s to the present day* (pp. 139–169). Frankfurt/New York: Campus.

King, R., Lulle, A., Conti, F., & Mueller, D. (2016). Eurocity London: A qualitative comparison of graduate migration from Germany, Italy and Latvia. *Comparative Migration Studies, 4*(3), 1–22. https://doi.org/10.1186/s40878-016-0023-1.

Lafleur, J.-M., & Stanek, M. (2016). Lessons from the South-North migration of EU Citizens in times of crisis. In J.-M. Lafleur & M. Stanek (Eds.), *South-North migration of EU citizens in times of crisis (IMISCOE Research Series)* (pp. 215–224). Dordrecht: Springer. https://doi.org/10.1007/978-3-319-39763-4.

Leal, J. (2017). *O Culto do Divino. Migrações e Transformações*. Lisboa: Edições 70.

Leite, A. C., Cardoso, S. G., Marques, A. G., & Morais, C. (2017). Believing is adapting': Belief in a just world and emigrants' identification and satisfaction with the host country. *Revista de Psicología Social, 32*(2), 424–439. https://doi.org/10.1080/02134748.2017.1291743.

Mamede, R. P. (2016). A crise existencial do euro. In E. P. Ferreira (Ed.), *União Europeia. Reforma ou declínio*. Lisboa: Vega.

Marques, J. C., & Góis, P. (2013). Portuguese emigrants and the state: An ambivalent relationship. In M. Collyer (Ed.), *Emigration nations policies and ideologies of emigrant engagement* (pp. 252–276). Basingstoke: Palgrave Macmillan.

Observatório da Emigração. (2015). *Portuguese emigration factbook 2015*. Lisbon: Observatório da Emigração, CIES-IUL, ISCTE-IUL. https://doi.org/10.15847/CIESOEMFB2015. http://observatorioemigracao.pt/np4EN/4924.html. Accessed 9 Nov 2017.

Observatório da Emigração. (2017a). *Data/Global estimates*. Data. http://observatorioemigracao.pt/np4EN/Dados/

Observatório da Emigração. (2017b). *Portuguese emigration factbook 2016*. Lisbon: Observatório da Emigração, CIES-IUL, ISCTE-IUL. https://doi.org/10.15847/CIESOEMFB2016. http://observatorioemigracao.pt/np4EN/5810.html. Accessed 9 Dec 2017.

Observatório da Emigração. (2018). *Portuguese emigration factbook 2017*. Lisbon: Observatório da Emigração, CIES-IUL, ISCTE-IUL. https://doi.org/10.15847/CIESOEMFB2017. http://observatorioemigracao.pt/np4EN/5999.html. Accessed 9 Mar 2018.

OECD. (2011). *International migration outlook. SOPEMI 2011*. Paris: OECD Publications.

Oliveira, I. T. d., Candeias, P., Peixoto, J., Azevedo, J., & Malheiros, J. M. (2016). Regresso e circulação de emigrantes portugueses no início do século XXI. *Sociologia, Problemas e Práticas, 2016*(81), 11–35. https://doi.org/10.7458/SPP2016817155.

Parutis, V. (2014). 'Economic migrants' or 'middling transnationals'? East European migrants' experiences of work in the UK. *International Migration, 52*(1), 36–55. https://doi.org/10.1111/j.1468-2435.2010.00677.x.

Pedroso, P. (2014). *Portugal and the global crisis – The impact of austerity on the economy, the social model and the performance of the state*. Berlin: Friedrich-Ebert-Stiftung. http://library.fes.de/pdf-files/id/10722.pdf. Accessed 9 May 2016.

Peixoto, J. (2000). A emigração. In F. Bethencourt & K. Chaudhuri (Eds.), *História da expansão portuguesa* (pp. 152–181). Lisboa: Círculo de Leitores.

Peixoto, J. (2012). A emigração portuguesa hoje: o que sabemos e o que não sabemos. In *SOCIUS Working Papers* (pp. 5–2012). Lisboa: Instituto Superior de Economia e Gestão (ISEG).

Peixoto, J., Oliveira, I. T. D., Azevedo, J., Marques, J. C., Góis, P., Malheiros, J., & Madeira, P. (2016). *Regresso ao futuro – A nova emigração ea sociedade portuguesa*. Lisboa: Gradiva.

Pereira, C. (2015). *Vidas partidas. Enfermeiros portugueses no estrangeiro*. Loures: Lusodidacta.

Pereira, C., Pinto, N., & Pires, R. (2015). Portuguese nurses in the UK 2014/Enfermeiros portugueses no Reino Unido 2014. *OEm Fact Sheets*, 3, Observatório da Emigração. CIES-IUL, ISCTE-IUL. https://doi.org/10.15847/CIESOEMFS032015-pt-en. http://observatorioemigracao.pt/np4EN/4317.html. Accessed 19 Sept 2016.

Pinho, F., & Pires, R. P. P. (2013). Espanha, *OEm Country Reports*, 1. Lisbon, Observatório da Emigração, CIES-IUL, ISCTE-IUL. https://doi.org/10.15847/CIESOEMCR012013. http://www.observatorioemigracao.pt/np4/3725.html. Accessed 7 Aug 2014.

Pires, R. P., & Espírito-Santo, I. (2016). Saldos migratórios 2000–2013. *OEm Fact Sheets*, 4,1–19. Observatório da Emigração, CIES-IUL, ISCTE-IUL. https://doi.org/10.15847/CIESOEMFS042016. http://observatorioemigracao.pt/np4/5603.html. Accessed 1 Mar, 2017.

Pires, R. P. (Ed.), Machado, F. L., Peixoto, J., Vaz, M. J. V., with Pinho, F., Azevedo, J., Sabino, C., & Chalante, S. (2011). *Portugal: An atlas of international migration*. Lisboa: Tinta da China.

Pires, R. P., Pereira, C., Azevedo, J., Espírito-Santo, I., Vidigal, I., & Ribeiro, A. C. (2015). *Emigração portuguesa. Relatório estatístico 2015*. Lisboa: Observatório da Emigração e Rede Migra, CIES-IUL, ISCTE-IUL, e DGACCP. https://doi.org/10.15847/CIESOEMRE022015.

Pires, R. P., Pereira, C., Azevedo, J., Vidigal, I., & Veiga, C. M. (2017). *Emigração portuguesa. Relatório estatístico 2017*. Lisboa: Observatório da Emigração e Rede Migra, CIES-IULISCTE-IUL, e DGACCP. https://doi.org/10.15847/CIESOEMRE042017.

PORDATA-INE. (2017). *População desempregada: total e por grupo etário*. Emprego e mercado de trabalho. https://www.pordata.pt/Portugal/População+desempregada+total+e+por+grupo+etário-40. Accessed 25 May 2017.

Raffini, L. (2014). Quando la Generazione Erasmus incontra la Generazione Precaria. La mobilità transnazionale dei giovani italiani e spagnoli. *OBETS. Revista de Ciencias Sociales, 9*, 139–165. https://doi.org/10.14198/OBETS2014.9.1.05.

Reichlin, L. (2014). Monetary policy and banks in the euro area: The tale of two crises. *Journal of Macroeconomics, 39*, 387–400. https://doi.org/10.1016/j.jmacro.2013.09.012.

REMIGR. (2017). Inquérito aos Portugueses no Estrangeiro, 2014-15, base de dados [Survey to Portuguese Abroad, 2014-15, database]. *Observatório da Emigração*. http://observatorioemigracao.pt/np4EN/524. Accessed 25 June 2017.

Rocha-Trindade, M. B. (1976). Comunidades migrantes em situação dipolar: análise de três casos de emigração especializada para os EUA, para o Brasil e para França. *Análise Social, XII*(48), 983–997.

Rocha Trindade, M. B., & Arroteia, J. (1984). *Bibliografia da emigração portuguesa*. Lisboa: Instituto de Português de Ensino à Distância.

Ros, C. R. (2013). Londres minusculastierra prometida. La emigración de jóvenes titulados universitarios catalanes a Londres. *Perifèria. Revista de Recerca I Formació En Antropologia, 18*(2), 158–174.

Santana-Pereira, J., & Horta, A. P. H. (2017). A global nation? The evolution of emigration and diaspora policies in Portugal (1960–2016). In A. Weinar (Ed.), *Emigration and diaspora policies in the age of mobility* (Vol. 9, pp. 121–137). Cham: Springer International Publishing. https://doi.org/10.1007/978-3-319-56342-8.

Santos, I. d. (2013). L'émigration au Portugal, avatar d'un pays 'semi-périphérique', métropole postcoloniale. *Hommes et Migrations, 1302*, 157–161.

Teixeira, A. A. C., Silva, E., & Mamede, R. P. (Eds.). (2014). *Structural change, competitiveness and industrial policy: Painful lessons from the European periphery*. Routledge: Taylor & Francis Group.

Triandafyllidou, A., & Gropas, R. (2014). *'Voting with their feet': Highly skilled emigrants from Southern Europe*. American Behavioral Scientist, May, 1–20. https://doi.org/10.1177/0002764214534665.

Triandafyllidou, A., & Isaakyan, I. (Eds.). (2016). High-skill migration and recession. *Gendered perspectives*. London: Palgrave Macmillan UK. https://doi.org/10.1057/9781137467119.

United Nations. (1998). Recommendations on statistics of international migration – Rev 1. *Statistical Papers* Series M (58). http://unstats.un.org/unsd/publication/SeriesM/SeriesM_58rev1E.pdf. Accessed 12 Dec 2012.

Vidigal, I. (2018). Emigração portuguesa para o Canadá, 1966–2016, *OEm Fact Sheets*, 7, Observatório da Emigração, CIES-IUL, ISCTE-IUL. https://doi.org/10.15847/CIESOEMFS072018. http://observatorioemigracao.pt/np4/6133.html. Accessed 1 June 2018.

6

Contemporary Portuguese Migration Experiences in Brazil: Old Routes, New Trends

Marta Vilar Rosales and Vânia Pereira Machado

Introduction

Emigration is deeply rooted in Portuguese history and culture. Over the centuries, people of different groups, religions and origins have moved to a multitude of places for diverse reasons, pursuing a wide range of goals. Contemporary transatlantic movements between Portugal and Brazil are, as they were in the past, characterised by bidirectional flows of people and things. These flows have constructed a migration path marked by colonialism, a shared language and, from the Estado Novo until the present, Freyre's *Luso-Tropicalism*. The first migrations took place in the fifteenth century and were driven in part by Portuguese colonial expansion policy (Feldman-Bianco 2001). From then on, the Portuguese community has been the largest foreign community residing in Brazil. The recent global financial crisis had a strong impact on the Portuguese economy, resulting in high rates of unemployment and stagnant economic growth. Contrariwise, the Brazilian economy flourished during the same period (2008–2011), making the country attractive as a migration destination for diverse populations.

This chapter is one outcome of an extensive research project that investigated a specific trend in the recent wave of Portuguese emigration. This project's main research goal was to describe and analyse the on-going Atlantic Crossings between four major cities – Lisbon, Oporto, Rio de Janeiro and Sao Paulo – in order to reveal how the circulations of people and things between these cities mutually reinforce one another. Our research was based on a comparative ethnographic approach that included a vast array of methods (questionnaires, multi-sided participant and direct observation, interviews, statistical data analysis), and drew on the theoretical and methodological *transnationalism approach* of Glick-Schiller et al. (1994). It focused on the contemporary movements of people and things, their intersections and

M. V. Rosales (✉) · V. P. Machado
Instituto de Ciências Sociais, Universidade de Lisboa (ICS-UL), Lisbon, Portugal
e-mail: marta.rosales@ics.ulisboa.pt; vania.machado@ics.ulisboa.pt

juxtapositions, and on the significance of old and new networks and relationships for the establishment of present-day migration routes. The four cities were selected on the basis of previous research results (Feldman-Bianco 2001; Malheiros 2011; Peixoto 2012), which identified them as major migration hubs on each side of the Atlantic. Our methodological design allowed us to gather substantive quantitative and qualitative data. We consider combining qualitative and quantitative data key to the analysis of the migration experiences, aspirations and values of the subjects involved, as well as for the framing of their experiences in the historical, political and economic context of Luso-Brazilian relations. Hence, this methodological approach allowed us to integrate different levels of analysis – descriptive and interpretative – while promoting a productive dialogue between structure and agency, universalism and particularism.

In this chapter, we will in particular explore the results of an extensive questionnaire that was distributed to all the households[1] included in the research. This questionnaire's main objective was to produce descriptive sociographic profiles of the subjects and their families, as well to gather qualitative descriptive data on their migration trajectories and backgrounds, their networks of belonging, and their domestic material culture and consumption practices (Burrell 2008; Rosales 2010). Our analysis in this chapter will mainly focus on the data gathered from the households we interviewed in Rio de Janeiro and São Paulo, who had recently[2] settled in these cities after arriving from Lisbon and Oporto. Even if the data we gathered cannot be considered representative of this particular migration trend, it produced significant information on original features of the contemporary Atlantic crossings – features such as the particular social composition of the households involved and their transnational positioning strategies. Our data also introduced new angles of analysis on the significant migration movements that have long existed between the two countries.

The chapter is structured around five topics: Portuguese migration to Brazil (a brief overview); Portuguese migration to São Paulo and Rio de Janeiro; profiles of the new migrant families; projects and expectations; and settling in a Brazilian city: materializing identity, belonging and positioning strategies.

Portuguese Emigration: Waves and Numbers

From 2008 to 2016, Portugal experienced a severe economic recession. This period of crisis had a strong impact on most of the country's institutions and affected all social spheres, including the migration movements in and out of the country. From an emigration perspective, the crisis significantly increased the number of people leaving the country (Peixoto and Iorio 2011) altering, for the first time in a

[1] A total of 100 interviews, 25 in each research site.

[2] The families arrived in Brazil between 2008 and 2015.

considerable period, the balance of migration movements from positive, in 2010[3], to negative, in 2011. Once a major structural dimension of Portuguese history – but absent from core academic and public debates for decades – emigration now regained its status as a significant research topic.

The consistent study of Portuguese migration is well documented and goes back to the beginning of the *colonial project*. In the fifteenth century, large contingents of mainland population left the continent and established themselves in Madeira and the Azores. Later on, Portuguese and European settlers migrated to the Portuguese African territories, to India and to Brazil.

By the second half of the eighteenth century, migration movements towards Brazil had become progressively more prominent, and before the turn of the century Brazil was already the main destination for those leaving Portugal in search of a better life. Migration to Brazil maintained quite a regular pattern, although its impacts were especially felt at times of internal political, social and economic turbulence. The most intense period of migration was the first decade of the twentieth century (1901–1911). The number of migrants decreased in the period between the two world wars, mainly due to the *great depression* (Pereira 2007) and the restrictive migration policy of the Vargas[4] administration. The end of the long Portuguese dictatorship, in 1974, and accession to the EU, in 1986, had a significant impact on Portuguese emigration, both in terms of its intensity and social composition. On the one hand, a large contingent of people returned to the country as a result of decolonization. This incoming movement was paralleled by a significant decrease, as a whole, of the emigration flows that consistently drained the country's population during the 1960s. On the other hand, emigration to Brazil continued – both from Portugal and from the former African colonies – due to the radical political and economic changes imposed during the post-revolutionary period (Graça 2009). Unlike the emigration flows during the previous historical periods, which mainly consisted of people from the working classes, the second movement mostly involved people from the middle classes and the elites who had been in favour of the *ancien regime*. In the 1990s, Brazil received a new wave of Portuguese emigration, this time due to the Fernando Henrique Cardoso administration's policy of privatization[5]. During this period, known as "the return of the caravels" (Feldman-Bianco 2001), some of the largest Portuguese corporations regarded Brazil once more as a promising country to invest in, which led to a further migration wave.

More recently, the Brazilian economy experienced a boost as the country received intense media attention, not only because of its economic growth, but also because of two major global events: the Football World Cup (2014) and the Olympics (2016). This good economic period in Brazil coincided with a severe global economic crisis that had especially negative effects in Portugal. The Portuguese media quickly began to depict Brazil as an important alternative for the thousands of Portuguese

---

[3] Source: http://www.pordata.pt/Portugal/Saldos+populacionais+anuais+total++natural+e+migratorio-657 [03/09/14].

[4] Getúlio Vargas, Brazilian. Served as President twice: 1930–1945 and 1951–1954.

[5] Former Brazilian President, from 1995 to 2002.

that opted – or were forced – to emigrate due to unemployment, financial problems and increasing social and politic instability. However, according to several official reports from Observatório da Emigração (Pires et al. 2014), Brazil received only 1% of the Portuguese people who decided to migrate, with the great majority (80–85%) of the overall contingent choosing European destinations.

Even if some of their statistical data on entries and exits seems to be incomplete and/or contradictory, the Brazilian Federal Police claim that the number of Portuguese who entered the country during 2001 was lower than 700. The figures increased moderately in the next 7 years and in 2009 the situation clearly changed, with more than 3000 Portuguese entering the country. This trend reached a peak of 5700 people in 2013 and slowly decreased from then on to the present-day. This change reflects rising political and economic instability in Brazil, which has been affecting the country since 2014.

Portuguese Emigration to Rio and São Paulo

The Portuguese are the largest community of residents in Brazil who were born outside the country (making up 23% of the total population born outside Brazil in 2010). Most of the 137,973 individuals within this category reside in São Paulo (47%) and in Rio de Janeiro (37%) and arrived in these cities before 1970, which makes them a considerably old group[6]. The number of entries of Portuguese citizens decreased during the following decades, until 2011, when the number of arrivals increased more than 100% compared with the previous period and continued to grow until 2013. Forty-four percent of all residence permits issued to Portuguese nationals during that year were for the São Paulo area and 20% for the Rio de Janeiro area. This data only covers official requests for residence permits and does not include other migration situations, such as family reunions and people who entered the country with tourist or student visas. This new group of Portuguese migrants coexists with the previous one – the group that arrived in the 50s and 60s – which allows the two contingents to be compared. This comparison enables a more comprehensive view of Portuguese migration to Brazil and its impact on the relationship between the two countries.

Who Are They?

The people interviewed during this research do not constitute a representative sample of all recent Portuguese migrants. However, even though representativeness was not a significant concern from the beginning, the different social, economic and legal statuses of the subjects approached during fieldwork was visible from the start

[6] IBGE, Censos 2010.

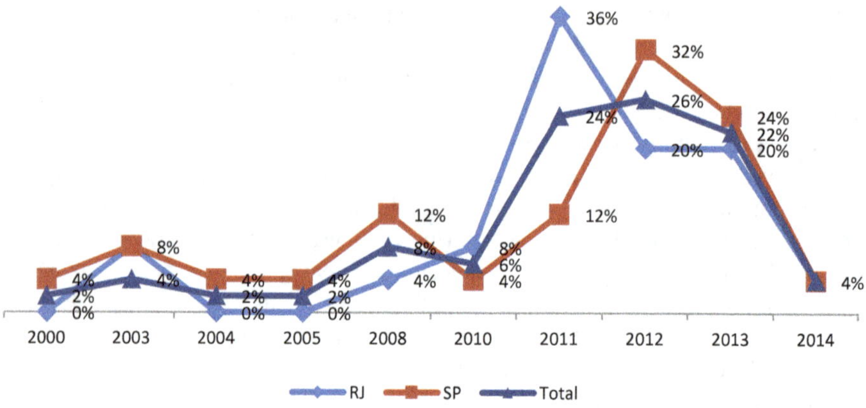

Fig. Year of arrival of Portuguese migrants in Brazil by destination (%).
Source: Survey on materiality, contemporary movements and policies of belonging. ATLANTIC CROSSINGS Project

and, therefore, taken into account during the selection stage. The sample includes a diverse range of subjects in terms of gender, formal education, professional backgrounds, migration backgrounds and origin (Oporto and Lisbon). Recognising this diversity within the small group of 50 Portuguese migrants and their families involved in our research helped illuminate the particularities of their social profiles, as well as of their future projects, desires and hopes[7].

Both the quantitative and qualitative stages of the research revealed a significant difference in the number of migrants originating from Lisbon and from Oporto (only 16% of all subjects in Rio de Janeiro and 12% in São Paulo are from Oporto). The fact that migration movements are often *structured* transnational networks – which help to prevent the dangers associated with emigration (Glick-Schiller et al. 1994; Vertovec 2007) – might explain this difference. These numbers may reveal the existence of a more solid migration network out of Lisbon than out of Oporto.

Figure presents emigrants' year of arrival in the two Brazilian cities. The data is in keeping with the overall picture painted by official Brazilian statistics on the entries of foreign citizens. The number of entries increases significantly from 2008 to 2012 (with spikes in 2011 (Rio 36%) and 2012 (São Paulo 32%)).

The ratio of men and women included in the research sample – 46% and 54% respectively – partially contradicts the figures of the Brazilian authorities, which show a much higher presence of male than of female migrants (65% and 35%, respectively). The age profile is also moderately different in the two cities. The average age in Rio is 34, where 65% of the subjects are between 25 and 34 years old. The subjects residing in São Paulo are older than those in Rio, with an average age of 40 (52% of them older than 40). The difference between the two groups' professional profiles helps clarify the reason for the age gap between them. The typical profile of

[7] The research only included individuals and their families who migrated from Lisbon and Oporto to Rio de Janeiro and São Paulo after 2000.

a Portuguese citizen residing in Rio is that of a young person who has recently graduated in the arts, architecture or engineering. In São Paulo, the typical profile is that of a mid-career professional working in the business or finance sectors. Most subjects in these groups are married. This trend is particularly significant in São Paulo, where only 16% of emigrants are single. And even if the number of single people in Rio is higher (44%) – mainly due to the respondents' youth and lack of professional stability – the majority of these migration projects are planned as collective, and often family-oriented, projects. The two groups are also similar in their formal education qualifications. Most subjects have got degrees, and half of them have completed post-graduate programmes (48% in Rio and 56% in São Paulo). This contrasts with the level of formal education of the former migrant contingents, which were mainly made up of low-income and low-skilled individuals. The majority of higher education qualifications were obtained in Portugal. However, the percentage of degrees completed outside Portugal is considerable (24%). All the qualifications were obtained before migration. This fact illustrates the importance of internationalization and mobility in structuring the respondents' professional and personal trajectories – as well as the significance of *cosmopolitanism* as a general added value which "has been further heightened by the elaboration of a public discourse within many industrialised countries that trumpets the importance of 'international experience' within a globalizing economy" (Amit 2011 [2007]: 6).

The qualitative data we gathered during fieldwork revealed that there were few *job opportunities* at the time for unskilled Portuguese workers in Brazil. Even if Rio and São Paulo were undertaking major urban transformations and experiencing an investment boost in all sectors, the existence of large contingents of low-cost Brazilian workers living in the cities' peripheries resolved the extraordinary need for manpower. Hence the subjects' high social and cultural capitals (cf. Bourdieu 1979) reflect the specificities of the job market, which mostly needed highly-skilled workers at that time.

As mentioned before, the groups involved in our research coexist in the cities with other Portuguese migrants who arrived in the 50s and 60s. These older groups are well organised as migrant communities. In both cities, there is a plurality of migrant associations and social clubs offering a wide range of cultural activities, as well as very active economic associations created to defend community business interests. All these associations and clubs are well integrated in their city's social, economic and political spheres and are fully recognised by Brazilians.

The social profiles of the subjects and their families were explored mainly through an analytical lens that privileged qualitative data. *Habitus* (Bourdieu 1984 [1979]) and all the conceptual tools related to this central concept, such as *taste* and *lifestyle*, were key to investigating the subjects' expectations and trajectories as recent migrants in Rio and São Paulo. The great majority of the subjects have got Portuguese nationality (96% in São Paulo and 76% in Rio) and do not plan to apply for Brazilian citizenship (74%). The subjects justify their lack of interest in *becoming Brazilian* by arguing that holding a European passport has got an added value that holding a Brazilian one does not have and, also, that they feel a great lack of identification with, in their words, the *Brazilian identity*. Both thoughts show a clear valorisation of Europe that is complementary to a paternalistic attitude towards Brazil, which is still influenced by the colonial past and post-colonial present-day relations between the two countries. On the one hand, Brazil is considered a *friendly* and *familiar* context in which to live, i.e. a place where the local population understand and positively value the Portuguese people and culture. On the other hand, according to the subjects, while the Portuguese *feel at home* in Brazil – i.e. they are familiar with the culture and the population's *ways of life* – they do not necessarily identify with Brazilian people.

The families' income is mainly from work (72% in Sao Paulo and 84% in Rio). In São Paulo, the centrality of work is especially evident for males, since the subjects claiming to be living off other family members' income (16%) and off scholarships (12%) are predominantly female. These figures draw attention to the fact that the number of Portuguese women that do not work in the city is comparatively high. These women migrated to Brazil due to their husbands' professional projects and do not carry out any remunerated activity. The majority of those who engage in remunerated professional activity have full-time positions (76% in São Paulo, 84% in Rio). Of these, 20% are self-employed professionals, who are mainly based in Rio. It is also worth noting that the percentage of business owners in São Paulo is considerable (24%) and, finally, that underemployment and unemployment are not widespread and mainly affect women residing in São Paulo.

As expected, the migrants' professional profile is strongly related to their capital. In Rio, 95% of the subjects belong to the category "Specialists in the Academic and Scientific sector". In São Paulo, half of the subjects work in this sector (48%), while the other half fall into the category of "Senior Partners in the Business sector" (33%). Even if this data paints a positive picture of the migrants' professional status in Brazil, it is important to stress that some of them are working without a formal contract, which is described as normal practice in general, and in Rio in particular. A considerable proportion of the subjects who stated they were full-time employees are, in fact, in a vulnerable position since they are paid below-average salaries and are not entitled to any kind of health, social or unemployment benefit. The lack of a formal contract affects many aspects of life. It makes it impossible to formally rent a house or open a bank account. This situation contradicts the migrants' initial expectations about life in Brazil and introduces a note of permanent insecurity and instability in their daily lives.

The difficulty of getting academic qualifications and degrees formally recognised constitutes a second major problem, especially for those who want a job in the public sector. The bureaucratic complexity of the process is a major factor behind most situations of underemployment, and is especially problematic amongst lawyers, architects and engineers, who see their attempts to join the professional orders blocked by lack of recognition of their diplomas.

We compared data on the subjects' last professional position in Portugal and their present position in order to identify and explore possible mobility trajectories. In Rio, most subjects kept the same profession (80%) they had in Portugal, while in São Paulo this tendency, even if dominant, is less evident (65%). Being able to *work and hold good professional positions in one's professional field* is considered a very important goal for the group. In fact, it is the main reason for their migrating to Brazil since, according to them, Portugal was not offering them the opportunity to accomplish it. Arguments about the quality and specificity of their professional skills are also used to draw a line between themselves and the other Portuguese migrants from previous waves who were, in their words, *uneducated people – mainly bakers and small retail businessmen.*

A significant number of subjects – even very qualified migrants – said they found their jobs through informal contacts (35%), a statement that attests to the significance of social networks. Only 15% of jobs (mainly those in the public sector) came from a formal job application.

Life Projects

The decision to migrate plays a very significant part in the group's short- and long-term plans. Our research explored these migrants' expectations in order to identity the main features of their trajectories.

The subjects' discourses confirm the existence of a plurality of reasons motivating their decision to migrate. There is a clear cleavage between the discourses gathered in the two cities. The São Paulo group says that the *economic opportunities (in terms of jobs and business)* that the city was offering at the time were a great incentive to migrate, while the migration of the group based in Rio was mainly due to their need to *experience something new and different from their life in Portugal.* Interestingly, both groups explicitly avoid connecting their decision to migrate to the economic crisis Portugal was facing. There is no direct mention of economic factors such as unemployment, job insecurity or lack of career prospects. On the contrary, all the emigrants' arguments are constructed around the advantages Brazil had to offer at the time in economic and social terms, and underline that their *quality of life* significantly improved with migration, in spite of their basically solid professional integration and income level in Portugal. This original trend echoes the arguments put forward by some contemporary authors, who draw attention to the fact that *lifestyle* motivations are gaining weight in contemporary migration (Benson and O'Reilly 2009). The group members we studied share a quest for *better life conditions*, i.e. better quality of life, with the great majority of the world's migrant population. *Quality of life* is, according to our research subjects, mostly the result of two factors: the new place of residence – i.e. the Brazilian cities they now inhabit – and the fact that migration allowed them to *restart their lives* – i.e. that migration provided both the setting and the tools for a transformative process to occur, a process that allowed them to be more in tune with *their true self* and *true identity* and to materialise a *new way of living* (Amit 2011; Benson and O'Reilly 2009).

Migration is defined, in most cases, as a *natural option*, resulting mainly from an individual or a couple's decision. Once more, the group distances itself from the other Portuguese emigrants who arrived before them who, in their opinion, *did not have a choice*. Unlike most of their fellow countrymen and women – for whom migration was a *last resort, a sacrifice made in order to escape poverty* – the group defines itself as mobile by preference. This self-definition establishes a direct connection between migration and cultural capital and justifies their decision to migrate as a decision to *upgrade* their own knowledge of the world.

Emphasising personal experience and cosmopolitanism does not, however, indi-cate that the group devalues work and economic capital. In fact, and in spite of their praise for a *cosmopolitan lifestyle* and for the *quality of life* in Brazil, the data gath-ered suggests that this group's careers are an important dimension of their daily lives. In fact, the data gathered on this topic illustrates that the existence of *job opportunities* strongly influenced their choice of destination city, especially amongst the migrants who opted to live in Rio. The figures in Table show that this was considered the most significant *pull factor* both in Rio (52%) and in São Paulo (48%), which corroborates the claim that economic factors play a significant role in contemporary Portuguese skilled emigration.

The importance of a common historical past, the existence of strong colonial and post-colonial ties between Portugal and Brazil, and the fact that the countries share the same language is considered the second main pull factor in Rio (48%) but is less significant for the São Paulo group (24%). The latter considers the positive international representation of Brazil more significant (40%), since it directly influences their professional careers and the business climate. Previous knowledge of the city (24%), the existence of social networks of support (32%), and a positive representation of Brazil (36%) are particularly significant for the group residing in Rio. However, for the Rio group – unlike the São Paulo group – this last factor is not valued because it translates into economic and professional gains, but rather because it shows that Brazil is valorised as a vibrant cultural context with beautiful landscapes, populated by easy-going and happy people. Family regrouping is also considered a strong motivation for migration amongst the group (28% in Rio de Janeiro and 32% in Sao Paulo). Although this reason is given almost exclusively by women, it is possible to identify different situations in each city. In São Paulo, women (as well as children) tend to follow their husbands, who migrated mostly due to their professional careers. In Rio, there are two distinct trends: a trend of

Table: Migration pull factors by destination

	RJ (%)	SP (%)	Total (%)
Job opportunities	52	48	50
Positive representations of the country	36	40	38
Cultural and linguistic affinity	48	24	36
Family reunification	28	32	30
Friendship network	32	12	22
Attractive climate	28	16	22
Previous knowledge of the city	24	16	20
Family network	4	12	8

Source: Survey on materiality, contemporary movements and policies of belonging. ATLANTIC CROSSINGS Project

mixed couples (where one spouse is Brazilian) migrating; and a trend of one partner deciding to follow the other partner who has already migrated.

Moving to a significantly different context is always stressful, and is mediated by numerous concerns, fears and expectations. Experiencing difficulties in adapting to and integrating into a new social context is more significant among the São Paulo group (40%), than among those settling in Rio de Janeiro (20%). The fear of not finding a proper job is not significant for the São Paulo group (8%), since almost all subjects had already found a suitable job before leaving Portugal. In contrast, the Rio group expressed considerable concern at not being able to find and hold secure and stable jobs (20%). It is worth mentioning that, once more, the shared history of the two countries played a significant part in attenuating anxieties about the new urban contexts they were entering.

The data gathered on preparation for migration (Table) suggests the existence of different migrant profiles among the group.

São Paulo seems to be the preferred city for those openly seeking job opportunities for highly qualified people. This group stated that they had also looked for positions that would boost their careers in other destinations such as the USA, other stronger European economies, and some of the former Portuguese African colonies (e.g. Angola and Mozambique). Their migration projects are highly structured and carefully planned, and represent an important milestone in the subjects' professional and personal biographies. The Rio group, however, presents a profile that contrasts with this. Rio de Janeiro is represented as an attractive context for very young qualified people, who are in the early stages of their professional careers. Subjects evaluate the city positively with respect to job opportunities, especially when compared to Lisbon and Oporto at the time they migrated. But the most significant theme in their discourse about the city is how great Rio is as a place to live, its

Table: Other destinations considered by respondents

São Paulo	N	Rio de Janeiro	N
USA	5	Argentina	3
Germany	2	Australia	2
UK	2	Brazil	2
Uruguay	1	Mexico	2
Denmark	1	Norway	2
Cape Verde	1	New Zealand	1
Mozambique	1	Angola	1
Angola	1	Colombia	1
Canada	1	USA	1
Switzerland	1	India	1
		UK	1
		Macao	1
		Mozambique	1

Source: Survey on materiality, contemporary movements and policies of belonging. ATLANTIC CROSSINGS Project

wonderful weather and its relaxed way of life. The allure of life in Rio is the main reason why most of the respondents migrated without pre-arranging a job, housing and, in some cases, even a visa permit. Many of them define themselves as cosmopolitans, true citizens of the world who embrace a lifestyle that revolves around permanent mobility and transition (Fig.).

The subjects based in Rio are highly mobile. Not only have a high proportion migrated previously (68%); in most cases they had previously migrated more than twice in addition to their current migration. They consider these previous experiences key to their current migration. Many of the subjects had visited Rio previously, and nearly half of them had migrated in the past to other destinations such as the USA, the Portuguese-speaking African Countries, the Middle East, and Australia (Fig.).

In São Paulo, only 32% of the respondents had a previous migration experience. Their destinations were also more restricted than those of the Rio group. The subjects for whom this is their first migration experience are all married (or divorced)

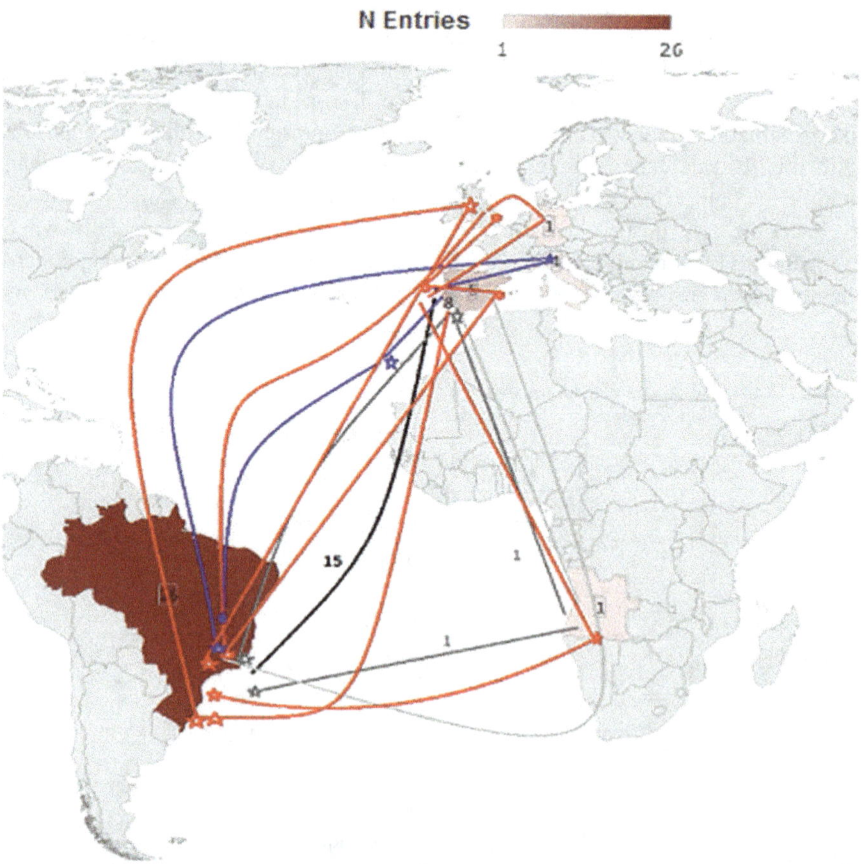

Fig. Migratory routes of Portuguese people living in Rio de Janeiro

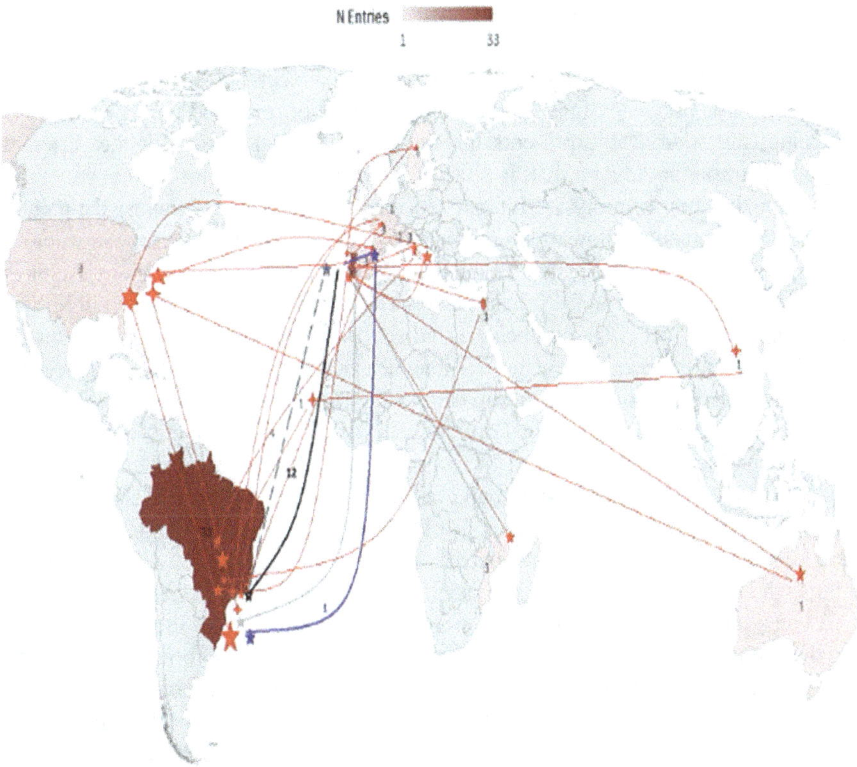

Fig. Migratory routes of Portuguese people living in São Paulo

and their spouses and children migrated with them. Their previous migration destinations were most often Spain, the Netherlands, Angola and the US. These experiences were interrupted by a period of time in Portugal, before the subjects departed again for Brazil.

Future migration plans were, at the time, still unclear for most of the subjects in the two cities. A considerable part of the São Paulo group (20%) aims to return to Lisbon after a short time. The idea of returning home coexists with the idea of migrating to the USA, the UK or Australia (18%) in the near future. The group from Rio is not very interested in returning to Portugal (only 8% said that was a possibility) and 24% of the subjects are considering future migration to new destinations such as Canada, the UK and the USA, but not in the near future.

Lifestyles and Leisure Activities

How different is life in Brazil, when compared with the subjects' past life in Portugal? And how do they evaluate their current routines and ways of living?

The groups' quest for a better existence was explored through a series of topics related to life quality. The research used a Likert scale (1 – I am doing much worse now; 6 – I am doing much better now) to grade the subjects' responses. The respondents were also asked to signal if their current situation matched their expectations preceding migration. Table presents the mean and median values for the different topics. It is important to note that, in spite of the negative values for several structural factors (e.g. housing, security, health services, education and cost of living), the gain in personal achievements following migration was positive at the time (4.4 mean value).

The reason behind the negative evaluation of the health and educational systems is the cost of these services in the private sector. The low quality of Brazilian public services has pushed most of the families we studied towards the private sector. This fact is considered a major downgrade when compared with the situation they experienced in Portugal. According to our research subjects, the quality of these basic services is good, but they cost much more than in Portugal. The families who cannot afford private healthcare and schooling mentioned the low quality and the near nonexistence of public services in both cities. The housing market is, in most cases, also negatively evaluated. The high prices and the small dimensions of most houses, especially in the city centre, were frequently mentioned. More than half of the families said that they were surprised at the high rents and that they had to make adjustments to their expectations.

A considerable number of respondents devalue the lack of a solid welfare system and the instability of the job market in Rio. As was mentioned before, the possibility of experiencing new situations, meeting new people and being mobile compensates for the economic instability experienced by some of the subjects based in Rio. In São Paulo, this adventurousness is only embraced by some of the younger families. The more senior research subjects (40%) mention the lack of time to be with their families, since both the working hours and the traffic in the city are much heavier

Table: Previous and current situation by destination

	RJ		SP		Total
	Mean	Me	Mean	Me	Mean
Personal achievements	4.4	4	4.3	5	4.4
Free time and leisure	4.6	5	4	4	4.3
Career opportunities	4.4	5	3.7	4	4.1
Integration and belonging	3.8	4	4.3	4	4.1
Travel and sports' activities	3.9	4	3.9	4	3.9
Income	4.1	4	3.6	4	3.9
Freedom	3.7	4	3.5	3	3.6
Expenses	2.9	3	3.5	3	3.2
Housing	2.8	3	3.5	3	3.2
Education	2.7	2	3.4	4	3.1
Health care	2.3	2	3.2	3	2.8
Safety	1.8	2	2.3	2	2.1
Total	3.4		3.7		3.6

Source: Survey on materiality, contemporary movements and policies of belonging. ATLANTIC CROSSINGS Project

than in Portugal. In contrast, most families in Rio state that they have more free time now than they have ever had. This free time will, in their words, hopefully allow them to materialise their romantic dreams of a life on the beach, playing sport daily and travelling – i.e. a very different picture from the image of hard work and money saving commonly associated with Portuguese migration. Whether this idyllic picture will ever be realised is a major topic to be explored in another article.

Final Remarks

The contemporary movement of Portuguese people to Rio de Janeiro and to São Paulo is the most recent episode of a longstanding trend – a trend that has been central in the history of Atlantic Crossings from Southern Europe to South America. This is an old migration route, travelled many times in contexts of economic and/or political instability by the Portuguese, who have crossed the Atlantic to pursue better lives for themselves and for their families. The fact that the two countries share a colonial past has always played a significant part not only in their political, cultural and diplomatic relations, but also in the positions that each nation's citizens occupy, as migrants, in the other country. As was argued before, present-day Portuguese migrants in Brazil do not identify themselves as migrants. Instead, they define themselves as cosmopolitans or travellers in search of new life experiences and/or professional internationalization in two great Brazilian cities. Colonialism and post-colonialism appear to facilitate this particular positioning strategy. By promoting cultural attachment and naturalizing the movements of Portuguese people towards Brazil and, simultaneously, diminishing Brazilian culture, institutions and health and educational systems, this new Portuguese migration wave seems to be contributing to the reification of a hierarchical relationship between the two countries, as well as to the exoticization of the "easy" Brazilian way of life.

Funding Research funded by the Fundação para a Ciência e a Tecnologia (Foundation for Science and Technology, FCT) (PTDC/CS-ANT/119803/2010) for the project "Atlantic Crossings: materiality, contemporary movements and politics of belonging" (*Travessias do Atlântico: materialidade, movimentos contemporâneos e políticas de pertença*). The proofreading of this chapter was funded by the Portuguese Emigration Observatory (Observatório da Emigração).

References

Amit, V. (Ed.). (2007). *Going first class?: New approaches to privileged travel and movement* (Vol. 7). London: Berghahn Books.

Benson, M., & O'Reilly, K. (2009). Migration and the search for a better way of life: A critical exploration of lifestyle migration. *The Sociological Review, 57*(4), 608–625.

Bourdieu, P. (1984 [1979]). *Distinction: A social critique of the judgement of taste*. Cambridge: Harvard University Press.

Burrell, K. (2008). Managing, learning and sending: The material lives and journeys of Polish women in Britain. *Journal of Material Culture, 13*(1), 63–82.

Feldman-Bianco, B. (2001, December). Brazilians in Portugal and Portuguese in Brazil: Constructions of sameness and difference. *Global Studies in Culture and Power, 4*(8), 607–650.

Glick-Schiller, N., Basch, L., & Blanc-Szanton, C. (1994). *Nations unbound: Transnational projects, postcolonial predicaments and deterritorialized Nation-States*. Amsterdam: Gordon and Breach Science Publishers.

Graça, M. Q. (2009). Portugueses no Brasil no pós-25 de Abril, um testemunho contra os estereótipos. In B. Padilla & M. Xavier (Eds.), *Revista Migrações – Número Temático Migrações entre Portugal e América Latina* (Vol. 5, pp. 288–290). Lisboa: ACIDI.

Malheiros, J. M. (Ed.). (2011). *A Imigração brasileira em Portugal*. Lisbon: ACIDI.

Peixoto, J. (2012). *A emigração portuguesa hoje: o que sabemos e o que não sabemos* (SOCIUS Working Papers, 5).

Peixoto, J., & Iorio, J. (2011). *Crise, imigração e mercado de trabalho em Portugal*. Cascais: Principia.

Pereira, M. H. (2007). A Emigração portuguesa para o Brasil e a geo-estratégica do desenvolvimento Euro-Americano. In AAVV (Ed.), *População e sociedade: A emigração portuguesa para o Brasil*, Parte I, 14.

Pires, R. P., Pereira, C., Azevedo, J., & Ribeiro, A. C. (2014). *Emigração Portuguesa: Relatório Estatístico 2014*. Observatório da Emigração e Rede Migra, CIES-IUL, ISCTE-IUL.

Rosales, M. V. (2010). The domestic work of consumption. Materiality, migration and home-making. *Etnográfica, 14*(3), 507–525.

Vertovec, S. (2007). Introduction. New directions in the anthropology of migration and multiculturalism. *Ethnic and Racial Studies, 30*(6), 961–978.

7

Entrepreneurship Among Portuguese Nationals in Luxembourg

José Carlos Marques

Introduction

Along with other countries in Europe, Luxembourg has once again become a destination for contemporary Portuguese emigration, which intensified during the recent economic crisis. The intensity with which this migratory flow has developed in recent years should not, however, obscure the fact that Portuguese emigration to Luxembourg has been a continuous reality since the 1960s, and has had different rhythms and intensities over time. This chapter's analysis of Portuguese immigrants' economic integration in Luxembourg (and in particular their entrepreneurial practices) reflects this long history of Portuguese emigration to this country.

The first part of the article briefly describes the evolution of Portuguese emigration to Luxembourg and its insertion in Luxembourg's labour market. The second part seeks to deepen the understanding of Portuguese immigrants' entrepreneurial activities (an area that, as the latest literature on Portuguese emigration shows, has not so far benefited from in-depth study[1]) and to analyse the different factors that influence the creation and development of entrepreneurial practices by the Portuguese abroad. A survey conducted in 2012 among Portuguese entrepreneurs in Luxembourg is used for this analysis.

[1] In this body of academic literature on Portuguese emigration between 1980 and 2013, there are only six references that address, sometimes indirectly, the practices of Portuguese immigrants' entrepreneurship (Candeias et al. 2014).

J. C. Marques (✉)
Instituto Politécnico de Leiria, Centro Interdisciplinar de Ciências Sociais FCSH/UNL (CICS.NOVA.IPLeiria), Leiria, Portugal
e-mail: jose.marques@ipleiria.pt

The Portuguese in Luxembourg

Since the late 1960s the Portuguese have been one of the main groups of immigrants arriving in Luxembourg – and since 1986 they have been at the top of the numerical hierarchy of foreign citizens arriving in the country every year.[2]

Data on the inflow and outflow of Portuguese nationals in Luxembourg (Fig.) allows the identification of two key moments in the formation of the Portuguese community. The first was between the late 1980s and mid-1990s, during which period the inflows were always more than double the annual outflows. The second, from 2003 onwards, saw the same flow observed in the first moment repeated, but this time at higher levels.

Until the end of the 1990s the inflow of Portuguese workers to Luxembourg was not significantly influenced by the country joining the European Economic Community in 1986 or by the end of the transition period for the free movement of people (in 1992). The intensification of the migratory movement after 2003 and, in particular, after 2007, occurred in a context in which the free movement of Portuguese citizens in the EU had already been consolidated. It is true that part of this migratory flow has benefited from a mobility regime more favourable to the pursuit of work opportunities in other EU countries. But the transformation of the institutional context in which the Portuguese movement to Luxembourg (and other EU countries) occurred didn't significantly change the nature of the migration flow: as shown in a recent study on Portuguese emigration (Schiltz et al. 2016), in spite of a diversifica-

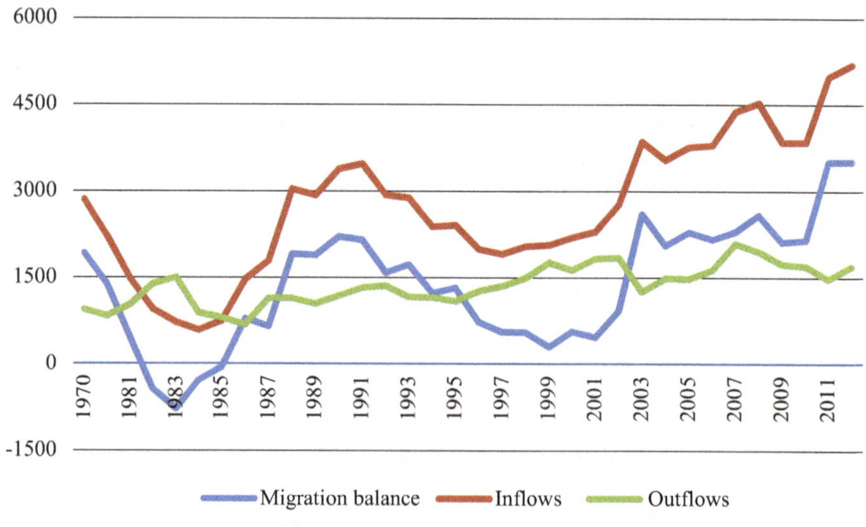

Fig. Inflow and outflow of Portuguese nationals in Luxembourg, 1970–2012.
Source: STATEC (various years, available at http://www.statistiques.public.lu)

[2] For a thorough analysis on the history of the Portuguese emigration in Luxembourg, refer to Beirão (1999) and Arroteia (1986).

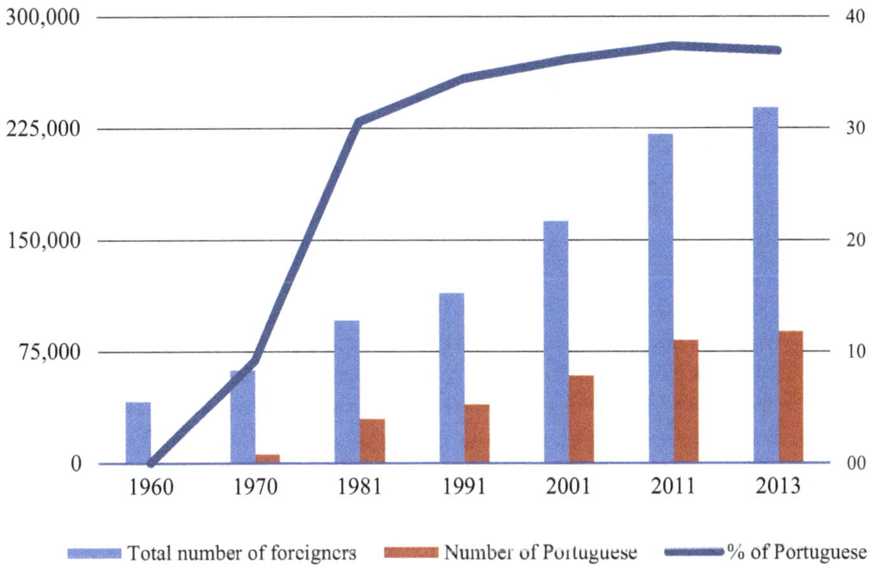

Fig. Evolution of the foreign and Portuguese population in Luxembourg, 1960–2013. Source: STATEC (various years, available at http://www.statistiques.public.lu)

tion of emigrants' sociodemographic characteristics in the last few years, the majority of Portuguese emigrants to Luxembourg have migration trajectories similar to those followed by emigrants of the 1970s and 1980s, which allows us to continue to analyse these flows as emigration rather than as internal mobility.

As a result of the evolution of the migratory flow described above, from 1981 onwards the Portuguese became the main community of immigrants in Luxembourg; in 2013 they made up 36.9% of all foreigners residing in the country and 16.4% of the total population (Fig.).

Demographically, the Portuguese population in Luxembourg can be characterised as young (with an average age of 32.9) and with a slightly higher percentage of males (52.5%)[3] than females.

This is a population with predominantly low levels of education (45% of those over 14 years of age only attended primary education and 24% lower secondary education[4]), and intermediate levels of further education (especially of a vocational nature). Analysis of education levels by age group confirms that these low levels of education prevail across practically all age groups, although younger age groups tend to be more highly educated. Thus, 80% or more of Portuguese nationals in their forties and above have only primary or lower secondary education (a percentage that rises to over 90% among immigrants aged 55 and over). In younger age groups

[3] Data referring to the population census of 2011.

[4] Lower secondary education is equivalent to the 9th grade in Portugal (Ordinance No. 699/2006 of 12 July).

Table: Portuguese nationals' main activity sectors (total and 15–29 year-olds), 2011 (%)

	Total	15–29 year-olds
Industry	7.9	7.4
Construction	29.1	21.7
Trade, hotel and restaurants	24.6	31.0
Scientific, technic, and administrative activities	15.4	17.6
Public administration, education, health and social support	11.2	12.0
Other sectors	11.8	10.3

Source: STATEC (http://www.statistiques.public.lu)

the proportion with lower levels of education reduces to 69.2% for those aged 35–39 and to 45.4% for those aged 25–29. We are thus witnessing an increase in the level of education among Portuguese nationals in Luxembourg over time, although this remains below the level registered among the total population[5] (STATEC 2013).

It is interesting to note that although this is mainly labour migration, only 51.2% of Portuguese nationals in Luxembourg are active in the labour market. This results from family reunification processes and the formation of Portuguese families in Luxembourg. Hence, of the inactive population, 22.7% are students, and 7.3% are retired. A further 4.9% of inactive individuals are unemployed.

The integration of Portuguese nationals in Luxembourg's labour market is characterised by the concentration of a large proportion of immigrants in the 'traditional' activity sectors of construction (23.6%) and trade, and hotels and restaurants (16.5%) (Table).

In addition to these sectors it is important to point out the significance of the support services sector, which employs 10.3% of Portuguese nationals. Data about the sectors in which young people (15–29 year-olds) are active show some differences in relation to the sectors in which the Portuguese emigrant population as a whole are active, though the global occupational pattern is preserved. Young people are slightly less active in the construction sector (21.7%) and more so in the trade, hotel and restaurant sectors (31.0%), as well as in sectors generally occupying fewer Portuguese people: scientific, technical, and administrative activities (17.6%), public administration, education and health (12.0%).

As for their current economic activity status, the overwhelming majority of active Portuguese nationals are employed (92.1%). In 2011 3.5% of active individuals were self-employed (a total of 1384 people) and the remaining 4.4% were either active in training (2.0%) or did not indicate their professional status (2.4%).[6]

Following this brief overview of the characteristics of the Portuguese population in Luxembourg, we will now look at their entrepreneurial practices.

[5] In the total population, the percentage of those with lower levels of education is 19.2% for youths between 25 and 29 years of age, 21.7% for those between 30 and 34 years old and 27.1% for the population between 35 and 39 years of age (STATEC 2013).

[6] These data on the economic status of Portuguese nationals come from a survey requested from the statistical service of Luxembourg (STATEC).

Portuguese Nationals' Entrepreneurship in Luxembourg

The data presented above on Portuguese immigrants' economic integration in Luxembourg shows that the percentage of those who are self-employed is not very significant in quantitative terms. As recognised by several authors, however, notwithstanding the relative importance of immigrant entrepreneurship[7] activities for the economies of host countries and the substantive meaning and practical implications of these activities for the immigrants themselves should not be neglected. To understand their significance we must find out whether self-employment is a response to unemployment, whether it creates job opportunities for an individual and/or their co-nationals, whether it provides economic resources, whether it allows or is based on maintaining transnational relations, etc. (Light et al. 1994, Portes and Sensenbrenner 1993).

The distribution of a questionnaire among Portuguese entrepreneurs in Luxembourg sought specifically to contribute to an understanding of these aspects, by including a set of questions intended:

1. to characterise Portuguese emigrants' entrepreneurial activity;
2. to identify the main determinants of the development of entrepreneurial practices, thus determining the influence of individual and group resources and the action of push and pull factors;
3. to analyse the problems and the need for support experienced by entrepreneurs of immigrant origin and, in particular, the importance of family and 'co national' resources in the entrepreneurial development process;
4. to register the development and maintenance of external economic relations by Portuguese entrepreneurs abroad, especially economic relations with the country of origin.

Characterization of Respondents

Before proceeding with the analysis of the survey data, it is important to briefly present the respondents' characteristics. The survey was distributed between January and February 2012 to 156 Portuguese entrepreneurs in Luxembourg (i.e., approximately 11% of Portuguese nationals who, according to the 2011 Census, were self-employed). Naturally, the number of respondents and the sampling

---

[7] Designations such as 'immigrant entrepreneurship' and 'ethnic entrepreneurship' will be used interchangeably throughout the text. However, it is recognised that ethnic entrepreneurship refers to self-employed practices among a segment of society whose members share (or believe they share) a common ethnic and cultural origin and who engage in shared activities in which this common origin is a central factor, while the notion of immigrant entrepreneurship is limited to individuals who actually migrated themselves (therefore excluding those born in the host country) (Volery 2007; Yinger 1985).

methodology[8] used did not allow the results to be extrapolated to the majority of Portuguese emigrant entrepreneurs in Luxembourg. This was not, however, the main objective of the investigation, which was guided by an interest in expanding our understanding of Portuguese immigrants' entrepreneurial activities – an area that, as mentioned in the introduction, has received little attention in existing studies of Portuguese emigration.

Of the 156 respondents, 58% were male and a little over two thirds (70.5%) were between 35 and 54 years old (Fig.). 32.3% first emigrated in the 1990s and 21.9% in the first decade of the twenty-first century. Data on the inflow to Luxembourg, especially during the last decade of the twentieth century, indicate that the Portuguese migratory flow to this country remained at this level even after politicians announced in the 1990s that Portugal was no longer a country of emigra-tion. The economic sectors in which the emigrants worked before becoming inde-pendent were the hotel and restaurant sector (32.1%), construction (13.7%), trade (15.3%), the real estate sector (6.1%), and the sector of 'other services' (11.5% related primarily to the provision of domestic services, cleaning and personal services, etc.).

Entrepreneurial Activity

Most of the survey participants' companies were created in the twenty-first century and from 2006 onwards in particular (44.2%). During this period, it was immigrants who arrived in Luxembourg in the last decade of the twentieth century or the first decade of the twenty-first century who were most likely to begin entrepreneurial activity (32.4% and 38.2% respectively).

As to how the activity was started, almost all respondents (99.3%) bought an existing company and only a minority went through the whole process of starting up a company from scratch. The legal form chosen was most often that of a limited liability company (55.6%), followed by forms of individual ownership (35.3%) and single-member companies (5.2%) (Table).

The main resources used by Portuguese nationals when creating their company were either their own (40.9%) or came from institutions (i.e. bank credit: 39.0%). Resources coming from the community (family or friends) made up a very small proportion (only 7.1% said they used this kind of help). This relatively small reliance on the community's economic resources is noteworthy, given that a lack of economic resources is one of the main difficulties experienced by Portuguese emigrant

[8] 'Snowball' sampling was used to identify respondents. This technique is particularly useful in a more exploratory study such as this one, which is intended to be an initial examination of the sub-ject that will help to support and develop further study. The 'snowball' technique was constrained by imposing quotas relating to type and sector of activity. The aim has been to include active immigrants in different sectors of activity and a significant proportion of both men and women, assuming that both genders have different opportunities in the labour market and in the pursuit of independent economic activity.

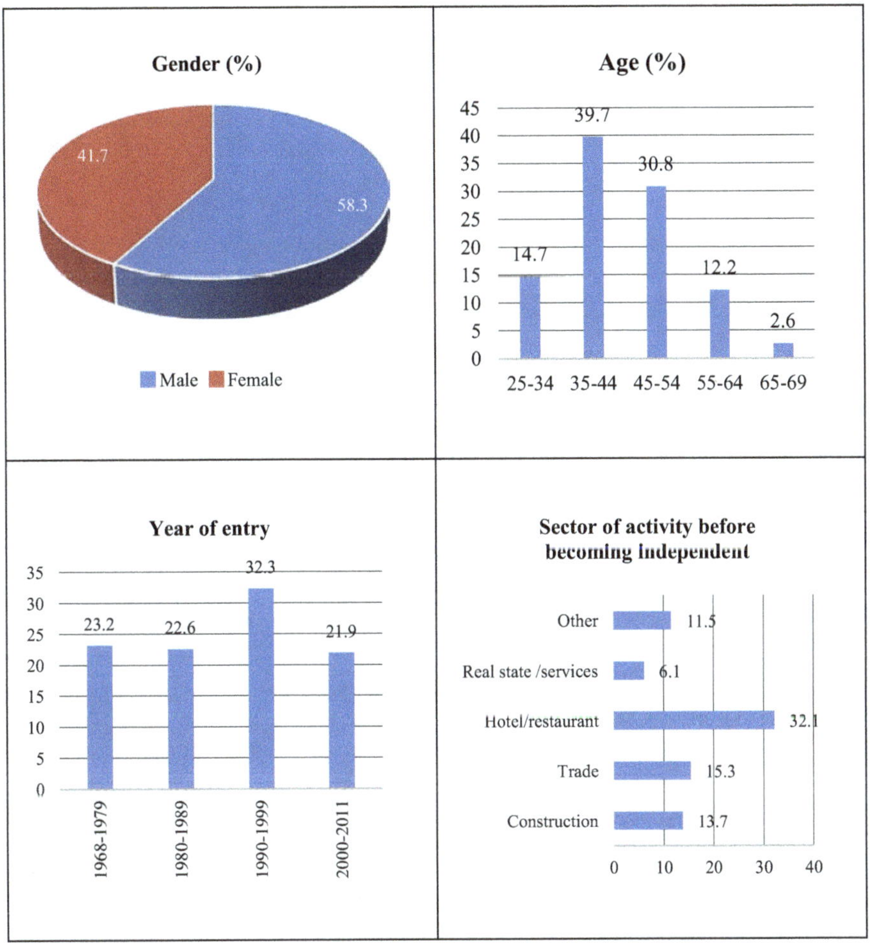

Fig. Social and demographic characteristics of respondents.
Source: Survey of Portuguese entrepreneurs in Luxembourg, 2012

entrepreneurs. It thus appears that, contrary to what is often suggested in the literature on immigrant entrepreneurship (cf., e.g., Light 1987; Light and Gold 2000; Smallbone et al. 2003), the scarcity of equity capital is not, in the case of Portuguese entrepreneurs, compensated for by the financial solidarity of the community or family.

A high proportion of companies created by the respondents are of small or medium scale both in terms of the number of employees (up to 9 employees), and in terms of turnover (usually lower than € 75,000) (Table).

Analysis of the sectors in which Portuguese emigrants constituted their companies shows that these are roughly the same sectors in which they were last employed before becoming independent, namely: the hotel and restaurant sector (57.8%), trade (16.9%) and real estate and provision of services (11.7%). Of all the main

Table: Characteristics of the companies created

	%	N
Year of creation		
Up to 1980	5.2	8
1981–1990	10.4	16
1991–2000	20.1	31
2001–2005	20.1	31
2006–2011	44.2	68
Form of ownership		
Sole proprietor	34.6	54
Single member limited liability company	5.1	8
Limited liability company	54.5	85
Other	3.9	6
Form of financing		
Personal savings	40.9	63
Bank credit	39.0	60
Loans from families/friends	7.1	11
Savings and bank credit	11.7	18
Other	1.3	2

Source: Survey of Portuguese entrepreneurs in Luxembourg, 2012

Table: Characteristics of companies

	%	N
Area of activity		
Hotel and restaurants	57.8	89
Trade	16.9	26
Real estate and provision of services	11.7	18
Construction	3.2	5
Other	10.3	16
Number of employees		
None	17.5	27
1–9	67.5	104
10–29	9.7	15
30 and over	5.2	8
Turnover		
Up to 75,000€	86.3	132
75,000–150,000€	13.7	21

Source: Survey of Portuguese entrepreneurs in Luxembourg, 2012

sectors in which Portuguese nationals work, the construction industry has the lowest share of self-employed workers. We believe that this is due to the high levels of capital investment usually associated with entrepreneurial activity in this sector.

Cross-tabulation of the sector of activity prior to entrepreneurial activity with the entrepreneurial development sector in Luxembourg shows that for 40.5% of respon dents there was no change, and for the remainder the change was mostly from construction to hotels and restaurants, from trade to hotels and restaurants, or from trade to the provision of services. Although it reveals an interesting relationship between the last sector of employment and the first sector of self-employment, this comparison does not clarify the emigrant's entire previous professional experience. From interviews conducted with some informants (serving mainly to supplement the information obtained from the survey) it is possible to conclude that a substantial part of the Portuguese entrepreneurs in Luxembourg created their company in a sector in which they had been employed at an earlier stage. Thus, for example, many decided to become self-employed in the restaurant sector because they worked for some time as employees in this sector, which allowed them to acquire skills related to its operation (relating to customers and suppliers, identifying opportunities for profit, etc.).

The low level of family involvement in the initial financing of the company, mentioned above, does not mean that the family or the rest of the Portuguese com-munity remains detached from the company's operation after its formation. Thus almost 40% of respondents reported that they employed at least one member of their family and nearly three-quarters of the respondents indicated that their employees were exclusively Portuguese (Table).

Data on the nationality of employees, customers and suppliers allows us to see that the companies formed by Portuguese citizens – although retaining a strongly national character in terms of their employees and customers – do interact with Luxembourg society, which plays a central role in the supply of goods to companies owned by Portuguese nationals. This is to be expected and is due largely to the sector in which most of these companies – restaurants and small retailers – operate, which relies on local suppliers near the companies' area of influence.

A distinction is often made in the studies of immigrant entrepreneurship between businesses operating in closed or niche markets made up of co-ethnics or co-nationals, on the one hand, and those operating in open markets, on the other. Portuguese entrepreneurs in Luxembourg are not limited to a specific market, and thus fall neither wholly on one side of this distinction or the other (Table): when it comes to suppliers, the open market plays a larger role; when it comes to customer

Table: Nationality of employees, customers and suppliers (%)

	Nationality of most employees	Nationality of most customers	Nationality of main suppliers
Portuguese	78.3	43.1	9.0
Portuguese and other	7.8	30.7	9.7
Luxembourg	3.9	19.0	72.9
Other	10.1	7.2	8.4
N	129	153	155

Source: Survey of Portuguese entrepreneurs in Luxembourg, 2012

base, the situation is mixed (although Portuguese nationals predominate); and when it comes to employees, community resources and the co-national market play a greater role.

Key Factors in Entrepreneurship Development: Push and Pull Factors

Various authors who have analysed immigrant entrepreneurship have identified the influence of a number of factors leading to self-employment among immigrant populations. Studies that suggest a multidimensional approach and recognise the relevance of the interaction between individual factors and environmental or situational conditions have been particularly relevant in recent years (Kloosterman and Rath 2001; Waldinger et al. 1990).

As Oliveira (2004) notes, it is not only community resources and opportunities in the host society that drive entrepreneurship, but also the individual's ability to use the resources and opportunities provided.[9] Opportunities include the ability to access the market, the ability to meet the labour market's operating conditions, and the ability to access resources – all of which may be characteristics shared by a given group that constitute a pathway to self-employment (Putz 2002).

In sum, the following factors have been presented as explaining the development of immigrant entrepreneurship:

(a) **Individual Resources, in Particular the Availability of Human and Financial Capital**

Though there may be limited access to the financial resources necessary to fund entrepreneurial activities, this has, according to several studies, been compensated for by resources available in the immigrant community and in particular by family support (Sanders and Nee 1996; Smallbone et al. 2003).

(b) **The Resources of the Ethnic or Co-National Group and Social Capital**

Ethnic resources and social capital – which may be both material and immaterial resources – can be mobilised by members of ethnic groups to pursue their entrepreneurial activities (Granovetter 1985; Portes and Sensenbrenner 1993).

(c) **Structural Factors**

Conditions in the country of destination – i.e. the existing opportunities in the host society – are highly significant in the development of immigrant entrepreneurship. Special attention is devoted to the action of markets and the labour market structure, as well as to legal and institutional factors (Rath 2000, Waldinger et al. 1990).

---

[9] See also Portes and Zhou (1999).

(d) **Incentives and Pressures (Push and Pull Factors)**

Two sets of extreme reasons for the development of entrepreneurial activities are identified: reasons related to self-realization (pull) and reasons arising from an economy of necessity (push). The desire for autonomy, independence and freedom of choice predominates among the first type of reason, while in the latter the predominant factors are the response to a situation or threat of unemployment, or dissatisfaction with the employment relationship (including dissatisfaction with salary) (Clark and Drinkwater 2000; Dawson and Henley 2012; Dawson et al. 2009; Hillmann and Rudolph 1997).[10] It is recognised that the initiation of entrepreneurial activity is almost always the result of various incentives and pressures, so that the simple categorization of motivations as belonging to only two extreme poles is not sufficient for a complete understanding.

It is assumed in this study that entrepreneurial initiatives are not determined only by the available (human and financial) resources, but also by certain incentives and pressures, and that decisions regarding the development of a business activity are complex, combining – to a variable degree – a number of diverse motivations. Identifying these incentives and pressures (or these push and pull factors) is particularly important if we want to understand the reasons that led to the pursuit of self-employed activity by immigrants.

For this study it was considered important to understand the reasons that led to self-employment and, in particular, to learn whether this was originally motivated by factors of attraction or by pressure resulting from limited opportunities in the labour market. Though we do not intend to discuss in detail the action of all these factors in Luxembourg-based Portuguese immigrants' move to self-employment, we will look at the incentives and pressures acting on these immigrants in order to identify, as part of this initial examination, the reasons that led them towards entrepreneurship. These are mainly subjective factors mentioned in survey responses. It was not possible to ascertain from the survey data the relative significance of each factor in the decision-making process (Table).

The data in the table indicates that the factors of attraction (incentives) are the most important in the decision to set up a business (in total, 89.3% of responses mentioned these factors). The recognition of opportunities, together with understanding the business sector, are mentioned as important reasons for pursuing self-employment (39.4% of responses), suggesting that knowledge of the economic sector (arising, for example, from prior work experience) is an important factor in setting up a businesses. Respondents' desire for independence or to make their own profit were also mentioned in a large number of responses (33.6%). They attributed less importance, in the decision making process, to push factors (or pressure), such

---

[10] In the academic literature – especially the literature produced in the context of the Global Entrepreneurship Monitor – the push and pull factors that led to entrepreneurship are also referred to using the terms necessity entrepreneurship and opportunity entrepreneurship (Reynolds et al. 2002).

Table: Incentives and pressures leading to entrepreneurial activity[a]

Question	Reason/indicator	Factor	%
Family idea	Family	Incentive	4.7
Change in family circumstances	Family	Pressure	1.3
I had that goal when I emigrated	Disposition/realization	Incentive	0.6
I had capital to invest	Disposition	Incentive	3.9
Felt that need	Disposition/realization	Incentive	1.3
Wanted to be self-employed	Autonomy	Incentive	19.3
Opportunity for own profit	Autonomy	Incentive	14.3
Had a good business idea	Opportunity recognition	Incentive	4.7
Had good contacts for business partners	Opportunity recognition	Incentive	1.1
The opportunity arose	Opportunity recognition	Incentive	26.3
Knew the business sector well	Opportunity recognition	Incentive	13.1
Was unemployed	Unemployment	Pressure	1.3
Wasn't satisfied with my previous condition	Dissatisfaction	Pressure	9.0

Source: Survey of Portuguese entrepreneurs in Luxembourg, 2012
[a]The reasons that led to self-employment were assessed through a multiple-choice question (limited to a maximum of three answers). The percentages of indicated responses are presented in the text

as dissatisfaction with their previous employment situation, or unemployment (respectively 9.0% and 1.3% of responses).[11]

Categorising the reasons for beginning independent business activity in terms of push and pull factors – while interesting from an analytical point of view and useful for the development of policies promoting entrepreneurship – ignores the fact that both sets of factors frequently and often jointly intervene in the decision-making process. For example, respondents who felt that the source of their entrepreneurial initiative was dissatisfaction with their work situation (push factor), also indicated as a motivation the identification of an opportunity or desire to work on their own (pull factors). In total, 33.3% of respondents identified both a push factor and a pull factor and the remaining individuals only identified push factors. It is thus important to recognise that both types of motivation intervene, to varying degrees, in the initiation of independent business activity. It therefore becomes necessary to distinguish the relative importance of each *type* of factor, as well as the relative importance of each *particular* factor present in the decision making process (which cannot be done with the survey data collected for this study).

[11] Like most of the answers to questions about past events, the answers given by the respondents may have been influenced by biased retrospection that tends to overestimate the positive effects, i.e. the pull factors (Pearson et al. 1994).

Difficulties in Establishing and Conducting the Independent Business Activity

The decision to set up in business is associated with the identification of resources (knowledge, economic capital, etc.) available to pursue the entrepreneurial initiative. In this section we intend, above all, to identify the constraints experienced by migrants in the creation and development of their business. Respondents were asked about problems experienced in two different periods: during the establishment of the company and during its operation.

As shown by the data in the following table, the difficulties encountered by Portuguese entrepreneurs in Luxembourg when creating the company were mainly due to structural issues (funding, staff problems, an insufficient number of customers, and difficulty in finding facilities). Insufficient financial resources and difficulty in accessing bank credit emerge as particularly constraining structural factors when setting up a business. Discrimination or racism was mentioned by a similar number of respondents as mentioned difficulty in obtaining bank credit. It is not straightforward to establish a causal relationship between these two variables, but of those who mentioned discrimination or racism as a difficulty when establishing their business, 60% also stated that they had difficulty getting credit from financial institutions. Since an almost identical percentage (59.3%) identified lack of economic resources as a difficulty, it could be hypothesised that perceptions of discrimination or racism are related to difficulties in acquiring financial capital from the banking system to establish a business. Constraints faced by small minority businesses in the credit system are commonly identified as caused by discrimination (Blanchflower et al. 2003) and discrimination in credit markets helps explain higher rates of loan denial, as well as higher interest rates among immigrants (Alden and Hammarstedt 2016). These two factors (loan denials and higher interest rates) could account for the percentage of Portuguese entrepreneurs that identified discrimination or racism as an obstacle both during the establishment and (to a lesser extent) the development of their business (Table).

It is also worth pointing out the relevance attributed to the shortage of human resources. This is particularly interesting given that, as mentioned above, most of the employees working in respondents' companies are of Portuguese nationality.[12] Further structural obstacles are the bureaucratic issues (contact with the institutions and management of the administrative process) that emerge, although with less significance, as the third set of difficulties encountered by Portuguese entrepreneurs at the beginning of their business activity. The lower importance assigned to these two factors can be explained by respondents' prior understanding of the functioning of Luxembourg society and, in particular, the sector of activity in which the Portuguese emigrants set up their company.

[12] It is possible that the scarcity of workers identified by employers is addressed, after the business has been established, by recruiting co-nationals in Portugal.

Table: Difficulties encountered during the initial period of the business' establishment (% of positive answers)

	%	Total of responses
Problems with partners	14.2	141
Insufficient knowledge of management techniques	18.3	142
Absence of economic or financial resources	44.4	144
Lack of qualified labour	27.5	149
Absence of a business idea or opportunity	4.1	128
Difficulty contacting institutions in the host country	12.5	144
Ignorance of the laws of the host country	19.0	147
Difficulty in defining a business strategy	4.8	146
Difficulties with organization and operation	6.1	148
Difficulty in obtaining the adequate information	10.8	148
Problems in the supply of goods	6.8	147
Lack of customers	28.4	148
Difficulties in finding the appropriate facilities	20.7	150
Difficulties accessing bank credit	19.1	141
Racism or discrimination	19.0	147
Difficulties in managing the administrative process with the official authorities	10.2	147

Source: Survey of Portuguese entrepreneurs in Luxembourg, 2012

In addition to structural difficulties, personal obstacles may also hamper the company's establishment. Among these, ignorance of the country's laws or of management techniques emerge as the most significant factors for respondents, followed by problems with business partners. Difficulties related to factors traditionally considered fundamental in the creation of a company (business idea and strategy, and organizational skills) are considered less important.

Overall, the Portuguese emigrants surveyed attach less importance to personal factors than to structural ones. This is not surprising, given that setting up a business requires, in addition to other factors, certain personal characteristics (for example, knowledge of the sector, predisposition for risk, etc.) which, when absent, inhibit entrepreneurial activity from the outset. Since the survey was distributed only to those who have succeeded in setting up a business and who still have a business, the sample has been positively selected, i.e. it is one in which such personal (and also structural) factors, while obstacles, were not enough to render the establishment of a business impracticable.

Once the initial obstacles to the establishment of a company are overcome, immigrants thereafter observe a clear decrease in difficulties – both structural and personal (Table). Again, inadequate financial resources are identified as the main difficulty, followed by labour and consumer market constraints (specifically difficulties in recruiting qualified staff, and a shortage of customers). It is interesting to note that once the business is up and running, personal factors are considered even less of a constraint, pointing to immigrants' ability to overcome their initial

Table: Difficulties during the company's operation (% of positive answers)

	%	Total of answers
Problems with partners	5.6	141
Insufficient knowledge of management techniques	6.9	145
Absence of economic or financial resources	18.5	146
Lack of qualified labour	12.9	148
Difficulty contacting institutions in the host country	4.1	146
Ignorance of the laws of the host country	6.1	147
Difficulty in defining a business strategy	4.1	147
Difficulties in organization and operation	4.1	147
Difficulty in obtaining the adequate information	4.8	147
Problems in the supply of goods	5.4	147
Lack of customers	14.4	146
Difficulties in finding the appropriate facilities	6.8	147
Difficulties accessing bank credit	6.9	146
Racism or discrimination	10.2	147
Competition	9.4	149
Difficulties in managing the administrative process with the official authorities	6.1	147

Source: Survey of Portuguese entrepreneurs in Luxembourg, 2012

individual limitations (for example, lack of management techniques, insufficient information, and lack of knowledge about laws) and to deal with the country's specific conditions in a more informed way.

Construction and Maintenance of External Economic Relations by Portuguese Entrepreneurs Abroad

Having analysed the characteristics of Portuguese entrepreneurship in Luxembourg, it is important to identify to what extent this activity makes use of the links that emigrants maintain with their country of origin to improve the business' operation. The question here is, essentially, to assess the extent and intensity of transnational entrepreneurship[13] practices among Portuguese entrepreneurs in Luxembourg. To this end, the survey contained a set of questions to firstly assess the emigrants' relationship with their country of origin and, secondly, to collect information about the use of contacts with Portugal in the development of their business.

The majority of the Portuguese emigrants surveyed express a close relationship with their country of origin, maintained particularly through regular holidays in

[13] For more on transnational entrepreneurship see, among others, Portes et al. (2002) and Drori et al. (2009).

Portugal,[14] or through investments in the country (mainly in property, aimed at home ownership). Most respondents (56.8%) claimed to have already invested in Portugal and, of those who have not made investments in the country, 35.3% indicated that they intended to do so in the future. This relatively small percentage of respondents intending to make future investments in the country can partly be explained by the unfavourable economic conditions Portugal was experiencing at the time of the survey. The survey data does not confirm this claim, but does suggest a significant relationship between the respondents' future plans and their investment intentions. Of those who indicated having no intention of investing in Portugal, 70.5% stated that they intend to stay permanently in Luxembourg and 20.5% revealed that they did not yet have definite plans for the future.

Another traditional way of maintaining relations with the country of origin is to send remittances, but the majority of respondents (73.5%) claimed not to send money to Portugal.

Aside from the links between Portuguese immigrants and their country of origin mentioned above – which are not exclusive to immigrant entrepreneurs – the relationships that Portuguese entrepreneurs in Luxembourg establish with companies in Portugal are also worth noting. These external economic relations may represent an important potential both in the initial stages of business development, as well as once the business is in operation. Contacts with companies, suppliers and distributors in the country of origin may allow privileged access (in terms of cost and time) to important resources for their businesses. The lack of language and cultural barriers and the explicit and implicit understanding of the country of origin's formal and informal structures may facilitate the development of Portuguese entrepreneurs' trade relations with business partners in Portugal. The construction and development of these transnational relations is not, however, an obvious or natural activity for all emigrant entrepreneurs. Spatial and temporal distances (e.g. the difference between the time of demand and the time of supply of goods and services), the type of industry and the nature of the product or marketed service may all have a strong influence on the existence and the intensity of migrant entrepreneurs' external economic relations.[15]

Portuguese entrepreneurs in Luxembourg have regular (29%) or occasional (41.9%) trade relations with the country of origin. Business relationships with companies, suppliers or distributors in Portugal are more intense in economic sectors based on the commercialization of products of Portuguese origin. Most respondents who maintain a regular or occasional relationship with companies in Portugal operate either in the trade sector (16.5%) or in the hotel sector (61.5%).

External trade relations are not limited to companies located in the country of origin. They may also involve other companies owned by Portuguese immigrants

[14] 49.7% of respondents reported going on regular vacations to Portugal and 41.3% stated that they occasionally went on holiday to Portugal. Only 0.6% of Portuguese entrepreneurs who responded to the survey said they do not go on holiday to Portugal.

[15] The regulatory and institutional framework of the different countries must be added to these factors.

located in other host countries. Although it is important to evaluate the relationships established between Portuguese emigrant entrepreneurs residing in different countries and to analyse their potential benefits, the survey used for this study did not include questions to this end.

Final Comments

From the data on Portuguese nationals' entrepreneurial practices in Luxembourg, it is possible to build up an initial picture of their activity. This picture reflects a specific point in time – the time at which the survey was conducted – however, and therefore does not allow a longitudinal evaluation of this business activity. Neither the success of the businesses established (particularly those founded recently), nor changes in the situation of the companies surveyed are known. Notwithstanding this limitation, it can be noted that Portuguese entrepreneurship in Luxembourg is a significant reality for the Portuguese community residing there, both because of the visibility of the kind of activities it involves, and because it is a space for the labour (and social) integration of many Portuguese emigrants. Concentrated mainly in the retail and hotel sectors, Portuguese entrepreneurship principally results from the identification of specific opportunities in the labour market and less from constraints imposed by the emigrant's career history (for example, unemployment). Identifying these opportunities and experiencing a low level of bureaucratic difficulty in establishing oneself in business results from knowledge about how the economic sector works – knowledge acquired while these entrepreneurs were working as employees, often in the same sector.

The initiation of entrepreneurial activity was mainly motivated by reasons related to self-realisation rather than by a response to push factors like, for example, unemployment or job dissatisfaction. But further scrutiny of the constraints faced by entrepreneurs in setting up and developing their business shows that aside from these reasons for self-employment, individual, social, and structural factors play an important role. Host-country conditions were considered particularly constraining when setting up a business. Personal characteristics were deemed less significant inhibitors of entrepreneurial activity. Whereas personal reasons were the primary motivation *pulling* Portuguese immigrants into self-employment, structural factors acted mainly to *constrain* this project's realisation. The interplay between individual and structural factors thus influences the constitution of a constellation of entrepreneurial activities, many of which are conducted in sectors where entrepreneurs were previously employed and which did not require these entrepreneurs to invest a high level of financial capital.

The results of this study of Portuguese entrepreneurship in Luxembourg constitute a preparatory step in the study of Portuguese emigrants' entrepreneurial practices. In the long term it is expected that the research will be extended to the analysis of other national contexts. This will provide a better understanding of both the contemporary development of Portuguese emigrants' entrepreneurial practices and, above all, the development of transnational entrepreneurial practices – both among Portuguese emigrants living abroad and between these emigrants and their country of origin.

Acknowledgments and Funding This chapter is an updated and extensively revised version of an original text published in Portuguese (Marques 2015). The research was funded by the Instituto Politécnico de Leiria, Leiria, Portugal. The revision of the text was financed by the Polytechnic Institute of Leiria, CICS.NOVA (pole of Leiria) by means of the project UID/SOC/04647/2013.

References

Aldén, L., & Hammarstedt, M. (2016). Discrimination in the credit market? Access to financial capital among self-employed immigrants. *Kyklos, 69*, 3–31. https://doi.org/10.1111/kykl.12101.

Arroteia, J. C. (1986). *A emigração portuguesa no Grão Ducado do Luxemburgo*. Porto: Secretaria de Estado das Comunidades Portuguesas.

Beirão, D. (1999). *Les Portugais au Luxembourg*. Paris: L'Harmattan.

Blanchflower, D. G., Levine, P. B., & Zimmerman, D. J. (2003). Discrimination in the small business credit market. *The Review of Economics and Statistics, 85*(4), 930–943.

Candeias, P., Góis, P., Marques, J. C., & Peixoto, J. (2014). *Emigração portuguesa: bibliografia comentada*. (1980–2013). SOCIUS Working Papers, 01/2014. Lisboa: ISEG. http://pascal.iseg.ulisboa.pt/~socius/publicacoes/wp/WP01.2014.pdf. Accessed 25 July 2016.

Clark, K., & Drinkwater, S. (2000). Pushed out or pulled in? Self-employment among ethnic minorities in England and Wales. *Labour Economics, 7*(5), 603–628.

Dawson, C., & Henley, A. (2012). "Push" versus "pull" entrepreneurship: An ambiguous distinction? *International Journal of Entrepreneurial Behaviour & Research Bulletin, 18*(6), 697–719.

Dawson, C., Henley, A., & Latreille, P. (2009). *Why do individuals choose self-employment?* (IZA Discussion Paper, 3974). Bonn: Institute of Labour Economics (IZA). http://ftp.iza.org/dp3974.pdf. Accessed 1 Feb 2018.

Drori, I., Honig, B., & Wright, M. (2009). Transnational entrepreneurship: An emergent field of study. *Entrepreneurship Theory and Practice, 33*(5), 1001–1022.

Granovetter, M. (1985). Economic action and social structure: The problem of embeddedness. *American Journal of Sociology, 91*(3), 481–510.

Hillmann, F., & Rudolph, H. (1997). *Redistributing the cake? Ethnicisation processes in the Berlin food sector* (WZB Discussion Papers, FS I 97-101). Berlin: Wissenschaftszentrum Berlin für Sozialforschung (WZB).

Kloosterman, R., & Rath, J. (2001). Immigrant entrepreneurs in advanced economies: Mixed embeddedness further explored. *Journal of Ethnic and Migration Studies, 27*(2), 189–201.

Light, I. (1987). Die unternehmer und ethnische unternehmer. *Kölner Zeitschrift für Soziologie und Sozialpsychologie, 28*, 93–215.

Light, I., & Gold, S. (2000). *Ethnic economies*. San Diego: Academic.

Light, I., Sabagh, G., Bozorgmehr, M., & Der-Martirosian, C. (1994). Beyond the ethnic enclave economy. *Social Problems, 41*, 65–80.

Marques, J. C. (2015). *Empresários portugueses no Luxemburgo: uma primeira aproximação* (*OEm* Working-Paper, 01). Lisboa: Observatório da Emigração, CIES-IUL, ISCTE-IUL. https://doi.org/10.15847/CIESOEMWP012015

Oliveira, C. R. (2004). *Estratégias empresariais de imigrantes em Portugal*. Lisboa: Alto-Comissariado para a Imigração e Minoriais Étnicas.

Pearson, R. W., Ross, M., & Dawes, R. M. (1994). Personal recall and the limits of retrospective questions in surveys. In J. M. Tanur (Ed.), *Questions about questions. Inquiries into the cognitive bases of surveys* (pp. 65–95). New York: Russell Sage Foundation.

Portes, A., & Sensenbrenner, J. (1993). Embeddedness and immigration: Notes on the social determinants of economic action. *American Journal of Sociology, 98*(6), 1320–1350.

Portes, A., & Zhou, M. (1999). Entrepreneurship and economic progress in the 1990s: A comparative analysis of immigrants and African Americans. In F. D. Bean & S. Bell-Rose (Eds.), *Immigration and opportunity. Race, ethnicity, and employment in the United States* (pp. 143–171). New York: Russell Sage Foundation.

Portes, A., Guarnizo, L., & Haller, W. (2002). Transnational entrepreneurs: An alternative form of immigrant economic adaptation. *American Sociological Review, 67*(2), 278–298.

Putz, R. (2002). Culture and entrepreneurship – Remarks on transculturality as practice. *Tijdschrift voor Economische en Sociale Geografie, 94*, 554–563.

Rath, J. (2000). *Immigrant businesses: the economic, political and social environment*. Houndmills/New York: Macmillan/St. Martin's Press.

Reynolds, P., Camp, S. M., Bygrave, W. D., Autio, E., & Hay, M. (2002). *Global entrepreneurship monitor 2001, executive report*. Babson Park/London: Babson College/London Business School.

Sanders, J. M., & Nee, V. (1996). Immigrant self-employment: The family as social capital and the value of human capital. *American Sociological Review, 61*(2), 231–249.

Schiltz, A., Candeias, P., & Ferreira, B. (2016). A emigração portuguesa recente para o Luxemburgo: novidades na continuidade. In J. Peixoto et al. (Eds.), *Regresso ao futuro: A nova emigração e a sociedade portuguesa* (pp. 141–167). Lisbon: Gradiva.

Smallbone, D., Ram, M., Deakins, D., & David, D. (2003). Access to finance by ethnic minorities in the UK. *International Small Business Journal, 21*(3), 291–314.

STATEC. (2013). *Les Portugais au Luxembourg. Recensement de la population 2011 – Premiers résultats n° 18*. Luxembourg: STATEC.

Volery, T. (2007). Ethnic entrepreneurship: A theoretical framework. In L. P. Dana (Ed.), *Handbook of research on ethnic minority entrepreneurship: A co-evolutionary view on resource management* (pp. 30–41). Cheltenham: Edward Elgar.

Waldinger, R., Aldrich, H., & Ward, R. (1990). Opportunities, group characteristics and strategies. In R. Waldinger, H. Aldrich, & R. Ward (Eds.), *Ethnic entrepreneurs. Immigrant business in industrial societies* (pp. 13–49). Newbury Park: Sage.

Yinger, M. J. (1985). Ethnicity. *Annual Review of Sociology, 11*, 151–180.

8

Portuguese Emigration to Angola (2000–2015): Strengthening a Specific Postcolonial Relationship in a New Global Framework?

Pedro Candeias, Jorge Malheiros, José Carlos Marques, and Ermelinda Liberato

Empirical and Theoretical Background

Historical Relations and Migrations Between Portugal and Angola

It is impossible to think about current Portuguese emigration without thinking of Angola which, both as an independent country and a former colony, has played an important role in the history of migration from Portugal. After 2004–2005, when emigration to the country began to increase again, Angola became one of Portuguese emigrants' main destinations. Despite the scarcity of statistical data, we know that Angola retained this status until 2013, after which it lost significance in absolute

P. Candeias (✉)
Universidade de Lisboa, Instituto de Ciências Sociais (ICS) and Instituto Superior de Economia e Gestão (ISEG), Investigação em Ciências Sociais e Gestão (SOCIUS/CSG), Lisbon, Portugal
e-mail: pedro.candeias@campus.ul.pt

J. Malheiros
Universidade de Lisboa, Instituto de Geografia e Ordenamento do Território (IGOT), Centro de Estudos Geográficos (CEG), Lisbon, Portugal
e-mail: jmalheiros@campus.ul.pt

J. C. Marques
Instituto Politécnico de Leiria, Centro Interdisciplinar de Ciências Sociais FCSH/UNL (CICS.NOVA.IPLeiria), Leiria, Portugal
e-mail: jose.marques@ipleiria.pt

E. Liberato
Faculdade de Ciências Sociais, Universidade Agostinho Neto, Luanda, Angola
e-mail: Ermelinda.Silvia.Liberato@iscte-iul.pt

and relative terms, basically owing to its weakening economic growth and to the increasing difficulties associated with immigration and expatriation of capital in foreign currencies.

Certain characteristics distinguish Portuguese emigration to Angola from Portuguese emigration to other countries in the Global South, including, for example, Brazil and Mozambique. These result from the close, long-standing historical ties that exist between Portugal and Angola – notwithstanding the moments of tension and reconciliation inherent in the complex relationship that developed between the two as a result of the lengthy colonial period. Angola was Portugal's oldest and largest colony in Africa, and it experienced a large influx of Portuguese colonists during the 1950s and 1960s (Castelo 2007; Santos 2013). Considered the "jewel in the crown" during the final stage of Portuguese colonialism, it was the last colony to attain its independence (November 1975). One of the most significant immediate outcomes of the decolonisation process was the return to Portugal of more than 300,000 people (Pires 2003, 189), a number that increased during the following years with the arrival not only of the so-called returnees (*retornados*)[1], but also Angolans who were seeking better living conditions well away from the civil war that began soon after independence and was to last until 2002. During this period, the inverse process, that is, Portuguese emigration to Angola, was practically non-existent. The exception lay in some solidarity workers or "cooperantes" settling in the country for fixed periods determined by their labour agreements (Pereira 1991). Furthermore, during this period, a number of small-scale entrepreneurs and shop owners stayed behind in Angola and made the new country their home (Galito 2015; Santos 2013).

The end of the civil war and the establishment of peace in 2002 provided the necessary conditions for substantial changes in the country. In political terms, democratisation was made a priority. In social terms, it was necessary to provide social and medical assistance to the population, which had suffered in the war. In economic terms, market-economy principles were introduced and applied with the supposed objective of stimulating production and distribution so as to lessen the country's external dependency. Therefore, the years following the end of the war were characterised by measures to reunite families and repatriate populations to their birthplaces after landmines had been removed. Economic growth was stimulated by rebuilding infrastructure (roads, bridges, railway lines, buildings, etc.) which had been destroyed. This process has encouraged the interest and presence of foreign companies, with consequences for both investment and immigration – and particularly for the arrival of highly and technically skilled migrants.

[1] The term retornado (returnee) applies to people born in Portugal or their descendants who returned to Portugal after living in the former Portuguese African colonies during the decolonisation period. This process of return reached its peak in 1975.

Political, Social, Demographic and Economic Aspects

The end of the civil war and the maintenance of political stability under the almost exclusive control of a single political party and its elite[2] paved the way for social change. Peace gave Angolan families the chance to reunite and allowed them to move away in search of greater security. Poverty was also reduced (from 68% of the population in 2001 to 37% in 2009 according to INE – Statistics Angola 2010), although, for most of the population, generalised deprivation as well as deep-reaching social inequalities remain important realities. In fact, the 2015 World Bank Report stated that 43% of the population lived on less than 1.25 dollars a day (World Bank 2015).

Until the beginning of the present decade, the last census in Angola dated back to 1970, during the final stage of the colonial period. Since then, the instability caused as much by the colonial war/the liberation struggle as by the civil war made holding a new general census of the population extremely difficult. Therefore, a new census was only carried out in 2014. The preliminary results of this census show that Angola's population – 24.4 million people in total – is largely young, and the majority (62%) live in urban areas. 27% of Angola's inhabitants are concentrated in Luanda province, in which the capital city is located (INE – Statistics Angola 2014).

The end of the civil war led to measures aimed at revitalising the economy (Ferreira and Gonçalves 2009; HRW 2010; Rocha 2013). To this effect, Angola's government opted for "an economic model situated between a centrally planned economy and a market economy" (Rodríguez et al. 2014, 105). In the years after 2005, the country became one of the world's most dynamic economies, registering growth of 20.6% GNP in 2005, 18.6% in 2006 and approximately 27% in 2007 (OECD 2010, 40).

Economic growth remained high until 2008, mainly due to the increase in oil production[3], which benefitted from high transaction prices on the international market. In 2009, following the global economic crisis, Angola entered a period of recession and the International Monetary Fund (IMF) awarded a loan of 1.4 thousand million dollars to the Angolan government (*Jornal de Negócios,* August 29, 2012).[4]

---

[2] The Movimento Popular de Libertação de Angola – MPLA (Popular Movement for the Liberation of Angola) has governed Angola since the country became independent in 1975. In the 2017 elections for the National Assembly (Parliament), it won again. According to Human Rights Watch (HRW 2010: 6. April 13. "Transparency and Accountability in Angola"), the MPLA and José Eduardo dos Santos, Party leader and President of Angola for almost 40 years (the country's new president João Lourenço, was sworn in on the 26th of September 2017), "have secured a near stranglehold on political power", governing without any opposition.

[3] According to data provided by the Central Intelligence Agency (CIA), oil production comprised 85% of Angola's GDP between 2004 and 2008, while the diamond industry comprised 5%. Available at: https://www.cia.gov/library/publications/the-world-factbook/geos /print/country/countrypdf_ao.pdf

[4] Retrato da Economia Angolana (Portrait of the Angolan Economy). Available at: http://www.jornaldenegocios.pt/economia/detalhe/retrato_da_economia_angolana.html

From 2010 to 2014 the Angolan economy made a comeback, although at slower rate than before.

It should be noted that economic growth has persisted mainly due to activities that exploit the country's natural resources (Jover et al. 2012; Rocha 2013; Schubert 2010), particularly oil production (in 2008 it made up approximately "91% of Angola's exports" – Santos 2012, 32 – increasing to 98% in 2012). In addition, 80% of Angola's public fiscal revenues also come from oil production (Jover et al. 2012, 7). Moreover, Angola is the fifth oil-producing country in the world and the second oil exporter in Africa (Rocha 2014, 12).

Despite its sizable economic growth and the development of the oil production sector, the Angolan economy is characterised by a very high level of informality that has increased during the last few years due to the social imbalances and employment constraints associated with expanding market economies. The informal sector – which is characterised by its heterogeneity and its dynamism is responsible for the livelihood of the Angolan population and plays a highly significant role in the country's economy (Lopes 2002). Therefore merely analysing the indicators connected with Angola's formal economy – such as the unemployment rate or formal registered wages – is both incomplete and inaccurate.

Portuguese Emigration to Angola: An Introduction to Factors of Attraction

As mentioned above, after 2004–2005 there was a significant increase of Portuguese emigration to Angola in general, and Luanda in particular. According to data on Portuguese emigrants' arrivals compiled by the Portuguese Emigration Observatory (Observatório da Emigração) in 2015, Angola was still the fourth most popular destination for Portuguese emigrants – despite a dip in flows after 2012 (Pires et al. 2016) [5]. The dynamism of the Angolan economy – associated with the country's physical rebuilding and its stronger financial and commercial ties with Portugal – was among the structural factors that contributed most to consolidating Angola's attractiveness as a destination country. Its aforementioned economic growth – which mainly took place during the second half of this century's first decade – attracted Portuguese investment. A scarcity of skilled human resources in Angola also helped drive an increase in emigration flows. It is also worth pointing out that, with commercial relations cemented between Angolan and Portuguese businesses, it has become a common practice for Portuguese companies – particularly the larger ones – to open branches in Angola in such sectors as banking, the construction industry and telecommunications. Accordingly, the recruitment of Portuguese staff occurred along two fronts: by Portuguese companies, which transferred both highly

[5] The indicator used by the the Portuguese Emigration Observatory (Observatório da Emigração) was based on the number of permanent immigration visas issued.

qualified professionals as well as less skilled workers to Angola, and by Angolan firms, which selected Portuguese nationals to occupy top positions (Åkesson 2016).

If the structural reasons for this increase in emigration are predominantly economic, they cannot help but intermesh with Portugal's status as Angola's former colonial metropolis, which justifies a long and well established relational framework grounded in profound mutual acknowledgment. At an individual level, the former colony's status explains the transnational ties left over from colonial days. These ties were reactivated by both the returnees and their descendants after the civil war had ended (Santos 2013).

In some cases, there is the additional factor of dual nationality. Many Portuguese emigrants heading to Angola already have some prior relationship with the country, either because they were born there and left while still young, or because they have family ties to the country that give rise to post-memory.[6] Legally, this allows them to acquire Angolan nationality – an essential condition for getting a job owing to the difficulty of obtaining a work permit.

In cultural terms, Lusophony may also act as a factor attracting not only Portuguese nationals but also Brazilians and citizens coming from other Portuguese-speaking African countries because it makes communication easier.

Finally, we should note the role of social networking in the generation and maintenance of these migration flows. The fact that most Angolan and Portuguese emigrants chose Portugal as their destination when they left Angola in search of better living conditions gave rise to a closer connection between the two states. Portugal is clearly a key destination for Angolans because many of them have family or friends living there. Moreover, the similarity between the countries' educational systems leads many Angolan students to choose to pursue their studies at Portuguese higher education institutions, thus helping to generate social networks that are often maintained after the students have returned to Angola (Liberato 2013).

In this context it is not surprising that, at the turn of the millennium, Angola was one of the three African countries with the highest number of Portuguese residents, together with Mozambique and South Africa (Ferreira 2001). We should note the duality of current Portuguese emigration to Angola: on the one hand, there are the middle-class expatriates who often have high levels of technical training as well as very highly-skilled professionals living in luxury housing and hotels whose expenses are paid by the companies employing them; on the other hand, there are some traditional low-skilled working-class emigrants (Santos 2013). A recent survey-based study of the socio-demographic profiles of Portuguese emigrants residing in Angola (Sangreman et al. 2015) indicates that the population is mostly adult, male and with higher-education qualifications.

---

[6] The term post-memory, coined by Hirsch (2001), normally refers to memories of the children of survivors of traumatic events such as wars. These memories are not experienced in the first person but rather are reconstructions of the past mediated by their parents' experiences (see, for example, Ribeiro et al. 2012, 16–17). Nevertheless, we may ask whether this same intersubjective construction of memory passed down from one generation to the next also applies to an older generation's positive memories. Descendants may similarly interiorise the past experienced by their parents and integrate it into their own identities as part of a kind of mythicised "golden age".

Undertaking research about Angola is a challenge due to the fact that "data from and about Angola are scarce" (Jover et al. 2012, 4). The civil war, the post-independence socialist-oriented political system, a scarcity of human resources, the destruction of infrastructure and the enforced removal of local populations are only some of the factors that have prevented broad, systematic statistical data from being produced. This continues to be the case because state agencies still follow practices designed for collecting information for themselves rather than making it available to the public. Angola's war and its political model discouraged the dissemination of information based in the argument that doing so would jeopardise the efficiency and the efficacy of Government's activities.

Due to this state of affairs, together with other factors such as the recency of the increase in migration, academia still knows very little about contemporary Portuguese emigration to Angola. In a review of 806 academic publications about Portuguese emigration published between 1980 and 2013, Angola was one of the least-studied countries (Candeias et al. 2014, 21).

Theoretical Challenges to Portuguese Emigration to Angola

Portuguese emigration to Angola can understood as part of a new, post-colonial, work-related type of migration that characterises contemporary North-South flows (Santos 2013). Studies in this area are, for the most part, yet to be undertaken. According to some estimates, these North-South flows make up 3–6% of total global emigration (Laczko and Brian 2013). Though some of these flows consist of Portuguese emigration to Angola, Mozambique and Brazil, similar movements originate from other countries in the North and flow to other countries in the South– e.g. Spanish emigrants going to Ecuador, Mexico or Argentina.

Migrations to the South take place as a result of the increasing global integration of Southern countries' financial and commercial systems – as well as their labour markets – and the consequent global economic and political significance of certain countries in Latin America, Asia and Africa. If the BRICS located in the South (Brazil, India, China and South Africa) provide the best example of this process – combining physical and economic modernisation with very competitive dynamic urban regions and the availability of relatively abundant although disputed natural resources – it is possible to identify similar situations in several other smaller countries. Various studies undertaken during the last few years have pointed to a process of economic recovery and progressive integration into global economic systems experienced by African countries since the start of the twenty-first century. Evidence of this process includes: a high mean GDP growth rate (higher than the mean world rate); a fall in the levels of absolute poverty; a notable increase in foreign investment; an integration in the ICT value chain, for instance due to coltan production; a greater involvement in world trade, albeit largely based on raw materials, and a reorientation of economic relations to Asian markets (Jerven 2010; Carmody 2010; Africa in Progress Report 2013).

Greater economic dynamism, more investment and an higher involvement in the global circulation systems has inevitably meant more migration – both more people leaving Africa, but also more people coming to the continent. These two kinds of movement are connected: some of the migrants wanting to go to Africa may be African born people – who may even have changed their nationality – returning to their original birthplace, or eventually their descendants.

Rising unemployment caused by the economic recession that started in 2008 in fact primarily affected immigrants who had settled in Europe and the USA, as the data published by the OECD-SOPEMI show (OECD 2012). This underpinned an increase in return movements (Laczko and Brian 2013) that was also driven by the lower impact of the recession in several African countries. Despite these findings, it is vital to understand whether the North-South economic migrations that have grown during the last few years are more than just a process of cyclical response and whether they will assume a more structural and permanent nature. It is therefore necessary to study these migrations' characteristics and identify the factors that may lead to their sustainability.

Migratory flows to Angola may further be interpreted in the light of migratory systems theory (Zlotnik 1992), namely by situating this movement in a broader system of relations often called the Lusophone migratory system. The concept was coined by Peixoto (2004) in order to classify migration to Portugal from Brazil and the Portuguese-speaking African countries (Países Africanos da Língua Oficial Portuguesa – PALOP) and later elaborated upon by Malheiros (2005). However, like any other country, Portugal belongs to more than one migratory system (Baganha 2009).

To begin with, the Lusophone migratory system only consisted of Portugal and Brazil, but after the 1974 Revolution in Portugal it extended to the former colonies (Baganha 2009). This system was distinguished by the bidirectional nature of its flows (Góis and Marques 2009). It is this characteristic that, according to migratory systems theory, would explain the fall in migration from Angola to Portugal and the current inversion in the direction of migratory flows. On this model, Portugal would behave as a semi-peripheral country as defined by world systems theory; but according to new refinements of this theory, its status as a semi-peripheral country might change depending on the context (Góis and Marques 2009). In more recent studies, the Lusophone migratory system has been considered a three-pronged system containing three nodes: Portugal, Brazil and Angola (Marques and Góis 2012).

Portuguese Emigration to Angola in the Statistics

Notwithstanding the scarcity of statistical data about the Portuguese and other foreigners in Angola, it is possible to collect some data that allow us to learn, even if sketchily, how many Portuguese emigrants have made Angola their destination. The

Table: Resident population and foreign-born population, 1990–2014

	1990	1995	2000	2005	2010	2014
Total population	10,662,000	12,539,000	14,280,000	16,618,000	18,993,000	24,383,301
Total foreign-born	33,517	37,502	46,108	56,055	65,387	–
Percentage of foreign-born	0.31	0.30	0.32	0.34	0.34	

Source: From 1990 to 2010 – UNDP 2014 – preliminary results, 2014 Census. Available from the website of the Portuguese Emigration Observatory (Observatório da Emigração): http://www.observatorioemigracao.pt/np4/paises.html?id=9

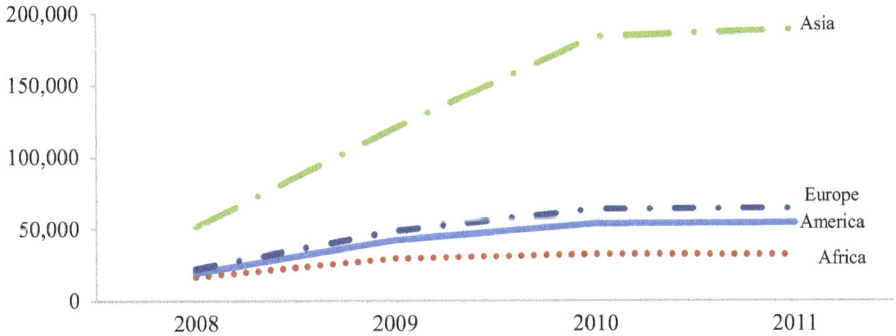

Fig. Population holding a residence or work permit by year and continent of origin. Source: Migration and Foreigners Service, Ministry of the Interior, Angola (INE – Statistics Angola, 2013 pp.28–29) (Authors' calculations). Available at: http://www.ine.gov.ao/xportal/xma in?xpid=ine&xpgid=publications_detail&publications_detail_qry=BOUI=30173945

total resident Portuguese population in Angola (Table) increased by about 78% between the start of the 1990s and 2010, while during the same period the foreign population nearly doubled (an increase of 95%). However, in relative terms, the growth in the foreign population led to it increasing only very slightly as a proportion of the total number of residents in Angola: from 0.31% in 1990, to 0.34% in 2010.

A preliminary analysis of the foreign population with resident or work permits in Angola by continent of origin, allow us to draw up an initial profile. From 2008 to 2010, almost all the large groups of foreign-born nationals increased in size, with Asian immigrants the largest contingent (more than 50% of the total). From 2010 to 2011, the size of the various groups of foreign nationals stabilised (Fig.).

If these data are broken down by nationality (Table), it can be seen that a high number of immigrants come from China, Portugal and Brazil. In 2011, Chinese immigrants accounted for 47% of the work or residence visas issued, while the Portuguese accounted for 13% and the Brazilians 19%. In the 4 years under study, the number of permits issued to Portuguese citizens tripled. Nevertheless, the high-est increase was not registered among Portuguese nationals but rather among Indian citizens whose numbers in 2011 had increased fivefold when compared with 2008.

Table: Population holding a residence or work permit/visa between 2008 and 2011

	2008	2009	2010	2011
South Africa	3747	14,557	15,875	15,694
Cape Verde Islands	3449	3493	3604	3623
Gabon	916	984	1027	1032
Mauritania	714	905	1745	1778
São Tomé and Príncipe	6185	6447	7184	7209
Others from Africa	2752	2780	2837	2645
Brazil	12,513	28,905	35,546	36,317
Cuba	2879	6163	9925	10,285
USA	3.599	6421	7676	7141
Others from the Americas	260	262	265	265
France	4157	8080	10,532	9989
Others from Europe	575	583	590	600
Portugal	12,051	31,666	43,656	44,761
United Kingdom	3513	5845	6769	6801
Russia	1655	2048	2121	2145
China	45,036	103,546	155,282	160,262
India	1914	5129	9572	9813
Philippines	2214	6116	9777	9696
Vietnam	2126	5288	9110	8979
Total	108,882	239,238	333,093	339,035

Source: Migration and Foreigners Service, Ministry of the Interior, Angola (INE – Statistics Angola 2013: 28–29)

The number of Philippine, Vietnamese and South African nationals multiplied by more than four in this period.

Data about the visas issued shows that immigration to Angola has a marked South-South component involving three of the BRICS in particular: China, Brazil and South Africa. Moreover, other Asian countries deserve mention – particularly India, the Philippines and Vietnam, each of which account for about 3% of visas – as well as Cuba. On the other hand, in 2011, documented African immigrants[7] comprised less than 10% of the foreign population. Almost half of them come from South Africa, while age-old inter-colonial relations – especially with the São Tomé and Principe islands and the Cape Verde archipelago – also carry some weight, accounting for 22% and 11% respectively of African immigration.

Meanwhile the majority of legal North-South migratory flows consist of European emigrants (19% of the total in 2011) among which the Portuguese predominated (70% of the Europeans), followed by the French (15%) and the British (10%). It should be noted that from 2008 onwards the Portuguese overtook

[7] African immigrants account for the largest number of illegal aliens in Angola, so the real number would actually be much higher.

Table: Consular registrations of Portuguese emigrants, 2008 to 2015

Year	2008	2009	2010	2011	2012	2013	2014	2015
Consular registrations	72,706	86,374	94,767	100,000	113,194	115,595	126,356	134,473

Source: The Portuguese Embassy in Angola for the Directorate-General of Consular Affairs and Portuguese Communities (DGACC) via the Portuguese Emigration Observatory (Observatório da Emigração). (Available at: http://www.observatorioemigracao.pt/np4/paises.html?id=9)

the Brazilians as the second most numerous foreign presence, at least as far as legal immigration is concerned.[8]

Data based on registrations made at the Portuguese consulates (Table) are fairly restricted and only cover a reduced period of time (8 years). During this period, the number of registrations increased from about 73,000 Portuguese emi-grants in 2008 to more than 134,000 in 2015, which represents an increase of about 85%. It should be pointed out that in the first half of this period (2008–2012), the growth rate (an annual mean of 14%) was much sharper than that of the second half (2012–2015), when a mere 6.3% average annual growth was registered. This backs up what was stated above about a reduction in Portuguese migration to Angola. The discrepancy between the official Angolan statistics and the Portuguese consular reg-isters is due to some limitations associated with both sources. First, work visas are only one of various types of visa that allow emigrants to stay in Angolan territory. Although it is the visa corresponding to labour immigration, this does not prevent migrants from entering the country with other types of visa such as the temporary stay or privilegiados (entrepreneurs') visas. Consular records also have some limita-tions, not only because registration is not compulsory but especially because of difficulties in updating information. File clearing in particular seems to be slow and several Portuguese nationals who have left Angola are still registered. Furthermore, double registration at two consulates (Benguela and Luanda) may also occur (Galito 2015). Finally, the higher number of consular records may also result from the reg-istration of individuals with dual nationality, who do not count for Angolan for-eigner's statistics but who nonetheless register at the Portuguese consulate.

Current Portuguese Emigration to Angola – Processes and Characteristics

While existing empirical data may help to give an overview of the Angolan context that frames and to a certain extent explains contemporary Portuguese emigration to this country, detailed studies on the topic are still very scarce.

[8] Note that, even so, the number of Portuguese nationals may have been under-calculated compared with the number of Brazilians, because there are a significant number of individuals with both Portuguese and Angolan (i.e. dual) nationality. Since these individuals have not been included in the foreigners' statistical databases, they have not been counted here.

Owing to the fact that Angola has become the main destination of contemporary extra-continental Portuguese emigration, we believe that it is essential to deal with this phenomenon directly and examine it more deeply. We therefore need to accept that we are dealing with a migration flow that has distinct features when compared with emigration to European destinations and even to Brazil, although it shares with both Brazil and Mozambique the characteristic of being "emigration to former colonies of the South". To treat Portuguese emigration to Angola as a specific phenomenon, the study has been structured around four fundamental themes: (i) the relationship between macroeconomic dynamics and emigration; (ii) identifying the specific characteristics of the emigrants; (iii) the post-colonial nature of emigration and its possible link to the past, and (iv) the limits to "integration" (in Angola) and the "orientation" towards Portugal.

The empirical material used to examine these themes derives from the questionnaire-survey run by the project "REMIGR-Portuguese emigration and relations with the country of origin" (Peixoto et al. 2016). This was designed to study all Portuguese people (both Portuguese nationals and/or Portuguese-born emigrants) who had been living outside the country for a period exceeding 3 months. The sampling process consisted of what might be considered convenience sampling, as criteria of randomness were not applied, nor were attempts made to obtain a statistically representative sample.

Fieldwork was carried out between May 2014 and May 2015. The questionnaires were completed both online and in hard copy in a traditional face-to-face setting. The online version received 4428 responses from around 100 countries. The paper version, distributed in France, the UK, Luxembourg, Brazil, *Angola* and Mozambique, was answered by 1658 people.

The strategy of employing online surveys is justified by its ease of implementation from Portugal and also by the reduction of costs when compared to face-to-face surveys. However, this technique is not without limitations, the most significant being the over-representation of highly qualified emigrants. Thus conducting face-to-face surveys was aimed at compensating for this over-representation.

579 questionnaires were answered by emigrants living in Angola. Of these, 349 (60%) were in hard copy. Although some of the questionnaires (23) were answered in the Angolan Consulate in Lisbon, the survey was conducted almost exclusively in Angola and predominantly in three provinces; Benguela, Huíla and Luanda (74% of the face-to-face questionnaires were conducted in the province of Luanda). Although Luanda accounted for a large proportion of the online questionnaires completed, the digital version managed to reach almost all the other provinces in Angola (Table).

Macroeconomic Dynamics and Emigration to Angola

First, it is our intention to test the effect of contextual macroeconomic factors (at source and in the destination country) on emigration to Angola. Our hypothesis is based on Lee's proposal (1966: 53) that "the volume of migration varies with

Table: Distribution of the sample according to province and version

	Online		Paper		Total	
Provinces	N	%	N	%	N	%
Benguela	22	9.6	22	6.3	44	7.6
Huíla	7	3.0	18	5.2	25	4.3
Luanda	165	71.7	263	75.4	428	73.9
Lunda-Sul	11	4.8	–	–	11	1.9
Others	22	9.2	1	0,3	23	4.2
No answers	3	1.3	45	12,9	48	8.3
Total	230	100	349	100	579	100

Source: Survey of Portuguese Nationals Abroad – REMIGR Project

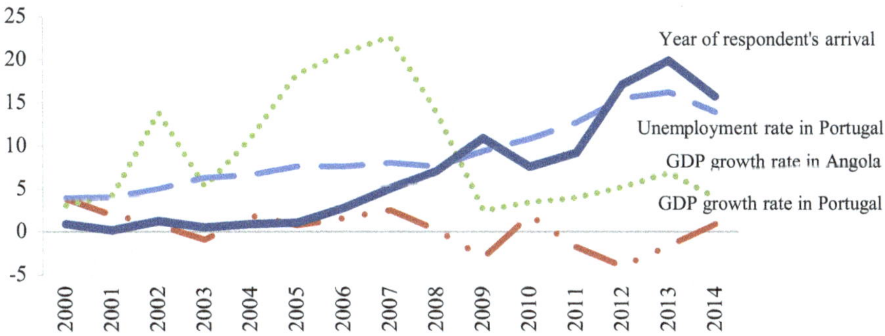

Fig. GDP growth rate and unemployment rate in Portugal; GDP growth rate and year of arrival in Angola (%).
Sources: Pordata-Unemployment Rates (See: www.pordata.pt), GDP Growth Rates -World Bank (See: www.worldbank.org/), Percentage of survey responses according to year of arrival – Survey of Portuguese Nationals Abroad – REMIGR Project

fluctuations in the economy". This hypothesis was tested by Jerome (1926)[9], who saw that fluctuations in migration resulted largely from changing economic conditions in the country of origin or destination. Similar studies have demonstrated that in the case of Latvia, for example, recent emigration can be explained by macroeconomic factors such as a fall in exports and foreign investment, but also by a decrease in public spending and a drop in domestic consumption (Apsite et al. 2012).

In our case, the following indicators associated with macroeconomic compo-nents have been taken into account: in Portugal, the variation in the GDP growth rate and the unemployment rate; in Angola, the GDP growth rate and the date of emigrant arrivals (Fig.).

According to Fig., annual arrivals in Angola are negatively correlated with Portugal's GDP growth rate and follow the increase in Portugal's unemployment rate, directly and very clearly. This seems to show that emigration occurs more as a

[9] In his analysis of emigration cycles from Europe to the USA during the nineteenth and twentieth centuries, Jerome concluded that these cycles were driven mostly by the destination country's economic situation, particularly during the Great Depression.

result of concrete factors such as lack of employment rather than economic growth in general (although both contextual factors interact). Similar results were found in a study on immigration to the United Kingdom where the same factors were tested (Dobson et al. 2009).

However, the relationship between growth in Angolan GDP and the arrival of Portuguese nationals in this country seems less clear. Despite the fact that between 2009 and 2014 both measures surged and later declined, the correlation was not statistically relevant. This may be due to the high oscillations observed, especially the drop that occurred between 2007 and 2009.

Therefore, in accordance with a push-pull model, the unemployment that affected Portugal may be seen as a structural push factor. But it is less clear that Angola's increasing GDP constitutes a structural pull factor. This may be due to Angola's economic productivity being heavily based on oil exports and oil prices, contributing to more frequent and sharp fluctuations in economic indicators that are consequently more difficult to align with migratory flow data. It should be pointed out that the macro analysis does not take into account the socio-professional profile of Portuguese migrants to Angola, which has changed over the years. According to Åkesson (2016), the first significant contingent of emigrants was composed of construction workers who started returning to Portugal in 2015 when oil prices fell. The arrival of highly qualified professionals started to increase from 2004 to 2005, gaining impetus from 2008 when the economic and financial recession hit Portugal.

The Profile of Portuguese Emigrants in Angola

Second, our aim is to trace the profile of Portuguese emigrants in Angola, considering the following factors: socio-demographics, migration strategies, reasons given for leaving Portugal, existence of former migration experiences, and the time spent looking for a job after arriving in the destination country.

Socio-Demographic Profile

Two aspects of the demographics of Portuguese emigrants in Angola (Fig.) stand out: these emigrants are mostly men (65%), and they are also relatively old: two thirds of the sample are over the age of 35.

Schooling

Concerning schooling levels (Table – Educational profile), it can be seen that a high proportion of emigrants to Angola possess a good level of formal education, particularly given the relatively older age of the sample. However, it should be underlined that the level of school qualifications decreases as the age of the

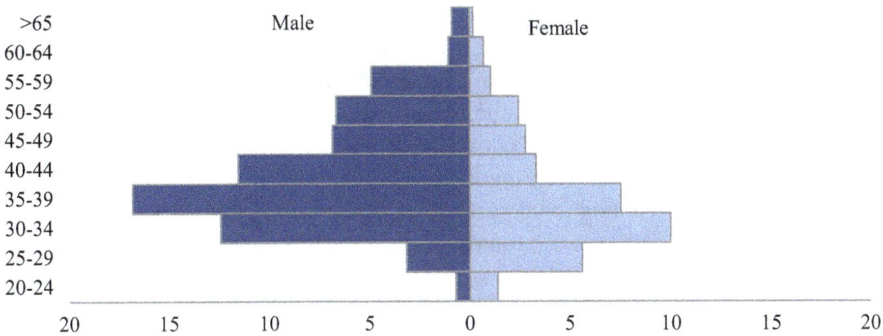

Fig. Age pyramid, Portuguese nationals in Angola (%). Source: Survey of Portuguese Nationals Abroad – REMIGR Project

Table: Educational profile

Educational level	%
Higher /tertiary	68.8
Upper Secondary school	23.6
Up to ninth grade (third cycle)	7.6

Source: Survey of Portuguese Nationals Abroad –REMIGR Project

Portuguese emigrant advances. Given these factors, the profile of people coming to Angola looks different from that seen in other Portuguese migration destinations, particularly those in Western Europe. Portuguese emigrants in Angola are more highly qualified, more mature, with greater levels of professional stability, and very often attached to their companies.

Migration Strategy

On analysing the migration strategy of Portuguese emigrants to Angola, the relative weight of independent emigration stands out (66%). Given this high rate of independent emigration, and also given that we are dealing with a group with a low proportion of single people (32%), we might expect to find most of these single people emigrating independently. On the other hand, the high proportion of married individuals in the sample collected in Angola (54%) might lead us to expect to see relatively high levels of family migration. However, this is not the case: emigration involving a couple, whether married or not, only covers about 20%. The proportion of married individuals emigrating alone is the most interesting detail that emerges from this analysis of migration strategies. To some extent, family reunification is discouraged by the country's image as a hostile and unsafe place, by the difficulty of finding a school for children owing to the weaknesses and costs of the educational system, and also the problems faced by women in integrating professionally and socially. Our analysis of migration strategy thus points to a type of emigrant who does not plan on staying for lengthy periods or permanently, and who views returning to Portugal as an "immediate" and highly-valued goal. Curiously, the current migratory profile perpetuates certain characteristics seen in Portuguese emigration during the previous colonial period in the 1960s. The earlier wave was also predominantly male and viewed Angola as a hostile, risk-filled country where one would go alone with the individual goal of "earning a living" and, from a macroeconomic point of view, of "contributing to the progress" of the "African Province" within the framework of the colonising power's interests.

Reasons for Leaving Portugal

Among the reasons that led the respondents to leave Portugal, the most frequent answer was "to acquire new experiences" (Table). The idea of not having a future in Portugal, although important, was not the most common answer. In general, these results are in line with the more mature and more stable profile of the emigrants in Angola. References to opening new businesses, as well as dissatisfaction with the incomes earned in Portugal, should not be disregarded.

It is also possible to find these two reasons in the literature: on the one hand, young graduates interviewed by Santos (2016) stressed that they were emigrating by "choice" rather than due to 'necessity'; on the other hand, the reasons identified by Åkesson (2016) had to do with the chance to pursue a profession, escape unemployment in Portugal and benefit from the high salaries offered abroad. Nevertheless, both of the above-mentioned studies have apparently focused on samples with a younger age profile than the sample analysed in this chapter.

Table: Reasons for leaving Portugal

Reasons	%
Acquire new experience	40.6
Did not see any future in Portugal	25.9
No opportunities to pursue a professional career	24.4
Was employed, but earned a lower income	22.8
Was unemployed	15.0
Chance to pursue business opportunities	11.9
Wanted to study or undergo professional training	2.8
Family reasons	10.2
Other	10.9

Source: Survey of Portuguese Nationals Abroad – REMIGR Project

Time Spent Looking for a Job

When it came to work, most emigrants had left Portugal with the assurance of a job to go to (73%). Some factors may complicate or prevent a person from leaving for Angola in pursuit of "an adventure", the most important probably being the cost of living in this country, as may be seen in newspaper reports: "Luanda is still the world's most expensive city" ("Luanda continua a cidade mais cara do mundo") (*Jornal de Notícias*, 17th of June 2015).[10] Secondly, it seems difficult to obtain employment individually using formal channels – such as responding to a job advertisement – given the specificities of the Angolan economy. In addition, the absence of a dense network of co-nationals who can provide accommodation and basic information on arrival also acts as a barrier to more spontaneous and independent emigration.

Emigration Experience

Most of the respondents declared that this was the first time they had emigrated (77%). Given the relatively advanced age profile of Portuguese nationals in Angola, one might expect these individuals to have emigrated at an earlier stage in their life cycles. Nevertheless, they only decided to do so when they were older and when a job opportunity with their employer came up. This is therefore emigration of a very particular kind, marked by conjuctural economic opportunity and by an attempt to reduce the risk of individual mobility. It occurs in a context of close economic relations between the two countries – as mentioned before – which leads various Portuguese companies to operate in Angola, often transferring their own personnel to conduct business abroad.

North-South Post-Colonial Emigration – With Past Reminiscences?

We will now dedicate our attention to identify latent networks that have emerged from the colonial past and the importance such networks are likely to have in the contemporary migration of Portuguese nationals. These networks may either be composed of Portuguese settlers who stayed in the country after decolonisation, or ancestors of present-day migrants who lived in Angola during colonialism. Given the existence of these networks, it is appropriate to refer to contemporary Portuguese migration to Angola as "post-colonial migration". More concretely, what we aim to analyse is whether contemporary Portuguese migration to Angola is a case of *ancestral return* (King and Christou 2011). This means a desire to return to a country

[10] "Luanda continua a cidade mais cara do mundo" ("Luanda is still the world's most expensive city") Available at: http://www.jn.pt/PaginaInicial/Mundo/Interior.aspx?content_id=4628585

in which individuals feel they have family ties, even if these ties have been built on the basis of post-memory – a construct based on a bond and a desire to learn by getting in touch with people that have experienced the place directly and witnessed the remembered situations. These people are normally ancestors willing to "tell the story". Sometimes, this migration is influenced by or is the outcome of a desire to return owing to a *family narrative of return* (Reynolds 2008), when a second generation is socialised in an environment where a possible return or a desire to return is frequently voiced.

Some of these desires have been found in the discourse of the "returnees" (*retornados*) in Portugal, as reported by Santos (2016) in her ethnographic study. She detected a frequent, emphatically-expressed nostalgia for life in Africa. Such feelings have grown stronger over the last 40 years and have been nourished through socialising and sharing photographs over the internet. Although the emigrant descendants of the returnees have never acquired any first-hand experience, they have received it second hand through their families. The memory of the colonial past was also revealed in Åkesson's (2016) study when the people she interviewed had lived in Angola when they were young or during their childhood, and used the phrase "going back to Angola" instead of "emigrating to Angola".

An alternative to the proposition that this is a post-colonial movement of return would be to interpret this contemporary emigration as part of a more general North-South migration – a movement driven by specific contingent circumstances resulting from economic and social crises impacting strongly on some countries in the North. Moreover, and as mentioned before, this movement is more than likely to be linked to global geo-economic restructuring processes involving the greater integration of certain southern countries and urban regions in global circulation and production systems, which inevitably leads to the expansion of transnational firms (Laczko 2013). This proposition is supported by looking at pairs of countries that did not have any past colonial relations, such as Italy and certain African countries, Germany and Turkey, or the USA and South Africa (Laczko 2013). Besides, this broader movement may also cover return migration, as we see with Brazilians, for example, who have returned to Brazil from Portugal in the last few years (Castro et al. 2015).

In order to test these two propositions, the following indicators are analysed: the major difficulties felt during the integration process, the help that emigrants received, the factors influencing their choice of country, and situations involving dual nationality.

Regarding the integration of Portuguese nationals in Angola, the most obvious difficulties lie in the amount of bureaucracy that has to be dealt with – which is in some ways an extension of the Portuguese administrative tradition in this domain. Difficulties are also experienced due to the increasing implementation of ever more complex – although not necessarily more efficient – systems of formal control that are so characteristic of neoliberal societies nowadays. As administrative response mechanisms tend to be slow moving and, in various cases, not at all clear to emigrants, one way of getting round such problems is to resort to bribes, which are commonplace due to the fact that various kinds of civil servant earn very low wages in Angola. Furthermore, antagonistic personal relations can exist between

Table: Support networks (%)

	Support			
Provider	Information about the country	Funding the trip	Finding/obtaining accommodation	Finding/obtaining work
Family	30.6	8.1	11.9	9.2
Portuguese friends	33.5	1.4	3.3	7.6
Recent Portuguese acquaintances	10.4	0.5	1.6	1.2
Employer	43.2	77.4	74.6	71.8

Source: Survey of Portuguese Nationals Abroad – REMIGR Project

Portuguese emigrants and the local population (Åkesson 2016), and these are often supported by old reciprocal stereotypes stamped by the colonial imaginary (inefficient black Angolans vs. white Portuguese workers who think they are superior and more capable of organising Angola).

As far as the networks providing support to emigrants in Angola (Table) are concerned, the role of the employer figures prominently in all fields. At the same time, the importance of Portuguese friends is relatively weak – a result that would be inverted and register higher values if the network left over from the past were at all important.

However, the network of Portuguese friends gains relevance when it comes to supplying information about the country (Angola), which leads one to think that the link does exist, even though it plays a smaller and more indirect role that one would suppose. In other words, this network is in place and is activated whenever emigration occurs, but it does not propel this emigration.

The employer's considerable importance should be seen in the light of the higher level of schooling attained by emigrants to Angola. Such results are to be expected if we recall that higher-status socio-economic groups depend more on the social networks established with their work colleagues and organisations (companies) than they do on family networks, which predominate among the less qualified workers (Meyer 2001).

Among reasons weighing in favour of choosing Angola as a destination country (Table), economic factors show up very clearly and they include job offers and opportunities as well as positive economic expectations. It is worth remembering the simultaneous downward trend in Portugal's GDP growth and the increase in Angola's GDP – mentioned earlier – as well as the results of the study carried out by Åkesson (2016).

In testing the hypothesis of the existence of a latent network, we expected to see a higher proportion of respondents choosing the category "Friends/family residing there for many years". However, the values obtained for Angola were lower than for the REMIGR project's sample overall, which leads us to conclude that old ties with the country do not motivate emigration to Angola although such ties do exist to a small extent, as may be seen below.

Table: Factors of attraction

Factors	%
Job offers or opportunities	68.6
Positive economic perspectives	46.1
Knowing the language	28.5
Quality of life	2.4
Friends/family residing there for many years	11.7
Friends/family residing there for a few years	9.8
Portugal within reach	0.7
No visa necessary	2.6
Others	10.4

Source: Survey of Portuguese Nationals Abroad – REMIGR Project

One reliable indicator of the existence of previous ties is dual nationality. Individuals in possession of passports from both states have full rights (as well as full duties) in both countries (Faist 2000). In the present case we have identified a small although significant number of individuals with dual nationality (14,7%), 87% of whom hold Angolan nationality.

We are therefore mostly dealing with individuals whose migration has been facilitated by their company's interests, and whose employer has been their main source of help. However, the high proportion of respondents identifying "friends and family" as having supplied information about the country may still be due to a large number of Portuguese nationals having lived in the country when it was still a colony[11].

"Weak Integration" and Strong Ties with Portugal

Lastly, we will show that the profile of contemporary Portuguese emigrants in Angola also includes strong ties with Portugal: many of these emigrants' social practices are organised around Portugal and have this country as an almost exclusive reference. The strong transnational link with Portugal is observed in three fields: financial, labour and social.

[11] Contracting individuals who are able to acquire Angolan nationality may be favoured by some companies, who can then declare in their annual reports that they employ a percentage of nationals and thus demonstrate that they are doing their bit to abide by Government dictates promoting the Angolanisation of labour power.

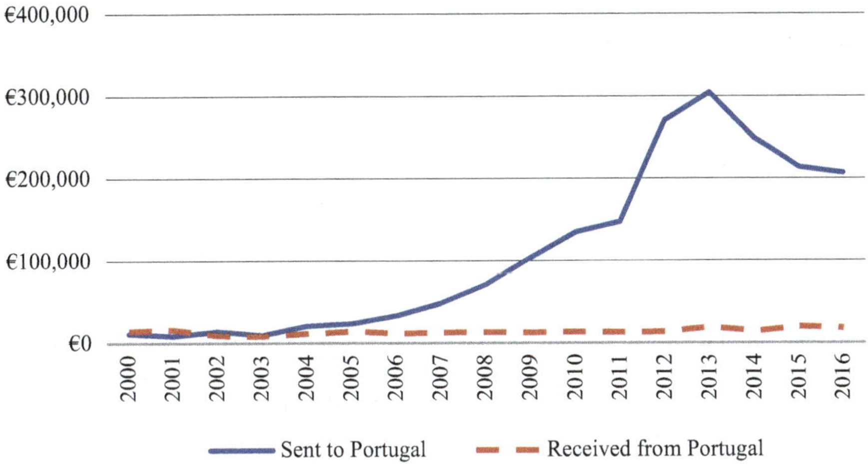

Fig. Remittances in thousands of euros, 2000–2016.
Source: Bank of Portugal. Available at: http://www.bportugal.pt/EstatisticasWEB (Follow links: Exploração multidimensional/Estatísticas de balança de pagamentos/Remessas de emigrantes/imigrantes com detalhe geográfico/dimensão: território)

Remittances (Financial Transnationalism)

Financial remittances are commonly used as an indicator of transnational relations (Vertovec 2002). Money can be sent back home for purposes related either to the individual alone or to their family, the latter being more pertinent here. Remittances for family purposes may be used to pay for the upkeep of both home and family as well as receiving the approval of close relatives (Lianos and Cavounidis 2008).

If we analyse the flows of remittances between the two countries between 2000 and 2013 (Fig.), we can see that: (1) at the start of the millennium, the amounts transferred totaled 12 million euros per year; (2) the balance was even negative for some years, specifically between 2000 and 2002, when more money was sent back by Angolan immigrants in Portugal than by Portuguese emigrants in Angola.

The amounts sent home by Angolan immigrants in Portugal have not significantly changed over the last few years, averaging 14 million euros annually, with limited variations. However, the money received in Portugal started increasing significantly from 2005 onwards, reaching a peak in 2013 (300 million euros). The most recent data show a downward trend since 2013 (when the Angolan economy's current recession started), which was the first year in which remittances from Angola had fallen since 2003. Therefore, it comes as no surprise that about three quarters (74%) of the Portuguese emigrants answering the REMIGR questionnaire in Angola are sending money back home.[12]

[12] In the aforementioned study by Sangreman et al. (2015), also based on a survey consisting of a questionnaire to Portuguese nationals in Angola, the proportion of respondents who said they sent money back home was 87.7%. However, their nationality was relevant to their attitude to remittances: the proportion of individuals with dual nationality who sent remittances was much smaller than that of emigrants with only Portuguese citizenship.

The volume of remittances sent from Angola back to Portugal may be determined by factors such as: Angola's high cost of living combined with its reduced opportunities for consumption and leisure; the idea that the period spent abroad has a fixed duration that depends on the length of one's professional activity, which in practice excludes consumer activities; and the fact that there are family dependents who remain in Portugal, which encourages emigrants to maintain their roots in their home country. In some cases wages (or part of them) are also deposited directly in the country of origin, which means that the lives of immigrants in Angola are almost totally placed within the boundaries set by the companies they are working for.

Once we consider the profile of Portuguese emigrants in Angola in conjunction with the factors that research suggests will determine the amount of remittances sent home, the trends identified above can be partially explained by existing theoretical frameworks. Nevertheless, certain details make the case of Angola unique. Firstly, the theory states that temporary migrants tend to send more money home (Hertlein and Vadean 2006). This is in line with the fact that the year in which respondents in Angola arrived in their destination country is on average slightly more recent than the average year of arrival for the REMIGR sample as a whole. Nevertheless, there is a second relevant factor in this case that gives rise to apparent inconsistencies with the theory. The existing literature states that, as a rule, low-skilled emigrants send a greater proportion of their income home, whereas more highly-qualified emigrants send money back to pay off debts accrued on university loans (Hertlein and Vadean 2006). Neither of these two observations is supported by our study: Portuguese nationals in Angola have a higher level of education relative to the sample and remit significantly and these remittances are not used to pay former university loans because in Portugal the practice of borrowing money to pursue tertiary education is not common. Even if emigrants had borrowed money for this purpose, the debt would probably have been paid off already given that respondents in Angola tend to be older.

As we will see later, migration to Angola seems to be predominantly temporary in nature, so the high volume of remittances is also linked to a reduction in costs normally associated with permanent migration, for example, buying a home or expenses related with socialising and leisure activities (Glytsos 2003).

Home Visits (Social Transnationalism)

Visiting Portugal is an important indicator because, despite the ease of communicating using inexpensive virtual means, visits allow irreplaceable face-to-face interaction to take place whenever certain family events occur (weddings and funerals, for example) (O'Flaherty et al. 2007). Given this significance, it is also important to consider visiting home as a way of preparing for a future return and keeping latent ties with friends and family alive.

Table: Home visits

Frequency	%
At least once a month	1.5
At least once every three months	41.6
At least once every six months	37.8
At least once a year	16.9
Less than once a year	1.7
Never	0.6

Source: Survey of Portuguese Nationals Abroad – REMIGR Project

Table: Plans for family reunification

Situation of the partner	%
She/he is already living and will continue to live in the country I currently reside in	43.5
She/he will probably come to the country I currently reside in	15.0
She/he will probably won't come to the country I currently reside in	19.0
We haven't made any definite plans	19.0
Other situations	3.6

Source: Survey of Portuguese Nationals Abroad –REMIGR Project

Portuguese emigrants in Angola visit Portugal frequently (Table). Receiving a high salary in the destination country and having close family in Portugal may weigh heavily in favour of such journeys. Frequent visits may also be the result of agreements with the companies employing the emigrants. They may form part of the "contract package" that, in addition to wages, may include payment for regular trips home –whether this figures in an explicit clause in the labour contract or as a process enabling the renewal of employees' visas, which often allow for only tem-porary stays.[13]

Strategies for Family Reunification

Finally, it should be noted that the aspiration to reunite with family (Table) is a relatively unimportant motivation for Portuguese nationals to emigrate to Angola: only 44% state that their partner lives there too. The sum of the other three explicit responses is higher (53%) and include the cases of the dominant heterosexual couples living apart and maintaining transnational relationships, with one partner in Angola (typically the male) and the other in Portugal. This is another indicator of the non-transference of affective and family bonds to Angola, with emigration

[13] A visa lasts 30 days and is renewable for equal periods up to a maximum of three months. At the end of this time, the foreigner is obliged to leave the country and apply for a new visa at the Angolan consulate in the country of origin.

assumed by many individuals to be a temporary process that does not incorporate the development of longstanding bonds with the destination country.

Concluding Remarks and Questions to Explore

Between 2000 and 2013, Portuguese emigration to Angola significantly increased. This transformation was accompanied by an identical increase in emigrants' tendency to send remittances to Portugal, as the sixfold increase in these private financial transfers that occurred between 2007 and 2013 illustrates. This has made Angola the third main source of legal remittances to Portugal, following France and Switzerland (according to the Bank of Portugal). It should be pointed out that there is no reliable source available to quantify the current stock of Portuguese nationals settled temporarily or permanently in Angola, nor is there data providing robust evidence about recent emigration flows from Portugal to Angola. Portuguese consulate registers refer to 134,000 people in 2015 although it is accepted that this number may be an overestimation because the 2014 Angolan Census counted only 45,000 Portuguese citizens. Nevertheless, the latter source is not only slightly more out-of-date, but also suffers from underestimation – for example of Portuguese emigrants on temporary visas who frequently move between Angola and Portugal. On the other hand, consulate registers may overestimate the number of Portuguese nationals in Angola due, for instance, to slowness in clearing the files of those who have left Angola.

Whatever the precise number is, the increase in the presence of Portuguese nationals in Angola and the formation of a sizeable *Luso community* during the last few years cannot be doubted. However, it seems clear that the process slowed down from 2013 to 2014 onwards, and it is likely to be reversed. This seems to have been accompanied by an identical downward trend in the volume of remittances sent back to Portugal. This current trend cannot be separated from the cooling down of the Angolan economy, and it naturally calls for more specific studies that, for example, will allow an assessment of the more or less circumstantial nature of Portuguese emigration to Angola.

The profile of contemporary Portuguese emigration to Angola, situated in a global context, is one of a North-South movement taking place in a post-colonial setting, contrary to the more common South-North or even South-South flows. It is characterised by its deep entrenchment in companies with business interests in Angola that transfer their employees, who are mostly male, often aged 35 or over and possess medium-high levels of qualification. Portuguese emigration to Angola may therefore be interpreted as a flow of specialised labour, facilitated by job offers and higher salaries, that intensified during a period of recession in Portugal and a favourable economic climate in Africa, and which is also marked by an increasing presence of Portuguese businesses.

If it is clear enough that a macroeconomic framework helps explain Portuguese emigration to Angola, it is less clear whether this explanation should be combined with the idea of *ancestral return* rooted in previous sentimental bonds with Angola. This despite the detection of some factors (e.g. the influence that family and friends exert in transmitting information about Angola, the importance of having dual nationality) that indicate the not negligible role that post-memory narratives play.[14] The links that at least some emigrants – or their relatives – have to friends or family previously in Angola should be more thoroughly studied. To sum up, while the character of Portuguese emigration to Angola – facilitated by a series of historical links between the two countries – supports the hypothesis that North-South migration flows have increased due to the emergence and insertion of Southern countries and urban regions in global economic networks, the same cannot be said about the theory of *ancestral return*.

Lastly, Portuguese emigration to Angola appears to be characterised by significant, fairly intense transnational activity in various domains (remittances, visits to Portugal, professional links to the country of origin). Compared with Portuguese emigration to other countries, emigration to Angola (or at least a substantial part of it) – with its weaker links to family reunification – is more temporary in nature and more actively sustaining social relations with and references to Portugal. Being professionally integrated in Angola does not always mean being socially integrated too, even if Angolans think that the Portuguese are more African than European, and that their integration in the different dimensions of Angolan life is usually quite straightforward.

Acknowledgments and Funding This chapter is based on the research project "Back to the future: new emigration and links to Portuguese society" (*Regresso ao futuro: a nova emigração e a relação com a sociedade portuguesa – REMIGR*), funded by Fundação para a Ciência e a Tecnologia (Foundation for Science and Technology, FCT) (PTDC/ATP-DEM/5152/2012). This chapter is an updated and extensively revised version of an original text published in Portuguese (Candeias et al. 2016).

References

Africa Progress Panel. (2013). *Africa in progress report 2013-Equity in extractives. Stewarding Africa's natural resources for all. Africa Progress Panel*. Switzerland: Africa Progress Panel. http://africaprogresspanel.org/en/publications/africa-progress-report-2013/. Accessed 6 Oct 2017.

Åkesson, L. (2016). Moving beyond the colonial? New Portuguese migrants in Angola. *Cahiers d'études africaines, 1*(221), 267–286.

Apsite, E., Krisjane, Z., & Berzins, M. (2012). *Emigration from Latvia under economic crisis conditions*. 2nd international conference on social science and humanity. IPEDR31, pp. 134–138.

[14] The fact that the questionnaire did not include questions about the respondent's parents' place of birth prevents a deeper analysis of the influence of family narratives involving ancestors in Angola.

Baganha, M. I. (2009). The lusophone migratory system: Patterns and trends. *International Migration, 47*(3), 5–20.

Candeias, P., Ferreira, B., & Peixoto, J. (2014). Emigração portuguesa: o que temos vindo a estudar e o que nos falta saber – Uma análise bibliométrica entre 1980 e 2013. *População e Sociedade, 22*, 11–31.

Candeias, P., Malheiros, J., Marques, J. C., & Liberato, E. (2016). A nova emigração para Angola: integração diferenciada e forte ligação a Portugal. In J. Peixoto, I. T. de Oliveira, J. Azevedo, J. Carlos Marques, P. Góis, J. Malheiros, & P. M. Madeira (Eds.), *Regresso ao futuro. A nova emigração e a sociedade portuguesa*. Lisboa: Gradiva.

Carmody, P. R. (2010). *Globalization in Africa: Recolonization or renaissance?* London: Lynne Rienner.

Castelo, C. (2007). *Passagens para África: o povoamento de Angola e Moçambique com naturais da metrópole (1920–1974)*. Porto: Afrontamento.

Castro, M. d. C. G. d, Botelho, P., & Knup, S. A. P. (2015). Contexto migratório de retorno. Perspectiva das famílias de brasileiros retornados de Portugal. In J. Peixoto, B. Padilla, J. Carlos Marques, & P. Góis (Eds.), *Vagas atlânticas. Migrações entre Brasil e Portugal no início do século XX* (pp. 159–176). Lisboa: Mundos Sociais.

Dobson, J., Latham, A., & Salt, J. (2009). On the move? Labour migration in times of recession what can we learn from the past? *Policy Network Paper*.

Faist, T. (2000). Transnationalization in international migration: Implications for the study of citizenship and culture. *Ethnic and Racial Studies, 23*(2), 189–222.

Ferreira, M. E. (2001). Emigração portuguesa para África: residual e concentrada. *Janus – Anuário de Relações Exteriores*, 154–155.

Ferreira, M. E., & Gonçalves, F. R. (2009). Diplomacia económica e empresas de bandeira. Os casos da Galp e da Unicer em Angola. *Relações Internacionais, 24*, 115–133.

Galito, M. S. (2015). Emigração Portuguesa em Angola. *CI-CPRI*, AI, 22, 1–14.

Glytsos, N. P. (2003). Remitting behaviour of "temporary" and "permanent" migrants: The case of Greeks in Germany and Australia. *Labour, 11*(3), 409–435.

Góis, P., & Marques, J. C. (2009). Portugal as a semiperipheral country in the global migration system. *International Migration, 47*(3), 19–50.

Hertlein, S., & Vadean, F. (2006). Remittances – A bridge between migration and development? Focus migration. *Policy Brief*, 5.

Hirsch, M. (2001). Surviving images: Holocaust photographs and the work of postmemory. *The Yale Journal of Criticism, 14*(1), 5–37.

HRW. (2010). *Transparência e responsabilização em Angola: Uma actualização*. New York: Human Rights Watch.

INE. (2010). *IBEP: Inquérito integrado sobre o bem-estar da população 2008–2009*. Luanda: Instituto Nacional de Estatística.

INE. (2014). *Recenseamento Geral da População e Habitação (RGPH) – Resultados Preliminares*. Luanda: Instituto Nacional de Estatística.

Jerome, H. (1926). The Influence of economic conditions in the countries of emigration. In H. Jerome (Ed.), *Migration and business cycles* (pp. 153–209). New York: National Bureau of Economic Research.

Jerven, M. (2010). African growth recurring: An economic history perspective on African growth episodes, 1690–2010. *Economic History of Developing Regions, 25*(2), 127–154.

Jover, E., Pintos, A. L., & Marchand, A. (2012). *Angola – Perfil do Sector Privado do País*. African Development Bank.

King, R., & Christou, A. (2011). Of counter-diaspora and reverse transnationalism: Return mobilities to and from the ancestral homeland. *Mobilities, 6*(4), 451–466.

Laczko, F. (2013). *North-South migration to developing countries*. Paper presented at the European Migration Network Conference, Dublin, June 14.

Laczko, F., & Brian, T. (2013). North-South migration: A different look at the migration and development debate. *Migration Policy Practice, III*(3), 14–19.

Lee, E. S. (1966). A theory of migration. *Demography, 3*(1), 47–57.
Lianos, T. P., & Cavounidis, J. (2008). Immigrant remittances, stability of employment and relative deprivation. *International Migration, 48*(5), 118–141.
Liberato, E. (2013). *Educação e desenvolvimento.* A formação superior de angolanos em Portugal e no Brasil (PhD thesis in African Studies). Lisboa: ISCTE.
Lopes, C. (2002). Luanda, cidade informal?: estudo de caso no bairro Rocha Pinto. *Cadernos Estudos do Desenvolvimento CESA,* ISEG,6.
Malheiros, J. (2005). Jogos de relações internacionais: repensar a posição de Portugal no arquipélago migratório global. In A. Barreto (Ed.), *Globalização e Migrações* (pp. 251–272). Lisboa: Imprensa de Ciências Sociais.
Marques, J. C., & Góis, P. (2012). A evolução do sistema migratório lusófono. Uma análise a partir da imigração e emigração portuguesa. *Revista Internacional em Língua Portuguesa – Migrações,* (24), 213–231.
Meyer, J.-B. (2001). Network approach versus brain drain: Lessons from the diaspora. *International Migration, 39*(5), 91–110.
O'Flaherty, M., Skrbis, Z., & Tranter, B. (2007). Home visits: Transnationalism among Australian migrants. *Ethnic and Racial Studies, 30*(5), 817–844.
OECD. (2010). *Economic diversification in Africa. A review of selected countries.* Organization for Economic Co-operation and Development.
OECD. (2012). *International Migration Outlook: SOPEMI 2012.* Paris: OECD Publishing.
Peixoto, J. (2004). *País de emigração ou país de imigração? Mudança e continuidade no regime migratório em Portugal* (SOCIUS Working Papers, 2).
Peixoto, J., de Oliveira, I. T., Azevedo, J., Marques, J. C., Góis, P., Malheiros, J., & Madeira, P. M. (Eds.). (2016). *Regresso ao futuro. A nova emigração e a sociedade portuguesa.* Lisboa: Gradiva.
Pereira, G. (1991). *Caracterização socio-profissional dos cooperantes portugueses* (p. 21). Lisboa: Instituto de Estudos para o Desenvolvimento/Cadernos IED.
Pires, R. P. (2003). *Migrações e integração. Teoria e aplicação à sociedade portuguesa.* Oeiras: Celta.
Pires, R. P., Pereira, C., Azevedo, J., Espírito-Santo, I., & Vidigal, I. (2016). *Emigração Portuguesa. Relatório Estatístico* (p. 2016). Lisboa: Observatório da Emigração e Rede Migra/CIES-IUL/ISCTE-IUL.
Reynolds, T. (2008). *Ties that bind: Families, social capital and Caribbean second-generation return migration* (Sussex Centre for Migration Research Working Paper, 46).
Ribeiro, M. C., Vecchi, R., & Ribeiro, A. S. (2012). The children of the colonial war: Post-memory and representations. In I. C. Gil & A. Martins (Eds.), *Plots of war – Modern narratives of conflict.* Berlin: De Gruyter.
Rocha, M. J. A. d. (2013). *As transformações económicas e estruturais na África Subsariana 2000–2010.* Luanda: Mayamba.
Rocha, A. d. (2014). *As perspectivas de crescimento económico de Angola até 2020.* CEIC-UCA working paper, 2.
Rodríguez, J.-L. G., Rodríguez, F. J., García, G., Castilla, C., & Major, S. A. (2014). Petróleo, pobreza y medio ambiente en Angola. *Boletín de la Asociación de Geógrafos Españoles, 64,* 101–126.
Sangreman, C., Lopes, C. M., & Galito, M. S. (2015). *Diáspora portuguesa em Angola – Um perfil em 2002–2012.* Fundação Portugal África.
Santos, M. (2012). *Borracha e tecidos de algodão em Angola (1886–1932) – O efeito renda* (WP/CEAUP/FF 2012/2).
Santos, I. S. d. (2013). L'émigration au Portugal, avatar d'un pays "semi-périphérique", métropole postcoloniale. *Hommes & Migrations, 1302,* 157–161.
Santos, I. D. (2016). L'Angola, un Eldorado pour la jeunesse Portugaise? Mondes imaginés et expériences de la mobilité dans l'espace lusophone. *Cahiers d'études Africaines, 1*(221), 29–52.

Schubert, J. (2010). Democratisation' and the consolidation of political authority in post-war Angola. *Journal of Southern African Studies, 36*(3), 657–672.

UNDP. (2014). *Human Development Report 2014. Sustaining human progress: Reducing vulnerabilities and building resilience*. New York: United Nations Development Programme.

Vertovec, S. (2002). *Transnational networks and skilled labour migration* (ESRC transnational communities research programme working papers, 02-02).

World Bank. (2015). *Global economic prospects: The global economies in transition*. Washington, DC: World Bank.

Zlotnik, H. (1992). Global and regional migration systems: Empirical identification of international migration systems. In M. Kritz, L. L. Lim, & H. Zlotnik (Eds.), *International migration systems: A global approach* (pp. 19–40). New York: Clarendon Press.

9

New Emigration and Portuguese Society: Transnationalism and Return

João Peixoto, Pedro Candeias, Bárbara Ferreira, Isabel Tiago de Oliveira, Joana Azevedo, José Carlos Marques, Pedro Góis, Jorge Malheiros, Paulo Miguel Madeira, Aline Schiltz, Alexandra Ferro, and Eugénio Santana

Introduction

Emigration was the subject of abundant research in Portugal until the 1970s. Outflows to escape poverty, often targeting the less privileged segments of the labour markets in the host countries, had been common since the late nineteenth century. For decades, most of these flows followed a post-colonial pattern and went to Brazil. Later, from the late 1950s to the early 1970s, Portugal was one of the main suppliers of migrant workers to Western Europe. Emigration reached its peak between the late 1960s and early 1970s. Afterwards, the statistics showed a significant decrease in outflows. This led some scholars to believe in its progressive disappearance. Scientific research and public opinion at first followed the apparent decrease in outflows but gradually lost interest in the subject.

However, episodic studies on recent emigration have shown that the flows never disappeared, even during the period of economic expansion and collective optimism

J. Peixoto (✉) · B. Ferreira
Universidade de Lisboa, Instituto Superior de Economia e Gestão (ISEG), Investigação em Ciências Sociais e Gestão (SOCIUS/CSG), Lisbon, Portugal
e-mail: jpeixoto@iseg.ulisboa.pt; bferreira@iseg.ulisboa.pt

P. Candeias
Universidade de Lisboa, Instituto de Ciências Sociais (ICS) and Instituto Superior de Economia e Gestão (ISEG), Investigação em Ciências Sociais e Gestão (SOCIUS/CSG), Lisbon, Portugal
e-mail: pedro.candeias@campus.ul.pt

I. Tiago de Oliveira
Instituto Universitário de Lisboa (ISCTE-IUL), Centro de Investigação e Estudos de Sociologia (CIES-IUL), Lisbon, Portugal
e-mail: isabel.oliveira@iscte-iul.pt

J. Azevedo
Instituto Universitário de Lisboa (ISCTE-IUL), Centro de Investigação e Estudos de Sociologia (CIES-IUL), Observatório da Emigração, Lisbon, Portugal
e-mail: joana.azevedo@iscte-iul.pt

of the late twentieth and early twenty-first centuries. Research on emigration after the mid-1980s helped to counterbalance the one-sided vision of a country of immigration (see Baganha 1993; Baganha and Peixoto 1997; Baganha and Góis 1998/1999; Baganha et al. 2002; Peixoto 2004; Marques 2008; Pires et al. 2010; Malheiros 2011, among others). These studies demonstrated that emigration continued, though some of its traditional forms and geographical routes were changing.

The global economic crisis that broke out in 2008 led to a surge in the number of Portuguese nationals leaving the country and so drew attention back to Portuguese emigration. The Portuguese economy had in fact been deteriorating since the early part of the twenty-first century. But the prolonged recession that started in 2008 led to a substantial increase in unemployment, a new impetus in emigration, a virtual halt on immigration and an increase of foreign immigrants returning home – especially after the Eurozone sovereign debt crisis and the austerity measures that followed in Portugal in 2011. Although the crisis reduced emigration to some former destinations such as Spain, this was offset by the appearance of new destinations, such as the emerging economies of Angola and Brazil. Public opinion turned its attention back to outflows and emigration became a topic of heated debate.

Despite the renewed significance of Portuguese emigration, prior to our study there had been rare comprehensive, up-to-date analysis of recent outflows, undertaken in order to understand the continuities and changes in relation to traditional emigration. The research project on which this chapter is based – "Back to the future: new emigration and links to Portuguese society" (REMIGR) – sought precisely to understand the extent and characteristics of recent emigration, especially the relationships that emigrants kept up with their country of origin, including new patterns of return (for an overview of the project's main results, see Peixoto et al. 2016).

J. C. Marques
Instituto Politécnico de Leiria, Centro Interdisciplinar de Ciências Sociais FCSH/UNL (CICS.NOVA.IPLeiria), Leiria, Portugal
e-mail: jose.marques@ipleiria.pt

P. Góis
Universidade de Coimbra, Faculdade de Economia and Centro de Estudos Sociais (CES), Coimbra, Portugal
e-mail: pedro.gois@uc.pt

J. Malheiros · P. M. Madeira · A. Schiltz
Universidade de Lisboa, Instituto de Geografia e Ordenamento do Território (IGOT), Centro de Estudos Geográficos (CEG), Lisbon, Portugal
e-mail: jmalheiros@campus.ul.pt; paulo.madeira@campus.ul.pt

A. Ferro
Centro de Investigação e Estudos de Sociologia (CIES-IUL), Lisbon, Portugal
e-mail: Aferro@iom.int

E. Santana
Universidade de Lisboa, Instituto de Geografia e Ordenamento do Território (IGOT), Centro de Estudos Geográficos (CEG), Lisbon, Portugal

Universidade Eduardo Mondlane, Escola de Comunicação e Arte, Maputo, Mozambique
e-mail: eugeniosantana@igot.ulisboa.pt

At a theoretical level, the project's main research question was about the kind of relationship that new emigrants had with Portugal. This question is particularly relevant in view of the new features of recent outflows and the new context in which they occur. On the one hand, the new flows involve more skilled individuals than in the past, being also more temporary and more circular. On the other hand, the technological context has changed, thanks to ease of transportation and communication. In economic terms there has been greater deregulation of labour markets, and politically speaking it is easier to move around within the European Union.

The project sought to assess the dynamics and size of emigrant flows to different countries in the last decade; emigrants' sociodemographic characteristics; their main motivations (push or pull factors, supply or demand factors, individual or family-related factors); emigration strategies (short- or long-term migration, individual or family migration); the nature of contacts with Portugal (travel, family contacts, remittances); and future plans (settlement in the destination country, return or re-emigration). Knowledge of the duration of emigration (temporary or permanent, meaning by this the intention to remain abroad for less or more than 1 year) and ties with Portugal would help assess whether new emigrants were Portuguese nationals temporarily locating outside the country's borders or whether their emigration marked a profound change to Portuguese society. Significant evidence was also drawn from return movements in recent decades.

One of the main concerns of the project was how emigration would evolve after the crossroads at which Portugal found itself after the 2008 economic crisis and the subsequent bailout in 2011. Would new emigration be highly dependent on the economic situation, coming to an end after the country's economic recovery and then giving way to a new predominance of return and foreign immigration? Would it be a new kind of movement, creating new forms of transnationalism, in which circulation and international contacts would remain the norm? Or would it result in a long-term damage for Portuguese society, including the loss of many of its elites and much of its labour force – accentuating its peripheral status in Europe?

The situation in Portugal seemed to give rise to some issues that other European countries were experiencing, such as an increase in the outward mobility of their citizens – including of highly skilled people – to diverse destinations, and a simultaneous increase in different types of emigration (short-term, long-term, seasonal, etc.). Some of these issues had arisen from free movement in the EU, but others had not (like the choice of non-EU countries as destinations). After the global economic crisis, other general trends became even more significant. Several of the former "new immigration countries", such as Spain, Greece and Ireland, experienced a decrease in immigration, while an increasing number of their nationals resorted to emigration again.

The evidence set out in the following sections covers part of the research project. First, we present a brief overview of recent theoretical trends on transnationalism and return, two understudied characteristics of Portuguese emigration. Second, using the data collected through the project's survey, we present an empirical reading of the transnational practices of recent Portuguese emigrants based on the links they maintain with their home country. Their plans for the future – settlement, return and re-emigration – are also identified and discussed. Third, the chapter examines data on returning emigrants extracted from the 2011 Census – focusing especially on those who returned between 2001 and 2011. The evidence discloses a significant number of returns – at both working and retirement ages, and at all skill levels – thus revealing the unexpected complexity of recent movements.

Transnationalism and Return: Conceptual Remarks and Approaches to Portuguese Emigration

The use of the transnational perspective in migration studies started in the early 1990s, when some researchers, mostly anthropologists (Vertovec 2009), called attention to migrants living in more than one "chessboard", that is, migrants whose daily lives involved multiple and diverse types of interconnection across national borders, establishing public and social identities with reference to more than one nation-state (Basch et al. 1994; Faist 2000). These so-called transmigrants develop a set of practices (economic, social, political…) that materialise links between space (or spaces) of destination and space of origin. They are inserted into the local labour markets of destination countries, have daily contact with these countries' institutions and may participate in their political life. But, at the same time, they have regular virtual and/or physical connections with their places of origin, often contributing to their local economies (through remittances or business connections), to religious and civil society institutions (through the transfer of assets or money, or even by helping to run these organisations), to politics (through emigrant voting and even participation in political parties) or to cultural activities (Portes et al. 1999; Itzigsohn et al. 1999; Malheiros 2001; Baubock and Faist 2010).

Though this sort of double involvement of migrants in destination and origin societies is not exactly a new phenomenon, contemporary circumstances attributable to globalization and international mobility may have contributed to its increase. The reduction of relative distances attributable to the development of transport and communication, the continuous and relatively up-to-date information about what takes place everywhere in the world, the complexity of investment flows, the emerging elements of a global culture, and the increasing international integration of various labour markets have all facilitated the increase of transnational practices and contributed to the establishment of transnational social fields. These transnational social fields correspond to social practices and institutions built or used by migrants that connect their homelands and destinations countries, in which goods, capital, ideas and other resources circulate. But these social fields involve more than just exchange, because these resources are transformed and used up as they circulate (Levitt and Glick Schiller 2004).

Over the past 25 years, the transnational approach has become well established in migration theory. Even if transnational migrant practices are not an entirely new phenomenon, the transnational approach provides "the lens" that enables a better reading of the contemporary circulation both of migrants and of the goods, capital and ideas generated by migration, allowing us to break with crystalized perspectives and old dichotomies (e.g. migration and return; emigrants and immigrants; places of destination and places of origin) (Portes 1999; Levitt and Sorensen 2004; Vertovec 2009). The development of the transnational perspective led to a refinement in academic approaches to migration and in the construction of categories, leading some authors to distinguish between domains (economical, political, cultural…) or levels of institutionalisation (Portes, Guarnizo and Landolt 1999; Itzigsohn et al. 1999), as well as levels of intensity (Góis 2005). The ideas of transnationalism "from above", associated with multinationals or nation-state institutions, and "from below", associated with migrants and grassroots organizations, have also been explored (Portes 1999; Malheiros 2001).

Research about Portuguese emigration that uses the transnational perspective has experienced significant growth in the past 20 years, accounting for approximately 13% of academic research on Portuguese emigration published between 1980 and 2013 (Candeias et al. 2014a, b). Nevertheless, this number encompasses research employing the transnational perspective broadly understood, including specific analysis of remittances and return, two well-established topics that may relate to transnational practices. In addition to these, in the late 1990s and early 2000s some studies focused on the circulation of Portuguese emigrants during the 1960s and early 1970s and its economic and social impact. The idea of *va-et-vien* – used to describe mobility between the place of destination, in particular France, and the homeland – was developed by a French team within this framework (Charbit et al. 1997).

Portuguese political transnationalism in particular, especially voting from abroad, has also attracted researchers since the early 2000s (Malheiros and Caldeira 2003; Abrantes et al. 2012), as have issues related to the role of media and communication technologies in facilitating the circulation of information between destinations and homeland. Scholars have also investigated the construction of transnational identities (Klimt 2000), as well as processes of Portuguese economic transnationalism that contribute to the regional development of places of origin. This began with the pioneering work of Silva et al. (1984); more recent perspectives have adopted a more explicitly transnational approach (Marçalo and Peixoto 2012).

Despite these developments, research about the transnational practices of the most recent – highly skilled – wave of emigrants is very scarce, justifying the approach developed in this chapter. Identifying and interpreting contemporary Portuguese emigrants' transnational practices should help us understand the nature of the transnational social fields of young, highly skilled migrants who leave their homelands in developed countries and travel abroad.

The notion of migrants' return, meanwhile, is much longer-established in the literature. The idea that return entails a permanent move back to or at least a long-term stay in the country of origin underlies most studies on the subject. Even recent work, such as that of King and Christou (2011, 452), indicate that return migration should be understood as "a physical relocation of the migrant with the intention of staying for some time, maybe permanently, in the place of origin". It is true that this notion has been questioned by those who emphasise the fluidity and the temporary nature of many return movements. Yet, in most cases, migrants' return is presented as relatively long-lasting - as with emigration itself.

The study of return may be as old as that of emigration. But the academy's widespread interest in the subject is relatively recent. According to Cassarino (2013), this began in the 1960s. References increased in the following decade, when the first large return movements were recorded after the oil shock of the 1970s and the economic change that followed. This event interrupted the recruitment of migrant workers to Western Europe, which affected workers from the Mediterranean countries. Starting in the 1980s, policies to encourage return were put in place by the host countries' authorities. This phenomenon led to a vast literature on the subject (King and Christou 2011). Gradually, the focus of academic studies of return has fallen on its impacts in countries of origin (Cassarino 2013).

Already in the 2000s there was a resurgence of interest in return, not so much as a consequence of a variation in its numbers, but more its theoretical reconceptualization (King and Christou 2011). This resulted in an increase in references to transnationalism. The contribution of this theoretical perspective on returns has been substantial, calling into question the traditional conceptualization (Cavalcanti and Parella 2013, Cassarino 2013; Carling and Erdal 2014). The idea that there may be multiple returns (and departures), or that double residences are common, diminishes the heuristic capacity of theories that regarded return as "permanent" and definitive. Attention was also drawn to the "porous boundaries" between long-term return and frequent visits, calling into question the classic paradigm of returns (Carling and Erdal 2014).

Despite their importance, studies on return account for only a minority of academic publications on emigration in Portugal; they are scarce and have several shortcomings (Rato 2001; Cairns et al. 2014). The bibliometric analysis undertaken by Candeias et al. (2014a, b) indicates that they account for about 8% of all publica-tions. Still, according to these authors, publications on return became more com-mon in the 1980s. Some of the main texts from this period are the already cited Silva et al. (1984) and Monteiro (1994).

From the end of the twentieth century, the literature on Portuguese emigration underwent an important quantitative and qualitative shift (Pires et al. 2010). Firstly, it was believed that outflows would remain at residual levels – a prediction that would not be confirmed. At the same time, there was a marked change in the char-acteristics of emigration. On the one hand, long-term departures were increasingly replaced by temporary movements. On the other hand, the profile of the emigrants changed, as departures of skilled workers and people from urban areas became more common. Studies about transnationalism and return in this new context, par-ticularly after the turn of the century, are very scarce. As regards return, the most notable exceptions are studies on the second generation (Portuguese descendants, who in some cases were even born in the countries of origin) (e.g. Neto 2010; Sardinha 2011) and the return of scientists and researchers (Delicado 2010). It was only more recently that Oliveira et al. (2016) sought to present a comprehensive view of the subject. Even so, the new trends of return remain largely unknown, due to the emergence of new emigrant profiles, new destinations and a new global con-text of international migration.

Transnational Links of Recent Portuguese Emigrants

This section aims to analyse the relations that recent emigrants establish with Portugal, based on some of the results of the survey carried out during the project mentioned in the introduction to this chapter – "Back to the future: new emigration and links with Portuguese society" (REMIGR). We will discuss the total number of responses as well as those responses that referred to the six countries that constitute our case studies.

Methodology

The project's methodological design was based on mixed quantitative and qualitative techniques. In addition to the collection of official statistics in Portugal and abroad, this approach included the use of extensive methods – such as an online and paper questionnaire survey – complemented by 45 semi-structured interviews with privileged informants, emigrants and institutional representatives in Portugal and in the countries of destination analysed in the project: the United Kingdom, France, Luxembourg, Brazil, Angola and Mozambique.

The quantitative data presented below resulted from a questionnaire distributed online and in paper form. Both online and paper questionnaire surveys have some associated limitations. By using both formats we sought to minimise these limitations and to fulfill two objectives: on the one hand, to cover the largest possible number of Portuguese emigrants, with particular emphasis on the residents of the countries under analysis; on the other hand, to diversify the profile of the respondents as much as possible.

The research subjects were all individuals older than 18 years of age residing in a foreign country, who either had Portuguese nationality or were born in Portugal, and who had left Portugal after 2000. The questionnaire was disseminated on the Internet between May 2014 and May 2015. Over the same period, the team proceeded with fieldwork in the countries under review, distributing the survey in the United Kingdom, France, Luxembourg, Brazil, Angola and Mozambique. Fieldwork ran from mid-2014 to late 2015. The total number of valid responses was 6086, of which 4428 were online and 1658 on paper. The data were then processed and analysed using SPSS statistical analysis software.

The study's methodology had several limitations. First, and above all, the non-representativeness of the sample means that results cannot be generalised for new Portuguese emigration, either as a whole or by country of destination. The main bias is towards highly skilled emigrants, who do not constitute the majority of recent departures. They account for about 70% of respondents, while several sources confirm that this segment was not predominant among emigrants in recent years (Pires et al. 2014). Second, aggregating responses at the country level ignores diversity within the host country, which in some cases is very high.[1] Third, given the high number of responses in the United Kingdom – about 24% – the "total countries" category is largely influenced by the responses obtained in this country. Finally, the importance of the context *versus* individual characteristics has not been tested, i.e. it is not known whether there is any context effect that justifies a future multilevel analysis, or whether the trends identified result exclusively from subjects' individual characteristics.

Links with Portugal

The first indicator of transnational practices is emigrants' visits to Portugal (Fig.). In total, more than half of the respondents (56%) reported coming to Portugal frequently, i.e. at least once every 6 months. Those who indicated that they "never" or "rarely" came were only 13%. Some interesting contrasts emerge between the return patterns of emigrants from different destination countries. Unlike many of the indicators on recent emigration, the frequency of home visits does not seem to be linked – among these countries – to whether destination countries are inside or outside Europe, and nor is geographical proximity the dominant factor. Portuguese emigrants in Angola, a country farther away than European destinations, have the highest frequency of visits, slightly higher than those from the United Kingdom. Several factors may explain this relative absence of a geographical pattern. First, Angola may be a special case due to the existence in this country of work agreements that include home visits supported by the employer – often a Portuguese

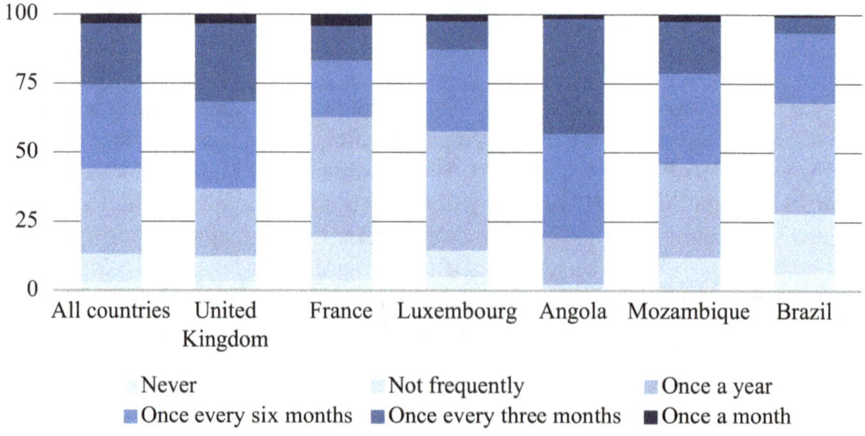

Fig. Frequency of home visits (%).
Source: Survey of Portuguese Abroad – REMIGR Project

[1] For example, the differentiation in the UK between residents of the London area and residents of the Norfolk area; or the differentiation in Brazil between residents of the States of Rio de Janeiro and São Paulo, and those in the Northeast.

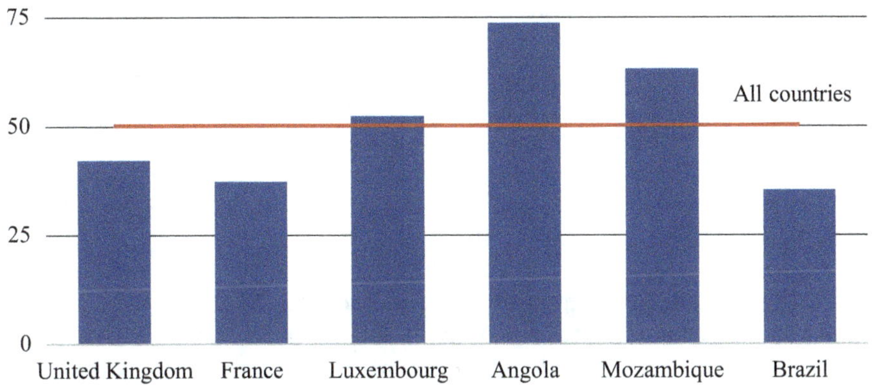

Fig. Proportion of respondents that sends remittances (%).
Source: Survey of Portuguese Abroad – REMIGR Project

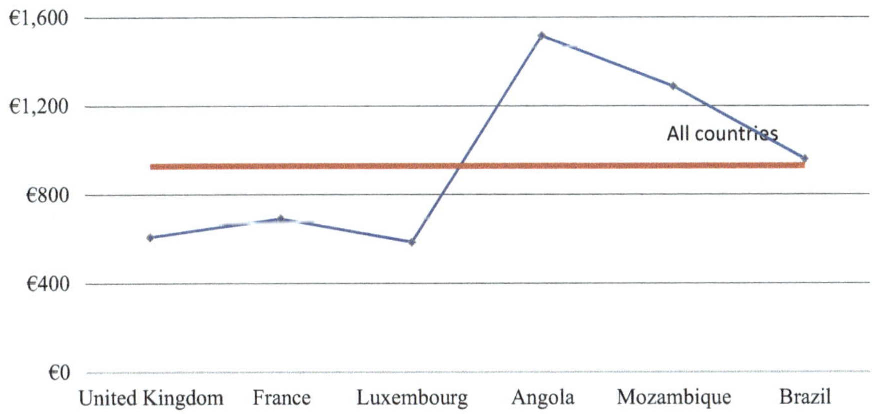

Fig. Average monthly amount of remittances (euros).
Source: Survey of Portuguese Abroad – REMIGR Project

company. Within Europe, the higher values registered in the United Kingdom can be explained by the fact that it receives more qualified emigrants who are less oriented towards saving money, unlike France and Luxembourg. The wider availability of low cost flights may also facilitate home visits.

A second indicator of transnational practices is the sending of remittances. The proportion of respondents that regularly sends remittances is about 50% (Fig.). Among the countries we studied, Angola, Mozambique and Luxembourg are the most significant in this regard. This may be due to a higher incidence of temporary emigration (in the case of African countries) or to the greater dependence of fami-lies in the country of origin on emigrants (in the case of Luxembourg, which experi-ences emigration closer to the traditional type).

As we can see by looking at the average monthly amount of remittances from destination countries (Fig.), European countries tend to be associated with reduced remittances. This is probably due to migrants here generally being younger – sometimes without dependents in the country of origin – and more orientated towards local consumption or with lower incomes. Among the group of non-European countries, Angola is the destination responsible for the highest volume of remittances, followed by Mozambique. In Angola's case, the fact that some companies pay their workers' salaries directly into Portuguese accounts contributes to these high values. The lower volume of remittances sent from Brazil may be explained by the high cost of living in certain Brazilian cities (Rosales and Machado 2015).

It should be noted, however, that the figures presented here do not match official statistics. According to data from 2013 (Vidigal and Pires 2014), the main countries from which remittances originated were, in this order, France, Switzerland and Angola, with France's figures close to three times Angola's. However, we must take into account the fact that official statistics on remittances record the volume sent by the entire emigrant community. Migrants arriving after 2000, who are naturally less numerous and in many cases in a worse economic situation, are not singled out.

Future Plans

Finally, we come to emigrants' plans for the future, which can be summarised under three headings: settlement in the country to which they emigrated, return to Portugal, or re-emigration to another country (Fig.). The largest group of respondents were those who declared themselves undecided – around 32%. Next came those who declared that they wanted to return to Portugal (29%) and those who intended to stay in the country to which they emigrated (28%). Despite the relatively balanced diversity of the answers (all categories accounted for around 30% of the total, with the exception of "re-emigrate", which accounted for only about 10%), as well

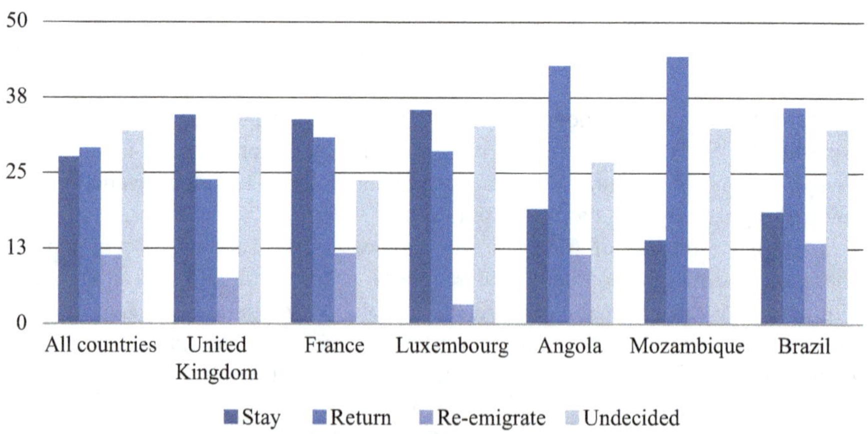

Fig. Plans for the future (%).
Source: Survey of Portuguese Abroad – REMIGR Project

as the uncertainty associated with all recent migration projects, aggravated by an unstable economic environment and a changing international political reality – the figures confirm that the intention to return is widespread and that many emigrants, at least implicitly, accept that their current migration project is not definitive.

In the three European countries, the plan to settle is the most prevalent. It is possible to explain this result by these countries' geographical proximity to Portugal, which allows for relatively regular trips; by their cultural similarity (which is of course also a factor in Portuguese-speaking destinations); and by their comparative economic and social stability. Even so, this plan is held by less than half of the respondents in the European countries under analysis.

The second option, the plan to return, was the most frequently selected in non-European countries, especially Angola and Mozambique, where more than 40% declared that returning was their intention. Perhaps the motivations that led the respondents to emigrate to these countries are relevant here – since they often consisted in the desire for "new experience" and engagement in temporary work projects – as is the context of instability in these countries (see Peixoto et al. 2016).

Onward migration plans are held by a minority of emigrants in all the countries studied, accounting for just over a tenth of the responses. The country where the highest proportion of onward migration plans was detected was Brazil. Such plans may be more prevalent where there is a higher proportion of emigrants who can be classified as cosmopolitan, and who fit the profile of global citizens with multiple affiliations, that often go beyond the borders of nation states (Vertovec and Cohen 2002). It is also among this group that lifestyle-based migration may predominate (Rosales and Machado 2015).

Many migrants, however, remain undecided: almost 1/3 of the total sample. Although this is not the predominant category in any of the countries under study, in the United Kingdom it has practically the same weight as the plan to settle. The significance of this category reveals that recent migratory paths are extremely fragile, and still highly dependent on factors affecting initial integration, as well as on changes in both the country of origin and destination.

Return Migration: The Other Face of Emigrants' Circulation

Research into returning emigrants reveals a special relationship between those who emigrated and their country of origin, namely the accomplishment of a temporary strategy of stay abroad, keeping the links with the sending country. A considerable number of emigrants have indeed come back to Portugal in recent decades. The 2011 INE census provided information on the number of individuals who had been born in Portugal, lived abroad for more than 1 year, returned to Portugal and resided there in 2011. This section provides information on this flow, focusing only on returns that occurred between 2001 and 2011.

Methodology

The last Portuguese Census introduced two new questions about previous residence outside the country.[2] The question asked in the 2011 Census was: "Have you ever lived outside Portugal for a continuous period of more than one year?" If the answer was yes, the respondents indicated the country and the year they had returned to Portugal. In this section we explore respondents' answers to these two questions in order to better understand return migration. Returned emigrants were defined as Portuguese-born respondents who had resided outside the country for at least 1 year.

According to the Census, there were about one million returned emigrants in 2011, i.e. almost 10% of the resident population. These figures are not a fully accurate indication of the number of returning emigrants, as they ignore both returnees who have died and those who have re-emigrated. Even so, the numbers from the last census point to the magnitude of return in the last decades: more than 213 thousand emigrants returned during the 1980s and more than 227 thousand during the 1990s. Between 2001 and 2011 more than 233 thousand emigrants returned to Portugal. This number includes only those who were born in Portugal and lived in a foreign country for at least 1 year (that is, short-term migration is not accounted for in these figures, since only periods of over 1 year are considered). The obvious conclusion is that emigration has not been one-sided over time, as many emigrants did not remain in their destination country, and later returned to Portugal.

Destination Country and Return

The first approach to examining the return flow in recent years (2001–2011) begins by looking at the returned emigrants' geographic dispersion (Table). The most significant flows were from France (26%), the country with the largest number of Portuguese emigrants (more than half a million), resulting from a major and long-standing migratory flow since the 1960s (Pires et al. 2010).

Two other countries associated with recent emigration – Switzerland, which has been a destination country since the 1980's (Marques 2008), and Spain, an important destination in the last decades but where the recessive effects of the post-2008 crisis were particularly significant (Pinho and Pires 2013) – became a significant source of returning emigrants (circa 13% and 11%). Next, we find emigrants returning from the United Kingdom (10%), a country for which the current wave of emigration is even more recent and intense (Pires et al. 2014). Germany, a traditional destination for Portuguese emigrants (Pires et al. 2010), is also an important source

[2] The Census also provides information about residence at specific moments. The 2011 census showed that about 85 thousand Portuguese-born respondents were living abroad on 31 December 2005 and about 43 thousand were living abroad on 31 December 2009.

Table: Countries of emigration of returned emigrants between 2001 and 2011

Countries	N	%
France	60,582	26.0
Switzerland	29,469	12.6
Spain	26,615	11.4
United Kingdom	23,077	9.9
Germany	18,809	8.1
USA	11,153	4.8
Brazil	7542	3.2
Luxemburg	5720	2.5
Canada	5525	2.4
Netherlands	4880	2.1
Angola	4715	2.0
Belgique	4431	1.9
Venezuela	3950	1.7
Andorra	2571	1.1
Italy	2446	1.0
South Africa	2250	1.0
Mozambique	2156	0.9
Cape Verde	1129	0.5
Ireland	1098	0.5
Bermuda	1090	0.5
Others	14,113	6.0
Total	*233,221*	*100*

Source: Own calculations, based on INE, Census 2011

of returning emigrants (8%). These five European destinations were the source of 70% of returning emigrants between 2001 and 2011.

These figures confirm the polarization of return migration from European countries, which have been the major destinations of Portuguese emigration over the past five decades. These figures reflect, on the one hand, the oldest emigration flows to European countries (France, Germany and Switzerland) and, on the other hand, the greater tendency towards short- and medium-term migration to new destination countries (Spain and the United Kingdom).

Countries with a strong history of Portuguese emigration – and therefore those with a large and older stock of emigrants, which also happen to be geographically more distant (US, Canada and Brazil) – are associated with a smaller number of returns than the new European destinations.

The larger geographical distance and a perception of emigration as a longer-term change in the life cycle probably contributed to a stronger tendency towards long-standing emigration to traditional non-European destinations, rather than to those that are geographically closer, where language barriers are less significant and long-term plans less frequent. Historical issues associated with the self-perception of some countries (e.g. Canada or the US; even Brazil) as "emigrant-based nations" may also contribute to the construction of a "culture of stay" which encourages

Table: Return rate between 2001 and 2011

Countries	%
France	10.1
Switzerland	21.9
Spain	34.3
United Kingdom	35.9
Germany	25.9
Brazil	4.3
Luxembourg	11.2
Canada	3.8
Netherlands	39.6
Italy	52.0
Ireland	77.4

Source: Own calculations, based on INE, Census 2011

definitive settlement. Portuguese emigrants, particularly of older waves, have not certainly been immune to this perception and its impact.

Emigrants' propensity to return can be identified by the return rate[3] (Table). The chances of return vary greatly depending on the destination country. Traditional destinations (especially Canada and Brazil, but also France and Luxembourg) have very low return rates, falling below 12%. On the contrary, for Portuguese emigrants in Ireland and Italy, return rates exceed 50%. Between these extremes, we find the return rates from the Netherlands, the United Kingdom and Spain (between 34% and 40%). Therefore, relatively recent emigration tends to be of a shorter duration and perhaps, in many cases, repeated migration. These figures also show that many returns occur not long after emigration.

Return and Life Cycle

Statistics on the age structure of returning emigrants show that many are young adults. This contradicts the usual idea that they come back at retirement age. In fact, the association between return migration and the elderly is strongly associated with the high proportion of older people among the population that emigrated several decades ago (Fig.).

The clear majority of recently returned emigrants are adults of working age (particularly between 25 and 50) and emigrants near retirement age (mainly between 60 and 75). The next sections focus on these groups.

[3] The return rate is the ratio between the returns from 2001–2011 and the average stock of Portuguese-born population in each country. Return rates measure the probability of an emigrant who has resided abroad during the past decade returning to their home country during the same period (regardless of the arrival date in the destination country).

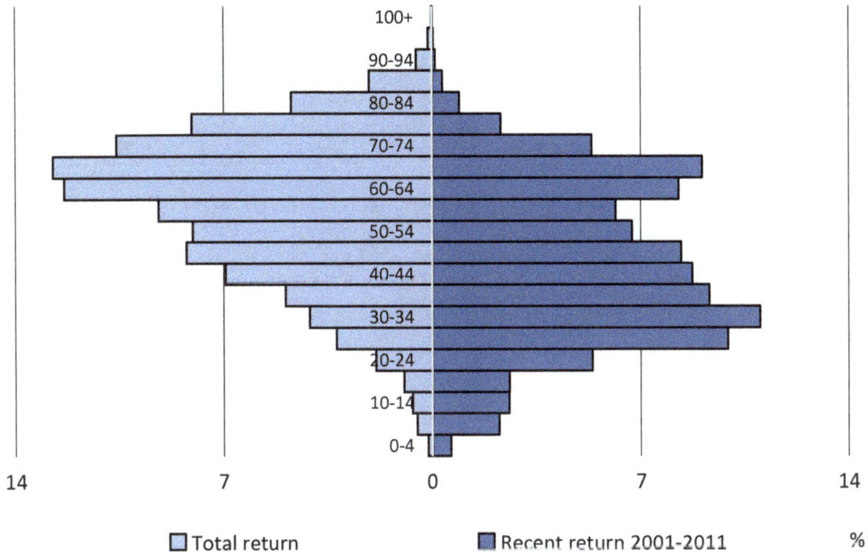

Fig. Emigrants' return, total and 2001–2011, by age group (%).
Source: Own calculations, based on INE, Census 2011

Returnees of Working Age

The working age emigrants who come back to Portugal account for the majority of returns, and are a much larger group than that of retirement-age returnees: about 153 thousand were between 20 and 59 years[4] in the 2011 census (almost 66% of the total flow during the decade).

These working-age returned migrants can be described according to several sociodemographic variables (Table). They tend to be predominantly men (more so than the older returnees): almost 60% of the total. They also have significantly higher levels of education than the older returnees. The two lowest education cate-gories account for 26% of working-age returnees, while they accounted for 88% of retirement-age returnees. Most common are individuals who have completed the sixth or the ninth grade (42%), though many also have higher qualifications: upper secondary (13%) and tertiary education (17%).

Returned emigrants aged between 20 and 59 are mostly in the labour market: 61% were employed and 16% unemployed. All other categories are of minor significance, with the exception of housewives (6%).

[4]We exclude individuals aged under 20 from the analysis for two main reasons: among recent returns, 94% of returnees aged 0–19 were family dependents; on the other hand, the criteria of place of birth in Portugal would exclude any children of emigrants born in destination countries (its proportion is not independent from the country of emigration, so no comparison is possible). It is also important to clarify that returnees' ages at the time of the census were not the ages at which they returned to Portugal. For recent returns (2001–2011) they were, on average, 5 years younger.

Table: Returned emigrants aged 20–59: sociodemographic characterization

Indicator	N	%
Sex		
Male	90,914	59.5
Female	61,887	40.5
Total	*152,801*	*100*
Education		
None	5434	3.6
Primary school	34,199	22.4
Lower secondary school	64,714	42.4
Upper secondary	20,543	13.4
Higher education	25,979	17.0
Total	*150,869*	*98.7*
Occupational status		
Pensioners	4795	3.1
Employed	92,698	60.7
Unemployed	23,762	15.6
Housewives	9623	6.3
Students	4272	2.8
Disabled	3844	2.5
Other	13,807	9.0
Total	*152,801*	*100*
Occupation (employed individuals)		
Managers and professionals	20,383	22.0
Technicians, clerks, service and sales workers	28,518	30.8
Skilled agricultural and fishery workers	3043	3.3
Craft and related trades workers, plant and machine operators and assemblers	27,742	29.9
Elementary occupations	12,578	13.6
Total	*92,264*	*99.5*
15 main countries of return		
France	25,599	16.8
Switzerland	24,465	16.0
Spain	22,500	14.7
United Kingdom	19,161	12.5
Germany	11,176	7.3
USA	6306	4.1
Brazil	4449	2.9
Luxembourg	3976	2.6
Netherlands	3973	2.6
Belgium	3345	2.2
Angola	3216	2.1
Canada	3047	2.0
Venezuela	2279	1.5
Italy	2146	1.4
Andorra	2106	1.4

Source: Own calculations, based on INE, Census 2011

Occupations were also recorded, but only for the population that was employed at the time of the census. There were two major categories. One comprised mid-level specialists, administrative staff and personal service, protection, security and sales workers, which accounted for 31% of the emigrants who had returned in the last 10 years. The other comprised skilled manufacturing workers, construction and craft workers, machine and equipment operators, and assembly professionals, accounting for 30%. The third largest category comprised emigrants in more highly qualified occupations, such as managers and intellectual and scientific specialists, accounting for 22%. Unskilled workers accounted for 14% and farm and fishery workers for very small percentages.

These emigrants returned from a wide range of countries of origin, showing that migratory destinations are currently less concentrated than before. Although France was still the main origin (17%), Switzerland accounted for almost the same percentage of returnees (16%), followed by Spain (15%) and the United Kingdom (13%). These four countries were far ahead of all the others and altogether were the origin of 60% of returning emigrants. A significant number of emigrants also returned from Germany and the United States, though at much lower percentages (7% and 4% respectively). All other origins accounted for a much lower proportion of returnees, although their presence in the census did show the significant geographical dispersion of Portuguese emigration.

Returnees of Retirement Age

Emigrants who returned when they stopped working or retired, i.e. those aged 60 and over at the time of the census, number almost 62 thousand (only 26% of the return flow in 2001–2011). Their sociodemographic characteristics (Table) show that they were mostly male (55%) and had low educational attainment: over half had only completed primary school (64%) and almost one quarter had not completed any level of education (24%). These low education levels account for 88% of the elderly. At the other end of the scale, there were very few who had higher education degrees (3%) or upper secondary school diplomas (2%). In most cases, these individuals were pensioners (82%), with only a few housewives (6%) and employed (5%).

Most of these emigrants came back from France (52%). All the other destinations were much less significant. Germany was the second most common (11%). The United States (7%) and Switzerland (5%) were also important. These four countries accounted for 74% of the elderly emigrants who returned during the 2001–2011 period. If we add two other traditional emigration destinations, Canada and Brazil, these together account for 81% of emigrants returning at the end of their migratory cycle.

Table: Returned emigrants aged 60 and over: sociodemographic characterization

Indicators	N	%
Sex		
Male	33,695	54.7
Female	27,933	45.3
Total	*61,628*	*100*
Education		
None	14,695	23.8
Primary school	39,654	64.3
Lower secondary	4163	6.8
Upper secondary	1327	2.2
Higher education	1777	2.9
Total	*61,616*	*100*
Occupational status		
Pensioners	50,612	82.1
Employed	2934	4.8
Unemployed	747	1.2
Housewives	3740	6.1
Disabled	926	1.5
Other	2669	4.3
Total	*61,628*	*100*
15 main countries of return		
France	32,279	52.4
Germany	6585	10.7
USA	4089	6.6
Switzerland	2759	4.5
Canada	2094	3.4
Brazil	1858	3.0
United Kingdom	1586	2.6
Venezuela	1560	2.5
Spain	1290	2.1
Luxembourg	1228	2.0
South Africa	1218	2.0
Angola	883	1.4
Belgium	698	1.1
Netherlands	585	0.9
Mozambique	553	0.9

Source: Own calculations, based on INE, Census 2011

Typology of Return Flows

A cluster analysis of the countries from which recent returns are occurring shows that the new Portuguese emigration is accompanied by new patterns of return, particularly among the younger population. The cluster analysis by country of

Table: Typology of returns - cluster analysis based on countries of emigration

	Traditional destinations	Continuity and change	Lusophone and others
Total flow	102,386 thousand (47.7%)	83,578 thousand (39.0%)	28,465 thousand (13.3%)
Male (%)	55.5	60.0	60.7
Mean age (years)	54.5	40.6	44.4
Education (in years)	5.6	8.3	10.4
Unemployment (%)	13.5	17.2	14.2
Retired (%)	13.6	8.0	14.5
Skilled occupations (%)	15.6	20.0	39.6
3 main countries	France (27.0%)	Switzerland (12.7%)	Other countries (6.5%)
	Germany (8.3%)	Spain (11.1%)	Brazil (2.9%)
	USA (4.8%)	United Kingdom (9.7%)	Angola (1.9%)

Source: Oliveira et al. (2016)

emigration reveals three different groups (Table)[5] (for more details, see Oliveira et al. 2016).

The first cluster includes the countries with a long tradition of emigration ("traditional destinations"). They account for almost half of returnees (48%). These returnees tend to be older, have very low levels of education and a significant percentage are retired. Within this group, France stands out because of its relative importance (accounting for more than half of the returnees in this group), but also because it is the country whose returnees best exhibit two of the fundamental characteristics of this group: low education and having retired. We can consider this a traditional cluster: these are old destinations from which emigrants return predominantly at the end of their working life.

The second cluster comprises new European destinations from which Portuguese emigrants are returning ("continuity and change"). It accounts for almost 40% of returnees in the decade. This group has different characteristics from the previous one: it has a greater percentage of men, and a much younger and more educated population. This cluster has the lowest proportion of retired returnees, but is the one with the highest incidence of unemployment. Switzerland, Spain and the United Kingdom are the most important origins in this cluster. In spite of its heterogeneity, this second cluster seems to be a group characterised by new patterns of return, albeit with elements of continuity: these are European destinations to which emi-

[5] The variables considered for each country were: sex (percentage of male migrants), age (mean age), education (average number of years of schooling, corresponding to the level of education completed), retirement (percentage of returnees who have retired), unemployment (percentage of returnees who are unemployed between the ages of 20 and 60), professional status (percentage in skilled occupations, i.e. in the categories "representatives of the legislative and executive administration, directors and executive managers" and "specialists in intellectual and scientific activities").

grants travel for both more and less skilled jobs and end up in very different post-return situations.

Finally, the third cluster comprises Lusophone countries and Italy, among other minority destinations (around 13%) ("Lusophone and others"). This group's returning migration flows are mostly male, with an average age between that of the two previous groups. Its returnees have the highest level of education of all the clusters and, therefore, it naturally has the largest proportion of individuals in qualified occupations. Unemployment and retirement have intermediate values, as occurs with age. It is a group whose returnees have different profiles. This cluster includes mostly Lusophone countries outside Europe that have experienced a recent reactivation of migratory flows (Brazil and countries in Africa), but which are also marginal destinations that lie outside the main trends of Portuguese emigration. This group tends to account for the more educated emigrants, who integrate better into the labour market upon return.

Conclusion

The available statistics and research, produced either in Portugal or in destination countries, support the statement that Portuguese emigration never actually ended and in fact recently increased dramatically. New outflows seem more complex than in the past, since temporary movements (i.e. of emigrants who intend to remain abroad for less than 1 year) have increased steadily, outnumbering permanent emigration (i.e. of emigrants who intend to remain abroad for 1 year or more). Both have shown resilience over the past few decades and both experienced an upsurge at the start of the new century. There seem to be four phases of evolution. Emigration remained steady and not very high between 1992 and 2000, increased between 2001 and 2007, dropped slightly in 2008–2010 and rose sharply after 2011. However, more recently, with the improvement of the Portuguese economy and the emergence of a positive national image that is tentatively optimistic for the future, a new slowdown seems to be occurring.

Despite this continuity in Portuguese emigration and its increase between 2001 and 2014 (with a break in 2008–2010), there are still various gaps in our knowledge about the most recent emigration wave. The REMIGR project helps shed more light on the features of Portuguese emigration in the first decade of the twenty-first century, including the development of connections with emigrants' home country. This chapter has explored precisely some of these links, completing the analysis with an overview of Portuguese returns between 2001 and 2011. As mentioned at the beginning of the chapter, the recent reconceptualisation of return – incorporating issues such as temporary returns and international double residence strategies – enabled the development of theoretical (and empirical) approaches linking it with transnationalism. These have therefore been the two conceptual pillars of the chapter, which has empirically explored the links of recent Portuguese emigrants to their home country.

Recent Portuguese emigrants have sustained the two practices that serve as basic indicators of connections with the home country – visits to the country of origin and remittances – but have done more of the first (more than 50% visit Portugal more than once a year) and ultimately less of the second (only about 50% regularly send remittances). This picture, which hides some differences between the various destination countries, shows that emigrants – particularly those that are highly skilled – do exploit the increasing opportunities for international circulation (relatively low cost and high frequency of transport, etc.). This means that the myth of a definitive return to the home country is in the end being challenged by an increasingly mobile world (at least for some migrant groups). Having said this, the relatively high monthly average amounts remitted by Portuguese emigrants working in non-European countries, particularly Angola and Mozambique (between 1200 and 1600 euros per month), point to a focus on the origin country and also to the assumption that their current migration is temporary. In fact, these are precisely the two groups of emigrants that, when asked about their future intentions, mostly state that they want to return to Portugal.

Therefore, while we can identify changes in the mobility of some emigrants and an eventual reduction in their transnational financial practices involving the home country, other emigrants keep the home country as the centre of their social lives and hold on to returning as a goal, even if the interpretation of returning as a single and unified phenomenon is currently being challenged.

Indeed, 2011 Census data on individuals born in Portugal who have resided abroad for more than 1 year but currently live in Portugal show a surprising number and diversity of returns. Taken as a whole, almost 10% of the current Portuguese population has lived abroad and returned (although decolonization boosts this figure, since the ex-colonies are now classified as foreign countries). Moreover, the number of returns has increased since the 1980s and totalled more than 233,000 people between 2001 and 2011. These returned emigrants come from all over the world, particularly from the main destination countries such as France, though the number of those coming back from recent destinations, such as Spain and the UK, is increasing. This large flow is even more significant as it involves long- and medium-term and not just temporary emigrants. These data confirm that contemporary emigration is much more than a one-way path, since many outflows are followed by returns – and possibly by further circulation.

The characteristics of returning emigrants differ considerably depending on their country of origin and the age at which they return. People returning from traditional destinations, such as France, are mostly older and have reached retirement age. On the other hand, people coming from new destinations, such as Spain and the UK, are mainly young adults. The characteristics of older and younger returnees also diverge. The older ones fit into the traditional profile of Portuguese emigrants – low skilled people coming from well-known destinations. The younger ones represent an emerging profile – they have more heterogeneous skills and come from a wider range of destinations. These figures seem to tell different emigration stories. Traditional emigration flows are followed, as they always have been, by many returns at the end of the migratory cycle. New emigrants, on the other hand, become part of a mobile world, where emigration is not a single event followed by an eventual "final return". In fact, emigration seems more and more to consist of complex, fragmented and multilateral movements.

Acknowledgments and Funding This chapter is based on the research project "Back to the future: new emigration and links to Portuguese society" (*Regresso ao futuro: a nova emigração e a relação com a sociedade portuguesa – REMIGR*), funded by FCT – Foundation for Science and Technology (PTDC/ATP-DEM/5152/2012). The project involved researchers from Universidade de Lisboa (ISEG and IGOT), ISCTE-Instituto Universitário de Lisboa and Universidade de Coimbra. The final edition of the chapter was supported by FCT, under the project UID/SOC/04521/2013. Some sections were previously published in Peixoto et al., 2016 and Oliveira et al., 2016.

References

Abrantes, M., Azevedo, J., Belchior, A. M., & Lisi, M. (2012). Away inside: Emigrants and transnationalism through the eyes of political parties. *Perspectivas – Portuguese Journal of Political Science and International Relations*, (8), 61–82.

Baganha, M. I. (1993). Principais características e tendências da emigração portuguesa. In *Estruturas Sociais e Desenvolvimento - Actas do II Congresso Português de Sociologia* (pp. 819–835). Lisboa: Fragmentos.

Baganha, M. I., & Góis, P. (1998/1999). Migrações internacionais de e para Portugal. O que sabemos e para onde vamos? *Revista Crítica de Ciências Sociais*, 52–53, 229–280.

Baganha, M. I., & Peixoto, J. (1997). Trends in the 90's: the Portuguese migratory experience. In M. I. Baganha (Ed.), *Immigration in Southern Europe* (pp. 15–40). Oeiras: Celta.

Baganha, M. I., Ferrão, J., & Malheiros, J. (Eds.). (2002). Os movimentos migratórios externos e a sua incidência no mercado de trabalho em Portugal. In *Observatório do Emprego e Formação Profissional*. Lisboa.

Basch, L., Glick Schiller, N., & Szanton-Blanc, C. (1994). *Nations unbound: Transnational projects, postcolonial predicaments and deterritorialized nation state*. Langhorne: Gordon & Breach.

Baubock, R., & Faist, T. (Eds.). (2010). *Diaspora and transnationalism: Concepts, theories and methods*. Amsterdam: Amsterdam University Press/IMISCOE Research.

Candeias, P., Ferreira, B., & Peixoto, J. (2014a). Emigração portuguesa: o que temos vindo a estudar e o que nos falta saber – Uma análise bibliométrica entre 1980 e 2013. *População e Sociedade, 22*, 11–31.

Candeias, P., Góis, P., Marques, J. C., & Peixoto, J. (2014b). *Emigração portuguesa: bibliografia comentada (1980–2013)* (SOCIUS Working Papers 01/2014).

Cairns, D., Sardinha, J., & Tiesler e N. C. (2014). *Mapping the return migration research field* (CIES e-Working Paper N.° 197/2014).

Carling, J., & Erdal, M. B. (2014). Return migration and transnationalism: how are the two connected? *International Migration, 52*(6), 2–12.

Cassarino, J.-P. (2013). Teorizando sobre a migração de retorno: uma abordagem conceitual revisitada sobre migrantes de retorno. *REMHU – Revista Interdisciplinar da Mobilidade Humana, 41*, 21–54.

Cavalcanti, L., & Parella, S. (2013). El retorno desde una perspectiva transnacional. *REMHU – Revista Interdisciplinar de Mobilidade Humana, 41*, 9–20.

Charbit, Y., Hily, M.-A., & Poinard, M. (1997). *Le va-et-vient identitaire. Migrants portugais et villages d'origine*. Paris: PUF.

Delicado, A. (2010). O retorno dos 'cérebros': regresso e reintegração dos investigadores portugueses em mobilidade. *Revista Iberoamericana de Ciencia, Tecnología y Sociedad, 5*(15), 185–218.

Faist, T. (2000). *The volume and dynamics of international migration and transnational social spaces*. Oxford: Clarendon Press.

Góis, P. (2005). Low intensity transnationalism: The Cape Verdian case. *Wiener Zeitschrift fur Kritische Afrikastudien, Stichproben, 8*, 255–276.

Itzigsohn, J., Cabral, C. D., Medina, E. H., & Vazquez. (1999). Mapping Dominican transnationalism: Narrow and broad transnational practices. *Ethnic and Racial Studies, 22*(2), 316–339.

King, R., & Christou, A. (2011). Of counter-diaspora and reverse transnationalism: Return mobilities to and from the ancestral homeland. *Mobilities, 6*(4), 451–466.

Klimt, A. (2000). European spaces. Portuguese migrant's notions of home and belonging. *Diaspora, 9*(2), 259–285.

Levitt, P., & Glick Schiller, N. (2004). Conceptualizing simultaneity: A transnational social field perspective on society. *International Migration Review, 38*(3), 1002–1039.

Levitt, P., & Sorensen, N. N. (2004). The transnational turn in migration studies. *Global Migration Perspectives, 6*, 2–13.

Malheiros, J. (2001). Arquipélagos migratórios: transnacionalismo e inovação. Faculdade de Letras da Universidade de Lisboa. PhD dissertation (unpublished).

Malheiros, J., & Caldeira, M. J. (2003). El voto, arma del pueblo: la participación política de los emigrantes portugueses. In L. Calderón Chelius (Ed.), *Votar en la distancia La extensión de los derechos políticos a migrantes, experiencias comparadas* (pp. 457–488). México: Instituto Mora, México.

Malheiros, J. (2011). Portugal 2010: o regresso do país de emigração? *JANUS.NET e-journal of International Relations*, 2(1) Available at: observare.ual.pt/janus.net/pt_vol2_n1_not3

Marçalo, C., & Peixoto, J. (2012). Economic transnationalism and migration: Portuguese-American entrepreneurship and Portugal. *Interdisciplinary Journal of Portuguese Diaspora Studies, 1*, 43–70.

Marques, J. C. (2008). *Os Portugueses na Suíça. Migrantes europeus*. Lisbon: ICS.

Monteiro, P. F. (1994). *Emigração. O eterno mito do retorno*. Oeiras: Celta.

Neto, F. (2010). Re-acculturation attitudes among adolescents from returned Portuguese immigrant families. *International Journal of Intercultural Relations, 34*(3), 221–232.

Oliveira, I. T., Candeias, P., Peixoto, J., Malheiros, J., & Azevedo, J. (2016). Regresso e circulação de emigrantes portugueses no início do século XXI. *Sociologia, Problemas e Práticas, 81*, 11–35. https://doi.org/10.7458/SPP2016817155.

Peixoto, J. (2004). País de emigração ou país de imigração? Mudança e continuidade no regime migratório em Portugal. *SOCIUS Working Papers* 2/2004.

Peixoto, J., Oliveira, I. T., Azevedo, J., Marques, J. C., Góis, P., Malheiros, J., & Madeira, P. M. (orgs.). (2016). *Regresso ao futuro: a nova emigração e a sociedade portuguesa*. Lisboa: Gradiva.

Pinho, F., & Pires, R. P. (2013). "Espanha", *OEm Country Reports*, 1, Lisboa, Observatório da Emigração, CIES-IUL, ISCTE-IUL. https://doi.org/10.15847/CIESOEMCR012013.

Pires, Rui Pena (Ed.), Machado, Fernando Luís, Peixoto, João, Vaz, Maria João Vaz et al. (coord.). (2010). *Portugal: An atlas of international migration*. Lisbon: Tinta da China and Fundação Calouste Gulbenkian.

Pires, R. P., Pereira, C., Azevedo, J., & Ribeiro, A. C. (2014). *Emigração Portuguesa.Relatório Estatístico 2014*. Lisboa: Observatório da Emigração e Rede Migra, ISCTE-IUL, CIES-IUL, e DGACCP.

Portes, A. (1999). *Migrações internacionais*. Lisboa: Celta.

Portes, A., Guarnizo, L. E., & Landolt, P. (1999). The study of transnationalism: Pitfalls and promise of an emergent research field. *Ethnic and Racial Studies, 22*(2), 217–237.

Rato, H. (2001). O retorno dos emigrantes. *Janus – Anuário de Relações Exteriores*, pp. 164–165.

Rosales, M. V., & Machado, V. P. (2015). Travessias do Atlântico: aspirações, projetos e avaliações de portugueses no Brasil, *Seminário Aberto – A Emigração Portuguesa no Século XXI*. Instituto de Educação, Universidade de Lisboa.

Sardinha, J. (2011). Returning' second-generation Portuguese-Canadians and Portuguese-French return motivations and sense of belonging. *Journal of Mediterranean Studies, 20*(2), 231–254.

Silva, M., Amaro, R. R., Clausse, G., Cónim, C., Matos, M., Pisco, M., & Seruya, L. M. (1984). *Retorno, emigração e desenvolvimento regional em Portugal*. Lisboa: Instituto de Estudos para o Desenvolvimento.

Vertovec, S., & Cohen, R. (2002). Introduction: Conceiving cosmopolitanism. In S. Vertovec & R. Cohen (Eds.), *Conceiving cosmopolitanism: Theory, context and practice* (pp. 1–22). Oxford: Oxford University Press.

Vertovec, S. (2009). *Transnationalism*. New York: Routledge.

Vidigal, I., & Pires, R. P. (2014). Remessas 2013, *OEm Fact Sheets*, 2, Lisboa, Observatório da Emigração, ISCTE-IUL, CIES-IUL e DGACCP. DOI: https://doi.org/10.15847/CIESOEMFS022014.

10

'Pulled' or 'Pushed'? The Emigration of Portuguese Scientists

Ana Delicado

Introduction

The literature on international mobility of the highly skilled often makes the distinc-tion between 'pull' (which attract skilled workers to a country) and "push" (which repel workers away from the country of origin) factors. These factors are associated with, among other conditions, differential material and symbolic resources between countries. Thus, migration in scientific professions largely occurs from the periph-ery to the centre of the world system of science.

Portugal, as a semi-peripheral country, has traditionally been a sending rather than a receiving country for scientists. Exit trends were actively encouraged throughout the last few decades by national science policies (training of human resources that provided opportunities for studying and working abroad) and by European policies (of intra-EU mobility), sustained by an objective of capacity building that would later be capitalised by scientific research in the country of origin, through the return of these scientists or the formation of diaspora networks. Similarly, the growth of resources in the Portuguese scientific system came to be a factor for attracting foreign scientists to Portugal.

However, the current economic crisis and reduced investment in science may be dictating an increase of outflows and a change in the factors of attraction or repul-sion of Portuguese scientists in mobility.

This chapter aims to discuss some of these issues, based on a research project carried out between 2007 and 2009 on the international mobility of Portuguese scientists, in which a survey of Portuguese scientists abroad (N = 521) and semi-structured interviews with returning researchers (N = 32) were conducted.

A. Delicado (✉)
Instituto de Ciências Sociais, Universidade de Lisboa (ICS-ULisboa), Lisbon, Portugal
e-mail: ana.delicado@ics.ulisboa.pt

International Scientific Mobility

The international mobility of scientists is a particular type of skilled migration that has merited a great deal of attention from scholars in the past few decades. There is an abundance of studies commissioned or funded by supra-national entities such as the European Commission (such as the analysis of Marie Curie Grants performed by Ackers et al. (2001) and Van de Sande et al. (2005) or the FP7 funded project E*CARE – Ivancheva and Gourova 2011) or OECD (2001, 2002), as well as research on specific sending or receiving countries (see, for instance, the work coordinated by Louise Ackers on flows between Italy and the UK – Ackers 2005; Gill 2005; Morano-Foadi 2006) or on specific sectors (such as biomedical research – Diaz-Briquets and Cheney (2002) – or ICT and biotechnology – Casey et al. (2001)).

Even though the relative figures concerning the mobility of scientists may be small within skilled migration, it does have a significant socioeconomic impact. Public and private investment in science has grown considerably in recent years and research institutions compete for the best researchers and students.

Mobility trajectories in science tend to follow fairly predictable patterns: from the periphery to the centre of the science world system and between centres. Scientists are attracted to scientific systems which are large (measured by the number of researchers, for instance), wealthy (in terms of R&D expenditure), more productive (in terms of publications and patents) and highly internationalised, such as the UK and the US (Hirt and Muffo 1998; Alarcon 1999; Mahroum 2000; Casey et al. 2001; Diaz-Briquets and Cheney 2002; van de Sande Ackers and Gill 2005; Millard 2005; Morano-Foadi 2006; Szélenyi 2006; Baruch et al. 2007; Fontes 2007). However, exit countries can also receive scientists, but they usually come from even less scientifically developed countries.

Scientific mobility is also characterised by circulation (multiple movements) rather than linear flows (Mahroum 2000; Ferro 2004; Gill 2005; Morano-Foadi 2006; Ivancheva and Gourova 2011; Schiller and Diez 2012; Geddie 2013). Scientists often spend time in different institutions and countries throughout their career, either through successive work contracts or visiting fellowships. Mobility has many positive effects, such as the training of human resources, fostering the circulation of knowledge (Ivancheva and Gourova 2011; Schiller and Diez 2012) or building diaspora networks between the home and the host countries (Meyer and Brown 1999; Rizvi 2005; Thorn and Holm-Nielsen 2006; Meyer and Wattiaux 2006; Favell et al. 2006; Mahroum et al. 2006). However, it can also deprive some countries of their more valuable human resources, which has been characterised as 'brain drain' (Jalowiecki and Gorzelak 2004; Morano-Foadi 2006; Baruch et al. 2007; Ivancheva and Gourova 2011).

Scientific Mobility Trends in Portugal

Portugal has been mainly an exit country for researchers in mobility, although in the past decade the country has also attracted researchers from abroad. Public policies in place since the 1990s have favoured exit flows, in particular for advanced training of human resources (PhD and post-doctoral grants), thus aimed at temporary stays abroad. However, no specific incentives for the return of mobile scientists were included in these policies (other than the EU wide Welcome programme, aimed at European researchers working outside the EU). Conversely, some policy measures have also favoured the inflow of foreign researchers to Portugal, such as opening up PhD and post-doctoral grants to foreign nationals and the Invited Research Chairs Programme (2008).

Though official statistics are scarce, incoming and outgoing trends can be gleaned from proxy indicators, such as the grants allocated by the Foundation for Science and Technology (FCT) or the fellowships integrated in Marie Curie Actions.

Between 1994 and 2015, FCT has awarded 4599 grants for pursuing PhDs abroad (19% of the total grants) and 5476 grants for mixed PhDs (hosted by both a national and a foreign institution). However, during this period significant changes are noticeable (Fig.). Whereas in the 1990s PhD grants abroad represented close to half the total of grants, this ratio has been declining since the 2000s, reaching just 2% in 2015. Mixed grants show a reverse trend: fairly uncommon in the 1990s (below 15%), they almost doubled in later years (31% in 2015).

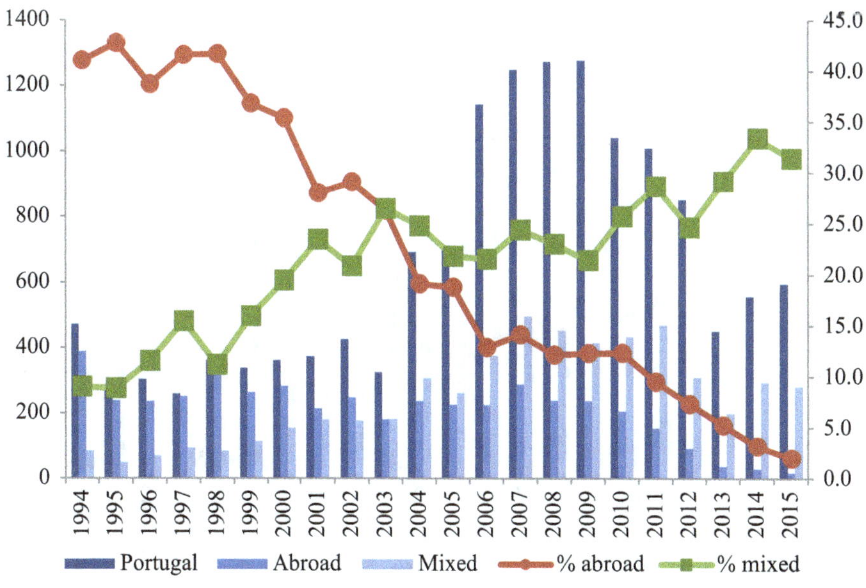

Fig. PhD grants awarded by FCT (1994–2015).
Source: FCT, http://www.fct.pt/estatisticas/bolsas/index.phtml.pt. Accessed 26 April 2018

Post-doctoral grants abroad have always been less-favoured that those hosted by Portuguese institutions (Fig.): only 756 grants were awarded between 1994 and 2015, representing just 9% of grants in this period. The downward trend is quite visible and since 2009 this type of grant has dropped below 5%. No such grants were awarded since 2012 (other than one in 2015). Mixed post-doctoral grants have fared a little better, with 1696 grants (20% of the total), although the numbers have been decreasing also in the past few years.

Conversely, the number of grants awarded to foreign nationals to carry out their PhD or post-doctoral research in Portugal has been growing (Fig.). PhD grants have yet to reach the levels of outgoing grants: 2299 PhD grants were awarded to foreign nationals between 1994 and 2015, which represents less than half the PhD grants abroad. But the 2544 post-doctoral grants awarded to foreign researchers (29% of the total grants) almost treble the post-doctoral grants for doing research abroad. Also, regarding the Programme 'Compromisso com a Ciência', that between 2007 and 2008 provided 5-year contracts in Portuguese research institutions for about 1200 researchers, 41% of the beneficiaries were foreign researchers, but 35% already had a PhD from a Portuguese university and a few more were working at a Portuguese institution before these contracts. This shows that Portugal has become an attractive country for researchers in mobility, though mainly from other peripheries: most of these foreign researchers came from Brazil, southern Europe (Italy, Spain), Eastern Europe (Russia, Bulgaria, Romania, Byelorussia, Ukraine), Asia (India, China) (FCT 2009).

These figures leave out the unknown amount of researchers that leave the country outside the scope of FCT programmes, with grants from other institutions or hired

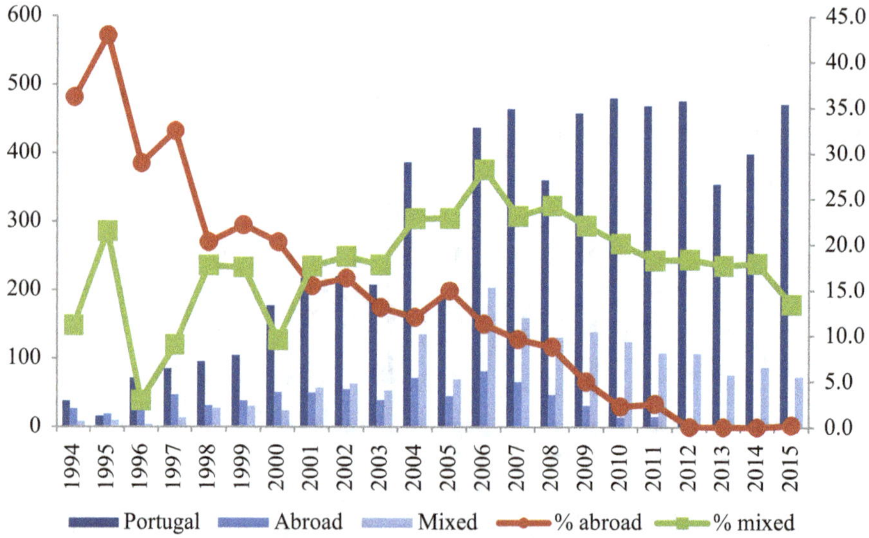

Fig. Post-doctoral grants awarded by FCT (1994–2015).
Source: FCT, http://www.fct.pt/estatisticas/bolsas/index.phtml.pt. Accessed 26 April 2018

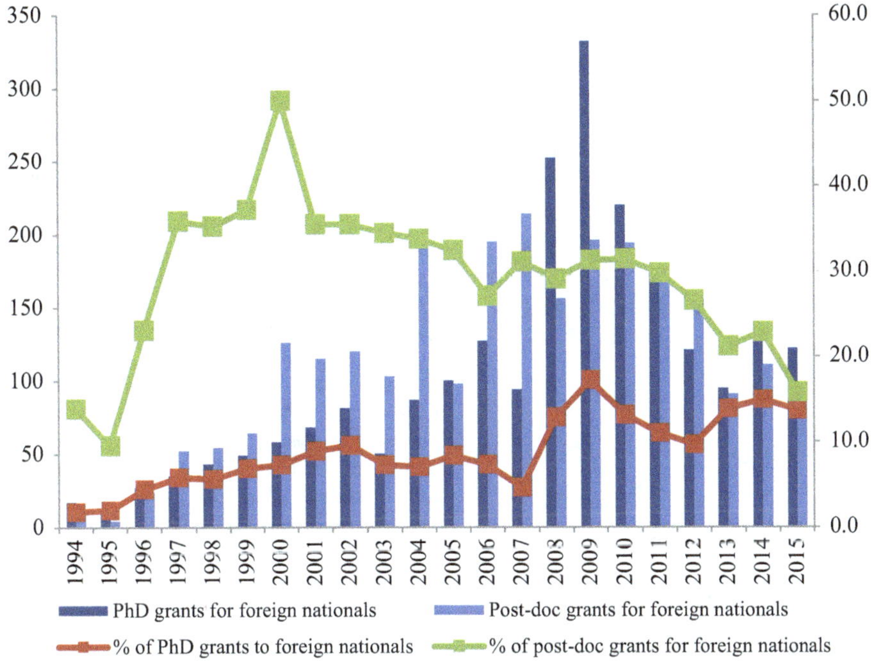

Fig. PhD and postdoctoral grants awarded by FCT to foreign nationals (1994–2015). Source: FCT, http://www.fct.pt/estatisticas/bolsas/index.phtml.pt. Accessed 26 April 2018

by research centres abroad. But they also leave out foreign researchers hired by Portuguese research centres and universities. However, these figures do show that outbound mobility sponsored by the main government funder of research in Portugal has been significant in the past few decades but is slowing down, whereas foreign researchers are entering the system, stimulated by the availability of grants. Unfortunately, there is no publicly available data on the origin of these researchers that could shed some light on if they are coming mainly from other peripheral countries in Europe or from other continents.

A more accurate indicator of inbound and outbound flows may be the Marie Curie Programme, which in the past decades has played a significant role in funding intra-European mobility (Table). It is noticeable that although an imbalance per-sists (the number of outgoing fellows is higher than the number of incoming fel-lows), it has been significantly reduced in the most recent editions of the programme.

Table: Number of participants in Marie Curie Actions: incoming fellows (foreign nationals in Portuguese host institutions) and outgoing fellows (Portuguese nationals in foreign host institutions)

	Outgoing	Incoming
FP4 and FP5 (1994–2002)[a]	173	69
FP6 (2002–2006)[b]	24	10
FP7 (2007–2014)[c]	24	21

[a]Includes all Marie Curie Actions, Van de Sande Ackers and Gill (2005, 16, 69)

[b]Intra-European Fellowships for Career Development (IEF) and International Outgoing Fellowships for Career Development (IOF), Pina (2009)

[c]Intra-European Fellowships for Career Development (IEF) and International Outgoing Fellowships for Career Development (IOF), FP7-PEOPLE Marie Curie Actions, Country fact sheet: Portugal, 26 May 2014, http://ec.europa.eu/research/mariecurieactions/documents/funded-projects/statistics/eu-countries/marie-curie-actions-country-fiche-pt_en.pdf

Pull and Push Factors

Circulation flows are often explained in terms of 'push' and 'pull' factors (Todisco et al. 2003; Jałowiecki and Gorzelak 2004; Thorm and Holm-Nielsen 2006; Baruch et al. 2007; Ivancheva and Gourova 2011; Schiller and Diez 2012). In general, the first concern conditions less conducive to scientific activities in the country of origin and the latter the favourable conditions in the country of destination. Among the most common factors of 'attractiveness' are not only scientific conditions (the resources available for scientific activity, namely funding and equipment; the quality of the research environment; development in cutting-edge areas; the opportunity to work in the team of a prominent scientist) and professional conditions (training and employment opportunities, wages, career progression) but also political (democratic regimes, incentives granted to skilled immigration) and cultural (language, lifestyle, cosmopolitanism, the presence of communities from the country of origin) (Todisco et al. 2003; Jałowiecki and Gorzelak 2004; Rizvi 2005; Thorm and Holm-Nielsen 2006; Favell et al. 2006; Baruch et al. 2007; De la Vega and Vessuri 2008).

The results of the survey of Portuguese researchers abroad carried out in 2007 (for a more detailed analysis, see Delicado 2010a) show that indeed scientists are 'pulled' to core countries of the science world system, in particular English speak-ing ones (Table): 29% were working in the United Kingdom and 27% in the United States. Close to two thirds are located in European Union countries that lead in the science field, in particular France, Netherlands and Germany. 4% of Portuguese researchers abroad are in Spain, which is explained more by geographical proximity than by scientific reasons. There are a few variations by scientific disciplines: the proportion of natural scientists in the US, of engineering researchers in Switzerland and of social scientists in English-speaking countries is slightly above average.

Table: Host countries of Portuguese researchers abroad (%)

European Union	64.9
UK	28.8
France	7.9
Netherlands	6.5
Germany	6.1
Spain	4.4
Other EU countries	11.2
Europe (non EU)	4.8
United States	26.9
Rest of the world	3.5

Source: Survey of Portuguese researchers abroad, 2007

Table: Motivations for leaving Portugal to work in research abroad (mean scores[a])

To learn new techniques/methodologies/theories	4.36
It is important for the scientific CV	4.24
Possibility to establish international scientific networks	4.19
To work in an underdeveloped area in Portugal	4.07
To use means or equipment unavailable in Portugal	4.00
To experience life in another country	3.77
Difficulties in enrolling in a PhD or finding a job in Portugal	2.70
Personal reasons (to be close to family and friends)	2.50
PhD students	
Quality of training is higher than in Portugal	3.73
To increase the possibility of working abroad after the PhD	3.52
To increase the possibility of finding work in Portugal	3.36
Senior researchers	
To obtain post-graduate training abroad	4.13
Getting a job in a foreign institution	3.55

Source: Survey of Portuguese researchers abroad, 2007

[a]Likert scale: mean score between 5 (very important) and 1 (Not at all important)

The motivations for leaving Portugal (Table) and choosing a host institution abroad (Table) also shed light on the importance of pull and push factors. On the one hand, researchers are pulled by the opportunities to learn new things, to improve

Table: Motivations for choosing a host institution (mean scores[a])

Prestige of the institution	4.34
Available resources (labs, computers, library)	4.10
Having received an invitation to work at the institution (senior researchers)	4.03
Wish to work with a particular scientist	3.74
Multidisciplinary team	3.54
Country where is situated	3.35
Having previously met a member of the institution (PhD students)	3.28
Multinational team	3.10
Contacts with business companies	2.78
Recommendation from a professor or colleague in Portugal	2.76
Having already studied at this institution	2.40
Exchange or collaboration agreements with Portuguese institutions	2.29
Portuguese researchers in the team	1.51

Source: Survey of Portuguese researchers abroad, 2007
[a]Likert scale: mean score between 5 (very important) and 1 (not at all important)

their CV, to join international networks, to work in a prestigious institution with specific material and human resources, to experience life in a new country. On the other hand, they are pushed abroad by the lack of means to perform research or lack of training opportunities in Portugal. However, this type of response was more common in researchers that had left the country longer ago, since the Portuguese scientific system has developed substantially in the past few decades and a wealth of PhD programmes in many scientific areas has been created.

The interviews with researchers that had returned to the country after doing their PhD abroad strengthen this argument.

Some mention as a motivation for leaving the country the lack of material resources:

> The area I was working in (and still do) required very expensive equipment that didn't exist in the country at the time. We had very limited apparatus, it was really difficult to do innovative things, and that led me to leave (PhD in the UK in the 1980s, exact sciences, professor at a public university)

Others refer the lack of skilled human resources to act as supervisors:

> There were very few people in Portugal with a PhD in Mathematics Education, less than a handful (…). I wanted to do my PhD in an area where we had nothing (…) one of my potential supervisors told me 'if you want to do it at this level, you have to go abroad because in Portugal no one knows anything about it (PhD in the UK in the 1990s, social sciences, lecturer at a polytechnic)

Others mention the scientific capital (Bourdieu 1975) they would earn through a PhD from a prestigious institution:

> By being in this PhD Programme, we had the opportunity of going anywhere and even though, obviously, there were already good research groups in Portugal, we can't compare the conditions we have at the top world laboratories, in the top universities, with those we

> have in Portugal. It never crossed my mind, since I had the opportunity to do the PhD anywhere in the world, not to do it in the best place, in a top place, so always outside Portugal. (…) it was an opportunity I must grab for what it would bring in terms of career, of human development, of professional development (PhD in the US in the 1990s, natural sciences, entrepreneur)

But not all researchers are solely motivated by scientific or career reasons. Living abroad in a pleasant city or a culturally stimulating country was also mentioned by some interviewees:

> Paris, you know, remains a cosmopolitan city, symbolically was the city of lights, but its universities are still an international benchmark and therefore this was the motivation. Since I'm a researcher in history, as we know, France is a paradise for historians. (PhD in France in the 2000s, humanities, post-doctoral fellow at a research institute)

Return Mobility

As mentioned above, scientific migrations are often composed of multiple journeys, from and to different countries. A much discussed issue is the return flows to the home country after a period working and studying abroad. This is considered a prerequisite to avoid brain drain and draw benefits from scientific mobility, such as an accrued capacity to perform high quality research, to publish in prestigious journals, to train new practitioners, to take part in international networks, raising the scientific profile of the home scientific system.

Though difficult to estimate without official statistics, the return rate of Portuguese researchers has been significant. In 2006, 29% (3200) of the Portuguese PhD holders working in Portugal had obtained their PhD abroad (survey 'Career of Doctorate holders', GPEARI 2006). An analysis of the close to 1100 beneficiaries of the Programme 'Compromisso com a Ciência' (see above) shows that 12% were Portuguese researchers who had done their PhD abroad and a few others were working outside the country just before signing these contracts.

Here again push and pull factor may play a role in stimulating return mobility. According to the survey of Portuguese researchers abroad, close to half had the intention of returning to Portugal in the near future (Table). But the motivations were quite different from the ones mentioned as reasons for leaving the country. Family reasons are strongly predominant, followed by the wish to contribute to the development of the home scientific system or of the country itself. Scientific and career motivations, such as job opportunities and conditions to perform research, exert a reverse effect, justifying the decision of remaining abroad.

The interviews with returnee scientists paint a not so different picture, albeit generational effects also have some impact.

Researchers that left the country in the 1980s often had a previous contract with a Portuguese institution (mostly universities), something that become much less common from the 1990s onwards, when government programmes supported PhD fellowships abroad for young researchers with no permanent positions (for details,

Table: Intention of returning to Portugal or remaining abroad and respective motivations (%)

Intention of returning to Portugal	49.3
Motivations	
Family reasons	80.5
Wish to contribute to the Portuguese S&T system	73.9
Wish to contribute to the development of Portugal	69.9
Quality of life in Portugal	62.4
Previous contract with a Portuguese institution	15.9
Job offer in Portugal	12.4
Good conditions for research in Portugal	6.4
Intention of staying abroad	50.7
Motivations	
Lack of job opportunities in Portugal	65.1
Difficulty in performing high quality research in Portugal	58.2
Wish to extend the research experience abroad	56.0
Difficulties in career progression in Portugal	51.7
Low salaries in Portugal	46.6
Quality of life in the host country	44.4
Family reasons	28.0
Job offer in another country	26.3
Contract with an institution in the host country	22.0

Source: Survey of Portuguese researchers abroad, 2007

see Delicado 2010b). For these older researchers, a return to the home country was not only expected but also came with a guarantee of a stable position:

> I had a job here and I think it never crossed my mind [to stay abroad]. Since the Portuguese government paid for my training, I had a moral duty to return. It didn't even cross my mind to stay. (PhD in the UK in the 1980s, natural sciences, professor at a public university)

But most researchers interviewed, both younger and older, stated that the main reason to come back was family ties:

> For purely personal reasons, there is no objective professional reason to return, both for me and my wife. Parents getting older, my siblings, missing them, missing some things in this country. We made this choice, just because of this. (PhD in the UK in the 1990s, health sciences, researcher at a research centre)

For those without the safety net of a permanent position, the return home was often marred with difficulties. Few employment opportunities, limited welfare and labour rights of fellowship holders and inbreeding in Portuguese universities generate professional and scientific instability.

> Employment opportunities don't really exist (…) the situation abroad is nothing like this. Your wage can be bad, the benefits can be bad, but we are workers, we have a contract, pay taxes. (…) I am not asking for a job for life, you also don't get it abroad, the contracts are for three or four years, but there are more opportunities, after this term one has other opportunities, applies and eventually gets another job. (PhD in the UK in the 2000s, natural sciences, post-doctoral fellow at a research institute)

> I tried a few Universities. I will not go into details but you ought to know already (…) I know that in this specific case were three vacancies, I know I was entitled to one of them thanks to my CV. I didn't get it because I think that anyone who is abroad and returns to Portugal has (…) less chances of getting a job here than those who stay and do a PhD here, especially if you do the PhD with someone you already have been working with for a long time and promises are made… (PhD in the US in the 2000s, engineering sciences, business company employee)

New Exit?

Since international scientific mobility is often composed of consecutive movements from one country to another, it is not guaranteed that returnees remain in Portugal. The interviews with researchers show that many are unwilling to leave again, mostly for family reasons,

> I would not want to leave Portugal for family reasons, for reasons, again, not related to the professional dimension I would not leave Portugal. But if I had no ties to the country and to the family probably I would have thought of returning abroad. This is because here I still do not have a sense of job security (PhD in Germany in the 2000s, engineering sciences, assistant professor at a public university)

and some even consider leaving science rather than leaving the country,[1]

> I want to stay. No doubt about it. In science or outside science, if I'm unable to find anything in science. But to stay. I do not say that in five or ten years I wouldn't consider spending some time abroad (…) I really enjoyed living abroad and really enjoy touring and traveling, but for now definitely not (…) I think I really like science but I think the personal life is more important (PhD in the UK in the 2000s, exact sciences, post-doctoral fellow at a research institute)

Others though envisage returning abroad if the conditions for performing research in Portugal worsen.

> I enjoyed doing science with some international impact, if that is possible in Portugal and since I'm being closer to the family, I do not mind staying in Portugal. If in order to do science with some international projection I have to go abroad again, I see no other choice (PhD in the United States in the 2000s, natural sciences, temporary contract researcher at a research centre)

---

[1] In fact, in the case of the following citation, this researcher ended up abandoning her scientific career and now works in the private sector, in an area unrelated to her training, since she was unable to get employment after her post-doctoral fellowship.

Current Trends

Most of the evidence presented above pertains to a period of expansion in Portuguese science (see Delicado 2010b). Mobility rates, both outbound and return, were high and we have seen how push factors became less significant, as Portugal became more attractive for young researchers wishing to pursue advanced training and even for foreign researchers. However, the economic crisis and the austerity measures implemented to deal with it, as well as some changes in science policy, may have created favourable conditions for an increase in brain drain.

According to the latest official statistics, the impact of the crisis is clearly noticeable in R&D expenditure and human resources. After several decades of continuous growth, expenditure in R&D started decreasing in 2009, both in absolute terms and as a percentage of the gross domestic product (Fig.). The number of researchers also shows a downward trend, particularly between 2011 and 2013 (Fig.), which may be a result of a number of factors: emigration, retirement of older researchers, a decline in enrolment in advanced degrees.[2] From 2015 onwards these trends started to reverse again, as austerity policies were eased.

This decline in R&D expenditure and personnel can be attributed to a reduction in funding from its main sources (Fig.). If business companies were already reducing their support from 2009 onwards (with a slight increase in 2016), government investment declined abruptly in 2010 and have been lower ever since, with small fluctuations. Funds from abroad are slowly rising, from the higher education sector have remained more or less stable and from the private non-profit sector have decreased.

The same trend can be seen in government budget allocations for science (Fig.). A steady increase between 2001 and 2009 has been followed by a decline steeper from 2011 to 2012, followed again by a slight rise, more noticeable since 2016.

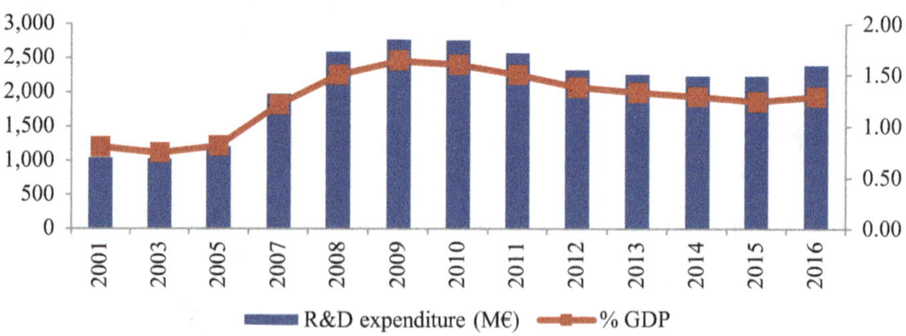

Fig. R&D expenditure in Portugal 2001–2015.
Source: GPEARI (2010) and DGEEC (2014c, 2018b)

[2] For instance, the number of new enrolments in PhDs has declined from 5247 in 2011/12 to 4575 in 2012/13 (DGEEC 2013a, 2014a).

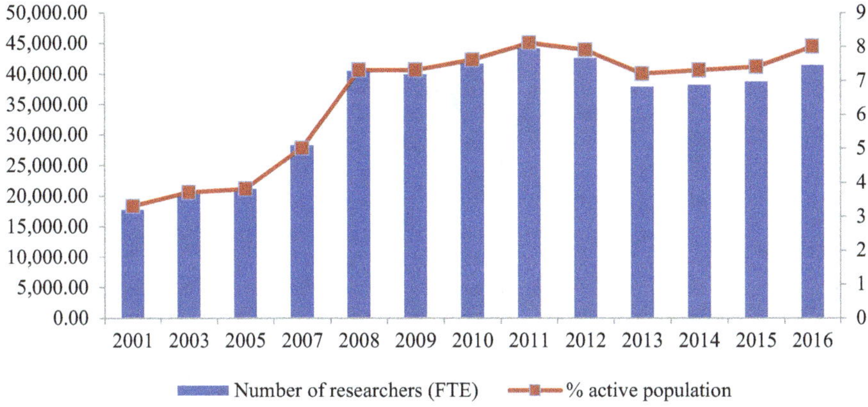

Fig. Researchers in Portugal 2001–2015.
Source: GPEARI (2010) and DGEEC (2014c, 2018b)

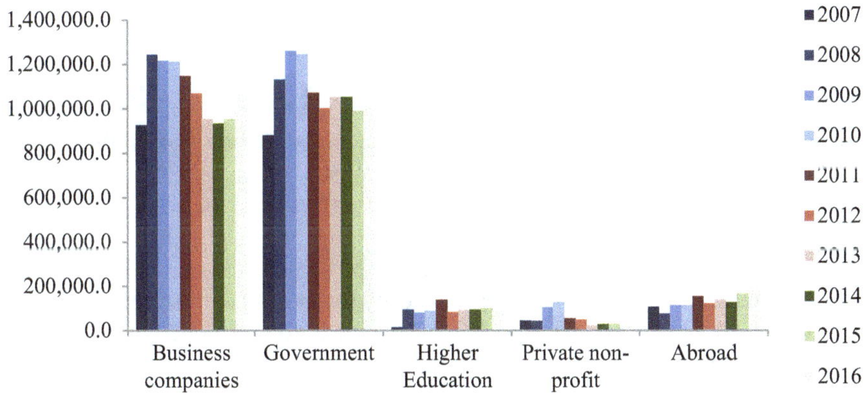

Fig. R&D expenditure by source of funding in Portugal 2007–2016 (thousands €).
Source: GPEARI (2009a, b, 2011a, b) and DGEEC (2012, 2013b, 2014d, 2015, 2016, 2017b, 2018a

This decrease in funding has been most noticeable in research units (the amount of money received is fairly unstable, but it reached a peak in 2008 of close to 90 M€ and its lowest point was in 2011, at 42 M€, rising again to 64 M€ in 2016), project grants (since 2012 general calls for projects have been infrequent and success rates have declined), training grants (declining since 2010) and fixed-term contracts (the Researcher FCT programme, announced as a replacement of the 'Compromisso com a Ciência' programme, hired only 802 researchers over 4 years). Additionally, other austerity measures also had an impact on the S&T system: salary cuts for researchers and university faculty, strict restrictions to hiring in universities and research centres, less support for PhD students. In the private university sector, a decline in enrolments has also led to reductions in faculty.

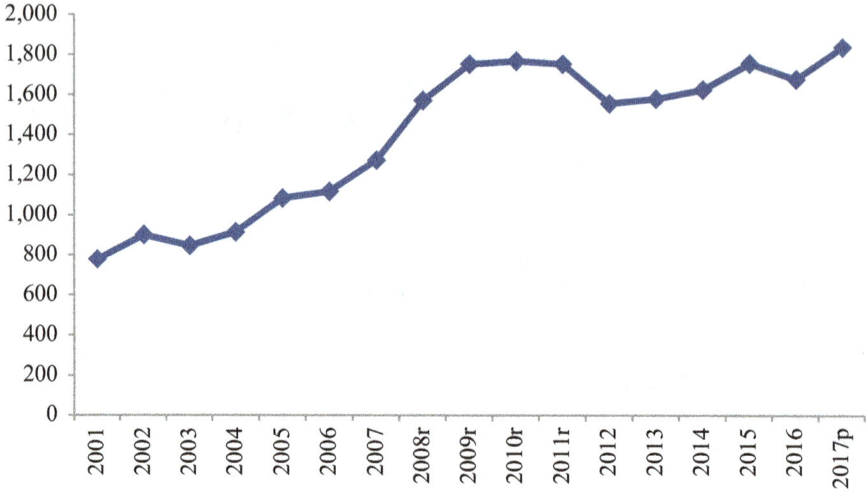

Fig. Government budget allocations for R&D 2001–2017 (M€). *r* revised value, *p* provisional data.
Source: DGEEC 2014b, 2017a

The financial cuts, coupled with the instability and unpredictability of policies, are bound to have had an impact over push factors for mobility, since they cause degradation in professional and scientific conditions.

Again, there is no official data on mobility trends that can help measure the impact of the crisis. But an exploratory analysis of the career paths of 'Compromisso com a Ciência' researchers[3] shows that 19% of the researchers hired in 2007 and 2008 are no longer in Portugal. The vast majority (over 80%) of the researchers who left the country are foreign nationals and half of the Portuguese ones had done their PhD abroad. Thus, it is the most mobile researchers (presumably the more internationalised) that are leaving the Portuguese scientific system. The situation of those who have stayed is unknown. Though some have managed to obtain new contracts (FCT Investigador, post-doctoral grants or as higher education lecturers) or to prolong the old ones (through funds from their host institutions), other may be unemployed or have abandoned research altogether.

Final Remarks

Scientific mobility is vital in science. It is barely possible to maintain a scientific career without spending time at different institutions, preferably in different countries. And mobility has many fruitful impacts on science, from the circulation of knowledge to the creation of international networks.

[3] Based on data available in the publication FCT 2009 and google searchers to ascertain the current positions of researchers.

However, mobility can also deprive some scientific systems of their best researchers. The huge disparity between countries in terms of R&D resources and labour conditions draws researchers to the centres and away from the peripheries. Though insufficient to turn the country into a "centre", in recent years the investment in science has made Portugal more attractive for some mobile researchers, both Portuguese trained abroad and foreign nationals. Nonetheless, slowing down this investment can have the reverse effect, pushing researchers to seek better professional and scientific conditions elsewhere.

References

Ackers, L. (2005). Promoting scientific mobility and balanced growth in the ERA. *Innovations, 18*(3), 301–315.

Ackers, L., et al. (2001). *The participation of women researchers in the TMR Marie Curie fellowships*. European Commission: Brussels.

Alarcon, R. (1999). Recruitment processes among foreign-born engineers and scientists in Silicon Valley. *The American Behavioral Scientist, 49*(9), 1381–1397.

Baruch, Y., Budwahr, P. S., & Khatri, N. (2007). Brain drain: Inclination to stay abroad after studies. *Journal of World Business, 42*, 99–112.

Bourdieu, P. (1975). La spécificité du champ scientifique et les conditions sociales du progrès de la raison. *Sociologie et Societes, VII*(1), 91–118.

Casey, T., Mahroum, S., Ducatel, K., & Barré, R. (2001). *The mobility of academic researchers: Academic careers and recruitment in ICT and biotechnology*. Seville: IPTS-JRC-EC.

De la Vega, I., & Vessuri, H. (2008). Science and mobility: Is physical location relevant? *Technology in Society, 30*, 71–83.

Delicado, A. (2010a). Going abroad to do science: Mobility trends and motivations of Portuguese researchers. *Science Studies, 23*(2), 36–59.

Delicado, A. (2010b). The international mobility of Portuguese researchers: Policies, trends and impacts. In D. Belyaev & Z. Roca (Eds.), *Portugal in the era of the knowledge society* (pp. 155–188). Lisbon: Edições Lusófonas.

DGEEC. (2012). *IPCTN10: Sumários estatísticos*. Lisbon: DGEEC.

DGEEC. (2013a). *Estatísticas da educação 2011/12*. Lisbon: DGEEC.

DGEEC. (2013b). *IPCTN11: Sumários estatísticos*. Lisbon: DGEEC.

DGEEC. (2014a). *Estatísticas da educação 2012/13*. Lisbon: DGEEC.

DGEEC. (2014b). *Dotações orçamentais para C&T e I&D – 2014*. Lisbon: DGEEC.

DGEEC. (2014c). *IPCTN12: Principais resultados*. Lisbon: DGEEC.

DGEEC. (2014d). *IPCTN12: Sumários estatísticos*. Lisbon: DGEEC.

DGEEC. (2015). *IPCTN13: Sumários estatísticos – Dados globais*. Lisbon: DGEEC.

DGEEC. (2016). *IPCTN14: Dados globais*. Lisbon: DGEEC.

DGEEC. (2017a). *Dotações orçamentais para C&T e I&D – 2017*. Lisbon: DGEEC.

DGEEC. (2017b). *IPCTN15: Dados globais*. Lisbon: DGEEC.

DGEEC. (2018a). *IPCTN16: Dados globais*. Lisbon: DGEEC.

DGEEC. (2018b). *IPCTN16: Principais resultados definitivos (2012–2016)*. Lisbon: DGEEC.

Diaz-Briquets, S., & Cheney, C. C. (2002). *Biomedical globalization: The international migration of scientists*. New Brunswick: Transaction Publishers.

Favell, A., Feldblum, M., & Smith, M. P. (2006). The human face of global mobility: A research agenda. In M. P. Smith & A. Favell (Eds.), *The human face of global mobility* (pp. 1–25). New Brunswick: Transaction Publishers.

FCT – Foundation for Science and Technology. (2009). *Mais cientistas para Portugal*. Lisbon: FCT/MCTES.

Ferro, A. (2004). Romanians abroad: A snapshot of highly skilled migration. *Higher Education in Europe, XXIX*(3), 381–391.

Fontes, M. (2007). Scientific mobility policies: How Portuguese scientists envisage the return home. *Science and Public Policy, 344*, 284–298.

Geddie, K. (2013). The transnational ties that bind: Relationship considerations for graduating international science and engineering research students. *Population, Space and Place, 19*, 196–208.

Gill, B. (2005). Homeward bound? The experience of return mobility for Italian scientists. *Innovations, 18*(3), 319–337.

GPEARI. (2009a). *IPCTN 2008: Resultados provisórios*. Lisbon: GPEARI-MCTES.

GPEARI. (2009b). *Sumários estatísticos IPCTN 07*. Lisbon: GPEARI.

GPEARI. (2010). *IPCTN09: Resultados provisórios*. Lisbon: GPEARI.

GPEARI. (2011a). *Sumários estatísticos IPCTN 08*. Lisbon: GPEARI.

GPEARI. (2011b). *Sumários estatísticos IPCTN 09*. Lisbon: GPEARI.

Hirt, J. B., & Muffo, J. A. (1998). Graduate students: Institutional climate and disciplinary cultures. *New Directions for Institutional Research, 98*, 17–33.

Ivancheva, L., & Gourova, E. (2011). Challenges for career and mobility of researchers in Europe. *Science and Public Policy, 38*(3), 185–198.

Jalowiecki, B., & Gorzelak, G. J. (2004). Brain drain, brain gain, and mobility: Theories and prospective methods. *Higher Education in Europe, XXIX*(3), 299–308.

Mahroum, S. (2000). Scientists and global spaces. *Technology in Society, 22*, 513–523.

Mahroum, S., Eldridge, C., & Daar, A. S. (2006). Transnational diaspora options: How developing countries could benefit from their emigrant populations. *International Journal on Multicultural Societies, 8*(1), 25–42.

Meyer, J. -B., & Brown, M. (1999). *Scientific diasporas: A new approach to the brain drain* (MOST Discussion Paper 41). http://unesdoc.unesco.org/images/0011/001163/116330eo.pdf. Accessed 26 Apr 2018.

Meyer, J.-B., & Wattiaux, J.-P. (2006). Diaspora knowledge networks: Vanishing doubts and increasing evidence. *International Journal on Multicultural Societies, 8*(1), 4–23.

Millard, D. (2005). The impact of clustering on scientific mobility. *Innovations, 18*(3), 343–359.

Morano-Foadi, S. (2006). Key issues and causes of the Italian brain drain. *Innovations, 19*(2), 209–220.

OECD. (2001). *Innovative people: Mobility of skilled personnel in national innovation systems*. Paris: OECD.

OECD. (2002). *International mobility of the highly skilled*. Paris: OECD.

Pina, D. G. (2009). *FP7 people programme: Marie Curie actions*. Slide presentation.

Rizvi, F. (2005). Rethinking "Brain Drain" in the era of globalization. *Asia Pacific Journal of Education, 25*(2), 175–192.

Schiller, D., & Diez, J. R. (2012). The impact of academic mobility on the creation of localized intangible assets. *Regional Studies, 46*(10), 1319–1332.

Szelenyi, K. (2006). Students without borders? Migratory decision-making among international graduate students in the US. In M. P. Smith & A. Favell (Eds.), *The human face of global mobility* (pp. 181–209). New Brunswick: Transaction Publishers.

Thorn, K., & Holm-Nielsen, L. B. (2006). *International mobility of researchers and scientists – Policy options for turning a drain into a gain* (Research Paper n. 2006/83, UN-WIDER). http://www.wider.unu.edu/publications/working-papers/research-papers/2006/en_GB/rp2006-83/. Accessed 26 Apr 2018.

Todisco, E., Brandi, M. C., & Tattolo, G. (2003). Skilled migration: A theoretical framework and the case of foreign researchers in Italy. *Fulgor, 1*(3), 115–130.

van de Sande, D., Ackers, H. L., & Gill, B. (2005). *Impact assessment of the Marie Curie fellowships under the 4th and 5th Framework Programs of Research and Technological Development of the EU (1994–2002)*. https://ec.europa.eu/research/evaluations/pdf/archive/fp6-evidence-base/evaluation_studies_and_reports/evaluation_studies_and_reports_2005/impact_assessment_of_marie_curie_actions_fellowships_in_fp4_and_fp5_2005.pdf. Accessed 26 Apr 2018.

11

A New Skilled Emigration Dynamic: Portuguese Nurses and Recruitment in the Southern European Periphery

Cláudia Pereira

Introduction

It was doing fieldwork among qualified Portuguese nationals[1] in London that led me to study Portuguese nurses in England and other countries. During the 5 months that I was in London in 2013 – interviewing and conducting participant observation among qualified Portuguese nationals for a post-doctoral project – I realised that Portuguese nurses stood out clearly from other professional groups, whether information technology personnel, economists, managers, teachers, musicians or others. I found myself meeting more Portuguese nurses in London, and heard frequent references to their increasing numbers, both in the capital and elsewhere. This prompted me to look into the statistics. They showed clearly how "numbers speak"; indeed, since the previous year (2012), Portuguese nurses had been the second main nationality among foreign nurses in England. It was clear that some major change was taking place because in 2008, 91 Portuguese nurses had arrived in the country, in 2010 the number had almost tripled to 249, and by 2012 it had increased to 781. At this point, I was still unaware that in 2013 the number of nurses that had started working in the country surpassed the milestone of 1000 to stand at 1211. The investigation continued and the interest of the Portuguese Nurses' Council in the study led to my interviewing 20 Portuguese nurses resident in 12 countries (Pereira 2015). The statistical investigation of the number of Portuguese nurses was expanded and supplemented with a survey of 349 nurses in the United Kingdom (UK) conducted in collaboration with others (Pereira et al. 2015), as well as interviews with four recruitment agencies that came to Portugal to recruit.

[1] The research refers only to people born in Portugal.

C. Pereira (✉)
Instituto Universitário de Lisboa (ISCTE-IUL), Centro de Investigação e Estudos de Sociologia (CIES-IUL), Observatório da Emigração, Lisbon, Portugal
e-mail: claudia.pereira@iscte-iul.pt

This topic is important because new dynamics of qualified emigration among nurses in particular reflect the dynamics of recent emigration in general within Europe. But also because emigration in this specific sector was distinguished by its unusually high numbers in the second decade of the twenty-first century, as well as by its demographic and socioeconomic impact. The implications have been considerable in both the origin and destination countries.

There are studies on the recent emigration of qualified people in the European Union (EU), originating from other European countries. There is also research on immigrant nurses in the countries with highest demand – such as Indian and Filipino nurses in the UK – but this focuses on the receiving country and on selection policies. There is a gap in the literature on the recent specific and very significant movement of nurses from the Eastern and Southern periphery of Europe to its Northern and Western countries, which it is important to relate to other emigration flows in Europe.

This study deepens research into the recent migration of Portuguese nurses within Europe, from the perspective of both origin and destination countries. It follows the recommendation of the geographer Raghuram (2008) that the contexts of emigration and immigration should be analysed together when considering the migration of qualified people.

The main finding is that although the push factor of economic recession and increased unemployment that hit the European periphery after the 2008 financial crisis played a role in the outflow of Portuguese nurses, it was a pull factor that was more significant. Health agencies started to recruit heavily among Portuguese nurses, which often led to their decision to leave the country with a guaranteed job abroad. However, these dynamics instigated by formal networks (a meso-level factor), were actually caused by a macro-level structural factor: the immigration policies of Portuguese nurses' main destination country, England, which erected barriers to the contracting of nurses from outside the EU, who were traditionally Indians and Filipinos. This government policy led British employment agencies and hospitals to recruit nurses inside the European area. By coincidence, in that same year, 2011, Southern European countries such as Spain, Italy and Portugal were undergoing economic recessions, and another of these countries – Romania – had entered the EU a few years earlier, in 2008, with nurses seeking employment. The decision to migrate is always individual (micro level) and the choice of the majority of the Portuguese nurses that emigrated was influenced by the fact that they were simultaneously experiencing a period of economic austerity – and thus knew that there would not be any job offers in Portugal – and an ideal life stage for mobility, completing their higher education degree and now searching for their first job, with many having been recruited even before they finished their university degree.

The second key finding is that this new mass emigration of Portuguese nurses is not just a Portuguese phenomenon but rather follows the model of South European migration (cf. King 2015). There is a general dynamic of migrants moving from the southern 'periphery' of Europe to its Northern and Western countries, principally the UK and Germany, which are in the geographic and economic 'centre' of the European area.

Recruitment and Economic Austerity in the Southern Periphery of Europe

A recent survey of Portuguese nurses in the UK found that more than three quarters (83%) were employed through agencies (Pereira et al. 2015, 4,5).[2] Another survey of UK-based foreign nurses from various different countries concluded that about two thirds were employed through recruitment agencies (Buchan et al. 2006). Portuguese nurses' main destination country is the UK (Pereira 2015), and recruitment by agencies plays a crucial role in their decision to move here.

The emigration of Portuguese nurses only took on significant dimensions after 2010–2011; up to this point Portugal had principally been a receiving country, welcoming primarily Spanish nurses (Ribeiro et al. 2014). Although recent, there are already studies on the departure of Portuguese nurses conducted in the sending country, Portugal (Gomes et al. 2014; Leal 2013; Leone et al. 2015; Reis 2016; Ribeiro et al. 2014), and some that complement this with the perspective of the receiving country (Pereira et al. 2015; Pereira 2015; Stoehr 2015).

Why did so many nurses began to emigrate from 2010–2011 onwards? In this chapter, I argue that the principal pull factor emerged at the macro level: from 2010 onwards, in a drive to limit immigration, the Conservative UK government erected barriers to the contracting of health professionals from countries outside the European Union[3] (Carvalho 2015; The Migration Observatory 2011). However, given that the British national health service is dependent on the work of foreign nurses and doctors (Bach 2010), the hospitals and employment agencies had to strengthen their recruitment efforts within the European Union. No longer able to resort to the nurses of India and the Philippines – who were predominant at the beginning of the twenty-first century – the British national health service and the recruiting agencies, among which were the four recruiting companies interviewed, started to recruit nurses from the Southern and Eastern peripheries of Europe, "pulling them" to work in the United Kingdom. Coincidentally, during that same period, while Northern and Western European governments slowly began to recover stability in the aftermath of the 2008 financial crisis, those of Portugal and other geographically peripheral countries in Europe, such as Spain, had to resort to external assistance to pay their sovereign debt. From 2010 to 2011 onwards, the peripheral countries descended into a period of austerity, during which the unemployment rate swelled, leading a large number of individuals to decide to seek employment in other countries (Observatório da Emigração 2014). So when agencies were

[2] The nursing profession and, consequently, the migrant nurse population, are largely female dominated.

[3] In addition to the barriers put in place against the immigration of health professionals from non-EU countries, the UK government reduced the number of places for nursing students in the country. However, the fact that it was no longer possible to contract such a high number of Filipino and Indian nurses had a far greater impact than the reduction of the number of education places for UK students, who were already unable to meet the system's requirements (cf. Buchan and Seccombe 2012; Bach 2010).

compelled to recruit within Europe, there was a considerable number of unemployed nurses available to work abroad.

A United Nations report highlights the role of intermediaries such as recruiters in contemporary migration, contextualising its value and cost:

> Despite this diversity among intermediaries, all except those who deceive and exploit migrants satisfy an overarching goal – bridging the gap between employers or sponsors and prospective migrants. Despite globalization, this gap has remained significant, allowing intermediaries to assume important roles. [...] Intermediaries [...] expand migrants' range of choice, increasing the possibility that they will be able to pursue lives that they value (Agunias 2009, 10).

In fact, the role of recruitment intermediaries in international labour migration is one of the most understudied (Martin 2005, 1). This is likewise the case for the role of recruitment in the emigration of Portuguese nationals, particularly nurses, to which very little research has so far been dedicated (Pereira 2015). Although recruitment is barely studied in international migration, its decisive role in global health care migration – including nurses' migration – has been identified (Maybud and Wiskow 2006; Connell and Stilwell 2006; Kingma 2006; Buchan 2007; Kroezen et al. 2015; Dussault et al. 2016). This chapter does not directly analyse the phenomenon of recruitment, but rather its role in Portuguese nurses' decision to emigrate.

The countries seeking to address critical shortages of nurses – which have consequently played the largest role in Portuguese nurses' recent recruitment – are those of Western and Northern Europe, in which there is already a higher number of nurses per inhabitant in comparison to Portugal (Barros and Moura 2015, 34, based on OECD Health Data): the United Kingdom, Germany and France. Indeed, the international recruitment of nurses has historically been one of the measures favoured by policymakers and officials to compensate for the scarcity of nurses (Gabriel 2013), although this has been a recent experience for Portuguese nurses.

The international migration and, consequently, recruitment of nurses crucially requires the existence of mutual recognition agreements on their qualifications (Yeates 2008, 158), even more so than the free movement of people between countries. Within the EU, despite the free movement of people there was actually very little internal migration of nurses as recently as 2003 (Buchan et al. 2003). It was only in 2005 that mutual recognition of diplomas and other documentation for the nursing profession was established in the EU, and this subsequently opened the gates to mobility for health professionals within Europe (Galbany-Estragués and Nelson 2016, 117).

The year of the financial crisis, 2008, marked the first time in the twenty-first century that the number of European nurses exceeded the number of nurses from Non-EU countries working in England, and have remained in the majority ever since. Moreover, since 2010 the number of nurses who have emigrated to England from other European countries has progressively increased (see Fig.). As we shall see in the section on "Findings", these nurses originate from countries of the Eastern and Southern peripheries of Europe.

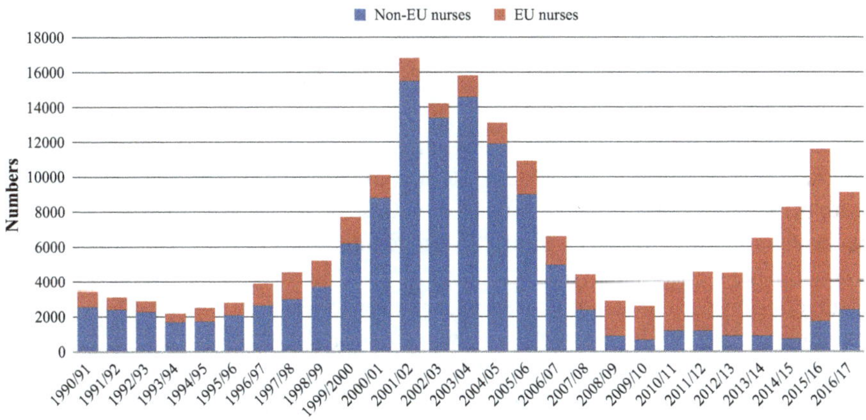

Fig. Number of EU and non-EU nurse registrations in England, 1990/1991–2016/2017. Source: Buchan et al. (2017, 29), based on data obtained from Nursing and Midwifery Council

Globally, 'the general flow [of nurses] is from countries on the *periphery of the world economy to countries at its core*' (Yeates 2008, 154, my emphasis). This means that the majority migrate from developing to industrialised countries, mainly in Europe, North America and the high-income countries of the Western Pacific (Sarfati 2003; Kingma 2007).

The novelty in the European continent is that this migration has shifted so that it *now flows from its own periphery to its core*. That is, mainly from the sending countries of Southern and Eastern Europe (Spain, Portugal, Romania and Poland) to the receiving countries of Westerm and Northern Europe. The OECD data confirm this: in Europe, Germany is the main destination country for foreign nurses, followed by the UK (OECD 2015, 115, from the Database on Immigrants in OECD Countries, DIOC, 2010/2011, Labour Force Survey, LFS, 2009/2012). The top destination for Portuguese nurses is England while Germany comes in second or third, depending on the year. The international mobility of nurses, as noted above, 'is not a new phenomenon, but its scope and importance in the current period has *intensified*' (Gabriel 2013). In this context, it is important to analyse the different conditions and motivations that lead to nurses' – in this case Portuguese nurses' – decision to migrate.

I will now move on to consider the chapter's theoretical framework, in particular the role of macro level dynamics (economic austerity and barriers to hiring nurses in England from outside the EU) in Portuguese nurses' decision to emigrate, together with the meso (recruitment) and micro (individual) level dynamics (cf. Goldin et al. 2011). This will be linked to the phenomenon of the 'new global cosmopolitan elite' (Bauman 2013).

Theoretical Framework

The primary theoretical basis for my analysis of Portuguese emigration is a framework that highlights the interplay of macro, meso and micro dynamics in the decision to leave home, highlighting immigration policies (macro) in the regulation of migrant flows (Massey et al. 2002; Goldin et al. 2011). This analysis is combined with the insights of the diagram produced by Coleman-Lindenberg (Coleman 1988; the analysis of the diagram by Pires 2014) to identify the results and causes of social phenomena, in this case, migration. Secondly, the case being studied fits the Southern European model of migration, suggesting migration with centre-periphery dynamics (King 2015). Lastly, the phenomenon under study is framed using the concept of the 'new cosmopolitan elite' (Bauman 2013).

The decision to migrate is a choice that can be influenced or constrained by diverse factors, such as networks. For our study, meso-level institutional networks (there are also social networks, family and friends) help to explain the beginning of any given migration. They

> … assist migration in areas where social networks are not sufficiently well developed to facilitate cross-border movement (Manolo, 2004). State-supported or private labor *recruiters help to initiate migrant flows by spreading (often limited) information* about the destination country and *offering jobs, accommodation, and support* for potential migrants (Goldin et al. 2011, 105, my emphasis).

As a (meso-level) social phenomenon, networks connect the individual agency of the migrant (micro level), with the economic, demographic and political structures (macro level), that influence the decision to migrate.

"Push" and "pull" factors are determinant on the macro level, driving the desire to leave the home country (push) and/or attracting towards the destination country (pull). For this study, at the macro level the economic and demographic conditions are important, and government policies – particularly immigration policies – appear to play a preponderant role. The volume of migrant flows is largely influenced, directly and indirectly, by immigration policies. In the words of the migration sociologist Douglas Massey and other co-authors, "In the world of the late twentieth century, distances are small but the barriers erected by governments are large, and the latter have become the principal factor determining the size and character of contemporary labor flows" (Massey et al. 2002, 14).

The actual decision to migrate is decided at an individual level by weighing up the meso and macro dimensions, taking stock of the risks, costs and uncertainties and contrasting them with potential opportunities and benefits. The decision to migrate is complex, and depends on the migrant's level of education, financial resources, social capital, access to information, among other factors (Goldin et al. 2011).

Through Coleman-Lindenberg's diagram, sociological theory shows that – put simply – when it comes to social phenomena, *macro-level effects* originate from *individual causes (micro)* – from individual actions – which in turn are influenced by macro-level causes (Coleman 1988; see the analysis of the diagram by Pires 2014). Applying this to Portuguese nurses' decision to migrate, we find the common sense empirical explanation that there was a massive emigration of nurses (*macro result*) due to the crisis and economic austerity (*macro cause*). Nevertheless, the diagram draws our attention to the fact that the ultimate cause lies in the micro sphere, at an individual level. In this case it could be the completion of a nursing degree and the search for a first job (*micro cause*), which, in turn, might have been hindered by the economic austerity that led to a reduction of employment offers (*macro causes*).

The Southern European model of migration frames current Portuguese migration taking place in Europe in the general context of migration from Southern European countries. The migration geographer Russell King shows that there is a historical sequence of migration common to the Southern European countries of Spain, Greece, Italy and Portugal, which started in the post-war period (King 2000) and is currently in its fourth phase. This fourth phase is characterised by the "'new emigration' of young, well-educated people seeking employment and new lifestyle experiences in Northern Europe, since the nineties, accelerating after 2008" (King 2015, 139).

King argues that two crises have combined to give rise to the present 'new emigration', one cyclical and the other structural, and both economic. The emigration of qualified young people from Southern Europe was the outcome of the 2008 financial crisis, but also reflected a much deeper structural crisis that had been pervasively entrenched for around two decades before this date: that of graduate unemployment (King 2015, 158).

According to the same author, this model is related to the 'centre-periphery framework'. Southern European countries' geographic peripherality overlaps with their economic peripherality, and their economies have been revealed as fragile with the reappearance of their structural dependency on the economies of the 'centre', i.e. Northern and Western European countries (Germany, the UK and others) (King 2015).

These conditions have been exacerbated for Southern European countries by conditions that operate as pull and push factors for the emigration of qualified young people such as nurses. The Portuguese Emigration Observatory (Observatório da Emigração) demonstrates the impact on emigration due to the 'push factor' of economic austerity: 'the asymmetrical nature of the sovereign debt crisis dating from 2010 and the recessionary effects of austerity policies have caused [Portuguese] emigration to rise faster than it had during the period before the crisis' (Observatório da Emigração 2014, 12). In the following year, 2011, the UK raised barriers to the contracting of qualified immigrants coming from countries outside the EU, a measure supposedly aimed at reducing immigration in this country (The Migration Observatory 2011; Carvalho 2015).

There are also non-economic, non-political factors that have influenced recent emigration, i.e. cultural factors – and specifically the phenomenon of a 'new global cosmopolitan elite'. Particularly for emigrants of Southern European countries, where '... a lengthening of young people's home, [...] and family dependency' was widespread, a new attitude has emerged due to the high graduate unemployment that has led to them to seek employment abroad (Domínguez-Mujica and Gracía 2017, 43). This change of mentality falls under the broader phenomenon identified by the sociologist and philosopher Zygmunt Bauman: the recent appearance of a new cosmopolitan elite that has emerged due to the weakening of the welfare state in Europe and is consequently 'seeking safety in an insecure world' through the idea of mobility. The 'permanent address' is that of the email or mobile telephone and is no longer a concrete physical location/country:

> Whatever else the new 'cosmopolitanism' of the new global elite may be, it is *born to be selective*. [...] What their lifestyle celebrates is the irrelevance of place, a condition most conspicuously beyond the reach of ordinary folks, of the 'natives' tied fast to the ground [...]. The message of the 'cosmopolitan' way of being is simple and blunt: it does not matter *where* we are, what matters is that *we* are there (Bauman 2013, 56).

> … because at no other social location has that certainty and security – and particularly the reassuring feeling of 'knowing for sure what is going to happen' – collapsed so spectacularly as in the underdefined, underinstitutionalized, underregulated and all too often anomic territory of exterritoriality inhabited by the new cosmopolitans (Bauman 2013, 60).

Mixed Methodologies

This study combines extensive and intensive methodologies. The extensive research focused both on the statistical collection and interpretation of data about Portuguese nurses in destination countries, as well as the analysis of a questionnaire-based survey conducted among nurses in the United Kingdom.

The intensive research consisted of ethnography conducted through interviews and participant observation among Portuguese nurses (and other qualified professionals). This took place in London over 5 months in 2013. The interviews sought to encompass the heterogeneity of the profiles of emigrant Portuguese nurses: 20 were interviewed in 12 different African, European and Asian countries; 3 were interviewed at different moments in 2013, 2014 and 2015, in order to follow the evolution of their expectations, and the remaining 17 were interviewed in 2015.

The interviewees included young recent graduates searching for their first job, but also others with a contract for an indefinite period who decided to leave the country. For a deeper understanding of what leads them to be selected in particular rather than nurses of other nationalities, interviews were conducted with four recruitment agency professionals and two hospital nursing officers in England with Portuguese nurses in their team. The interviews were conducted in person, through the Internet by Skype and in writing. Their total duration was between one and seven hours – depending on the flow of the conversation – and the majority lasted around four hours.

This study involved finding the numbers of Portuguese nurses that have gone abroad – statistics that have not been published internationally or even within the host countries. In order to discover the number of nurses that leave the country each year, the methodology used by the UN, OECD and World Bank – i.e. finding out the number of foreigners that arrive in the countries of destination, in this case Portuguese nurses – was followed to calculate the number of international immigrants. This means that the number of Portuguese nurses leaving the country was calculated based on data about entries recorded by institutions in the foreign countries in which they have to register.

During the statistical research into the number of Portuguese nurses in the destination countries, various difficulties emerged:

(a) not all the countries have socio-professional associations in which registration is compulsory (this is the case for Germany and Switzerland);
(b) the registration of nurses is calculated using various sources from institutions of a different nature (for example, the Norwegian Nurses' Association, the Federal Office for Migration in Switzerland, the Federal Employment Agency in Germany or the Ministry of Health in Belgium);
(c) where they exist, socio-professional nurses' organisations generally provide data on the number of nurses by country of qualification, and this does not always align with nationality;
(d) there are countries that simply do not authorise the disclosure of data on foreign nurses in the country (such as Saudi Arabia);
(e) the lack of response from some countries in which Portuguese nurses are found.[4]

The Numbers. Emigration of Portuguese Nurses and Countries Chosen

In the findings I shall begin by presenting the statistical research into the number of Portuguese nurses that left the country in the wake of the 2008 financial crisis. This analysis will be related to the emigration of nurses from Southern Europe, who are currently working in North and Western European countries. In the following section, this scenario will be contextualised using both the results of a questionnaire completed by Portuguese nurses and material from the 20 interviews conducted.

The emigration of Portuguese nurses intensified around 2011, the year when close to 1000 nurses left the country (see Table). Up until this date less than 500 emigrated per year. The departure of nurses reached its peak in 2013 and 2014 when the number surpassed 2000 per year. In other words, from 2012 to 2013 it increased to double, and this level was maintained in the following year. In 2015 and 2016 the number of nurses leaving to go abroad diminished, but even so still remained at high at around 1000. These numbers are drawn from the records of nurses in the destina-tion countries.

Over Half of the Portuguese Nurses Who Had Emigrated Chose England

The emigration of nurses can be related to that of the Portuguese population in general. According to the data of the Emigration Observatory, there was a general increase in emigration from 2011. The specific emigration of nurses reflected this general trend. In 2013 approximately 120 thousand Portuguese nationals emigrated

[4] This is the case of Ireland.

to other countries (Observatório da Emigração 2017, 20). The 2366 Portuguese nurses that moved abroad that year corresponded to around 2% of the total emigration of Portuguese nationals over the same period[5] – and this proportion was the same in 2014. The fact that nursing – in contrast to most other professions – accounts for more than merely a fraction of a percentage of total Portuguese emigration makes this a highly visible outflow.

Table: Portuguese nurse inflows in destination countries, 2009–2016

	2009	2010	2011	2012	2013	2014	2015	2016
Country	N	N	N	N	N	N	N	N
England	207	249	527	781	1210	1286	1102	717
France	..	..	..	..	515	446	53	92
Germany	..	..	..	..	206	251	..	..
Switzerland	129	150	271	259	228	181	154	104
Belgium	..	2	36	158	196	96	54	42
Norway	..	..	..	..	11	18	1	5
Total	336*	401*	834*	1198*	2366	2278	1364*	960*

Sources: Table by the author, based on the inflow of Portuguese nurses into the following countries: United Kingdom, Nursing and Midwifery Council; France, Ordre National des Infirmiers; Germany, Bundesagentur für Arbeit; Switzerland, State Secretariat for Migration SEM, Statistics Service; Belgium, Ministère de la Santé Belge, 2013, 2014 – SPF Service Public Fédéral Santé Publique, Commission de planification, Groupe Infirmier, 2015, 2016 – Service Professions de santé et Pratiques professionnelles, Direction Générale GS; Norway, 2013, 2014 – Norsk Sykepleierforbund; 2015, 2016 – Norwegian Directorate of Health, Department of Education and Health Workforce Planning

Notes: The symbol ".." refers to data not available. The symbol "*" means that this data is provisional as the numbers of nurses in the countries with this symbol ".." are still not available and could not be counted for this reason. The data was provided following a request for the purposes of this study. The values refer to the number of nurses who graduated in Portugal, except for Switzerland and Germany, where the data corresponds to nationality. In all the other four countries the figures by country of qualification and by nationality appear to be similar. The numbers of Portuguese nurses are detailed below by country: United Kingdom – number of nurse registrations, compulsory to work in this country; France – number of nurse registrations; Germany – number of Portuguese nurses that started working in the respective years; Switzerland – number of Portuguese nurses in the country, including those who have permanent and temporary authorisation; Belgium and Norway – number of nurse registrations. It should be noted that the Saudi Commission for Health Specialities of Saudi Arabia answered our request stating that the number of Portuguese nurses in the country is confidential information, and that they could not disclose the figures. Some Swiss cantons, though not all, require registration at the Red Cross and according to this source the numbers of Portuguese nurses registered in the country by year are as follows: 2010–38; 2011–61; 2012–114; 2013–204; 2014–224

[5] This proportion is an estimate based on values from heterogenous sources. However, both of the absolute values were calculated based on the records of Portuguese nationals in the destination countries in 2013 and while therefore unlikely to be highly accurate, this proportion is acceptable.

The Portuguese Nursing Council provides the number of requests for profes-sional equivalence to enable working abroad – but these values are numerically inflated as they record the intention to emigrate and not the effective outflow[6] (see Table). Nevertheless, the number of requests follows the same upward trend until 2014, falling in the two subsequent years, but maintaining a high absolute level.

Portuguese Nurses: Increased Intention to Emigrate

Over half of the Portuguese nurses emigrated to England. A major increase took place from 2011/12 onwards. An illustrative example is the fact that 91 Portuguese nurses started working in this country in 2008, while in 2013 this number stood at 1210 (see Fig.).

The same trend can be observed in Portuguese emigration in general, whose main country of destination since 2011 has been England, in the United Kingdom (Observatório da Emigração 2017). In fact, 4% of the total number of Portuguese nationals who moved to UK in 2013 (30,121) were nurses. This is a highly significant percentage given that it represents only one profession.

Table: Requests for professional equivalence to the Portuguese Nurses' Council, 2009 to 2016

	Nursing council, Portugal
Years	N
2009	609
2010	1030
2011	1724
2012	2814
2013	2516
2014	2850
2015	2717
2016	1614

Source: Table produced by the Portuguese Nurses' Council, based on requests for statements of the European Directives required to work in European countries

[6] Nurses who choose to work in European countries must ask the Portuguese Nurses' Association to issue a statement certifying that their nursing qualifications comply with European Directive 2013/55/EC (www.ordemenfermeiros.pt/comunicacao/Documents/2014/Diretiva_2013_55_EU_modernizacaoDiretiva2005_36.pdf).

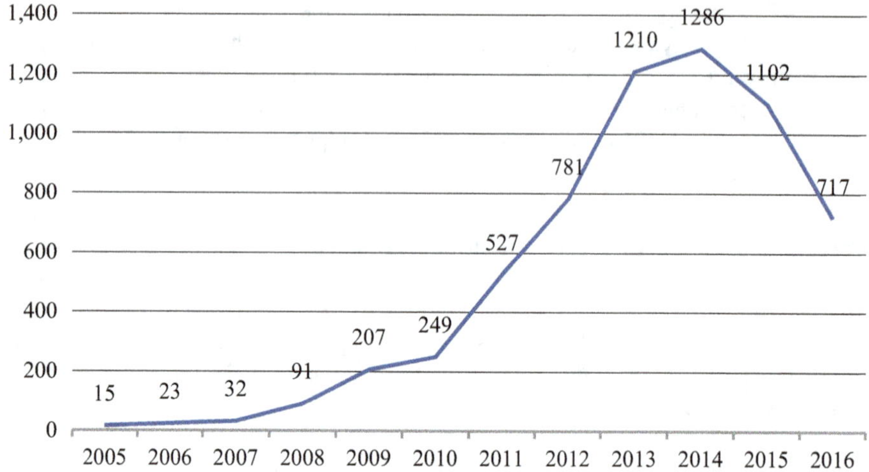

Fig. Portuguese nurse inflows into England, 2005 to 2016.
Source: Figure by the author, based on data obtained from the Nursing and Midwifery Council, UK. Note: The values refer to the number of nurse registrations, compulsory to work in this country

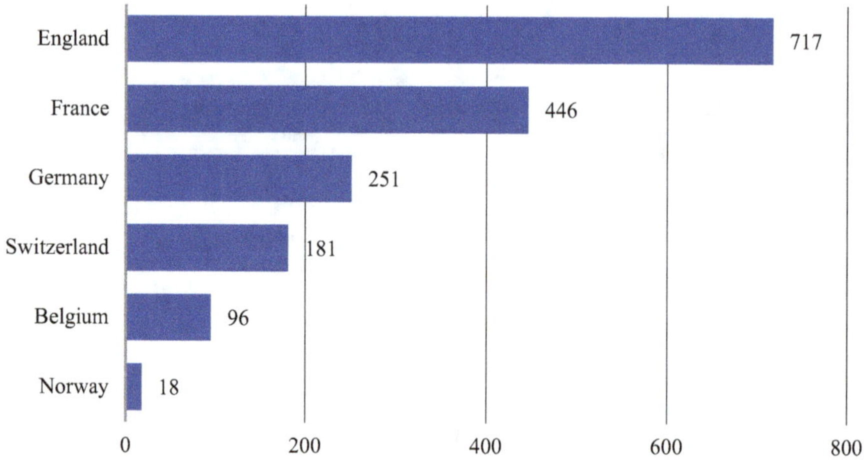

Fig. Portuguese nurse inflows by country of destination, 2016 (or nearest year).
Sources and notes: Same as Table

400% Increase in the Inflow of Portuguese Nurses into the United Kingdom, 2010–2014, and Recent Decrease While Maintaining High Values

The other countries chosen by Portuguese nurses are Germany, France, Switzerland and Belgium (see Fig.). As well as being "receiving-countries" of Portuguese nurses, these countries are also those that contract the most immigrant nurses in Europe (OECD 2015, 115, from DIOC 2010/11, LFS 2009/12), as noted above.

England, France, Germany and Switzerland: Main Destinations of Portuguese Nurses in 2016

Increased Emigration of Portuguese Nurses Compared With Spanish and Italian Nurses

In England, Portuguese nurses were the second main foreign nationality (following the Spanish) between 2012 and 2014. Portuguese nurses, combined with Spanish, Romanian and Italian nurses, substantially replaced the Indian and Filipino nurses in the United Kingdom between 2012 and 2014. In 2015 the emigration of Filipino nurses started to increase although they no longer represent one of the three top nationalities (see Fig.).

Portuguese Nurses in England Among the Top 5 Nationalities from 2012 Onwards

These four Southern and Eastern European nationalities (Portuguese, Spanish, Italian and Romanian) are also the principal nationalities of the nurses in Belgium, together with the French (see Fig.).

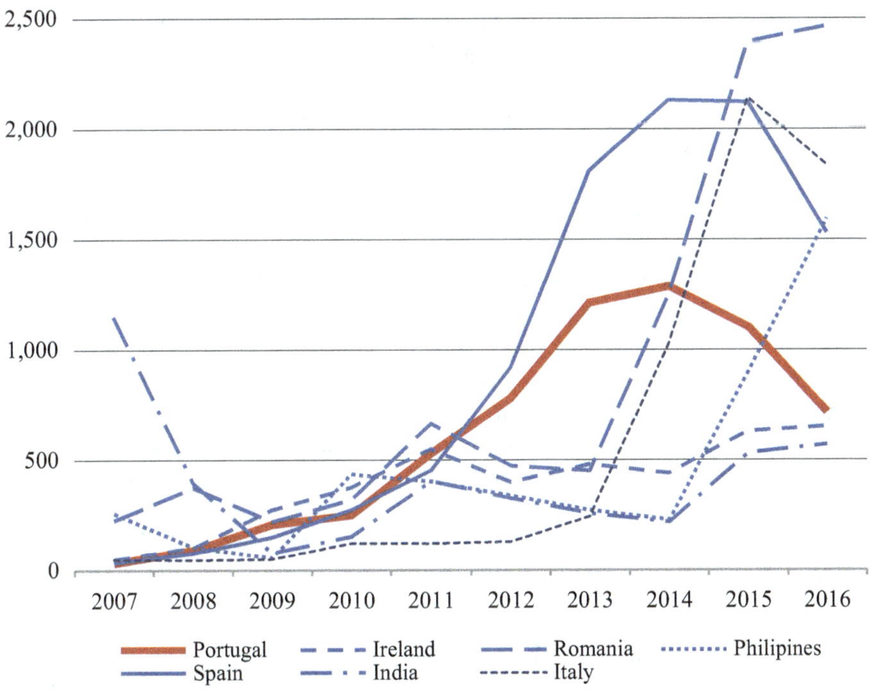

Fig. Inflows of the six main nationalities of nurses into England, 2007 to 2016.
Source: Figure by the author, based on data obtained from the Nursing and Midwifery Council, UK

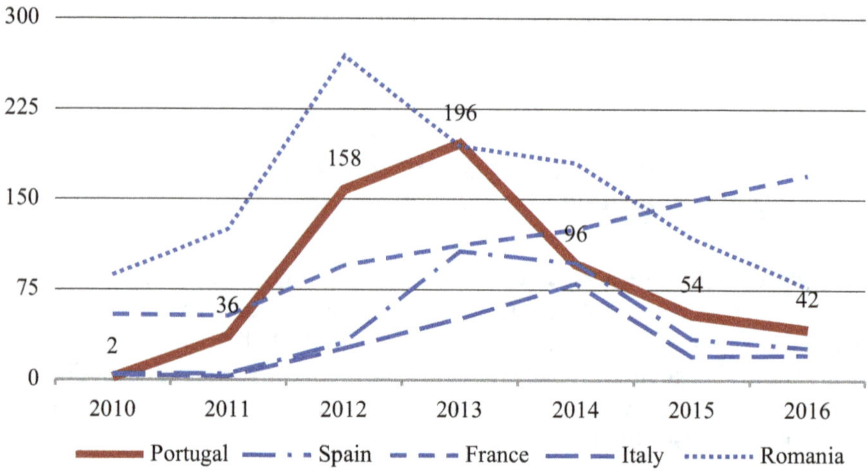

Fig. Inflows of foreign nurses into Belgium, 2010 to 2016.
Source: Figure by the author based on Ministère de la Santé Belge, 2010–2014, SPF Service Public Fédéral Santé Publique, Commission de planification, Groupe Infirmier, 2015, 2016 – Service Professions de santé et Pratiques professionnelles, Direction Générale GS

Portuguese Nurses Are the Main Foreign Nationality in Belgium in 2013

In terms of demographic impact, we can draw two conclusions. Firstly, nurses only flow outwards, constituting a migratory movement which is not offset by inflows of foreign nurses. This is due to the low (or null) attractiveness of the Portuguese employment market as a result of austerity policies in the National Health Service (cf. Correia et al. 2015). German nurses, for example, emigrate to work in Switzerland and the Scandinavian countries (among others), but the outflows are offset by foreign nurses who come into the country (Ognyanova et al. 2014), in contrast to what happens in Portugal, which no longer receives immigrant foreign nurses.

Secondly, based on the profiles of the Portuguese nurses who moved to England in 2013 – the destination country of over half the nurses that leave Portugal – the majority of emigrant Portuguese nurses appear to be women and young adults. The majority of Portuguese nurses in England are women (77%), consistent with a pro-fession that is largely female dominated. 75% are up to 29 years old (see Fig.). Of these, 40% are 24 years old or less, which means that nearly half moved soon after attaining their degree.

75% of Portuguese Nurses in England: Up to 29 Years Old

A survey of 349 emigrant nurses Portuguese nurses in the UK – the main destination country – reached similar numbers in 2014. The survey confirms that the profile is

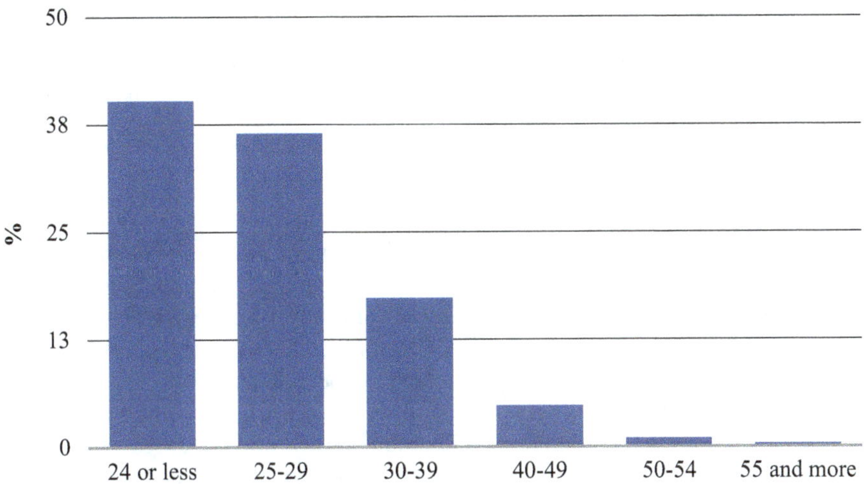

Fig. Portuguese nurse inflows into England by age group, 2015.
Source: Figure by the author, based on the data obtained from the Nursing and Midwifery Council, UK

generally of young single women, aged less than 30, who are recent graduates who found their first job in this country (Pereira et al. 2015). As a rule, their employment in the UK was obtained through employer agencies (83%) that recruit Portuguese nurses either in this country or in Portugal.

Professionally-organised formal recruitment processes therefore clearly predominate over informal and individual processes of emigration. Emigration not only enabled access to employment, both for recent graduates and unemployed professionals, but it also opened up paths towards professional promotion in the majority of the cases. Over half have no intention to return to Portugal before their retirement.

The Decision to Leave the Country. "At the Recruitment Company I Had Been Selected Even Before I Had Finished My Course"

In this section I focus on the actual voice of the nurses, specifically on their motivations for emigrating at the individual level (micro), which are related to the political-economic dimension (macro) and the role of the recruitment networks (meso) (cf. Goldin et al. 2011), as well as to their particular profile.

> My boyfriend and I – he is also a nurse – decided to wait for three months and if there were no alternatives we would emigrate. After three months, we contacted the company [...] that had already made a presentation at the School. I was torn between choosing England or Belgium because they were the countries presented as the best to work in. As I have always preferred the French language, I decided on Belgium. Then they explained all the steps that had to be taken: how to apply for authorisation to work as a nurse in Belgium, the French course, among others. [Cátia, 26 years old, nurse in Belgium, 2015][7]

At the network level, even before completing their university degree, various Portuguese nursing students had received information from employment agencies on working in countries such as the United Kingdom and Belgium. Other nurses, who finished their course before 2010, easily found advertisements on employment websites on the Internet and in Facebook groups, which listed opportunities in France, Switzerland, Germany and Ireland. Others heard about opportunities through friends and attended presentation sessions on working conditions in Saudi Arabia and the United Arab Emirates. Recruitment was also identified as the main driver for Portuguese nurses leaving to work in Germany, according to sociologist and German teacher Anne Stoehr (Stoehr 2015).

At an individual level, the twenty interviews conducted among emigrated nurses revealed that the causes "pushing" them to leave the country are heterogenous. For those who are unemployed or seeking their first job, it is the guarantee of being able to work in nursing. For those who are employed, it is professional demotivation due to three factors: (i) the impossibility of progressing professionally because career trajectories are frozen; (ii) the salary cuts due to economic austerity; and (iii) the scant communication with managers that makes them feel undervalued and, in their opinion, rather inefficient personnel management.

Moreover, the majority of the employed nurses have two jobs, one at a public hospital and another in a private institution. This is partly because overtime in public hospitals is not paid but exchanged for free time, which the senior staff decide when employees can take, informing the nurses only a few days beforehand, thus precluding the possibility of programming holidays. This dissatisfaction at work is exacerbated by the lack of communication along the hierarchical chain and particularly with the administrative boards, which are largely unreceptive to the complaints, needs and suggestions of the nurses:

> I left Portugal due to professional demotivation, especially in terms of recognition and the way that we are treated by our senior staff. [...] I knew that they were contracting for Saudi Arabia and I applied. [...] They should give nurses the opportunity to continue to study, facilitating their work hours so they can attend post-graduate, specialisation or doctoral classes. In my case, what did I want? I wanted more flexible work hours, not to take a course during work hours, but the possibility of adjusting them [Alexandra, 51 years old, a nurse that re-emigrated from Saudi Arabia to the United Arab Emirates, 2015].

The number of nurses searching for their first job increased from 2008 onwards. A questionnaire-based survey of the Portuguese Nurses' Council covering 730 professionals – around half of whom completed their university degree in 2008 – reveals

[7] The interviewees are given fictitious names in order to protect their privacy.

that 49% had not found a job 6 months later and 77% had not received any offer of employment in Portugal. The same survey revealed that only about 1% of the sample of nurses who graduated in 2006 and 2007 were unemployed (Fernandes et al. 2009, 7)). In the words of one nurse who completed her course in 2010 and searched for employment in nursing for over a year:

> I continued to look for job offers and I saw this opportunity here in Germany and another in England. That was when I decided, "OK, now I am going abroad" ... […] In the case of Germany it was wonderful opportunity because it offered accommodation at a ridiculously low price for a little over a year; it was the hospital that directly came to fetch the nurses and offered a German course at the Goethe-Institut. […] I saw the opportunity, I found it interesting and within a week it was settled [Sandra, 29 years old, nurse in Germany, 2015].

The high number of Portuguese nurses that emigrate has been widely disclosed not only in the national media,[8] but also by the British media, among others in *The Guardian* newspaper and on BBC radio.[9]

Due to the weakness of the welfare state, these nurses hold the contemporary mindset of a new global and cosmopolitan elite (Bauman 2013), among whom what has become permanent is their electronic contact details rather than their physical address. Both the interviews with nurses as well as the participant observation conducted in Lisbon and London revealed that nurses do not always remain in the country they first emigrate to beyond the year in which they emigrate: some return to Portugal; others re-emigrate from Saudi Arabia to England, from Saudi Arabia to the United Arab Emirates, from France to Switzerland, from Spain to Norway, from Spain to England. In the words of a nurse who emigrated to Spain and then re-emigrated to England:

> From another perspective, due to the lack of nursing employment in Portugal, I had met Spanish doctors and nurses who had worked in Portugal and then returned to Spain. (…) I was facing a dilemma, I would either go to Spain or Switzerland. I saw the advertisements of the agencies on the Internet and at Chaves Higher Education School [Portugal]. How come there's such a shortage of nurses in these places and how is it possible that they pay these wages and offer these conditions? I asked myself, why doesn't this exist in Portugal? In the meantime, I was called to a meeting at Chaves job centre about the recruitment of nurses to work abroad [Nuno, 28 years old, nurse who re-emigrated from Spain to England, 2015].

---

[8] Among various news items, this was disclosed in "Portugal trains nurses and Great Britain takes advantage" (Rádio Renascença: http://rr.sapo.pt/informacao_detalhe.aspx?fid= 31&did=117953) and "The nurses of the others" (Antena 1: http://www.rtp.pt /play/p309/e158192/reportagem-antena-1). For more news items, see Amaral and Marques 2013.

[9] For example: "West Suffolk Hospital recruits nurses in Portugal" (BBC: http://www.bbc.com/news/uk-england-suffolk-21181861); "NHS fills nursing shortage by turning to Spain and Portugal" (The Independent: http://www.independent.co.uk/life-style/health-and-families/health-news/nhs-fills-nursing-shortage-by-turning-to-spain-and-portugal-8877745.html); "Portuguese nurses arrive at troubled Barking, Havering and Redbridge University NHS Trust hospitals" (The Guardian: www.guardian-series.co.uk/news /11533329.Portuguese_nurses_arrive_at_troubled_hospitals_trust/?ref=mr); "NHS nurse recruitment from EU 'too aggressive'" (BBC: http://www.bbc.com/news/health-33691084).

Nurses are not an isolated case; other authors in this book, such as Peixoto et al., have analysed the return of Portuguese nationals to the country using the global perspective of the census, and still others, such as Queirós, the re-emigration of another professional sector – construction workers. Still, as indicated by the academic literature, nursing is undoubtedly a transnational profession (Prescott and Nichter 2014). Consistent with this observation, Portuguese nurses prove to be mobile, not only in their decision to leave, but also in their mobility between countries.

Conclusion

The emigration of qualified Portuguese nationals increased between 2001 and 2011, according to the censuses of their destination countries (Observatório da Emigração 2015; Pires and Pereira 2018; Pires et al. 2018). Recent research presented in this book shows that this number continued to increase from 2011 onwards. Due to the educational efforts of different governments, the Portuguese population is more highly qualified in this century than it has been previously – and, for this reason, it is only natural that a higher number of qualified Portuguese nationals have left the country than in previous decades.

Among Portuguese emigrants with higher education degrees, nurses have one feature that differentiates them from most other qualified professionals: they are obliged to register with the bodies equivalent to the Nurses' Council in the country where they are going to work. This enables investigation into the numbers of emigrants in this specific professional group. This registration takes place because the equivalence of higher education degrees in nursing is recognised by EU member states. Other professions – such as informatics, finance and teaching, among others – are also recognised but do not demand professional registration.

The statistical research conducted for this study showed that sometimes "the numbers speak for themselves". The significance of Portuguese nurses' emigration was revealed in its impact on not just the country of origin, but also the destination countries.

From the perspective of the sending-country, Portugal, there are three pertinent facts. First, there was a shift from fewer than 500 nurses leaving the country per year in around 2010, to more than 2000 in 2013 and 2014, a figure that has remained high ever since. Second, this specific trend in the outflow of Portuguese nurses reflected changes in Portuguese emigration in general. Both took on massive proportions in 2011 and England was the main destination country in both cases (Observatório da Emigração 2017 and Pires' chapter in this book). Third, because it stood at 2% of the total outflow of Portuguese nationals in 2013 and 2014, the outflow of this professional class has been highly visible.

From the perspective of the receiving country, the inflow of this group became highly visible in 2012 and 2013 because Portuguese was the second main nationality among new immigrant nurses working in England– and in 2013 the first in

Belgium. In other countries, such as Switzerland and Germany, its size increased considerably in comparison to previous years.

The causes that led to this phenomenon are heterogenous. One of the main findings of this research, supported by the theory of migrations (cf. Goldin et al. 2011), is that the beginning of this new emigration among qualified Portuguese nationals – and nurses in particular – was due to the visible emergence of recruitment networks (a meso-level factor). This in turn was driven by the preponderant factor – though this lacked visibility – of immigration policies in the United Kingdom (macro-level), which led to the individual decision (micro-level) of nurses to leave Portugal. The majority of these nurses were in the early period of a new stage of life: having completed higher education, they were searching for their first job. This change of life stage – through access to a profession – instigates geographic mobility according to Savage (1988, 560–63). In this study, through a questionnaire, statistics and interviews, I confirmed that the majority of nurses migrate to the United Kingdom right after finishing their course.

In this context, the 'pull factor' played a determinant role in the outflow of Portuguese nurses to England, their main destination. The fact that in 2011 British agencies and hospitals were barred from recruiting in countries from which nurses had historically emigrated, such as India and the Philippines, compelled them to search for nurses inside Europe. At the same time, coincidentally, austerity was taking place in Southern European countries. This pull factor performed the decisive role of the 'macro cause' – Portuguese nurses might have been facing economic austerity, with fewer job opportunities, but they could also work in other areas, even in unqualified jobs, or continue their job search. When employment agencies started to recruit in Portugal and "pull" them abroad, nurses in Portugal knew that under austerity new jobs would not be created, and those that were employed saw their salaries cut and their career trajectories frozen, preventing them from achieving professional fulfilment and from working in their speciality. In addition to a salary, the job vacancies in the United Kingdom offered paid overtime – and time spent on training or post-graduate study was recorded in the work schedule and paid. Therefore, the fact that British agencies and hospitals started coming to universities and job fairs to recruit Portuguese nurses directly – bringing them access to information about how to work in England as well direct employment offers – played a determinant role in their decision to leave the country from 2011 onwards.

Recruitment networks pulled together the macro political-economic structure and the micro individual reasons to leave; nonetheless, the decision to migrate is always individual. The argument is schematised below (see Fig.), based on Coleman-Lindenberg's sociological diagram of the causes and effects of social phenomena. In this case, the social phenomenon in question is the emigration of Southern European nurses, specifically Portuguese and Spanish nationals.

From the point of view of the employment agency professionals interviewed, so many Portuguese nurses are selected for jobs in the United Kingdom and other countries because their training includes a 4-year university course – which involves internships with a practical component from the first year onwards – and because they speak good English. In comparison, applicants from other European countries

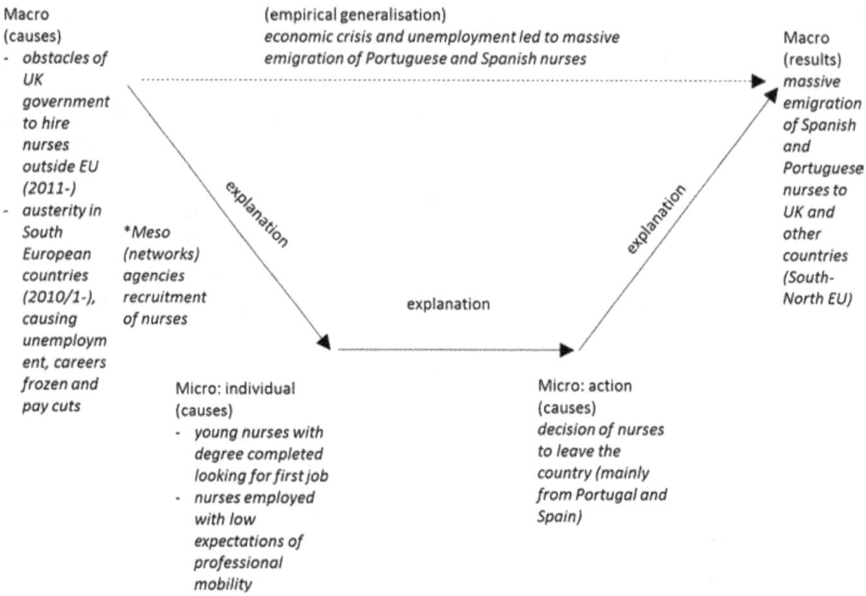

Fig. Macro, meso and micro dynamics in the decision of Portuguese and Spanish nurses to migrate (based on Coleman-Lindenberg's diagram).
Source: Macro, meso and micro dynamics in the decision of Portuguese and Spanish nurses to migrate. Text in italics by the author, based on Pires (2014: 38). Diagram Coleman-Lindenberg, from Coleman (1988). Notes: Data on Spanish nurses based on the research of Galbany-Estragués and Nelson (2016); *not originally in the diagram, by the author

have less training and practical experience. The same opinion is voiced by Debbie Knight (*NHS Professionals* 2014), who came to Portugal to recruit nurses to work under temporary and flexible arrangements in the south of England:

> We looked at nurses across the whole of the EU, but Portugal has the four-year training programme and is commensurate with the nursing training that we have here in the UK. They have the really good technical base to their training and their English is excellent.

The second key finding is that this new emigration of Portuguese nurses – following the general trend of rising emigration from the peripheral countries of Europe – is not only a Portuguese phenomenon but rather is in keeping with the Southern European model of emigration (cf. King 2015), in this case applied to European nurse emigration. Thus the dynamic of migration from the periphery to the centre continues. In the specific case of transnational care labour, in which nurses are included, these new dynamics in Europe further extend the general trend of a flow from the global south to the industrialised north (Peterson 2003), specifically from the peripheral east and south of Europe to the industrialised north and west. They also reflect the asymmetries of global – and in this case European – political economy.

Let us consider this issue from the perspective of the second main receiving-country of immigrant nurses (OECD 2015) and the first main receiving-country of

Portuguese nurses in the EU – the UK. During the twenty-first century, the immigra-tion of nurses to England primarily came from countries outside the EU until 2008–2009, as illustrated above in Fig. From this date onwards, the number of nurses arriving from EU countries surpassed those from non-EU countries. In 2010–2011 there was a significant increase in the immigration of nurses from EU countries – and this group has maintained its clear majority position in relation to those from outside the EU ever since. The numbers found for this study demonstrate that this emigration of European nurses to England, the 'core' country of immigration, essentially comes from the 'periphery' of Europe: from Romania in the east, and from Spain, Italy and Portugal in the south (see Fig.). As noted above, a decisive role was played in this shift by a structural factor of macro order: the barriers of UK immigration policy against nurses coming from outside the EU, from about 2011 onwards, which paved the way for nurses from other European countries experienc-ing economic recession to move.

Portugal is differentiated from the other European sending countries by the demographic and, consequently, socioeconomic implications of its nurses' emigra-tion. Considering that the total population of Spain (around 47 million) is four times higher than that of Portugal, that of Italy (around 60 million) is almost six times higher, and that of Romania (around 21 million) is double, we can conclude that the outflow of Portuguese nurses has a greater impact on the population of Portugal than the departure of nurses of other nationalities has on their Southern and Eastern European countries of origin. Moreover, Portuguese nurses' departure from the country is not offset by the entry of foreign nurses, in contrast to what happens in other countries. Now that the social and formal networks of this new emigration outflow have been created, it is possible that nurses will continue to leave. But it will be crucial to investigate just what the consequences of the UK government's barri-ers to the contracting of nurses within the European area will be in the wake of Brexit. Indeed, the specific emigration of Southern European nurses is simultane-ously reproducing existing socioeconomic inequalities and developing new profes-sional and geographic disparities.

Acknowledgments and Funding This research was supported by a grant (SFRH/BPD/78853/2011) from the Fundação para a Ciência e a Tecnologia (Foundation for Science and Technology, FCT) to carry out statistical and ethnographic research in London and Lisbon for the author's postdoctoral project, "Skilled Portuguese nationals in London and the financial crisis". The chapter received the support of the Fundação para a Ciência e a Tecnologia for its translation, through Strategic Funding: UID/SOC/03126/2013. The proofreading of this chapter was funded by the Portuguese Emigration Observatory (Observatório da Emigração).

Some data in the introduction, methodology and findings have been presented in the book published in Portuguese by the author, *Vidas Partidas. Enfermeiros Portugueses no Estrangeiro* [Divided Lives. Portuguese Nurses Abroad] (2015), and were further analysed and updated for this chapter. I would like to thank the nurses that I interviewed, as well as the recruitment agents. I would also like to thank the institutions that sent unpublished data on Portuguese nurses in the respective countries. I am grateful to Rui Pena Pires for the theoretical insights, in particular about the importance of the obstacles put in place by the United Kingdom to the entry of immigrants from outside the European Union, which consequently led to the recruitment of nurses in Portugal. I thank the anonymous reviewers for their insightful comments.

References

Agunias, D. (2009). *Guiding the invisible hand: making migration intermediaries work for development*. 2009/22. Research Paper – United Nations Development Programme (UNDP). http://hdr.undp.org/sites/default/files/hdrp_2009_22.pdf. Accessed 27 Dec 2017.

Amaral, S., & Marques, A. (2013). Emigração portuguesa de profissionais altamente qualificados: uma proposta de leitura a partir do discurso jornalístico e das perspetivas de atores envolvidos [Highly skilled Portuguese emigration: a Reading propposal from the journalistic discourse and the actors involved]. Paper presented in *Conference Federacion Espanola de Sociologia*. Madrid: Universidad Complutense de Madrid. http://www.fes-web.org/uploads/files/modules/congress/11/papers/2211.pdf. Accessed 7 Sept 2017.

Bach, S. (2010). Achieving a self-sufficient workforce? The utilization of migrant labour in healthcare. In B. Ruhs (Ed.), *Who needs migrant workers? Labour shortages, immigration, and public policy* (pp. 87–124). Oxford: Oxford University Press.

Barros, P. P., & Moura, A. C. (2015). Aspetos económicos da emigração de enfermeiros: uma primeira exploração [Economic aspects of emigration of nurses: a first exploration]. In C. Pereira (Ed.), *Vidas partidas. Enfermeiros portugueses no estrangeiro* [Divided lives. Portuguese Nurses Abroad] (pp. 27–39). Loures: Lusodidacta.

Bauman, Z. (2013). *Community: Seeking safety in an insecure world*. Oxford: Wiley.

Buchan, J. (2007). International recruitment of nurses: Policy and practice in the United Kingdom. *Health Services Research, 42*(3p2), 1321–1335. https://doi.org/10.1111/j.1475-6773.2007.00710.x.

Buchan, J., & Seccombe, I. (2012). *Overstretched. Under-resourced. The UK nursing labour market review*. Royal College of Nursing. https://www.rcn.org.uk/__data/assets/pdf_file/0016/482200/004332.pdf. Accessed 7 Sept 2015.

Buchan, J., Parkin, T., & Sochalski, J.. (2003). International nurse mobility: Trends and policy implications, WHO. Geneva: World Health Organization (WHO). http://www.who.int/iris/handle/10665/68061. Accessed 7 Sept 2015.

Buchan, J., Jobanputra, R., Gough, P., & Hutt, R. (2006). Internationally recruited nurses in London: A survey of career paths and plans. *Human Resources for Health, 4*(1), 14. https://doi.org/10.1186/1478-4491-4-14.

Buchan, J., Charlesworth, A., Gershlick, B., & Seccombe, I. (2017). *Rising pressure: The NHS workforce challenge. Workforce profile and trends of the NHS in England*. London: The Health Foundation.

Carvalho, J. (2015). Política migratória do Reino Unido e recrutamento de profissionais de saúde [UK immigration policy and recruitment of health professionals]. In C. Pereira (Ed.), *Vidas partidas. Enfermeiros portugueses no estrangeiro* [Divided lives. Portuguese nurses Abroad] (pp. 11–15). Loures: Lusodidacta.

Coleman, J. S. (1988). Social capital in the creation of human capital. *American Journal of Sociology, 94*, S95. https://doi.org/10.1086/228943.

Connell, J., & B. Stilwell. (2006). Merchants of medical care: Recruiting agencies in the global health care chain. In Christiane Kuptsch (Ed.), *Merchants of labour* (pp. 239–253). Geneva: International Labour Organisation (ILO). http://www.ilo.org/wcmsp5/groups/public/%2D%2D-dgreports/%2D%2D-dcomm/%2D%2D-publ/documents/publication/wcms_publ_9290147806_en.pdf. Accessed 9 Dec 2016.

Correia, T., Dussault, G., & Pontes, C. (2015). The impact of the financial crisis on human resources for health policies in three Southern-Europe countries. *Health Policy, 119*, 1600. https://doi.org/10.1016/j.healthpol.2015.08.009.

Domínguez-Mujica, J., & Gracía, T. P. (2017). The Economic crisis and the southern european migration model. In B. Glorius & J. Domínguez-Mujica (Eds.), *European mobility in times of crisis: The new context of European South-North migration* (pp. 17–48). Bielefeld: Transcript.

Dussault, G., Buchan, J., & Craveiro, I. (2016). Migration of nurses and doctors in the EU and the European Free Trade Association. In A. Triandafyllidou & I. Isaakyan (Eds.), *High-Skill migration and recession. Gendered perspectives*. London: Palgrave Macmillan UK. https://doi.org/10.1057/9781137467119.

Fernandes, R., Martins, B., Maurício, B., Matos, D., Ferreira, D., Afonso, L., Gouveia, M., et al. (2009). Estudo sobre situação profissional dos jovens enfermeiros em Portugal. Lisboa: Ordem dos Enfermeiros/Rede de Jovens Enfermeiros. https://www.ordemenfermeiros.pt/arquivo/documentosoficiais/Documents/estudo_empregabilidade_jovens_enf.pdf. Accessed 12 Aug 2015.

Gabriel, C. (2013). NAFTA, Skilled migration, and continental nursing markets. *Population, Space and Place, 19*(4), 389–403. https://doi.org/10.1002/psp.1780.

Galbany-Estragués, P., & Nelson, S. (2016). Migration of Spanish nurses 2009–2014. Underemployment and surplus production of Spanish nurses and mobility among Spanish registered nurses: A case study. *International Journal of Nursing Studies, 63*, 112–123. https://doi.org/10.1016/j.ijnurstu.2016.08.013.

Goldin, I., Cameron, G., & Blarajan, M. (2011). Leaving home: Migration decisions and processes. In *Exceptional people. How migration shaped our world and will define our future* (pp. 97–120). Princeton: Princeton University Press.

Gomes, B. N., Domingos, P., & Graça, T. (2014). *Factsheet: Preliminary data of the study The Emigration of Portuguese Nurses*. Lisbon: International Affairs Department of the the Ordem dos Enfermeiros (OE) Term in Office 2012–2015.

King, R. (2000). Southern Europe in the changing global map of migration. In R. King, G. Lazaridis, & C. Tsardanidis (Eds.), *Eldorado or fortress? Migration in Southern Europe* (pp. 1–26). London: Macmillan.

King, R. (2015). Migration and Southern Europe – A center–Periphery dynamic? In M. Baumeister & R. Sala (Eds.), *Southern Europe? Italy, Spain, Portugal and Greece from the 1950s to the present day* (pp. 139–169). Frankfurt/New York: Campus.

Kingma, M. (2006). Nurses on the move. In *Migration and the global health care economy*. Ithaca: Cornel University Press.

Kingma, M. (2007). Nurses on the move: A global overview. *Health Services Research, 42*(3p2), 1281–1298. https://doi.org/10.1111/j.1475-6773.2007.00711.x.

Kroezen, M., Dussault, G., Craveiro, I., Dieleman, M., Jansen, C., Buchan, J., Barriball, L., Rafferty, A. M., Bremner, J., & Sermeus, W. (2015, August). Recruitment and retention of health professionals across Europe: A literature review and multiple case study research. *Health Policy, 119*, 1517. https://doi.org/10.1016/j.healthpol.2015.08.003.

Leal, A. M. C. (2013). *Migração dos enfermeiros portugueses na Europa*. Universidade Nova de Lisboa. http://hdl.handle.net/10362/19150

Leone, C., Bruyneel, L., Anderson, J. E., Murrells, T., Dussault, G., de Jesus, É. H., Sermeus, W., Aiken, L., & Rafferty, A. M. (2015). Work environment issues and intention-to-leave in Portuguese nurses: A cross-sectional study. *Health Policy, 119*(12), 1584–1592. https://doi.org/10.1016/j.healthpol.2015.09.006.

Martin, P. (2005). *Merchants of labor: Agents of the evolving migration infrastructure* (DP/158/2005. Discussion Paper OIT). Geneva. http://www.oit.org/wcmsp5/groups/public/%2D%2Ddgreports/%2D%2D-inst/documents/publication/wcms_193617.pdf

Massey, D., Arango, J., Hugo, G., Kouaouci, A., Pellegrino, A., & Edward Taylor, J. (2002). *Worlds in motion: Understanding international migration at the end of the millenium*. Oxford: Oxford University Press.

Maybud, S., & Wiskow, C. (2006). 'Care trade': The brokering of health care professionals. In C. Kuptsch (Ed.), *Merchants of labour* (pp. 223–238). Geneva: International Labour Organisation (ILO). http://www.ilo.org/wcmsp5/groups/public/%2D%2D-dgreports/%2D%2D-dcomm/%2D%2D-publ/documents/publication/wcms_publ_9290147806_en.pdf.

NHS Professionals. (2014). NHS professionals' EU nurses programme. *NHS Professionals*. http://nhspbank.com/2014/05/02/nhs-professionals-eu-nurses-programme/

Observatório da Emigração. (2014). *Portuguese emigration factbook 2014*. Lisbon: Observatório da Emigração/CIES-IUL/ISCTE-IUL/DGACCP. https://doi.org/10.15847/CIESOEMFB2014.

Observatório da Emigração. (2015). *Portuguese emigration factbook 2015*. Lisbon: Observatório da Emigração/CIES-IUL/ISCTE-IUL. https://doi.org/10.15847/CIESOEMFB2015.

Observatório da Emigração. (2017). *Portuguese emigration factbook 2016*. Lisbon: Observatório da Emigração/CIES-IUL/ISCTE-IUL. http://observatorioemigracao.pt/np4EN/5810.html

OECD. (2015). Changing patterns in the international migration of doctors and nurses to OECD Countries. In *International migration outlook 2015* (pp. 105–182). Paris: OECD Publishing. https://doi.org/10.1787/migr_outlook-2015-6-en.

Ognyanova, D., Young, R., Maier, C. B., & Busse, R. (2014). Why do health professionals leave Germany and what attracts foreigners? A qualitative study. In J. Buchan, M. Wismar, I. A. Glinos, & J. Bremner (Eds.), *Health professional mobility in a changing Europe* (Vol. II). Copenhagen: World Health Organization. http://www.euro.who.int/__data/assets/pdf_file/0006/248343/Health-Professional-Mobility-in-a-Changing-Europe.pdf?ua=1

Pereira, C. (2015). *Vidas partidas. Enfermeiros portugueses no estrangeiro [Divided lives. Portuguese nurses abroad]*. Loures: Lusodidacta.

Pereira, C., Pinto, N., & Pires, R. P. (2015). Portuguese nurses in the UK 2014/Enfermeiros portugueses no Reino Unido 2014. *OEm Fact Sheets, 3*, 1–16. https://doi.org/10.15847/CIESOEMFS032015-pt-en.

Peterson, V. S. (2003). *A critical rewriting of global political economy: Integrating reproductive, productive and virtual economies*. London: Routledge.

Pires, R. P. (2014). Modelo teórico de análise sociológica [Theoretical model for sociological analysis]. *Sociologia, Problemas e Práticas, 74*, 31–50. https://doi.org/10.7458/SPP2012743199.

Pires, R. P., & Pereira, C. (2018). Migrações, qualificações e desigualdade social [Migrations, skills and social inequality]. In R. M. do Carmo, J. Sebastião, J. Azevedo, S. da Cruz Martins, & A. F. da Costa (Eds.), *Desigualdades sociais: Portugal e a Europa* (pp. 335–352). Lisbon: Mundos Sociais.

Pires, R. P., Pereira, C., & Azevedo, J. (2018). Portugal – An in-depth analysis of the emigration of skilled labour. In *Labour market policy thematic review 2018: An in- depth analysis of the emigration of skilled labour.* Brussels: European Commision/European Centre of Expertise (ECE). http://ec.europa.eu/social/main.jsp?catId=738&langId=en&pubId=8132&furtherPubs=yes. Accessed 18 Oct 2018.

Prescott, M., & Nichter, M. (2014). Transnational nurse migration: Future directions for medical anthropological research. *Social Science & Medicine, 107*(April), 113–123. https://doi.org/10.1016/j.socscimed.2014.02.026.

Raghuram, P. (2008). Governing the mobility of skills. In C. Gabrielle & H. Pellerin (Eds.), *Governing international labour migration. Current issues, challenges and dilemmas* (pp. 81–94). London: Routledge. http://oro.open.ac.uk/11808/1/Microsoft_Word_-_governing_the_mobility_of_skills_final.pdf

Reis, P. (2016). Reconhecimento de qualificações profissionais e competências no espaço europeu. In *Atas do IX Congresso da Associação Portuguesa de Sociologia*. Associação Portuguesa de Sociologia. http://hdl.handle.net/10362/22780

Ribeiro, J. S., Conceição, C., Pereira, J., Leone, C., Mendonça, P., Temido, M., Vieira, C. P., & Dussault, G. (2014). Health professionals moving to and from Portugal. *Health Policy (Amsterdam, Netherlands), 114*(2–3), 97–108. https://doi.org/10.1016/j.healthpol.2013.05.009.

Sarfati, H. (2003). Remuneration of nurses in Islamic countries: Economic factors in a social context. In N. H. Bryant (Ed.), *Women in nursing in islamic societies*. Oxford: Oxford University Press.

Savage, M. (1988). The missing link? The relationship between spatial mobility and social mobility. *The British Journal of Sociology, 39*(4), 554. https://doi.org/10.2307/590501.

Stoehr, A. L. (2015). A Emigração de enfermeiras portuguesas para a Alemanha [The emigration of Portuguese nurses to Germany]. In C. Pereira (Ed.), *Vidas partidas. Enfermeiros portugueses no estrangeiro* [Divided lives. Portuguese nurses abroad] (pp. 41–52). Loures: Lusodidacta.

The Migration Observatory. (2011). A loose fitting cap: Why is the limit on skilled non-EU workers undersubscribed? Oxford: COMPAS/University of Oxford. http://www.migrationobservatory.ox.ac.uk/wp-content/uploads/2016/03/Commentary-Loose_Fitting_Cap.pdf. Accessed 13 Mar 2013.

Yeates, N. (2008). Transnationalism, social reproduction, and social policy: International migration of care workers. In C. Moser & A. A. Dani (Eds.), *Assets, livelihood and social policy* (pp. 149–170). Washington, DC: World Bank. http://documents.worldbank.org/curated/en/502051468313757117/pdf/453960PUB097801SE0ONLY1May014102008.pdf. Accessed 24 June 2015.

12

Working Class Condition and Migrant Experience: The Case of Portuguese Construction Workers

João Queirós

Introduction

This chapter presents some results of fieldwork-based research into the transformations affecting the professional, geographical and social mobility strategies of construction workers throughout the years of economic and social crisis Portugal faced from the beginning of the 2000s – but especially after 2008. Its main goal was to arrive at an empirical and analytical sociological understanding of these transformations.

Building on the results of previous work on this topic (Pinto and Queiroz 1996a, b; Pinto 1999; Pinto and Queirós 2008, 2010; Queirós 2010; Monteiro 2014a), this research started with a multi-sited ethnography conducted in 2007 and 2008 in three distinct locations: two small communities in Northwest Portugal, where the migration of construction workers to Spain had become a salient aspect of local economic and social relations, and a small city in the Spanish region of Galicia, where a group of Portuguese construction workers was followed and accompanied in its everyday routines (Monteiro and Queirós 2009a, b, 2010; Queirós and Monteiro 2016). In both locations our research sketched the main features and implications of the (changing) work-related mobility of Portuguese construction workers coming from different areas of the northern and especially the north-western parts of the country. This initial sketch was then followed by a new study based on fieldwork once again in Galicia, in the same city visited in 2008, and in two locations in eastern France and western Germany. This follow-up study was conducted within the research project "Recent emigration trends in Northwest

J. Queirós (✉)
Instituto de Sociologia da Universidade do Porto and Escola Superior de Educação do Politécnico do Porto, Porto, Portugal
e-mail: jqueiros@letras.up.pt

Portugal: the case of construction workers", funded by the Secretary of State for Portuguese Communities, and its main goal was to document the impacts of the 2008–2010 financial, economic and social crisis on the life of an important segment of the Portuguese working class.

Since the early 2000s, circular migration to Spain had been the answer for thousands of workers affected by unemployment, low-paid and/or precarious jobs, and the overall lack of professional and social mobility prospects characterising areas in Northwest Portugal where "traditional" activities (textiles and clothing, footwear, wood and furniture, mining, construction) were facing severe constrains (see, for instance, Pinto and Queirós 2010; Pereira 2012; Monteiro 2014a). But the downfall of the Spanish economy and especially of its real-estate and construction sectors after 2008 threw up several new questions for those studying this phenomenon. As the importance of Spain as a work destination for Portuguese construction workers inevitably declined, it became of major interest to understand how these workers were dealing with this country's "crisis" (see Monteiro and Queirós 2009a; Monteiro 2014b; Queirós and Monteiro 2016).

Following our 2007–2008 study, the constitution of two new "sociological observatories" in France and Germany in the 2013–2014 period – as well as our return to the research site in Galicia, Spain – was envisaged as a way of gathering empirical evidence of the reconfiguration of the professional trajectories and work-related mobility of Portuguese construction workers formerly involved in circular migration to Spain. This chapter will discuss some of the most salient aspects and implications of these workers' migrant experience – as seen in Galicia, Spain, in 2008 and 2013. It will then show – through reference to data collected in the Bourgogne-Franche-Comté region in eastern France – how the new conditions and characteristics of Portuguese working-class migration to central and northern Europe are intertwined with both changing economic and social conditions in Portugal and accelerating processes of (uneven) economic integration within the EU. In fact, while producing new work patterns and work-related mobilities for Portuguese construction workers, the construction sector's significant recent transformations – at both national and European levels – seem to help reinforce the subordinate integration of southern countries' economies and their workers in the European economy.

A Brief Note on Method

Since it focuses on the different physical and social settings where migration is enacted – and on the ordinary practical and bodily experience of migrants – multi-sited ethnography enables researchers to overcome both the naturalistic and individualistic interpretations of migration typical of common sense discourses, as well as the simplistic second-degree explanations implicit in "push-pull" models and "rational choice" theory. It is necessary to identify and scrutinise interactions between the emigrants' social history as incorporated in schemes of thought and action – which Pierre Bourdieu would call their habitus (see, for instance, Bourdieu 1994; Wacquant 2016) – and the objective conditions in which these schemes are actualised and instantiated in practice, and which actually (re)produce migratory acts. This is why "following connections, associations, and putative relationships" – which lies at the heart of multi-sited ethnography – is essential for theoretically and analytically reconstructing a social reality, such as circular migration, that is coproduced in multiple geographically dispersed yet socially interconnected locations (Marcus 1995, 97; see also Marcus 1998; Fitzgerald 2006; Holmes 2013). By "following the people", this "circular" or "mobile" ethnography reconstructs the map of a phenomenon that is simultaneously geographical and social. It can thus be envisaged as an *ethnography of contemporaneity*, since the space-time of the research is created through the reconstitution of actual, effective social relations, allowing for a territorially fragmented object of study to attain a distinct and specific density, character and analytic coherence (Queirós and Monteiro 2016).

Fitzgerald (2006) advocates four methodological strategies that are useful for an ethnographic study such as that proposed here. Firstly, Fitzgerald (2006, 2) underlines the importance of direct contact with social agents in their multiple settings so as to "reveal the full scope of the migration experience and its impacts". Fitzgerald continues (2006, 2): "Despite the practical and epistemological problems of multi-sited fieldwork, it offers advantages for gaining access to members of multi-sited networks and explaining the effects of place on a variety of outcomes". Secondly, Fitzgerald (2006, 2) refutes the bias of methodological nationalism that frequently characterises migration studies. What multi-sited fieldwork does is to strip off "the national blinders that restrict the construction of the field", thus integrating in the analysis "both sending and receiving country sites". Thirdly, he emphasises the need to historicise migration processes and the constellation of places they interconnect. By deploying an eclectic methodological strategy – combining ethnographic fieldwork with local archival work, oral histories and the recovery of results of previous studies – it is possible to turn "the problem of the 'ethnographic present' into historical depth" (Fitzgerald 2006, 2, 12). Finally, Fitzgerald (2006, 3) recalls the need to develop "research programs in which ethnographic case studies contribute to the elaboration of migration theories". As he puts it (2006, 16), "ethnographers would do well to situate their studies in ways that strengthen claims to both empirical representativeness and theoretical significance". This implies conducting "intensive research in several connected sites selected for their potential theoretical yield": it is not just about "following the people" in their immediate displacement, but also about understanding "the influences of different kinds of boundary crossings and ecologies on their experiences in multiple domains" (Fitzgerald 2006, 20).

Living In-Between: Social and Symbolic Divisions and Everyday Life Among Portuguese Construction Workers in Spain

Economic Crisis and Working-Class Migration in Northwest Portugal

According to official data from the Spanish National Statistics Institute, close to 6.5 thousand Portuguese individuals entered Spain in 2015. This number was 12% higher than in 2014 and represented the second consecutive year of growth in the number of Portuguese individuals entering their neighbouring country, thus ending a period of sharp decline in this movement from 2008 through 2013. Although far below those registered from 2004 to 2007 – when official data reported an average of 18 thousand new Portuguese arrivals in Spain each year, reaching a peak of 27 thousand in 2007 – the 2015 figures represented the return to a pattern that made Spain one of the most significant destinations for Portuguese emigration (see Figs.also Pinho and Pires 2013; Vidigal 2016).

Resulting from the economic downturn that followed the 2008 financial crisis – which affected the majority of Spain's economic activities, and especially the real-estate and construction sectors – the sudden decrease in Portuguese workers arriving in Spain ushered in an era that contrasted sharply with the status quo since the first years of the twenty-first century. Especially between 2002 and 2008, these two countries' divergent socio-economic conditions had favoured the consolidation of Spain as a destination for several thousand Portuguese workers looking for better working and living conditions or simply trying to find a job in the midst of the "crisis back home" (Monteiro and Queirós 2009a; Queirós and Monteiro 2016; Pinho and Pires 2013).

Construction workers originating from different parts of the country, but especially from (post-)industrial and rural areas in the Northern and Central regions, made up one of the largest segments of Portuguese immigrants in Spain in those years. Low salaries, unemployment, and the lack of prospects for professional and social mobility all made the thriving Spanish construction sector very attractive for large numbers of Portuguese workers – especially low skilled men, whose migration frequently took the form of weekly or fortnightly international commutes to construction sites in the neighbouring country. The number of Portuguese nationals residing in Spain rose from 71 thousand in 2004 to almost 150 thousand in 2009. To these should be added Portuguese workers commuting to Spain on a weekly or fortnightly basis, who were estimated to number 80–100 thousand in the Northwest alone. In this period, construction always accounted for more than 40% of the total number of Spanish jobs held by Portuguese workers (see Figs.; Monteiro and Queirós 2010; Queirós and Monteiro 2016; see also Byrne 2011).

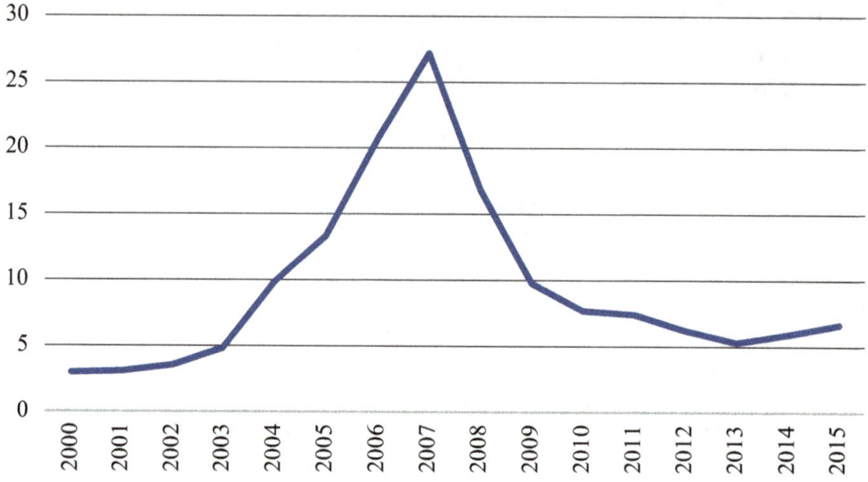

Fig. Portuguese entering Spain annually (2000–2015; thousands).
Source: Queirós and Monteiro 2016

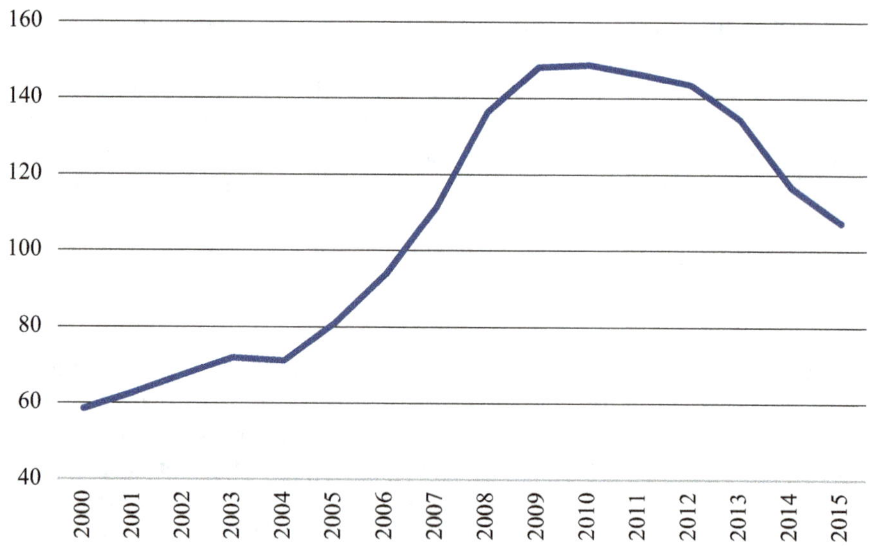

Fig. Portuguese-born residents in Spain (2000–2015; thousands).
Source: Queirós and Monteiro 2016

With economic growth "largely driven by a credit-fueled, often speculative expansion in residential house building" (Byrne 2011, 27), and a segmented labour market – albeit with average wages significantly higher than Portugal's – Spain became the preferred destination for many Portuguese workers who were either already unemployed or threatened by unemployment. As soon as the "swarm of micro and small subcontractors" prevalent in this sector started to operate on the ground, supply and demand converged. But rather than a supposedly spontaneous process of market equilibrium, the "compatibility between the propensities and interests incorporated in workers, on the one hand, and the objective system of opportunities and demands that encompass the transnational construction labour market, on the other", was in fact intensely promoted by this web of intermediaries, "which simultaneously compete and cooperate among themselves to form a floating, ready-to-use proletariat" (Monteiro 2014b, 11; see also Bosch and Philips 2003). The Spanish construction sector's status as one of the major destinations for north-western Portuguese workers has also been reinforced by the internationalisation strategies of many large Portuguese construction companies, as well as by improvements to infrastructure and transportation that significantly increased the possibility of communication and travel between European regions.

The Growing Importance of Circular Migration

The increase in circular migration that has been noticed in Portugal since the mid-2000s matches recent global trends in international migration. The intensification of transnational mobility has made this issue "all the rage in international policy circles" (Vertovec 2007, 2). In fact, several international agencies, inter-governmental forums and government departments are putting forward the idea that circular migration represents a "win-win-win" situation, since it brings benefits for both the receiving countries, through meeting labour market shortages, the sending countries, through guaranteeing remittances, and the migrants themselves, through offering employment and control over the use of their wages. As a result, many of these agencies, forums and departments are aiming to promote managed circular migration systems. Although the new policy measures are presented wholly as a way of maximising the developmental potential of circular migration (and of the remittances it generates), it is hard not to see their utility in creating a regulated workforce reserve to meet labour market shortages in specific moments of the economic cycle or in specific activity sectors, while reducing the social costs of permanent immigration and making immigration more amenable to public opinion, especially where there is growing resistance to policies surrounding the permanent accommodation of unskilled migrants (Vertovec 2007, 3–7; see also Burawoy 1976 on the separation migration systems produce between "reproduction of labour force" and "production from labour force").

Social and Symbolic Divisions and Everyday Life Among Portuguese Construction Workers in Spain

The repeated and long-lasting periods of social and economic constraint experienced by many segments of the Portuguese working classes – especially in the northern part of the country ("the situation in Portugal is very tight")[1] – lie at the origin of historically specific forms of interest ("I have to turn to somewhere"; "I have to look out for myself"), and thus underpin the formation of aspirations that are plausible because they are probable. Underlying apparently intentional economic "options" and "choices", it is possible to find the personal and collective histories of gradual familiarisation with the kind of social situations that generate the "hunches" and "preferences" justifying the reasonableness of – if not the urge for – certain alternatives ("you have to go"; "you have to make a living"; "you have a good body to work") instead of others ("staying at home"; "doing nothing"; "idling"). Jorge, an 18-year-old who had been working in Spain for over a year when he was interviewed in 2008, puts it in clear terms:

> I could have stayed in Portugal, but… you know… Meanwhile, when they asked me to go there [to Spain], I was going to earn a little bit more and I decided to go there. I've looked for jobs back here in Portugal, but there were no immediate proposals, I didn't want to stay at home… and then I decided to go. (…) I needed it back then. I looked in the newspapers, I sent my CV to several companies in Portugal and… (…) Then they offered me this job, I thought over it and, well, it wasn't good for me to stay at home for too long, at home you don't earn money, and then I went.

Insofar as it radically destabilises a "precarious economic balance, shattering the temporal and spatial rhythms that constitute the bonds of all social existence" (Bourdieu and Sayad 1964, 21), temporary or circular migration provides experiences as contradictory as the social conditions on which they are grounded. The "essentialisation" of the relation between spatial (dis)location and social (dis)connection resulting from circular migration – which is aggravated by the characteristics of construction activities – supports and explains the "dualistic view of the world" shared by these workers (Comaroff and Comaroff 1992, 45). From this dualistic view can be deduced the mode of "thinking in pairs" that shapes the discourse of contrast opposing "here" and "there".

The dichotomy of "living in Portugal and working in Spain" provides the axis of articulation for a series of symbolic oppositions juxtaposed to those that are immediately geographical (home versus workplace) and temporal (week versus weekend); Portuguese construction workers in Spain have two worlds of significance, since they have "two lives", the "life there" and the "life here", as Pedro, a 31-year-old working in Spain for over 7 years, puts it. The physical and temporal overinvestment in work, the domestic confinement typical of non-work hours (or, at

---

[1] Both the quotations between brackets and the indented quotations are direct translations of excerpts of the testimony of Portuguese workers interviewed in Portugal, Spain or France as part of the research presented here.

Fig. "Pensão Noroeste" and "Bar Soldado", in O Carballiño, Galicia, Spain, where a team of Portuguese construction workers was staying, in January 2008. (Photo: João Queirós)

best, the endogamous sociability within the "team"), and the austerity in consumption throughout the working week all define these migrants' range of probable experiences during their time in Spain. The weekends they spend back in Portugal, on the other hand, provide an opportunity for restoring self-esteem, for the unre-stricted use of time ("doing nothing"; "going for a walk"; "sleeping"), for the con-spicuous spending of money ("spending all the money on booze"; "going out with the lads here"), and for forms of socialising that had been temporarily interrupted or suspended ("spending time with the family"; "talking freely") – they thus enable migrants to engage in what Moodie (1991, 29) calls "practices of personal integrity" (Fig.).

The alternation typical of this bulimic pattern of appropriating time and space is indelibly etched in minds and bodies: "the imaginary, here, becomes body with biography" (Comaroff and Comaroff 1992, 55). Only if we remain open to understanding these workers' objectively unstable and contradictory status can we resist the impression of ambiguity, bad faith or ineptitude transmitted by their often duplicitous discourse, and attend to the conditions of possibility and reasonableness of the migrant's vision of the world – of his world.

The opacity of the personal consequences of migration is reinforced by migrants' internalisation and naturalisation of experiences of exploitation and domination. By contributing to the impression that this is an exceptional period or a period of respite ("this is just until I get my life back on track"; "I was living a difficult situation and then this opportunity arose"), the transitoriness of this type of migration helps deflect attention away from the conflicts attributable to power structures. It disguises these conflicts by depicting them as specific to a defensive sacrifice – as operating to restore the harmony of collective and personal existence by "establishing or re-establishing the limits, frontiers and frames legitimately constitutive of these structures of society and culture within which an ordered life can be lived" (Turner 1977, 215). This type of migration emerges as an "opportunity" that is of course both accessible and acceptable, but only for workers able and willing to see it as an effective way to cope simultaneously with necessity ("a guy needs money to pay his dues, to buy his things") and with the imperative of maintaining the social honour of the virtuous man ("walking tall"; "I could stay out of a job but that's even worse"; "I always liked to work"). Under these conditions, the mental and physical costs of work are reinterpreted using the logic of masculine stoicism and virtuosity ("many can't stand it") and justified by the financial compensation it brings ("as long as they pay me at the end of the month…").

De-justification is, however, the most powerful means of justification. The inertia of incorporated structures – which are transmuted physiologically and practically in bodily postures as well as discourses of deference that retranslate collective feelings of inferiority and illegitimacy ("you're in a country that's not yours"; "it's not they who have to adapt to you, it's you who has to adapt to the system") – explains how these workers help realise in everyday life the asymmetries of power present in the social conditions that lie at the root of their schemata of action and thought. The interiorisation of social inequalities – in the form of principles of classification (and hierarchisation) of behaviours, attitudes and appearances – inscribes the moral and physical violence experienced daily in the workplace ("you're in pain"; "you work till you drop dead"; "it was degrading"; "they don't respect anyone") within the order of the "normal" and even of the "deserved". These principles come to function as a "natural" sense of reality: "Because of these perceptions, the migrant body is seen as belonging effectively to the position that it occupies in the system which has meanwhile led to its deterioration" (Holmes 2006, 1787; see also Holmes 2013, ch. 4; Wacquant 2005). In Pedro's words:

> The easier, lighter work – it was them [the Spanish workers] who would do it and then… That happens but… In fact, I didn't tell you that, but, for me, for us, that was normal. I think it was good for us things were that way. You want to know why? That way you could prove to the overseer you really knew how to do things – and that way you were able to gain his respect. That was the thing that mattered there.

As the product of naturalised power relations, subordination is confirmed by the apparently spontaneous actions and words of the migrants themselves. As Ong (1987, 3) tells us: "The dominant meanings and practices shape the substance of everyday experiences: our expectations, meanings and lived practices constitute and are constituted by our sense of social relations and reality". The effect of evidence of reality ordinarily determines the unquestionable nature of the social world.

For migrant workers such as those described here, the long-term experience of hard labour, difficult social relations and harsh conditions reinforces common personal and collective beliefs about the unpredictability and even the malevolence inscribed in one's "fate" ("you have to be lucky"; "no one could have guessed what would happen"; "five minutes before and it would have been me, five minutes later and it happened to my colleague"). This long-term experience also tends to produce a self-image of vulnerability to the harshness of reality, aggravated by one's seeming invisibility and insignificance in the eyes of others ("no one respects you"; "they don't give a damn"; "you're just a number"; "from the moment you stop being useful to the company, you become disposable"). Workers' reduction to sheer economic value is linked to their loss of symbolic recognition, producing a loss of self-worth.

Facing the "Crisis in Spain"

As in many other countries, the eruption in Spain of the 2008 "financial and economic crisis" had immediate repercussions for the Portuguese migrants working there – particularly in construction and related sectors. The number of Portuguese workers entering Spain dropped from 27 thousand in 2007 to 17 thousand in 2008; and in the following years this trend only deepened, at least until 2014 (see Fig.). Specialists talk of a real "collapse" in Portuguese migration to Spain during this period (Pires et al. 2014, 47) – a "collapse" that was inevitably related to the sharp decrease in low-skilled circular and permanent emigration that resulted from the post-2007 slump in the Spanish construction industry, which generated a loss of around 1 million jobs (Byrne 2011; see also Monteiro 2014b).[2]

Although Spain may have lost its importance as a destination for Portuguese migrant workers, the number of Portuguese temporarily or permanently leaving their home country did not decrease. As a matter of fact, between 2008 and 2013, Spain was the only major European destination that witnessed a decline in the number of individuals coming from Portugal. Although it remained one of the most significant receiving countries (the fifth in 2014), Spain saw other European countries, such as Luxembourg, Switzerland, Belgium, the UK, France and Germany, increase (or regain) their relative weight as destinations for Portuguese

[2] Between 2007 and 2008, there was a decrease of around 20 thousand registered Portuguese workers in the Spanish construction sector (−27%). The total number of Portuguese construction workers registered for Spanish social security decreased by 17%, with a drop of −40% in the construction sector and −26% in mining and mining-related activities. Nevertheless, the percentage of Portuguese construction workers registered for Spanish social security was still very high: 25% of the total. Unemployment among Portuguese workers also increased dramatically during this time, especially among construction workers. Of the 15,713 total Portuguese workers registered in unemployment offices in Spain, more than 6 thousand (around 40%) were construction workers. Between 2007 and 2008 the number of construction workers registered in Spanish unemployment offices rose 233,5% (OEFP/OOSPEE 2009, 21–27).

Fig. One of many abandoned construction sites, in O Carballiño, Galicia, Spain, in 2013. (Photo: João Queirós)

working class migrants (on this point see Marques and Góis 2014; Observatório da Emigração 2015) (Fig.).

The dramatic alteration of Portuguese construction workers' prospects for professional and social integration in Spain resulted in their adopting one of the following three main alternatives: (i) returning to Portugal and transitioning to inactivity (especially for older workers), to unemployment, or eventually to employment in a different sector (with or without future re-emigration); (ii) transitioning to permanent residency in Spain – if employed or on unemployment benefits – often combined with a move to a more economically dynamic region; (iii) maintaining a career in the construction sector while diversifying and extending their geographical mobility following the multiplication of Portuguese (and Spanish) construction companies' business locations.

"Old Emigrants, New Emigrants": The Reconfiguration of Work-Related Mobility and Portuguese Working-Class Migrants' Experience in France

The European Construction Field and the Reconfiguration of Work-Related Mobilities

As Monteiro (2014b, 15) emphasises, the Portuguese construction sector's integra tion into the European market has been fast-tracked by the regressive economic situation of recent years, which has encouraged companies to turn to the external market in various different ways, broadening the geographical scope of their operations and thus opening up new mobility pathways for Portuguese construction workers.

The reconfiguration of work-related mobility in the construction sector is inextricably associated with the ongoing institutionalisation of an integrated European economic space in which construction companies operate and compete. This institutionalisation is advancing due to developments in legal integration; to the progressive liberalisation of markets; to the creation and consolidation of new statutes for workers, such as posted workers; to corporate concentration and restructuring, and to the rise of new economic mediators, among other factors. It has helped to enlarge and consolidate the transnational economic and social space of the migrant condition (Bosch and Philips 2003; Monteiro 2014b).

Although it has opened up new prospects for Portuguese construction workers wiling to avoid unemployment or looking for better jobs and especially better wages, the institutionalisation of an integrated European construction sector and the (imperfect) unification of the European labour market have also brought with them uncertainty and risk. The persistently unequal legal and regulatory frameworks that can be found within Europe – as well as tendencies towards the liberalisation and individualisation of contracts, the segmentation of labour markets and the lowering of wage standards and working conditions (Monteiro 2014b) – have raised new questions for the study of working class migration in Europe.

In Portugal's case – which in a certain sense may be considered unique in western Europe because of the country's long-term status as a provider of low and semi-skilled workers to central and northern European economies – there have been clear changes to the main characteristics and patterns of working-class emigration. Aside from the typically circular, volatile character of current working-class Portuguese emigration – which is particularly visible in the construction sector, and makes it substantially different from previous, typically permanent, emigration – the reconfiguration of work-related mobility in recent years has deeply affected the everyday life and experiences of working class migrants.

From "Double-Pole Communities" to "Double-Pole De-structuring"?

Focusing on construction workers, Pinto (1999, 21) has noticed how the threat of unemployment – whether short-term or long-term –, wage relations instability, and the compulsive flexibility of productive processes and management strategies all frequently lead to "a decrease not only of the exigency levels (both objective and subjective) regarding working conditions and increasing production rhythms, but also of self-esteem and self-confidence". This results in "the disruption of group solidarities, without which consciousness of labour issues and subsequent collective action are barely attainable". Under conditions of economic flexibility and the everyday uncertainty of mobile, unpredictable work trajectories, the socialising role of work is undermined, and workplaces can become places of "identity de-structuring", rather than identity-formation (Pinto 1999, 21–22). This fact is especially visible today, since construction workers are increasingly exposed to job instability and constant socio-geographic displacement. By living as contemporary "nomads" of a kind and having to cope with the risks associated with this condition, circular migrants and international commuters in the construction sector may suffer from what Michel Pialoux, referring to the effects of economic flexibility, calls "existential anxiety" (quoted in Pinto 1999, 22; see also Queirós 2010).

This pattern of migration, work, and everyday life clearly differs from that which could typically be found in eastern France in the 1960s and 1970s, when many thousands of low-skilled Portuguese workers arrived in the area to work in various sectors, and particularly in the Peugeot factories. With job contracts secured by a formal agreement between French and Portuguese authorities, these soon-to-be automotive industry workers were eventually able to establish themselves in the Montbéliard area, in the Bourgogne-Franche-Comté region, where they developed their careers, raised their families, and (re)constructed community ties and a sense of belonging (Fig.).

Contrasting with this social setting, working class migrants arriving in the region in recent years are typically industrial or, more commonly, construction workers with short-term contracts involved in circular migration who quickly move on to other places. Although there are occasional reports of malaise and competition between fellow-nationals, established migrants ("the old") tend to talk of a "generation" of Portuguese migrants ("the new") who simply "pass through" the area, and are often "almost invisible". These two very different "generations" of Portuguese migrants are not simply different generations in terms of age, but are also the product of different sociological modes by which working class migration is generated (Monteiro 2014b). These different modes result from different stages and configurations of state policies, economic settings, company strategies, and conjunctures in both departure and receiving countries.

In contrast to what typically occurred in the traditional destinations of Portuguese permanent emigration in central and northern Europe – where it was possible to

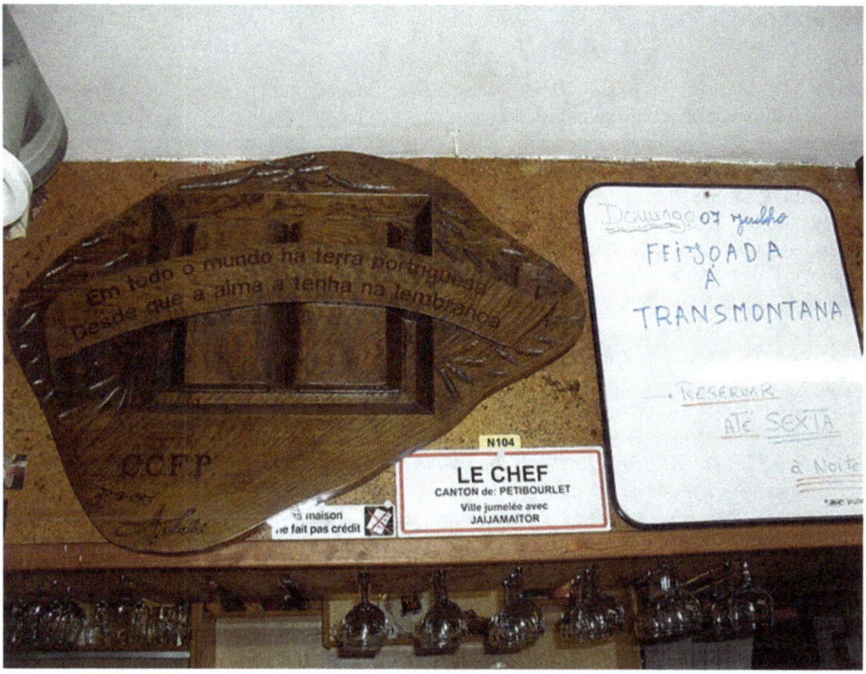

Fig. "All around the world there is Portuguese land as long as the soul has it in remembrance". In a Portuguese club in Mulhouse, Bourgogne-Franche-Comté, France, 2013. (Photo: João Queirós)

observe the steady constitution of what Rocha-Trindade (1976) termed "double-pole communities" – the transnational social space created by Portuguese construction workers' circular migration seems to be one in which social processes of double-pole de-structuring have unfolded, rather than the reconstruction of meaningful and durable relations through which migrants' social ties can be reinforced. In fact, under current conditions, while work and geographical trajectories become more individualised and uncertain, migrating construction workers seem increasingly to get trapped in the vicious circle of over-investment in work and interactional confinement: in their multiple, temporary destinations, it is very difficult to invest in the building and consolidation of solid social relations and renewed social networks; and back in their places of origin, social ties tend to weaken and life becomes increasingly atomised.

Acknowledgments and Funding The author would like to thank the Secretary of State for Portuguese Communities for funding the research presented in this chapter (project "Recent emigration trends in Northwest Portugal: the case of construction workers"). The preparation of the final version of this text also benefited from funding from the Portuguese Foundation for Science and Technology, through the Institute of Sociology of the University of Porto (Unit UID/SOC/00727/2013). The author would also like to thank Cláudia Pereira and Joana Azevedo for their patience and support.

References

Bosch, G., & Philips, P. (Eds.). (2003). *Building chaos. Regulation and deregulation in the building industry*. London: Routledge.

Bourdieu, P. (1994). Stratégies de reproduction et modes de domination. *Actes de la Recherche en Sciences Sociales, 105*, 3–12.

Bourdieu, P., & Sayad, A. (1964). *Le déracinement*. Paris: Les Éditions de Minuit.

Burawoy, M. (1976). The functions and reproduction of migrant labor: Comparative material from Southern Africa and the United States. *American Journal of Sociology, 81*, 1050–1087.

Byrne, J. (2011). Spain: The single market in practice? *CLR News, 1/2011*, 25–33.

Comaroff, J., & Comaroff, J. (1992). Le fou et le migrant. *Actes de la Recherche en Sciences Sociales, 94*, 41–58.

Fitzgerald, D. (2006). Towards a theoretical ethnography of migration. *Qualitative Sociology, 29*(1), 1–24.

Holmes, S. (2006). An ethnographic study of the social context of migrant health in the United States. *PLoS Medicine, 3*(10), 1776–1793.

Holmes, S. (2013). *Fresh fruit, broken bodies. Migrant farmworkers in the United States*. Berkeley: University of California Press.

Marcus, G. (1995). Ethnography in/of the world system: The emergence of multi-sited ethnography. *Annual Review of Anthropology, 24*, 95–117.

Marcus, G. (1998). *Ethnography through thick and thin*. Princeton: Princeton University Press.

Marques, J. C., & Góis, P. (2014). A emigração portuguesa contemporânea e o estado: uma nação dispersa, um estado longínquo. *População e Sociedade, 22*, 55–71.

Monteiro, B. (2014a). *Frágil como o mundo. Etnografia do quotidiano operário*. Porto: Edições Afrontamento.

Monteiro, B. (2014b). Portuguese construction workers in Spain: Situated practices and transnational connections in the European field of construction. *CLR News, 2/2014*, 8–32.

Monteiro, B., & Queirós, J. (2009a). Entre cá e lá. Notas de uma pesquisa sobre a emigração para Espanha de operários portugueses da construção civil. *Configurações, 5/6*, 143–173.

Monteiro, B., & Queirós, J. (2009b). Homens duros, vidas frágeis. Uma etnografia da experiência do trabalho migrante na construção civil em Espanha. *Actas do X Congresso Luso-Afro-Brasileiro de Ciências Sociais, 5/6*, 322–328.

Monteiro, B., & Queirós, J. (2010). Pela estrada fora. Apontamentos sobre a génese social da migração pendular de trabalhadores da construção civil portugueses para Espanha. In J. M. Pinto & J. Queirós (Eds.), *Ir e voltar. Sociologia de uma colectividade local do Noroeste Português (1977–2007)* (pp. 261–271). Porto: Edições Afrontamento.

Moodie, D. (1991). Social existence and the practice of personal integrity: Narratives of resistance on the South African gold mines. *African Studies, 50*(1), 39–63.

Observatório da Emigração. (2015). *Portuguese emigration factbook 2015*. Lisbon: Observatório da Emigração/CIES-IUL/ISCTE-IUL. https://doi.org/10.15847/CIESOEMFB2015.

OEFP/OOSPEE. (2009). *El mercado de trabajo y la movilidad laboral entre España e Portugal. Síntesis de datos/O mercado de trabalho e a mobilidade laboral entre Espanha e Portugal. Síntese de dados*. Lisbon: Observatório do Emprego e Formação Profissional/Instituto do Emprego e Formação Profissional (Portugal)/Observatório Ocupacional do Serviço Público do Emprego Estatal (Spain).

Ong, A. (1987). *Spirits of resistance and capitalist discipline: Factory women in Malaysia*. Albany: SUNY Press.

Pereira, V. B. (Ed.). (2012). *Ao cair do pano. Sobre a formação do quotidiano num contexto (des) industrializado do Vale do Ave*. Porto: Edições Afrontamento.

Pinho, F., & Pires, R. P. (2013). *Espanha, OEm country reports* (Vol. 1). Lisboa: Observatório da Emigração, CIES-IUL, ISCTE-IUL. https://doi.org/10.15847/CIESOEMCR012013.

Pinto, J. M. (1999). Flexibilidade, segurança e identidades sócio-profissionais. *Cadernos de Ciências Sociais, 19–20*, 5–37.

Pinto, J. M., & Queirós, J. (2008). Estruturas produtivas, escolarização e desenvolvimento no Vale do Sousa. Análise da reprodução da condição social periférica numa região metropolitana portuguesa. *Cadernos de Ciências Sociais, 25/26*, 309–356.

Pinto, J. M., & Queirós (Eds.). (2010). *Ir e voltar. Sociologia de uma colectividade local do Noroeste Português (1977–2007)*. Porto: Edições Afrontamento.

Pinto, J. M., & Queiroz, M. C. (1996a). Qualificação profissional e desqualificação social na construção civil. *Cadernos de Ciências Sociais, 15/16*, 41–85.

Pinto, J. M., & Queiroz, M. C. (1996b). Flexibilização da produção, mobilidade da mão-de-obra e processos identitários na construção civil. *Sociologia, Problemas e Práticas, 19*, 9–29.

Pires, R. P., Pereira, C., Azevedo, J., & Ribeiro, A. C. (2014). *Emigração Portuguesa. Relatório Estatístico 2014*. Lisbon: Observatório da Emigração e Rede Migra/CIES-IUL/ISCTE-IUL/DGACCP.

Queirós, J. (2010). Recent economic performance and changing configurations of workforce mobility in Northwest Portugal: Social consequences of unemployment and the rise of youth emigration. In D. Cairns (Ed.), *Youth on the move. European youth and geographical mobility* (pp. 95–106). Wiesbaden: Springer/VS Verlag für Sozialwissenschaften.

Queirós, J., & Monteiro, B. (2016). *Trabalhos em curso. Etnografia de trabalhadores portugueses da construção civil em Espanha*. Porto: Deriva.

Rocha-Trindade, M. B. (1976). Comunidades migrantes em situação dipolar: análise de três casos de emigração especializada para os EUA, para o Brasil e para França. *Análise Social, XII*(48), 983–997.

Turner, V. (1977). Sacrifice as quintessential process – Prophylaxis or abandonment? *History of Religions, 16*(3), 189–215.

Vertovec, S. (2007). Circular Migration: The way forward in global policy?. *Working Papers of the International Migration Institute*, 4.

Vidigal, I. (2016). Emigração portuguesa para Espanha volta a crescer. *Observatório da Emigração*. http://observatorioemigracao.pt/np4/5417.html. Accessed in July 2016.

Wacquant, L. (2005). Carnal connections: On embodiment, apprenticeship, and membership. *Qualitative Sociology, 28*(4), 445–474.

Wacquant, L. (2016). A concise genealogy and anatomy of habitus. *The Sociological Review, 64*, 64–72.

Permissions

All chapters in this book were first published in NORPEUFTPE, by Springer; hereby published with permission under the Creative Commons Attribution License or equivalent. Every chapter published in this book has been scrutinized by our experts. Their significance has been extensively debated. The topics covered herein carry significant findings which will fuel the growth of the discipline. They may even be implemented as practical applications or may be referred to as a beginning point for another development.

The contributors of this book come from diverse backgrounds, making this book a truly international effort. This book will bring forth new frontiers with its revolutionizing research information and detailed analysis of the nascent developments around the world.

We would like to thank all the contributing authors for lending their expertise to make the book truly unique. They have played a crucial role in the development of this book. Without their invaluable contributions this book wouldn't have been possible. They have made vital efforts to compile up to date information on the varied aspects of this subject to make this book a valuable addition to the collection of many professionals and students.

This book was conceptualized with the vision of imparting up-to-date information and advanced data in this field. To ensure the same, a matchless editorial board was set up. Every individual on the board went through rigorous rounds of assessment to prove their worth. After which they invested a large part of their time researching and compiling the most relevant data for our readers.

The editorial board has been involved in producing this book since its inception. They have spent rigorous hours researching and exploring the diverse topics which have resulted in the successful publishing of this book. They have passed on their knowledge of decades through this book. To expedite this challenging task, the publisher supported the team at every step. A small team of assistant editors was also appointed to further simplify the editing procedure and attain best results for the readers.

Apart from the editorial board, the designing team has also invested a significant amount of their time in understanding the subject and creating the most relevant covers. They scrutinized every image to scout for the most suitable representation of the subject and create an appropriate cover for the book.

The publishing team has been an ardent support to the editorial, designing and production team. Their endless efforts to recruit the best for this project, has resulted in the accomplishment of this book. They are a veteran in the field of academics and their pool of knowledge is as vast as their experience in printing. Their expertise and guidance has proved useful at every step. Their uncompromising quality standards have made this book an exceptional effort. Their encouragement from time to time has been an inspiration for everyone.

The publisher and the editorial board hope that this book will prove to be a valuable piece of knowledge for researchers, students, practitioners and scholars across the globe.

List of Contributors

Graça Índias Cordeiro
Centro de Investigação e Estudos de Sociologia (CIES-IUL), ISCTE Instituto Universitário de Lisboa (ISCTE-IUL), Lisbon, Portugal

Russell King
School of Global Studies, University of Sussex, Sussex, UK

João Sardinha
Instituto de Ciências Sociais (ICS), Universidade de Lisboa (UL), Lisbon, Portugal

Marco Lisi
Faculdade de Ciências Sociais e Humanas (FCSH), da Universidade NOVA de Lisboa and Instituto Português de Relações Internacionais (IPRI), Lisbon, Portugal

Ana Maria Belchior
Instituto Universitário de Lisboa (ISCTE-IUL), Centro de Investigação e Estudos de Sociologia (CIES-IUL), Lisbon, Portugal

Manuel Abrantes
Universidade de Lisboa, Instituto Superior de Economia e Gestão (ISEG), Investigação em Ciências Sociais e Gestão (SOCIUS/CSG), Lisbon, Portugal

Ermelinda Liberato
Faculdade de Ciências Sociais, Universidade Agostinho Neto, Luanda, Angola

Cláudia Pereira and Joana Azevedo
Instituto Universitário de Lisboa (ISCTE-IUL), Centro de Investigação e Estudos de Sociologia (CIES-IUL), Observatório da Emigração, Lisbon, Portugal

Marta Vilar Rosales and Vânia Pereira Machado
Instituto de Ciências Sociais, Universidade de Lisboa (ICS-UL), Lisbon, Portugal

José Carlos Marques
Instituto Politécnico de Leiria, Centro Interdisciplinar de Ciências Sociais FCSH/UNL (CICS.NOVA.IPLeiria), Leiria, Portugal

Pedro Candeias
Universidade de Lisboa, Instituto de Ciências Sociais (ICS) and Instituto Superior de Economia e Gestão (ISEG), Investigação em Ciências Sociais e Gestão (SOCIUS/CSG), Lisbon, Portugal

Isabel Tiago de Oliveira
Instituto Universitário de Lisboa (ISCTE-IUL), Centro de Investigação e Estudos de Sociologia (CIES-IUL), Lisbon, Portugal

Pedro Góis
Universidade de Coimbra, Faculdade de Economia and Centro de Estudos Sociais (CES), Coimbra, Portugal

Alexandra Ferro
Centro de Investigação e Estudos de Sociologia (CIES-IUL), Lisbon, Portugal

João Peixoto and Bárbara Ferreira
Universidade de Lisboa, Instituto Superior de Economia e Gestão (ISEG), Investigação em Ciências Sociais e Gestão (SOCIUS/CSG), Lisbon, Portugal

Eugénio Santana
Universidade de Lisboa, Instituto de Geografia e Ordenamento do Território (IGOT), Centrode Estudos Geográficos (CEG), Lisbon, Portugal
Universidade Eduardo Mondlane, Escola de Comunicação e Arte, Maputo, Mozambique

Jorge Malheiros, Paulo Miguel Madeira and Aline Schiltz
Universidade de Lisboa, Instituto de Geografia e Ordenamento do Território (IGOT), Centro de Estudos Geográficos (CEG), Lisbon, Portugal

Ana Delicado
Instituto de Ciências Sociais, Universidade de Lisboa (ICS-ULisboa), Lisbon, Portugal

João Queirós
Instituto de Sociologia da Universidade do Porto and Escola Superior de Educação do Politécnico do Porto, Porto, Portugal

Index

www.ingramcontent.com/pod-product-compliance
Lightning Source LLC
LaVergne TN
LVHW051047220926
848485LV00001BA/30